The Old Norse *Elucidarius*

Medieval Texts and Translations

Edited by
Evelyn S. Firchow (University of Minnesota)

Medieval Texts and Translations *founded and edited by Evelyn S. Firchow, comprise a group of significant works dealing with the Germanic Middle Ages translated into American English and edited by American, European, and Canadian scholars.*

Medieval Texts and Translations is published in the series
Studies in German Literature, Linguistics, and Culture
edited by James Hardin and Gunther Holst
(South Carolina)

The Old Norse *Elucidarius*

Original Text and
English Translation

by

Evelyn Scherabon Firchow

CAMDEN HOUSE

Copyright © 1992 by
CAMDEN HOUSE, INC.

Published by Camden House, Inc.
Drawer 2025
Columbia, SC 29202 USA

Printed on acid-free paper.
Binding materials are chosen for strength and durability.

All Rights Reserved
Printed in the United States of America
First Edition

Library of Congress Cataloging-in-Publication Data

Honorius, of Autun, ca. 1080-ca. 1156.
    [Elucidarius. English & Icelandic]
    The Old Norse Elucidarius : original text and English translation
  / [edited by] Evelyn Scherabon Firchow.
    p.   cm. -- (Studies in German literature, linguistics, and culture)
    Includes bibliographical references.
    ISBN 1-879751-18-6
    1. Theology, Doctrinal--Popular works. 2. Catholic Church--Doctrines. 3. Old Norse language--Texts. I. Firchow, Evelyn Scherabon. II. Title. III. Series: Studies in German literature, linguistics, and culture (Unnumbered)
BX1749.H6613 1992
230'.2--dc2   92-17547
                                                    CIP

Acknowledgments

This version of the Old Norse/Icelandic *Elucidarius* is derived from the diplomatic computerized manuscript text which formed the basis of the *Elucidarius* edition prepared by myself and Kaaren Grimstad, and published by the Arnamagnaean Institute at the University of Iceland in 1989 (Bibliography [8]). Parts of the original machine-readable texts have been re-arranged and some of the extant manuscript fragments have been combined and re-aligned in such a way as to provide the reader with the most coherent and longest possible Old Norse/Icelandic version of the *Elucidarius*. The technique used here also illustrates how computerized medieval texts can be used in various ways and combinations once they are available to the textual scholar. I hope that this new text will introduce medievalists to an important work and will help students get an idea of what to expect when they actually read medieval manuscripts. As an aid to the reader, I have also provided an accurate and idiomatic American English translation of the work.

It is a duty and pleasure to acknowledge the financial help that I have received from several sides for the preparation of this book, notably the Graduate School, the College of Liberal Arts, and the Academic Computing Services and Systems of the University of Minnesota. A number of individuals have also provided me with a great deal of support: Richard Hotchkiss, Deputy Director of Academic Computing, and Alice Hotchkiss, both of whom very ably put the computer to work and set up this book; the late Gordon W. O'Brien, Professor of English, who generously helped me with the numerous biblical references and allusions in the text; Anna A. Grotans, who carefully proofread and corrected the text; and, last but not least, Peter E. Firchow, who edited my English prose and provided much needed moral support. I want to thank them all.

Minneapolis, Minnesota
Evelyn Scherabon Firchow

This book is dedicated

to the memory of my parents

Raimund and Hildegard Scherabon

Contents

Introduction ix

Original Text and English Translation 1

   Book 1 2

   Book 2 54

   Book 3 78

Notes 109

Bibliography 111

Introduction

*T*he Old Icelandic *Elucidarius* is one of a number of translations into vernacular languages of this popular medieval Latin work, probably written in the early twelfth century by a monk called Honorius Augustodunensis. Honorius was born sometime between 1075 and 1080 and died in 1156. It is generally thought that he was either an Englishman from Canterbury or an Irish monk residing in Regensburg in Southern Germany. If so, however, his rather peculiar "surname" does not corroborate those origins, since it is difficult to associate "Augustodunensis" convincingly with either Canterbury or Ireland (or Regensburg, for that matter).

The only undisputed facts concerning his life are that he lived somewhere in Germany and that he purposely concealed his name in the preface to the *Elucidarius* because he was afraid of being accused of heresy. We also know that he referred to himself as a "presbyter et scholasticus," or priest and teacher, and that in the manuscripts he is called a "solitarius" and "inclusus," that is a hermit. Since Honorius lists an "Elucidarius" among his writings but his description thereof does not correspond precisely to the extant version, some doubt remains as to whether he was indeed the author of this work. Those scholars who do accept his authorship tend to believe that the *Elucidarius* must have been his first work, composed sometime during the first quarter of the twelfth century.

In the *Elucidarius* the author tried to provide a coherent, summary treatment of theological questions as they were discussed by the church fathers from the beginnings of ecclesiastical history until the close of the Middle Ages, and even beyond. If, however, Honorius did not succeed entirely in this attempt, that should not be surprising since virtually no one else did either. The faults that are apparent in the *Elucidarius* are perhaps due (if we can believe those who see this as Honorius' first literary production) to his relative immaturity and to his attempt to answer too many questions in too small a compass.

The work is composed in the form of a Socratic dialogue between a disciple and his teacher. The disciple asks the leading questions which propel the dialogue forward. Although the disciple is often permitted to express his own views, it is the teacher who pontificates about the whole of Christian theology, as the (modern) subtitle to the Latin *Elucidarius*, "dialogus de summa totius christianae theologiae," clearly indicates. Aside from the form and the language, there is very little that is original about the work, for Honorius simply incorporated into his text ideas and explanations provided by the church fathers and contemporary theologians, as Yves Lefèvre demonstrates convincingly in the notes to his critical edition of the Latin *Elucidarius* as it survived in France (Bibliography [9]). The arguments put forth sometimes proceed by strange leaps and bounds, and at times they appear illogical to the modern reader. Still, they are characteristic for a medieval mode of thinking which allows opposing views to be presented side by side, with the one side providing explanations according to the *lex naturalis,* and the other according to the *lex theologiae.* In this and in other respects, the *Elucidarius* mirrors the teachings (and the manner of teaching) of the Church in the Middle Ages, and as such it is a significant forerunner of the medieval *summa,* a genre which was to become the favorite scholastic form of writing during the period.

The Latin *Elucidarius* very quickly turned into a "bestseller." Its simple and naive explanations of theological questions were used to teach elementary Christianity to medieval Christians. Its audience consisted chiefly of the unlearned laity who esteemed the work for the straightforward and authoritative answers it contained. The success of the Latin version must have been immediate, since Yves Lefèvre found sixty manuscripts and fragments of the *Elucidarius* in France alone and even more have been discovered there since. The *Elucidarius* was translated into many vernacular languages; apart from Icelandic, there are extant versions in High German, Low German, French, Provençal, Italian, English, Dutch, and Swedish. At the request of Duke Henry the Lion (1129-1195) a work called *Lucidarius* was composed in Middle High German in the late twelfth century. This text is partially based on Honorius' *Elucidarius* and includes a good deal of material from other scholastic works as well. Like its predecessor, the *Lucidarius* became a very popular medieval book and was translated into numerous Western European languages including late medieval Icelandic.

The Old Icelandic translation is preserved in a total of eight parchment fragments written between approximately 1200 and the fifteenth century. They vary in length from 66 manuscript pages to a single paragraph and are all on deposit in the Arnamagnaean Collection at the University of Copenhagen:

AM 674a 4to	66 pages	7,826 words	1200 or earlier
AM 675 4to	32 pages	11,857 words	early 14th century
AM 544 4to	2½ pages	1,005 words	early 14th century
AM 229 fol. IV	1 page	1,725 words	second half, 14th century
AM 238 fol. XVIII	6 pages	3,728 words	second half, 15th century
AM 685b 4to	2 pages	642 words	second half, 15th century
AM 685d 4to	4½ pages	1,493 words	second half, 15th century
AM 238 fol. XIX	8 lines	114 words	1400 or early 15th century

Of the above manuscripts, one of the earliest translations of the original

Latin *Elucidarius* is the Old Norse/Icelandic version contained in AM 674a, 4to. Nothing is known about the translator, not even whether he was an Icelander or a Norwegian, for the two languages were at this time (c. 1200) very similar and the manuscript gives us no clues as to where it originated. For this reason I have chosen to call the language in which it is written "Old Norse/Icelandic." The manuscript itself was taken from Iceland by Árni Magnússon to Copenhagen. This fact in itself constitutes, however, no proof that it originated either in Iceland or in Norway.

Both AM 674a, 4to and AM 675, 4to, which are the two earliest manuscripts, are fairly extensive. AM 675, 4to originally formed part of the famous *Hauksbók* and appears to have been copied by a non-native scribe from an Icelandic original. It contains numerous idiosyncrasies and curious mistakes. Only two of the additional six smaller fragments are partially reprinted here: AM 544, 4to, a short insert in another part of the *Hauksbók* which was written by the so-called "first Norwegian hand;" and two of the three leaves of AM 238 fol. XVIII, which were written in Iceland like all the other fragments.

The edition which I offer here provides the longest possible version of the Old Norse/Icelandic *Elucidarius*. It is based on the diplomatic rendering of the four fragments described above which form part of the textual *corpus* prepared by myself and Kaaren Grimstad and used in our complete *Elucidarius* edition published in 1989 (Bibliography [8]). The text I have prepared for this book is an "advanced reader's version" and is meant to make the *Elucidarius* generally available to students of Old Icelandic. The corresponding English translation should not only serve as a guide through the some of the difficulties of the text but should also make it possible for students and scholars who do not read Old Norse to get a sense of what this text was actually like.

I have combined the extant Old Norse/Icelandic fragments and thereby offer an estimated 80% of the original total text, based on comparisons with Lefèvre's Latin edition. The oldest fragment AM 674a is printed in full; portions not found in this fragment but preserved in the next oldest, AM 675, are added; the next fragment, AM 238 fol. XVIII, is also provided in part, as is the last, AM 544. Thus, translations written in the course of three centuries are joined and printed here as one text even though there is no proof that they all go back to the same original version. But since the fragments from which the Old Norse/Icelandic texts are taken are clearly marked in this edition, I hope that philological "purists" will not be put out by such an unusual composite text. On the contrary, it is my hope that literary historians and critics will be pleased by an experiment of this sort, since they now have easy access to the longest possible version. For any specialized text-critical work, of course, the reader is referred to the Firchow/Grimstad edition (Bibliography [8]).

In establishing the present text, Yves Lefèvre's Latin edition served as an invaluable guide: I followed his arrangement and numbering of the disciple's questions both in the Old Norse/Icelandic and English texts to make the references easier for readers. Some questions and answers appear in a different sequence in the original fragments or have been mixed and combined. The numbering system used here reflects this inconsistency, for at times it is reversed and sometimes two or even more question numbers had to be combined. Where there are gaps in the numbering, no extant fragment has preserved the missing passage. Lefèvre's critical Latin text edition is based on the French manuscript tradition which did *not* form the basis for the Icelandic translations. Thus some of the differences between the Latin and the Old Icelandic text can be explained by a varying source text, especially in Book II, and are not simply the result of an inadequate translation.

According to Lefèvre's ordering, the sequence of the Old Norse/ Icelandic text is as follows:

Book I, questions	1–106	= AM 674a 4to, pp. 1–34
	106–139	= AM 675 4to, pp. 13–17
	140–146	= AM 674a 4to, pp. 35–36
	146–203	= AM 675 4to, pp. 18–25
Book II, questions	1–75	= AM 675 4to, pp. 25–32
	75–94	= AM 238 fol. XVIII, fol. 1^r–1^v
Book III, questions	7–21	= AM 238 fol. XVIII, fol. 2^r–2^v
	2–42	= AM 544 4to, fol. 11^r–12^r
	57–120	= AM 674a 4to, pp. 37–66

There are not only *lacunae* within the three books but particularly also between each of the three books: for example, II, 95–106; III, 1–6, 22–31, 43–56, and 121–122 are missing altogether. Parallel passages preserved in the various fragments were not included in this edition, since they represent duplications. It is not my intention here to present a critical text edition of the *Elucidarius* and for this reason the differences between the parallel passages are not given. The following parallel manuscript passages were omitted:

AM 675 4to, pages 1–13, 17–18	=	Book I, questions 1–106, 140–146
AM 229 fol. IV, fol. 2^v	=	Book I, questions 1–40
AM 685d 4to, fol. 8^v–10	=	Book I, questions 1–32
AM 238 fol. XIX, fol. 1^r–1^v	=	Book I, question 21
AM 685b 4to	=	Book II, questions 8–13
AM 544 4to, fol. 10^v–11^r	=	Book II, questions 75–76
AM 238 fol. XVIII, fol. 3	=	Book III, questions 69–100

Scholars interested in these passages are referred to the complete diplomatic edition.

The Latin *Elucidarius* is divided into three books: Book I deals with divine matters, particularly with the nature of the Trinity, genesis, the fall of Adam, the Incarnation and Redemption. Book II considers ecclesiastical concerns, especially man's salvation through the church and the sacraments. Book III discusses the afterlife and the Last Judgment, the fate of the damned in hell and the joys of those saved in Paradise. It should be noted, however, that in the Old Norse/Icelandic manuscripts the division into three books is not marked.

I have tried to prepare a reliable Old Norse/Icelandic text which is sufficiently detailed and accurate to be used for various kinds of study. The present text clearly reflects how Icelandic has changed during the three centuries when the vernacular fragments were written. I also hope to draw the attention of language students to the lack of homogeneity within the individual fragments as well as to the historical changes which occurred in the language during a span of 300 years. I hope to encourage investigators of Old Norse/Icelandic to return to a study of the language and to the texts as they are preserved in the medieval manuscripts. I feel very strongly that normalization and the process of "cleaning up" text versions to make them more readily accessible to readers have obscured many details and facts about Old Norse/Icelandic. Once scholars begin again to study the texts in their original form, many generalizations and simplifications about philological, linguistic, and literary matters will need to be revised. The basis of all scholarly work in the medieval period must always remain the extant manuscript texts themselves despite claims to the contrary. This diplomatic edition then was not prepared for such readers of Old Norse/Icelandic who need a "beautified" normalized and thus "easily readable" medieval text in order to understand it. It is meant for scholars (and students) who want to struggle to understand the preserved "raw" versions of the manuscripts without active intervention — or interference — by a contemporary editorial mind.

For all of these reasons I have refrained from producing a normalized and "corrected" *Elucidarius* version with the conventional pseudo-appearance of a standardized and uniformly written medieval text. Nevertheless, a number of (editorial) compromises did prove to be necessary. Though I did not "rewrite" sentences or phrases which were wrongly translated or copied in the manuscripts, I did indicate the most glaring instances of such errors in the notes. I did not "correct" the irregular spelling within each fragment or unify it for all fragments. I did not add punctuation marks but merely printed those found in the manuscripts. Periods which are part of abbreviations were omitted, however, when the abbreviations were resolved and the period did not stand at the end of a sentence. The abbreviations were resolved according to the spelling conventions within each individual fragment and marked in italics. Small capitals in medial or final word positions denoting double consonants were resolved as such and printed in italics. Small capitals in initial word positions are printed as regular capitals. A number of ligatures were resolved without comment since I did not want to clutter up the text with too many unusual letters and make it unattractive to use and difficult to cite. My computer expert Dick Hotchkiss originally designed all of these symbols but we decided against using them in the end. Other changes were made as follows: Periods above consonants have been omitted and double consonants were substituted. The manuscripts use various symbols for <u, v, y> such as: u, U, v, V, y, Y, ẏ, ɣ, ɣ̇, and these are reproduced here. All accent marks remain as they were found in the manuscripts, word divisions likewise. If a word is broken at the end of a line and hyphenated, it is indicated by a hyphen in the text. If there is no hyphen in the manuscript, I have indicated that the separated parts belong together by inserting a hyphen in square brackets to show broken words or compounds. I did not mark the end of manuscript lines, but the manuscript pages are indicated by manuscript number and page or leaf designation in bold face. Letters written above or below the line in the manuscripts are marked ∨ or ∧. As a consequence, the Old Norse/Icelandic text in this edition has a rather unconventional appearance. Scholars who wish to have additional information about the fragments are referred to the diplomatic and the facsimile editions (Bibliography [8], [1], [6], [7]) which show the manuscript abbreviations and, in the case of the diplomatic edition, the suggested resolutions throughout.

The symbols used in the Old Norse/Icelandic text are as follows: all fragments are indicated by manuscript number and page in boldface and enclosed in [[ ]]. Lefèvre's numberings of the Latin text are given at the beginning of each question of the disciple in Arabic numerals and enclosed in double guillemets « ». In many instances the Old Norse/Icelandic fragments do not write out *Discipulus* or *Magister*: these were placed in single pointed brackets by me < > and if the scribe used an abbreviation here, the actually preserved letter(s) are printed in regular script: <D*iscipulus*> therefore means that the scribe wrote only D and I have supplied the rest. A series of periods mark (major) *lacunae* and I have tried to indicate the amount of space left in the manuscripts in the case of shorter *lacunae*: each period corresponds to one missing letter; illegible or damaged passages or words are placed within [ ] if they were supplied from parallel texts; if there are no parallel texts available, missing or illegible words are indicated by [....]; words or letters supplied by the editors appear in < >, they are not found in the manuscripts.

In the English translation Lefèvre's numbers are also indicated. A series of periods again mark *lacunae*. References to quotations and allusions from the Bible are placed in parentheses ( ). The biblical references are based on the King James version of 1611; where the numbering differs from the Vulgate, Vulgate numbers appear first, separated by / from the King James Bible numbers. Additions of words as well as phrases missing in the Old Icelandic text and supplied from the Latin, as well as textual explanations supplied by the translator are printed in double guillemets.

Finally, a comment on the translation itself. I have tried to give as accurate a rendering of the fragments as possible without translating every "ok" and "en" contained in the original texts. This translation into contemporary American English is therefore not a word-for-word interlinear rendering of the medieval manuscripts. What I have hoped to avoid at all cost is to prepare a "trot" or a "crib," since my principal aim has been to make readers appreciate and enjoy the work. Occasionally, passages in the Old Norse/Icelandic text are not very clear, and some passages represent examples of typical scholastic "double think," while yet others can be interpreted in a number of different ways. I have noted the most glaring obscurities and errors in my notes without attempting to hide in any way the gyrations, contradictions and strange turns of mind present in this immensely influential and valuable work. The actual source of the Old Norse/Icelandic translation is unknown and so it is not certain whether the obscurities found are due to the Latin original or to the Scandinavian translator(s). I trust that I have not added to these obscurities in this translation.

Original Text and English Translation

[[674a:1]] Ofst va[s] ek be[þ]e*nn* af sa*m*lere suei[-]no*m* mino*m* at leysa or yandrẹþo*m* necq*u*erra sp*u*rninga oc syndesc m*er* o[-]maklect at neita þei*m* fyse sinne allra helzt af þvi at ek hreddo*mc* at fyr dømasc ef ek fela þegian[-]de i iorþo pund þ*at* es Goþ selde m[*er*] þ[*ui*]at Goþ tekr fra þeim auþ[o]ve es þei[-]ra vill ei*nn* niota *oc* spara [v]iþ þ*u*r[-]fanda. E*nn* af þvi [r]e[it] ek [*oc*] sendac boc þessa. at sysla mín stoþaþe *ei*ge at eins þessar tiþar m[*onno*]m he*l*dr *oc* þei*m* es siþa*rr* ero. E*nn* h*u*e*rr* biþe f*vrr* m*er* es þessa boc le*ss*. Bok þessa kalla ek elucidariu*m* e*nn* þ*at* es lvseng þu*i*at ihe*nn*e lysasc necq[*uer*er] mvrq[*ue*]r hlut*er*. E*nn* af þvi þagþa ek v[*uer* na]fne mino at *ei*ge [[674a:2]] egiaþe ov*vnn*d ohlvþna m*enn* at haf-na nvto v*er*ke. E*nn* sa es boc þessa le*ss* biþe at þ*at* nafn se ritet alifs bok a hi*m*ne. E*nn* þessa v*er*x grundvollr sc*al* setr vesa v*uer* biarg þ*at* es *cr*istus *oc* oll sia smiþ es studd meþ .iiii. stoplo*m*. E*nn* fvrsta stopol reiser spama*nn*a scýn-seme. en annan styþr postola tign. en þ*ri*þia efler speke feþra en e*nn* .iiij fester vitr. ahvggia lẹrefeþra. E*nn* sia boc es oll gór efst*er* tuegia viþr mẹle. þat es spvrianda lẹre-svei*nn*s *oc* svara*nn*da lerefoþor. Boc s[ia heit*er*] eluci[dari*us*]

«1.1» <Discipulus> Ek biþ þic dv*r*-legr lerefaþ*er* at þu suar*er* þvi es ek spvrk þic til nvtseme heilag[-]rar *cr*istne.

Magist*er*. Þat mon ek ge[-][[674a:3]]ra ef Goþ gef*rr*. m*er* afl til *oc* mon m*er* *ei*ge þvngia þ[*et*]ta erveþe.

«1.2» Discip*ulus*. Sva es sagt at ma*nn*ge veit h*u*at Goþ es e*nn* oss svnesc omaklect at vita *ei*ge h*u*at v*er* gofgo*m*. Af þvi sc*al* þ*at* uphaf vesa þessa mals at þu seg m*er* fvrst huat Goþ es.

M*a*gist*er*. Goþ es andlegr eldr at þvi es helzt ma sciliasc sua biart *oc* ou*m*broþelegr ifegrþ *oc* idv́rþ at englar es .vii. hlutu*m* ero fegre an sol fvssasc of valt at sia ha*nn* *oc* una viþ fegrþ ha*n*s.

«1.3» Discipulus. Huerso es ei*nn* Goþ iþrennningo.

M*a*gist*er*. Sua sem þu ser þre*nn*ing í solo. þ*at* es eldr *oc* hite *oc* lios. Þesser hlu[-]t*er* ero sua osundrskilleg*er* at enge ma fra oþrom scilia ísolo*nn*e. sua [[674a:4]] sem Goþ es osund*r*scillegr iþre*nn*ingo. Faþer es íeldlego ẹþle en son*rr* íliose. en heilagr ande ihita.

« Book 1 »

I have often been asked by my fellow disciples to answer questions and to clear up doubts. Hence I did not think it right to refuse their request especially since I was afraid to be damned, if, by remaining silent, I hid in the earth the talent that God has given to me (Matt. 25:25). For God takes away riches from those who use them for their own benefit only and who keep them from those in need. For this reason I wrote and published this book so that my efforts would be of use not only to contemporaries but also to posterity.

Let everyone who reads this book pray for me. I shall call this book *Elucidarius* — which means "Illuminator" — because some unexplained matters are illuminated here. And I shall not mention my name, so that no one will be prejudiced by envy to disregard a useful work. But whoever reads this book should pray that its name be recorded in the book of life in heaven, that the foundation of this work be set up on the Rock which is Christ (1 Cor. 10:4), and that the whole artifact be supported by four columns. The first column serves to hold up the understanding of the prophets; the second to support the honor of the apostles; the third to strengthen the wisdom of the fathers; and the fourth to uphold the wise concern of the teachers.

This book is made up entirely of a dialogue consisting of the questions of the Disciple and the answers of the Master. This book is called *Elucidarius*.

«1.1» Disciple: I request, dear esteemed teacher, that you answer my questions for the benefit of Holy Christianity.

Master: I will agree to do so if God grants me the strength and this task will not burden me.[1]

«1.2» Disciple: It is said that nobody knows who God is. Since it does not seem appropriate not to know whom we worship, could you at the beginning of this discussion tell me who God is?

Master: God is spiritual fire, which means: he is so brilliant and unchanging in beauty and glory that the angels, who are seven times brighter than the sun, desire always to gaze upon Him and rejoice in His beauty.

«1.3» Disciple: How can one God be a Trinity?

Master: You can see the Trinity in the sun, which consists of fire, heat and light. These aspects of the sun are so inseparable that they cannot be distinguished from one another. In the same way God is inseparable in the Trinity. The Father appears in the substance of

«1.4» D*iscipulus*. Fvr hui kal-lasc Go*þ* fa*þ*er.
M*agister*. Þu*i*at h*ann* es alz uphaf *oc* ero af ho*n*om aller hlut*er* scapa*þ*er en speke h*ann*s kallasc sonr h*ann*s.
«1.5» D*iscipulus*. Fvr hui sonr.
M*agister* Þu*i* at h*ann* es sua gete*nn* af fe*þ*r se*m* scin af solo. e*nn* begia þ*ei*ra ost nefnesc sp*iritus* s*an*c*tu*s.
«1.6» D*iscipulus*. Fvr hui heilagr ande.
M*agister*. Þu*i*at h*ann* ferr fra*m* af huoro*m*tueggia eilifle-ga svase*m* ande bl*es*[c] af mu*nn*ne. þ*at* afl Go*þ*do*m*s kallasc fa*þ*er es alla hlu[-]te scapa*þ*e. e*nn* sa kallasc sonr es heldr *oc* styrer ollo at e*i*ge faresc. E*nn* sa nefnesc heilagr ande es alt fegr*er oc* lifgar íábl*es*te sino*m*. Af fe*þ*r ero aller hlut*er oc* fvr son aller hlut[*er*] *oc* [[674a:5]] ihelgo*m* anda aller hlut*er*.

«1.7» D*iscipulus*. Ef Go*þ* kal-lasc dvr*þ oc* milde fvr hui heit*er* h*ann* fa*þ*er heldr án mo*þ*er.
M*agister* Þu*i*at af fe*þ*r es uphaf alz getna*þ*ar. sua s*em* af Go*þ*e es alz uphaf.

«1.8» D*iscipulus* Ef sonr kallasc dó*þ oc* speke. hui heit*er* h*ann* held*r* sonr an dott*er*.
M*agister* Þu*i*at sonr es fe*þ*r glikare an dott*er*.
«1.10» D*iscipulus*. Huar byggver Go*þ*.
M*agister*. Hvor-vetna es velde h*ann*s en þo es o*þ*le h*ann*s iscilni*n*gar hi*m*ne.

«1.11» D*iscipulus*. Huat es scilni*n*-gar himi*nn*
M*agister* Þrir ero hi*m*nar. Ei*nn* lica*m*legr sa es v*er* mego*m* sia. A*nn*a*rr* a*n*dlegr. þar es andlegar scepnor bvggua þ*at* ero englar. E*nn* þri*þ*e es scilni*n*gar himi*nn* þar es heilog þre*n*-ni*n*g bvggver. *oc* helg*er* englar me-go þar sia Go*þ*.

«1.12» D*iscipulus*. Huerso kallasc Go*þ* [[674a:6]] allr iollo*m* sto*þ*om vesa *oc* á valt allr sama*n oc* íeino*m* sta*þ*.
M*agister*. Iollo*m* sto*þ*om. se-gesc Go*þ* allr vesa. þu*i*at h*ann* es ia*m*mottogr íollo*m* sto*þ*om slict íhelvite se*m* íhimin-riki. Allr sama*n* segesc h*ann* vesa þu*i*at h*ann* styrer ollo*m* se*nn* íaustre *oc* ivestre. Of valt segesc h*ann* vesa íollo*m* sto*þ*om. þu*i*at h*ann* stvr*er* ollo ia*m*t áhv*er*re ti*þ*. Iengo*m* sta*þ* segesc h*ann* vesa. þu*i*at h*ann* es ólica*m*legr *oc* ma e*i*ge lica*m*legr sta*þ*r halda á Go*þ*e. enn h*ann* held*r* sama*nn* ollo*m* hluto*m oc* livo*m* v*er* iho*n*om *oc* ero*m*.

fire, the Son in the form of light, and the Holy Ghost in the embodiment of heat.

«1.4» Disciple: Why do we call God "Father?"

Master: Because He is the origin of everything and all things were created by Him. His wisdom is called "His Son."

«1.5» Disciple: Why "His Son?"

Master: Because He is begotten by the Father in the same way as the sunshine is begotten by the sun. Their love is called *spiritus sanctus*.

«1.6» Disciple: Why "Holy Spirit?"

Master: Because the Holy Spirit issues forth eternally from the Father and the Son in the same way as breath comes from the mouth. That godly power which created all things is called the Father, and He is called the Son who preserves and keeps everything so that nothing is lost. And He is called the Holy Spirit who beautifies and revives by His breath. For all things come from the Father, and all things are for the Son, and in the Holy Spirit all things are contained.

«1.7» Disciple: If God is called glory and kindness, why do we call Him "Father" rather than "Mother?"

Master: Because the father is the origin of everything begotten. In the same way God is the origin of everything.

«1.8» Disciple: If the Son is called omnipotence and wisdom, why do we call Him "Son" rather than "Daughter?"

Master: Because a son rather than a daughter is more like the father.

«1.10» Disciple: Where does God live?

Master: His Kingdom is everywhere, but His home is in the heaven of understanding.

«1.11» Disciple: What is the heaven of understanding?

Master: There are three heavens (2 Cor. 12:2): first a physical heaven which we can see; the second heaven is spiritual, where the spiritual beings called angels live; and the third is the heaven of understanding, where the Holy Trinity lives and where the holy angels can see God.

«1.12» Disciple: How can they say that God is One and in all places at once, and at the same time One in a single place?

Master: God is said to be One in all places at once because He is equally powerful everywhere, in hell as well as in heaven. He is said to be One because He rules everything at once in the East and in the West. He is said to be in all places always because He rules over everything at the same time. He is said to be in no particular place because He has no physical body, and no physical place can

«1.13» D*iscipulus*. Veit G*o*þ alt.
M*agister*. Fv*rer* sér h*ann* alla hlute lip̄na *oc* óorþna sua se*m* nulega *oc* visse h*ann* fv*rr* an h*ann* scapa[-]þe hei*m* þe*nn*a allra engla *oc* m*enn* nofn *oc* siþo *oc* vilia orþ *oc* verk *oc* hugre*nn*i*n*-gar.
«1.15» D*iscipulus*. Scolom ver þat ę̄tla at Goþ lifþe [[674a:7]] ei*nn*slego life aþ*r* h*ann* scapaþe hei*m*.
M*agister*. Sva es ritet. þat vas lif ísiolvo*m* Goþe es gort vas. Iþesso*m* orþo*m* scyresc at oll scepna vas á valt svneleg ífy*rer* etlon Goþs su es siþan varþ syneleg scepno*nn*e sial-fre. þaes hon vas scopoþ. Sua se*m* smiþr sa es h*us* vill g*er*a lit*rr* fyrst h*u*erso h*ann* vill hvatke g*er*a. *oc* riss su smiþ si-þan í v*er*ke es fy*rr* stoþ smiþoþ íhug-uite smiþsens. Af þvi kallasc Goþ eige fv*rr*e scepno sinne at tíþ held*r* at tign.

«1.16» D*iscipulus* Hver soc vas til þes at heim*r* vęre scapaþ*r*.
M*agister* Gø̄zka Goþs at þeir v*er*e es h*ann* mę́tte veítta miscu*nn* si*nn*a.

«1.17» D*iscipulus* h*u*erso vas heim*r* gorr.
M*agister* Sialfr mę̄lte Goþ *oc* voro þegar gorv*er* aller hlut*er*.

«1.18» D*iscipulus* Mę̄lte Goþ þat orþom.
M*agister* Þa mę̄lte Goþ orþ es h*ann* sca[-][[674a:8]]paþe alla hl*u*te fvr son es kallasc orþ foþor se*m* ritet es. Alt g*er*þ*er* þu í speke Goþs.

«1.19-20» D*iscipulus*. Vas h*on*om duol necqu*er* at scapa eþa scapaþe h*ann* alt se*nn*.
M*agister*. Aei-no avga bragþe scapaþe h*ann* alt se*nn* se*m* ritet es. Saes eiliv*er* scapaþe alt se*nn*. E*nn* h*ann* scifste ollo íhlute á .vi. dogo*m* hofoþ scepno*m* .iii*a*. daga en aþra .iii*a*. þei*m* hluto*m* es fvr i*nn*nan hofoþ skepnor ero. E*nn* fv*r*sta dag scop h*ann* eilifs dag þat es andlect lios *oc* alla andlega skepno. Annan dag scop h*ann* him*in* þa*nn* es skilr licam̄lega scepno fra andlegre. E*nn* en þriþia dag sę *oc* iorþ. E*nn* .iiii. dag scop h*ann* tiþlegan dag þat es sol *oc* tungl *oc* stiornor á e*nn*ne ofsto hofoþ [[674a:9]] skepno. þat es áhi*m*ne. E*nn* .v. dag sc[op] h*ann* fogla *oc* fisca. *oc* sette fogla ílof[-]ste e*nn* fisca ívatne. E*nn* .vi. dag scop h*ann* dyr *oc* ma*nn* ór e*nn*ne neþ[-]sto hofoþ skepno. þat es ór iorþo.

comprehend God. He holds together the whole universe and in Him we live and have our being (Acts 17:28).

«1.13» Disciple: Does God know everything?

Master: He knows all things, the past, the future as well as the present. And before He created this world, He knew the names of all the angels and men, their customs, desires, words, deeds, and thoughts.

«1.15» Disciple: Should we believe that God led a solitary life before He created the world?

Master: As is written: It was life in God Himself that was made (John 1:3-4). From these words we can see that the whole creation was always visible in God's design and later became visible to the creation itself after it was created. In the same way the mason who wants to build a house first plans how he will build it. After that the building, which before was only in the mason's mind, rises in reality. For this reason God is said to be before His creation not in time but in rank.

«1.16» Disciple: What was the reason for creating the world?

Master: The goodness of God, so that those beings would exist to whom He could show His grace.

«1.17» Disciple: How was the world created?

Master: God Himself commanded, and all things were created forthwith (Pss. 32/33:9).

«1.18» Disciple: Did God command with words?

Master: God spoke words when He created everything, through the Son who is called the Word of the Father (John 1:1), as is written: In the wisdom of God have you made all (Pss. 103/104:24).

«1.19-20» Disciple: Did it take Him long to create everything or did He create everything at once?

Master: He created everything in the twinkling of an eye, as is written: He who lives eternally created all at once (Eccl. 18:1). And He divided everything in six days: the elements in three days, and in the next three days those things which are contained in the elements. On the first day He created eternal day, which is spiritual light, and all spiritual creatures. On the second day He created heaven, which separates the earthly from the spiritual creatures. On the third day He created the sea and the earth. On the fourth day He created temporal day, that is sun, moon, and stars in the highest element which is heaven. On the fifth day He created the birds and the fish, and put the birds in the sky and the fish in the water. On the sixth day He created animals and man out of the lowest element which is earth.

«1.21» Discipulus Kennna scepnor Goþ.
Magister Etke gerþe Goþ þat es eige kennne hann. þuiat andlauser hluter ero oss dauþer. oc oscynsamer enn al-ler hluter lifa Goþe oc kennna scapera sinn. Himinn kennner hann þuiat hann snvsc of valt efster boþorþe hans sem ritet es. Goþ gerþe himna ískilningo. Sol oc tungl oc stiornor kennna Goþ þuiat þau varþ-veita staþe rasar sinnnar at vilia hans. Iorþ kennner hann. þuiat hon gefr ávoxt oc gros ásinnne tiþ. Ár kennna Goþ þuiat þę́r huerva afstr avalt til staþa sinna þa-[[674a:10]]þan es þę́r falla. Sęr oc vinndar kennna Goþ þuiat þeir stoþvasc at boþorþe hans. Dauþer menn kennna hann þuiat þeir risa up at raþe hans. Heluite kenner hann. þuiat þat geldr sem hann bvþr þa es þat glévpþe. Oll cvquende kennna Goþ þuiat þau hal[-]da logom þeim es hann gaf þeim.
«1.23» Discipulus. Scvr-þu alt framarr þetta.
Magister. Goþ almatte-gr konongr gerþe sser fyrst albiarta holl þa es hann kallaþe riki himna si-þan gerþe hann mvrqua stofo þat es heim þenna enn íþeire mvrquastofo sette hann dauþa grof þat es helvite. Til hallar sinnar set-te hann uisa tolo valra riþara þa er nauþ-svn vas at fvlla oc eige lofat viþ at auka. Enn þessa tolo valþe hann af monnom oc engl[om] oc greinnde .i .x. sueiter .ix engla [[674a:11]] en x.ndo manna.

«1.24» Discipulus. Fyr hui nio sueiter engla.
Magister Þuiat nio ero þrysvar .iii. þat es þrevold þrennning.
«1.25» Discipulus Fvr hui einn sveit manna.
Magister. At einn Goþ se gofgaþr i .iii°. oc þrennning íei-ningo af englom oc monnom.
«1.26» Discipulus Fvr hui vil-de hann eige alla tolo fylla af englom.
Magister Tuennnar hofoþskepnor gerþe Goþ. aþra andlega enn aþra licamlega oc vilde hann loyaþr vesa af huarre tyeggio af andlegre. þat es af englom. oc af licam-legre þat es af monnom.

«1.27» Discipulus Hue ner voro enn-glar scapaþer.
Magister Þa es Goþ męlte verþe lios.
«1.28» Discipulus Męlte hann þesse orþ.
Magister Eige męlte hann. heldr es oss svnt íþessom orþom tign eþles þei[-]ra es þeir kallasc lios.
«1.29» Discipulus Huert es eþle engla.
Magister. Andlegr eldr sem ritet es. Sa es gerþe engla ór elz loga.

«1.21» Disciple: Do all creatures know God?

Master: God made nothing which does not know Him. Although lifeless things seem dead and not rational to us, nevertheless all things live for God and know their Creator. Heaven knows Him and forever turns according to His command, as is written: God made the heavens by wisdom (Pss. 135/136:5). The sun, moon, and stars know God because they stay in their tracks according to His will. The earth knows Him and produces vegetation and grass at the appropriate times. The rivers know God and they always return to their source. The sea and the winds know God and they stop at His command. The dead know Him and they rise at His will. Hell knows Him and it returns those it devoured as He commands. All animals know God and they observe the laws which He gave them.

«1.23» Disciple: Can you explain all this in more detail?

Master: God, the Almighty King, first created a brilliant hall for Himself, which He called the Kingdom of Heaven. Then He fashioned a dungeon, which is this world, and in this dungeon He placed the pit of death, which is hell. Into His hall God ordered a certain number of chosen knights, as many as were necessary to fill it, but He did not permit any more than that. And He chose this number from among men and angels and divided them into ten hosts, nine consisting of angels and the tenth of men.

«1.24» Disciple: Why nine hosts of angels?

Master: Because nine is three times three or tripled Trinity.

«1.25» Disciple: Why one host of men?

Master: Because one God is honored in this Trinity and this Trinity is honored in the unity of angels and men.

«1.26» Disciple: Why did he not want to fill all the hosts with angels?

Master: God created two types of creatures, one spiritual and the other physical, and He wanted to be praised by both of them: by the spiritual creatures or angels, and by the physical beings who are men.

«1.27» Disciple: When were the angels created?

Master: When God said: Let there be light (Gen. 1:3).

«1.28» Disciple: Did He say these words?

Master: He did not actually speak them; rather in these words we are shown the sublime nature of these words, which is called light.

«1.29» Disciple: What is the nature of the angels?

Master: It is spiritual fire, as is written: He made the angels out of the flames of fire (Heb. 1:7).

«1.30» D*iscipulus*. Hafa [[674a:12]] englar nofn.
M*agister* Sua mikit es vit en*n*gla at þeir þvrfo e*i*ge nafna.

«1.31» D*iscipulus* Mi-chael gabriel raphael ero e*i*ge þat en-gla nofn.
M*agister* Hel*d*r ke*nn*ni*n*gar nofn þau es m*en*n gofo þei*m* af atburþ. Sua se*m* e*nn* fvrste e*n*ngell toc nafn af at[-]burþ *oc* vas kallaþr sataél þat es go-þs andscote.

«1.32» D*iscipulus*. Ihui vas h*ann* andscote. Goþs.
M*agister* Þa es h*ann* sa sic ollo*m* englo*m* oþra í dyrþ *oc* fegrþ. þa fyr leit h*ann* þat alt *oc* vilde vesa iafn se*m* Goþ eþa meire.

«1.33» D*iscipulus* H*u*erso iafn eþa meire.
M*agister* Oþre tign vilde h*ann* taka af nauþgo*m* Goþe an Goþ gaf hono*m* at raþa oþro*m* fyr of rike.
«1.34» D*iscipulus* Huat gerþesc þa.
M*agister*. Braut vas h*ann* re-ke*nn* ór kon*ong*s hollo *oc* setr ídvflizo *oc* varþ e*nn* liotaste es fvrst vas e*nn* [[674a:13]] fegrste. *oc* reke*nn* fra ollo*m* veg es fv*rr* vas prydr ollo*m* veg.

«1.35» D*iscipulus* Visse h*ann* fv*r*er fall sitt.
M*agister* Ollunges e*i*ge.
«1.36» D*iscipulus*. Hue len-ge vas h*ann* ahi*m*ne.
M*agister* E*i*ge alla eina stund þu*i*at h*ann* viltesc þegar es h*ann* vas scapaþr oc fvr let et sa*n*na.
«1.37-37a» D*iscipulus* Hui vas h*ann* e*i*ge þar lengr.
M*agister* Þu*i*at at h*ann* cnat-te engo bergia af hi*m*nesco*m* søtleik. þu*i*at h*ann* huarf þegar fra sonno liose oc fyldesc ildzco. es h*ann* vas scapaþr.
«1.38-39» D*iscipulus* Hvat misgerþo aþ*r*er englar.
M*agister* Þat es þeir urþo sa*m* huga viþ ofmetnoþ h*an*s. *oc* etloþo sic oþro*m* englo*m* øþre møn-do verþa ef h*ann* mette meira an Goþ.
«1.40» D*iscipulus* Hvat varþ þeim.
M*agister* Meþ hono*m* voro þeir abraut recn*er oc* send*er* sum*er* íhelvi-tes diup. e*nn* sum*er* i myrc*ra* lofst *oc* ha-[[674a:14]]fa þo qu*o*l se*m* hin*er* es ihelvite bre*nn*a.
«1.41» D*iscipulus* Hvi e*i*ge aller ihelvite.
M*agister* At þeir me-ge reyna goþa m*en*n *oc* illa ífreist-ne si*nn*e sua at helg*er* m*enn* se dyrþar verþ*er* fvr þat. e*nn* ill*er* eilifra qu*a*la.

«1.30» Disciple: Do the angels have names?
Master: So great is the intelligence of the angels that they do not need names.
«1.31» Disciple: Michael, Gabriel, Raphael — are those not names of angels?
Master: These are surnames which men gave them to characterize their nature. Just as the first angel got his name from his characteristics and was called Satael, that is God's adversary.
«1.32» Disciple: In what way was he an adversary of God?
Master: When he regarded himself as superior in honor and beauty to all other angels, he became dissatisfied and wanted to be equal to God or even higher (Isa. 14:13-14).
«1.33» Disciple: How did he want to be equal to God or even higher?
Master: He wanted a higher rank than God was willing to give him, so that he could rule over others in tyranny.
«1.34» Disciple: What happened then?
Master: He was driven away from the King's hall and put in prison, and he became the ugliest angel, he who first had been the most beautiful. And he was deprived of all honor, he who earlier had been adorned with all honors.
«1.35» Disciple: Did he know about his fall beforehand?
Master: No, of course not.
«1.36» Disciple: How long was he in heaven?
Master: Not even for a whole hour, because he went astray immediately after he was created and left the truth (John 8:44).
«1.37-37a» Disciple: Why was he not there longer?
Master: He could not enjoy heaven's sweetness because he turned away from the true light and was filled with wickedness as soon as he was created.
«1.38-39» Disciple: What did the other angels do wrong?
Master: They acknowledged his arrogance and wanted to be raised higher than the other angels since he seemed more powerful than God.
«1.40» Disciple: What became of them?
Master: They were driven away together with Satael. Some were sent into the depths of hell and some into the heights of darkness where they suffer pain like those who burn in hell.
«1.41» Disciple: Why were not all of them sent to hell?
Master: So that they may test both good and wicked men by temptation in such a way that the saints will be worthy of glory and the wicked will be assured of eternal pain.

«1.42-43» *Discipulus* Hvi hurfo þeir eige afstr.

Magister Eige motto þeir. þuiat enge barg þeim til upriso sem enge tevgþe þa til falz. Af þvi vas maklega fra þeim tekenn allr goþr vile. at þeir volþo sér sialfer ilt. oc mego þeir eige afstr huerua. þuiat þeir vilia aldrege gott.

«1.44» *Discipulus* Hui lęvste cristr þa eige sem menn.

Magister Englar voro aller senn scapaþer eige af einom engle sem menn ero getner af .i. manne. Englar ero o dauþleger oc motto þeir eige af þui leẏster verþa. at Goþ vildi eige annat [[674a:15]] hafa til lausnar an dauþann. oc leẏs-te hann af þui eige engla at hann matte eige deyia í engles eþle þot hann tø-ke þat af .i. engle

«1.45» *Discipulus* Hui scapaþe Goþ þa eige sua at þ[eir] mętte eige misgera.

Magister Fvr retlete at þeir mętte retta ombon taka fyr v[er]þleic sinn. Ef þeir vere sua scapaþer at þeir mętte eige misgera. þa hefþe þeir enge verþleic viþ Goþ þuiat þeir gerþe sua sem nauþger gott. Enn hann gaf þeim sialfręþe at þeir mętte oc vilde velia ser gott. Enn hann gaf þeim sialfręþe. at þeir mętte oc vil-de velia ser gott.[2] oc tøke þeir at retto íombon ef þeir velþe ser gott. at þeir mętte aldrege siþan misgera.

«1.46» *Discipulus* Hui scapaþe Goþ þa engla [[674a:16]] es hann visse fyrer at iller møndo ver[-]þa.

Magister Fyr pryþi verx sins. þuiat þa es huitr litr eþa rauþr es biartare. ef svartr es hia scrivaþr. Sua ero oc retlater þa dvrlegre es þeir ver-þa sundrleiter hia illom.

«1.47» *Discipulus* Hui sca-paþe Goþ eige aþra engla istaþ þei-ra.

Magister Eige otto aþrer englar at coma istaþ þeira nema sliker vere sem þeir ef þesser stoþesc at osenne pisl svnþugra. En þat matte eige ve[-]sa. þuiat þesser fello þegar ípisler es þeir misgerþo.

«1.48» *Discipulus* Uito dioflar alla hlute.

Magister Af engla eþle vito þeir ma[-]rt oc eige alt. oc sua sem þeira oþle es gløgsẏnna an manna. sua ero þeir oc slogre íollom velom an menn. Enn þa eina [[674a:17]] vito þeir oorþna h[lut]e es þ[ei]r ra[þa] at glikendom af liþnom hlutom e[þa] Goþ lętr þa vita. Enn enge ueit hugren-ningar manna nema Goþ einn. oc þeir es hann ui-trar þat.

«1.48a» *Discipulus* Hui møne eige dioflar vita illa hugrenning ef hon virþesc ofst sem unnit verk.

«1.42-43» Disciple: Why did they not return?

Master: They could not because nobody helped them until resurrection, just as no one had lured them to their fall. All good will was taken from them because they chose to be wicked; they can never return because they never wanted to be good.

«1.44» Disciple: Why did Christ not redeem them as He redeemed men?

Master: All angels were created at the same time. They are not descended from one angel, as men are begotten of one man. Angels are immortal and therefore could not be redeemed, because God did not want any redemption other than through death. He did not redeem the angels for He Himself could not die in the shape of an angel, even if He had assumed the nature of an angel.

«1.45» Disciple: Why did God not create the angels so that they could not sin?

Master: For the sake of justice, so that they could receive their just reward for their worth. Had they been created without the ability to sin, they would not have had any merit before God because they would have acted well only out of necessity. But He gave them the freedom of choice, so that they could and would choose to be good, and so that they could justly receive their reward, if they chose to be good, and would never sin again.

«1.46» Disciple: Why did God create the angels if He knew beforehand that they would turn wicked?

Master: To embellish His work. Just as white or red is more outstanding if black is written next to it, in the same way the righteous are more glorious when they are compared to the wicked.

«1.47» Disciple: Why did God not create other angels in their stead?

Master: Other angels could not have taken their place unless they were like them before they had seen the torture of the sinners. But that was impossible because they suffered torture at once when they sinned.

«1.48» Disciple: Do the devils know everything?

Master: Having the nature of angels, they know a great deal but not everything. Their nature is such that they are more sharp-witted than men and they are also more cunning in all crafts than men; they know the future because they guess at it from past events or because God lets them know it. However, nobody knows the thoughts of men but God alone and those to whom He reveals them.

«1.48a» Disciple: Why should the devils not know evil thoughts which are often considered the same as evil actions?

M*agister* Sia mego þeir sca-pasc ihugrenni*n*go sc*r*imsl þau es þeir casta íhug m*onn*om þuiat þegar scýggua necq*uer* svnþa myrkr andar lios. E*nn* þei*r* of sia e*i*ge asionor c*r*afsta þera es Go*þ* sende*r* íhug m*onn*om þ*ui*at þei*r* mego e*i*ge be[-]ra scin retle̜tes Go*þ*s held*r* an v*er* solar lios. þ*ui*at þeir mønd ͺo ́ e*i*ge freista heilagra. ef þeir visse sic mega yu*er* stigask.

«1.49» D*i*scipulus Me-go þei*r* alt þ*at* es þei*r* vilia.
M*agister* Etke mego þeir gott ne vilia. enþeir vilia huet[-][[674a:18]] [vetna ilt *oc* me]go þ*at* eitt es goþer en[-]glar lata þa mega.

«1.50» D*i*scipulus Huat seger þu fra goþo*m*.
M*agister* Efste*r* fall vandra engla styrcþosc þesser. sua at þei*r* motto aldrege siþan misg*er*a.
«1.53» D*i*scipulus Vas e*i*ge fall hi*nn*a stvrki*n*gar soc þessa.
M*agister* Eige. held*r* verþleikr þeirra sialu*r*a. þ*ui*at þesso*m* mis-licaþe þ*at* es hin*er* volþo ser ilt e*nn* þes-ser fylgþo þegar enogoþa. *oc* urþo þess íom̃bonþegar stvrcþer af Go*þ*e *oc* gørv*er* viser fvlse̜lo sinnar es þei*r* voro aþr oviser.

«1.54-55» D*i*scipulus Hui lica ásiono haua englar.
M*agister* Sua se*m* licneske es go ͺr ́t. ór vaxe ái*nn*sigle. sua es oc merkþ í þei*m* gliki*n*g Go*þ*s su es þei*r* ero olica*m*lect lios *oc* prvd*er* allre fegrþ.
«1.56» D*i*scipulus Vito þeir eþa mego alt þ*at* es þei*r* vilia.
M*agister* E*nn*ge [[674a:19]] scepna es leynd fyr. þei*m*. þ*ui*at þeir sia al-la hl*ut*e í Go*þ*e *oc* mego þeir auþveldlega g*er*a alt þ*at* es þeir vilia.

«1.57» D*i*scipulus Þva*rr* tala heilag ͺr ́a viþ fall vandra engla.
M*agister* Þvi vas maþ*r* scapaþr at fyldesc tala heilag*r*a.

«1.58» D*i*scipulus Huaþan vas h*ann* scapaþr.
M*agister* Af andlego oþle *oc* lica*m*lego.
«1.59» D*i*scipulus Hua[-]þan vas h*ann* lica*m*legr.
M*agister* Af .iiii. hofoþ scepno*m*. *oc* callasc h*ann* af þui e*nn* mi*nn*e heim*r*. þ*ui*at h*ann* hafþe hold af iorþo e*nn* bloþ af vatne blost af lofste e*nn* hita af elde. Hofoþ h*an*s vas bollot íglikí*n*g hei*m*ballar. Iþui ero augo tuav se*m* sol *oc* tungl. ahi*m*ne. Ibrioste es blóstr *oc* hoste se*m* vindar *oc* reiþarþrum-or ílofste. Qu*i*þr te̜cr viþ veco se*m* se̜r viþ

Master: They can see the monstrous ideas taking shape in their thoughts, which they cast into the souls of men, because a certain darkness of sin immediately overshadows the light of the soul. But they do not see the appearances of the power which God casts into the minds of men, because they cannot bear the light of God's righteousness, just as we cannot bear the light of the sun. For they would not tempt saints if they knew that they themselves could be overcome.

«1.49» Disciple: Are they allowed to do whatever they like?

Master: They cannot and will not do anything good. But they want to do whatever is evil and they can do only what the good angels allow them to do.

«1.50» Disciple: What can you say about the good angels?

Master: After the fall of the bad angels the others were strengthened so that they could never sin again.

«1.53» Disciple: Was their fall not the cause for strengthening the good angels?

Master: No. It was the merit of the good angels for they were displeased that the bad angels had chosen evil for themselves, but the good angels followed good forthwith. As a reward God strengthened them immediately and made them aware of their bliss which they had been unaware of before.

«1.54-55» Disciple: What do the angels look like?

Master: Just as a picture is imprinted in wax by a seal, so the picture of God is also imprinted upon them in such a way that they are disembodied light and adorned with great beauty.

«1.56» Disciple: Do they know everything? And are they able to do everything they wish?

Master: Nothing is hidden from them because they can see all things in God and can easily do anything they wish.

«1.57» Disciple: Did the number of saints decrease with the fall of the bad angels?

Master: Man was created to make up the number of the elect.

«1.58» Disciple: What was man made of?

Master: He was made of both a spiritual and a physical nature.

«1.59» Disciple: What is his physical nature?

Master: It consists of the four elements and man is therefore called microcosm, the small world. He got his flesh from the earth and his blood from the water, his breath from the air, and his warmth from the fire. His head is ball-shaped just like the globe. In his head there are two eyes just like the sun and moon in heaven. In his breast there are breath and cough, like the winds and claps of

votnom. Føtr halda up ollom licam [[674a:20]] sem iorþ berr allan hofga. Af himnes-com elde heuer hann svn. enn af eno øfra lofste heýrn. enn hilmning af eno neþra. bergning af vatne. enn hann-da kennning af iorþo. harþleik bei-na afsteinom. enn glikeng trea íno-glom hars voxt af grase. enn hann kenner sin sem kvquende þuiat þat alt licamlect eþle manz.

«1.60» Discipulus Huaþan es hann andlegr.
Magister Af andlegom elde. þat es efster licnes-ce Goþs.
«1.61» Discipulus Huert es licnesce Goþs í manne.
Magister Goþdomr es iþrennningo þetta licnes-ke hever ond. þuiat hon heuer minneng liþenna hluta oc oorþenna oc heuer hon skilning nvlegra oc svnelegra. oc heuer hon vilia þann es hon ma gera greinn Goþs oc ildz. I Goþe ero aller crafstar sua ma [[674a:21]] oc ond nema alla goþa hlute. Oc sua sem enge skepna ma halda á Goþe enn hann heldr ollom hlutum. sua ma oc enge sv-neleg skepna ondenagripa en hon ma igegnom fara alla svnelega hlute. þuiat eige ma himinnbyrgia fyr henne himnesca hlute. oc ma eige iorþ hulia fvr henne hel[-]vites diup.
«1.62» Discipulus Scapaþe Goþ menn meþ hondom.
Magister Heldr boþorþe eino. enn ó-stvrcleik eþles hans merkesc iþvi es hann segesc meþ hondom scapaþr ór iorþo.

«1.63» Discipulus Hui scapaþe Goþ mann ór sua herue-lego efne.
Magister Til ovegs dioflenom; at hann scammaþesc þa es iarþlegr maþr oc ostyrcr kome til þeirrar dvr-þar es hann vas fra rekenn fvr ofmet-noþ.
«1.64» Discipulus Huaþan toc adam nafn.
Magister [[674a:22]] Af .iiii. ottom heims þat es austr oc uestr norþr oc suþr. Enn at griksco male a d a m callasc anatole disis artos mesem-bria þat es sem griplor hende til nafns adams. Enn af þui toc hann nafn af fiorom ottom heims at kvn hans atte at coma íallar heims atter. Iþui haf-þe hann oc gliking Goþs ˋat´ hann scylde sua sty-ra ollo aiorþo sem Goþ reþr ollo áhimne.

«1.65» Discipulus Fyr hui scapaþe Goþ kyquende. þar es maþr þurfte þeira eige.
Magister Visse Goþ at maþr mvnde misgøra oc þvr-va þeira.
«1.66» Discipulus Scapaþe Goþ mv eþa kleg-gia eþa onnor meinkvquende.

thunder in the air. His belly takes in liquid as the sea takes in rivers. His feet support the whole body as the earth carries all its weight. He has his sight from the heavenly fire, his hearing from the upper heights and his smell from the lower levels. His taste comes from the water, and his sense of touch from the earth. He gets the hardness of his bones from the stones, and his nails bear the likeness of trees. The growth of his hair he gets from the grass, and he feels like an animal, for all that is the physical nature of man.

«1.60» Disciple: Where did his spiritual nature come from?

Master: From the spiritual fire according to God's likeness.

«1.61» Disciple: Where is God's likeness in man?

Master: Divinity is in the Trinity, and the soul has that shape. For the soul knows the past and the future and understands the visible present. It has the capacity to make distinctions between good and evil. In God are all powers, thus the soul, too, can receive all good things. And just as no creature can take hold of God for He holds everything, so no visible creature can take hold of the soul, since the soul can penetrate all visible things. And heaven cannot exclude the soul from heavenly bliss and the earth cannot hide the depths of hell from the soul.

«1.62» Disciple: Did God create man with His Hands?

Master: He created him only by command, but because man has a fragile nature is he is said to have been created with His Hands out of earth (Gen. 2:7; Job 10:8-9).

«1.63» Disciple: Why did God create man out of such wretched material?

Master: In order to embarrass the devil, so that he will be ashamed when this weak and mortal man enters the glory of heaven from which the devil was driven because of his arrogance.

«1.64» Disciple: How did Adam get his name?

Master: From the four compass points of the world, that is from East and West, North and South. In Greek these are called **Anatole, Dysis, Arktos, Mesembria**, and they form an acrostic of Adam's name. He got his name from the four corners of the earth, since his kin was expected to spread out in all directions over the earth. For that reason he took on the shape of God, so that he could rule everything on earth as God rules over everything in heaven.

«1.65» Disciple: Why did God create animals if man did not need them?

Master: God knew that man would sin and need them.

«1.66» Disciple: Did God also create mosquitoes, horseflies and other noxious animals?

M*agister* Meþ ia*m* mikille uandvirke scapaþe Go*þ* my *oc* mavra se*m* engla.

«1.67» D*iscipulus* Tilhuess scapaþe h*ann* þ*at*.
M*agister* Alt til lofs dyrþar [[674a:23]] sinnar. Mv. *oc* meinkv*qu*ende ero sco-poþ ígegn dra*m*be m*ann*a at þ*ei*r scile hue litet þ*ei*r mego þa es þ*ei*r hliota mein af eno*m* sm*ę*sto*m* kv*qu*endo*m*. Af þvi *qu*ol-þo *ei*ge birn*er* ne leones pharaone*m oc* liþ h*an*s. held*r* lýs *oc* kleggar. E*nn* maurar *oc* congorvofor *oc* þau cv*qu*ende es svslo fremia ero tilþess scopoþ at vér take*m* døme nýtz erveþes af þ*ei*ra syslo. Mikils es vert of alla scep-no Go*þ*s þar es su*m* heu*er* fegrþ se*m* blomar. e*nn* su*m* l*ę*cni*n*g se*m* gros. en su*m* fø\t/zlo se*m* acrar. en su*m* takn enna meire hl*u*ta se*m* foglar eþa dýr. Aller hluter ero goþ*er*. *oc* aller til m*ann*a þurfta scapaþ*er*.

«1.68» D*iscipulus* Huar vas ada*m* scapaþ*r*.
M*agister* Istaþ þei*m* es ebron heit*er*. þar es h*ann* do siþan *oc* [[674a:24]] vas g*r*ave*nn*. en h*ann* vas i paradisu*m*.
«1.69» D*iscipulus* H*ua*t es paradisus.
M*agister* E*nn* fegrste staþ*r* í austre. þar ero alzkvns tre *oc* alden ígegn meino*m* m*ann*a. Ef maþ*r* berg*er* amacleg*re* tiþ. af .i°. tre þahun[-]grar h*ann* ald*r*re siþan. Ef h*ann* b*er*ger af oþ-ro þa þýrster h*ann* *ei*ge. Ef h*ann* b*er*ger af eno iii*i*a þa møþesc h*ann* *ei*ge. En ef h*ann* b*er*ger aflifs tre. þa *ę*ldesc h*ann* *ei*ge ne svkesc ne deyr.

«1.70» D*iscipulus* H*ua*r vas kona scopoþ.
M*agister* Iparadiso ór riue souanda mandz.
«1.71» D*iscipulus* Hvi vas h*on* af karm*ann*e scopoþ.
M*agister* At sua v*er*e þau íeino*m* astar hug se*m* þau uoro í eino*m* lica*m*.
«1.71a» D*iscipulus* Hui licr vas suefn sia.
M*agister* Go*þ*s ande na*m* h*ann* up í hi*m*nesca paradi-su*m*. *oc* sa h*ann* þa þat at *ch*ristus *oc* *s*a*nc*ta *c*ristne mønde berasc ór h*an*s cyne. þvi spa-[[674a:25]]þe h*ann* of þau þegar es h*ann* vagnaþe
«1.72» [D*iscipulus*] Hui v*or*o *ei*ge aller se*nn* helg*er* me*nn* scapaþ*er* se*m* englar.
M*agister* Þui*a*t Go*þ* vilde e*nn* ada*m* la-ta íþui hafa sina gliki*n*g at alt ma*nn*-kvn køme fra h*on*o*m* sua se*m* aller hlut*er* ero af Go*þ*e.
«1.73» D*iscipulus* Hui scapaþe Go*þ* þau *ei*ge sua at þau m*ę*tte *ei*ge misg*er*a.
M*agister*. Go*þ* vilde at þau uelþe sér gott at vilia sino*m*. *oc* toke þ*at* íombon at þau m*ę*tte *ei*ge misgøra ne kvn þ*ei*ra.

Master: God created mosquitoes and ants with the same great care as the angels.

«1.67» Disciple: Why did He create them?

Master: To praise His glory. Mosquitoes and noxious animals are created against the arrogance of men, to make them realize how little they can do when they suffer injury from the smallest animals. Therefore it was not bears or lions that tortured the Pharaoh and his people, but lice and horseflies (Exod. 8:16, 21). Ants, spiders and other working animals are created so that we can see their labor as an example of useful work. All creatures of God are of great value: some possess beauty like flowers; some contain medicine like herbs; some provide food like fields; and some show signs of a higher existence like birds and animals. All things are good and all are created for the needs of men.

«1.68» Disciple: Where was Adam created?

Master: In that place which is called Hebron[3] where he died later and was buried. That place was Paradise.

«1.69» Disciple: What is Paradise?

Master: It is the most beautiful place in the East (Gen. 2:8). All kinds of trees and fruits useful against the diseases of men grow there. If a man tastes from a tree at the proper time, he will never be hungry again. If he tastes from another tree, he will never be thirsty again. If he tastes from a third, he will never be tired, and if he tastes from the tree of life, he will never become old or ill, nor will he ever die.

«1.70» Disciple: Where was woman created?

Master: In Paradise from the rib of man while he was sleeping.

«1.71» Disciple: Why was woman created from man?

Master: So that they could be one in their love as they are one in body.

«1.71a» Disciple: How was Adam's sleep?

Master: The spirit of God took man into heavenly Paradise and man realized then that Christ and holy Christianity would be born out of his kin. Therefore man foretold this when he woke up.

«1.72» Disciple: Why were not all saints created as angels right away?

Master: Because God wanted Adam to take His likeness, and He wanted all mankind to be descended from him in the same way as all things come from God.

«1.73» Disciple: Why did God not create men so that they could not sin?

Master: God wanted them to be able to choose good of their own free will and He offered them as reward that neither they nor their offspring could sin.

«1.74-76» Discipulus Huerso mondo menn aukasc eþa alasc íparadiso.
Magister Licams liþer møndo fremia embette sitt ón losta svnþar sua sem þa es menn takasc íhendr eþa siasc til enn born enn møndo vesa sotta laus oc ón allre øhreinson. Þegar møn[-]de huert barn męla scyrt oc ganga [[674a:26]] [es] alet vęre oc nevta aldens af þeim treom es þar ero viþ ollom meinom oc bergia siþan áfvrer ętlaþre tiþ af lifs tre.

«1.77-78» Discipulus Huerso lenge scyldo menn vesa íparadiso.
Magister Vndz fyldesc tala þeira engla es forosc oc su tala hei[-]lagra es fyllasc scylde íparadiso. þo at englar foresc eige. Oc sua sem nu berasc aþrer istaþ es aþrer deẏia. sua møndo oc þa feþr vesa up num-ner til betre vista siþann es þeir berg-þe af lifs tre en siþan huerr at bo-ge e`f´ster annan áfvrer ętlaþ`r´e tiþ en at nęst møndo aller saman verþa iafner sem englar ahimne.

«1.79» Discipulus Vo-ro ener fvrsto menn necþer scapaþer.
Magister Nec[-]þer voro oc scommoþosc enskes liþar [[674a:27]] sins heldr an augna.

«1.80-81» Discipulus Hui es sua fra þeim sagt efster svnþ. at þau sǫ́ sic necqueþ. sem þau séé þat eige fvrr.
Magister Efster synþ gerþesc fyse munoþliues ílicomom þeira. oc scomþosc þau þeira liþa sinna mest. es til synþar fys-tosc. þuiat þau visso þegar at [alt] cyn þeira mønde liggia under þeire enne somo svnþ.

«1.82» Discipulus So þau Goþ iparadiso.
Magister Sø þau hann ínecqueriom licneskiom sem hann vitraþesc siþan spa[-]monnom.

«1.83» Discipulus Fvr hui sueic diovoll þau.
Magister Þuiat hann ovunde þat es þau scvldo ko-ma til þess uegs es hann uas fra rekenn fyr ofmetnoþ. Enn fvr þann ofmet-noþ sueic hann þau þuiat þau drombo[-]þo af gifst sinne. oc hugþosc ei møn[-][[674a:28]]do [l]iu[a.

«1.84» Discipulus] Hui lét Goþ þeira freista þar [es] hann sa at þau møndo eige standasc.
Magister Þuiat hann visse hue mikla gøtzco hann mønde sẏna efster synþ þeira.

«1.85» Discipulus. Męlte ormren viþ þau.
Magister Heldr diovoll fvr ormenn sua sem nu męler hann fvr oþa menn.

«1.74-76» Disciple: How could men multiply and be born in Paradise?
Master: The limbs of the body could do their work without sinful lust, just as men use them now when they shake hands or look at each other. And the children would have been free from illnesses and all uncleanliness. Each child could have spoken clearly and walked as soon as it was born. It could have picked the fruits off the trees, which are there to guard against all diseases, and later at a pre-ordained time each child could have tasted from the tree of life.

«1.77-78» Disciple: How long were men supposed to be in Paradise?
Master: Until the number of the angels that had perished was made up, and the number of saints that were supposed to populate Paradise, had the angels not perished. Just as some are born now in place of others who die, in the same way fathers would have been taken then to the higher abode after they had tasted from the tree of life, one generation after another at a pre-ordained time, and, finally, all would have become equal to the angels in heaven.

«1.79» Disciple: Were the first men created naked?
Master: They were naked and not more ashamed of any limb of their bodies than they were of their eyes (Gen. 2:25).

«1.80-81» Disciple: Why is it said of them that after the fall they saw each other naked as if they had not noticed it before (Gen. 3:7)?
Master: After the fall the desire for a lustful life developed in their bodies. They were most ashamed of those limbs which desired to sin, because they knew right away that all of their kin would be subjected to the same sin.

«1.82» Disciple: Did they see God in Paradise?
Master: They saw Him in some visions as He later revealed Himself to the prophets.

«1.83» Disciple: Why did the devil betray them?
Master: Because he resented that they should receive the honor he had lost because of his arrogance. And aided by this arrogance, he betrayed them because they prided themselves on their gift and believed that they would live forever.

«1.84» Disciple: Why did God allow them to be tempted when He saw that they could not withstand this temptation?
Master: Because He knew how much goodness He would show them after their fall.

«1.85» Disciple: Did the snake speak to them?
Master: It was the devil speaking through the snake in the same way as he now speaks through possessed men.

«1.86» D*iscipulus* Hui he*ld*r fvr orm an an-nat cucq*u*ende.
M*agister* Ormr hrøquesc *oc* es háll. Sua u*er*þa *oc* aller þ*eir* es dioffoll syct. haler ísynþo*m* þ*at* ero galauser *oc* hrøcviser ívelo*m*. *oc* hafa eitr ímvnne þ*at* ero ill orþ.

«1.87» D*iscipulus* Vas vit*ra* Goþs eþa ildz íbonnoþo eple.
M*agister* E*ige* ieple he*ld*r ívuer stoplon Goþs laga. þ*ui*at maþr visse bęþe gott *oc* ilt aþr h*ann* misgerþe þo at h*ann* reyn[-]de þa gott eitt. e*nn* efst*er* synþ [[674a:29]] reynde h*ann* ilt *oc* munþe at ei[ns] gott.

«1.88» D*iscipulus* Mendo iller m*enn* alasc ípa-radiso.
M*agister* Goþer at eins.
«1.89» D*iscipulus* Hui a-lasc nu iller m*enn*.
M*agister* Til raunar *oc* dyrþar goþra.
«1.90» D*iscipulus* Hue lenge vo-ro þau í paradiso.
M*agister* Siau stund*er*
«1.91» D*iscipulus* Hui e*ige* lengr.
M*agister* Þ*ui*at cona viltesc þegar es h*on* vas scopoþ. At dag-molo*m* vas ada*m* scapaþr. *oc* gaf h*ann* nofn ollo*m* kvq*u*endo*m*. en at miþio*m* dege vas cona scopoþ. *oc* át h*on* þegar af bonnoþo tre. *oc* selde ma*nn*e sino*m* *oc* át h*ann*. *oc* rac goþ þau at aptne dags ór paradiso.

«1.92» D*iscipulus* H*u*at es cheru-bín *oc* loganda suerþ.
M*agister* Cheru-bín es engla varþald. en logan-da sv*er*þ es eldlegr. þ*ui*at engell [[674a:30]] [va]rþe ondo*m* en eldr licomo*m* dy*rr* paradisar efst*er* synþ.

«1.93» D*iscipulus* H*u*ert fór ada*m* þa.
M*agister* Þangat s*em* h*ann* vas scapaþr í ebron oc bvgþe þar *oc* ól sono. E*nn* efst*er* vig abel. sonar sins. þa c*om* h*ann* e*ige* í sa*m*a sęing kono si*nn*e .c. vet. En aldz *christus* vilde e*ige* berasc ór bol[-]voþo cyne caín. þa minte engell ada*m* at h*ann* hefþe sa*m*farar viþ cono sina. *oc* ólo þau son ístaþ abél þa*nn* es seth hét. ór þess cyne let *christus* be-rasc. E*nn* fra ada*m*s ęve til noa floþs c*om* e*ige* regn aiorþ. *oc* vas e*ige* regn-boge sén. *oc* óto m*enn* e*ige* kiot ne dr[-]ucko vin. Su tiþ vas oll sua s*em* vár tíþ *oc* vas þa gnott allra goþra hl*u*ta sues siþan. þva*rr* af svnþo*m* m*ann*a.

«1.86» Disciple: Why did he speak through a snake rather than through another animal?

Master: The snake wriggles and is slippery, and so all those whom the devil has deceived are slippery in their sins. They are careless and wriggly in their slyness and have poison in their mouths — that is, bad words.

«1.87» Disciple: Was the knowledge of good and evil contained in the forbidden apple?

Master: Not in the apple but in the trespassing of God's laws. For man knew both good and evil before he sinned, though he had experienced only good, but after his sin he experienced evil and then only remembered the good.

«1.88» Disciple: Could wicked men be born in Paradise?

Master: No, only good ones.

«1.89» Disciple: Why are wicked men born now?

Master: To be a trial and glory for the good.

«1.90» Disciple: How long did the first human beings remain in Paradise?

Master: For seven hours.

«1.91» Disciple: Why not longer?

Master: Because woman went astray as soon as she was created. At the beginning of the day, Adam was created and he gave names to all the animals. But in the middle of the day, woman was created and she ate at once of the forbidden tree. She gave some of the fruit to her man and he ate also. So in the evening of that day God drove both out of Paradise.

«1.92» Disciple: What are the Cherubim and the flaming sword (Gen. 3:24)?

Master: The Cherubim is the guardian of the angels, and the flaming sword is fiery. For after the fall, the angel guards the door of Paradise against the souls, and the fire guards against the bodies.

«1.93» Disciple: Where did Adam go then?

Master: To the place where he was created, to Hebron, and he settled there and begat sons. But after the death of his son Abel he did not come into his wife's bed for one hundred years. Since Christ did not want to be born of the cursed kin of Cain, an angel reminded Adam that he ought to have intercourse with his wife. And they begat a son in place of Abel who was called Seth. Out of his kin Christ was born. But from Adam's time until the flood of Noah, no rain fell upon the earth and no rainbow was to be seen; and men did not eat meat nor drink wine. This time was like eternal spring, and there

«1.94» Discipulus Huat [[674a:31]] mísgørþ[e [[675:11]] maðr er hann var abravt rekenn or] paradiso.
Magister Át hann af bonnoþo [tre] igegn boþorþe Goþs
«1.95» Discipulus Vas mikil [sýnd] at eta eple.
Magister Sua þung synþ vas su at eige matte. bøta ollom heime.

«1.96» Discipulus Sannaþu þat.
Magister Svnesc þér rétt at maþr hlvþe Goþs vilia.
«1.97» Discipulus Etke vas ret-tara an scynsamleg skepna þione vilia scapera sins.
Magister Synesc þér Goþs vile ollom heime øþre.

«1.98» Discipulus Vist es sua.
Magister Ef þu støþer fyr Goþe oc melte necquerr viþ þic at þu sneresc fra honom eþa ella møn-de allr heimr farasc. enn Goþ melte at þu scvlder eige snuasc fra honom. scvlder þu þa hafna Goþe oc leysa falvaltan heim.
«1.99-100» Discipulus Ollunges eige.
Magister Þat gerþe adam hann stóþ fvr Goþe oc leit fra honom oc ueic efster [[674a:32]] [[675:8]] fianda[-][[675:9]] nvm ok gorði sýnð þa er ollom] heime [[[675:9]] ýar þýngri] Sex hofoþ svnþer [[[675:9]] gerði adamr] iþesse .i⁰. oc hafþe .vi. heims [a]ldra idauþa.
«1.101» Discipulus Hueriar voro þér .vi.
Magister Fvrst ofmetnoþr. es hann vilde vesa glicrr Goþe. Of þa svnþ es melt. Ohreinn es sa fvr Goþe es drambar íhiarta sino. Onnor svnþ vas ohlyþne. es hann hlyd[-]de eige boþorþe Goþs oc vrþo honom þa al[-]ler hluter øhlyþner es aþr voro hlýþner; Ofþa svnþ es melt. Sua sem illtt es at vilia eige hluþa boþorþe Goþs En iii. synþ vas agirne. þuiat hann girnþesc framarr anhonom vere lofat oc tynde hann þa ollo þui es honom vas veit. Of þa synþ es melt. Agirne es scurþgoþa þio[-]nosta. Fiorþa synþ vas stuˈlˊþr enn mei[-][[674a:33]]re. þat es ór helgom staþ. þuiat hann toc ór helgom staþ þat ˋesˊ honom vas bannat; oc vas hann af þvi rekenn ór paradiso sem ritet es. Sa es rener helga staþe verþr abraut re[-]kenn ór helgom stoþom. Fimta synþ vas andlegr hordomr; þuiat ond hans vas gifst Goþe en hon fyr leit hann oc samtengþesc diofle oc tynde elsco ens sanna bruþ[-]guma sem ritet es. Glatasc huerr fra Goþe es hordom gerer.

was an abundance of all good things, which since then have decreased because of the sins of men.

«1.94» Disciple: How did man sin before he was driven out of Paradise?

Master: He ate of the forbidden tree against God's command.

«1.95» Disciple: Was it a terrible sin to eat the apple?

Master: So great was the sin that it could not be compensated for by the whole world.

«1.96» Disciple: Can you prove that?

Master: Does it seem right to you that man obeys God's will?

«1.97» Disciple: Nothing could be more right than for a rational creature to serve the will of its Creator.

Master: Does God's will seem more important to you than the whole world?

«1.98» Disciple: Yes, certainly.

Master: If you stood before God, and someone said to you that you should turn away from Him or else the whole world would perish, and God said that you should not turn away from Him, would you then forsake God and redeem this transitory world?

«1.99-100» Disciple: No, I would not.

Master: Adam did just that. He stood before God, looked away from Him and followed the devil; and he committed the sin which was the most terrible in all the world. Six mortal sins did Adam commit in this one sin and thereby bring death to six ages of the world.

«1.101» Disciple: What were those six mortal sins?

Master: The first was arrogance, for he wanted to be like God. Of this sin it is said that unclean is he before God who is proud in heart (Prov. 16:5). The second sin was disobedience. When he did not listen to God's command, all things became disobedient to Adam which had been obedient before. Of this sin it is said: It is evil not to want to listen to the command of God (1 Sam. 15:23). The third sin was avarice, for he desired more than he was permitted and then lost all which was granted to him. Of this sin it is said that avarice is the service of idols (Col. 3:5). The fourth sin was grave robbery, that is stealing from a holy place. For he took from a holy place that which was forbidden to him and he was driven out of Paradise for doing so, as is written: He who plunders holy places will be driven away from holy places (Lev. 22:3). The fifth sin was spiritual fornication, for his soul was married to God and it abandoned Him and joined with the devil and lost the love of the true bridegroom. It is written: Everyone is lost from God who goes a-whoring (Pss. 72/73:27).

Setta synþ vas mann-drap. þat es hann glataþe siolvom sér ídau-þa oc ollo cyne sino. Of þa synþ es mẹlt. Sa es vig vegr dauþa mon hann deyia. Af þvi do hann þegar ens iþra manz dauþa. oc la grauenn igrof licams sins.

«1.102» Discipulus Minkaþe eige þat synþ hans es hann uas teldr aflyge ens sløgsta [[674a:34]] anda.
Magister Ef necquerr byþe syslo þrẹ-le sinom oc synde honom talgrof at eige felle hann þar. es hann mette eige uprisa. enn hann fyr lete ounnet verk. oc felle viliande ígrofena. vẹre hann eige secr þa.

«1.103» Discipulus Heldr tuefaldre secþ. þuiat hann fyr[-]leit Goþ sinn oc gerþe sic omotkan til nytz verx.
Magister Sua gerþe adam hann haf-naþe Goþe oc fyrleit hlýþne oc fell í dauþa grof.

«1.104» Discipulus Huerso atte hann afstr at huerua.
Magister Gialda Goþe veg þann es hann tok fra honom. oc bøta synþ þa es hann gerþe. þat es rett at maþr gialde þat es hann tecr fra oþrom oc bøte gor óskil.

«1.105» Discipulus Huat toc maþr fra Goþe.
Magister Alt þat es hann ẹtlaþe at gera ór kyne hans.

«1.106» Discipulus Huerso scylde adamr gialda Goþe braut tekenn [[675:13]] væg
<Magister> Stiga iýir diofvlen sem hann var aðr ýfir stiginn ok gora sik sialfan ok alla vallda men slika sem þeir mvndv vera ef hann misgerði eigi

«1.107-108» <Discipvlvs> Hver[-]sso skýlldi hann ýfir bøta
<Magister> Gialda gvði nokot heimi bettra þvi at hann ˋmisgerði´ þat at heimi var þýngra en af þvi fo[rsk] hann idavða grọf at hann matti þat eigi gera

«1.109-110» <Discipvlvs> Hvi fýrir forsk hann eigi með ollv
<Magister> Gýðs fýrir ettlan matti eigi farazc þvi at gvð hafði raðit at fýlla tolo heilagra or hann kýni en ef hann gallt eigi makliga væg þann þa heimti gvð þat at honom navðgvm i hermðar pislvm

«1.111» <Discipvlvs> Hverssv er pisl manz vegr gvðs
<Magister> Maklict var at flýiandi kenndi reði gvðs i pislvm þat er hann villdi eigi ælska hann sem sonr foðvr idýr

The sixth sin was manslaughter through which he destroyed himself and all his kindred in death. Of that sin it is said: He who commits manslaughter will die the death (Lev. 24:17). Therefore, he died the death of the inner man at once and lay buried in the grave of his body.

«1.102» Disciple: Did it not diminish his sin that he was betrayed by the lie of the most cunning spirit?

Master: If someone gave his slave a task to do and showed him the pit, so that he would not fall into it as he might not be able to get out again; and if that slave left the task undone and fell into the pit intentionally, would he then not be guilty?

«1.103» Disciple: He would be doubly guilty because he despised his God and made himself unfit to do the necessary work.

Master: That is what Adam did. He abandoned God, scorned obedience, and fell into the pit of death.

«1.104» Disciple: How could he return to God?

Master: By returning to God the honor which he had taken from Him, and by atoning for the sin which he had committed. It is right that a man should restore what he has taken from others and compensate for unfair dealings.

«1.105» Disciple: What did man take from God?

Master: Everything which He meant to make of Adam's kindred.

«1.106» Disciple: How should Adam have restored the honor he had taken away from God?

Master: By defeating the devil as he was defeated before, and by making himself and all the elect just as they would have been if he had not sinned.

«1.107-108» Disciple: How should he have atoned?

Master: By repaying God with something better than the world, because he committed a sin that was greater than the world. Because he did not do so, he fell into the pit of death.

«1.109-110» Disciple: Why did he not perish altogether?

Master: God's providence could not be undone. God decided to complete the number of saints out of Adam's kin. But if man did not yield to God the honor due to Him, then God could claim the debt and compel man into the torment of His wrath.

«1.111» Disciple: How can man's torment be God's honor?

Master: It was appropriate that the fugitive should know the wrath of God through suffering (Gen. 4:13-14), because he did not want to love Him as a son loves his father in glory.

«1.112» <Discipvlvs> Ef gvð er miskvn*n*samr hvi fvrir gaf h*ann* ho*nom* eigi allt *ok* leidi h*ann* til dý́ðar allz h*ann* villdi bøta ef h*ann* metti *ok* mat*t*i eigi

<Magister> En gvð firir gæfi eigi þa ýere h*ann* omattolig*r* [[675:14]] þv*i*at h*ann* helldi eigi ýeg fýrir ætlan sin*n*ar Een ef h*ann* tæke sýndvgan vpindan idýrð þaðan er h*ann* rak abravt engil fýrir hvgren*n*ing þa veri h*ann* eigi re[tt]latr Er sýndar tati at hæfna at eki færi at oskipvðv iriki gvðs þv*i* at engi mvn leggia gi*m*stein vþvegin iork sina þan*n* er aðr hef*i*r i savr fallit

«1.113» <Discipvlvs> Til hvers anda atti þet*t*a at koma

<Magister> Flýiandi þræll hliopsk fra gvði sinv*m* með stvld til hins grim*m*asta vikings Af þv*i* var sendr kono*n*ngs son or hi*m*nariki imýrkv\a´ stofo eft*i*r þræli at sa stigi ýf*i*r viki*n*nge*n*n *ok* leiddi aft*r* þræl með fe*n*gi *ok* sætti h*ann* með kononge

«1.114» <Discipvlvs> Hvi mat*t*i maðr eigi aft*r* hverýa eftir sýnd

<Magister> Sva sem h*ann* teýgði an*n*ar til fallz sva var *ok* makligt at an[-]nar teýgði h*ann* til vprisv þeirar er h*ann* villdi *ok* matti eigi

«1.115» <Discipvlvs> Hvi sen[-]di gvð eigi engil at læýsa ada*m*

<Magister> Ef engill læýsti man*n*en þa ve[-]ri maðr engils þrell en engill mat*t*i eigi læýsa man*n* i sinv æðli þv*i* at h*ann* matte eigi dæýia en h*ann* gærðiz maðr þa mætti h*ann* en*n* min*n*a

«1.116» <Discipvlvs> Hvi skapaði gv eigi an*n*an man*n* or iarðv *ok* sendi þan*n* eft*i*r hinv*m* glata[-]ða

<Magister> En gvð skapade nýian man*n* *ok* sendi þan þa kemi engi or a[-]dams kýni Sý lavns er allt kýn endr bøt*i*r

«1.117-118» <Discipvlvs> Hvi sendi gvð eigi spa man*n* sin*n*

<Magister> Spa maðr var gettin*n* i sýnd *ok* mato þeir eigi læýsa man[-]kýn or pislv*m* af þv*i* tok sýn gvþs fvllan mando*m* asik til lavsnar ollo mankýni *ok* gerðiz ẹin*n* itvæn*n*v æðli Jþv*i* æðli er h*ann* var gvð stæig h*ann* ýf*i*r diofvlen þan*n* er svẹ\i´k ada*m* *ok* lavk vpp himnv*m* fýr*i*r ollo*m* mon*n*om sinv*m* *ok* gærðe ia*m*na englo*m* en þat mat*t*i gvð ein*n* En i þvi er h*ann* var maðr tok h*ann* davða v ýærðr *ok* bøtti þa sýnd er ollo*m* hæimi var þvngri en þat atte maðr at gera

«1.119» <Discipvlvs L>ofat se mal mvnz þins þv*i* at þv ert san*r* son*r* gvðs af himni hvi tok son*r* gvðs lika*m* helldr en faðir eða hæilagr andi

«1.112» Disciple: If God is merciful, why did He not forgive him for everything and lead him to glory? For man wished sincerely to repent if possible, but was not able to do so.

Master: If God had not forgiven him, He would be powerless, because He had not placed honor before His divine plan. Moreover, if He had accepted a sinner unchastised into that glory from which He excluded an angel because of a single thought, He would not have been just. But sins must be atoned for, so that nothing shall fall into disarray in God's kingdom. For nobody would place an unwashed gem on his chest after it had fallen into the dirt.

«1.113» Disciple: What might have been the result of all this?

Master: A fleeing slave ran away from his God with his booty and went to the most villainous viking. For this reason the Son of the King was sent from the heavenly kingdom into the dungeon in search of the slave, so that He might vanquish the viking and lead the slave back with his booty and reconcile him with the King.

«1.114» Disciple: Why could man not turn back after the fall?

Master: Just as someone had lured him to his fall, so it was fitting that someone else should lead him to resurrection, exactly as he desired but was unable to do.

«1.115» Disciple: Why did God not send an angel to redeem Adam?

Master: If an angel had redeemed man, man would have been the slave of the angel. Because of his nature, an angel could not redeem man because he cannot die. And if the angel had become a man, he would have been even less able to redeem man.

«1.116» Disciple: Why did God not create another man out of earth and send him in place of the man who had fallen?

Master: If God had created a new man and had sent him, it would not have been Adam's kin who redeemed the whole of mankind.

«1.117-118» Disciple: Why did God not send His prophets?

Master: The prophets were begotten in sin and thus could not redeem mankind from suffering. Therefore, God's Son became a man in order to redeem all mankind and He who had two natures became One. In His godly nature, He overpowered the devil who had betrayed Adam, and unlocked heaven for all His men and made them equal to the angels. Only God could have done that. In His human nature, He suffered death undeservedly and atoned for the sin which was greater than the whole world. Only a man could have done that.

«1.119» Disciple: May the words of your mouth be praised, for you are the true son of God from heaven. Why did the Son of God rather than

<Magister> En faðer eða heilagr an[-]de tæki mandom þa ýrði týæir sýnir i þrenningo annar gvðs son en annar m manz son Sonr kallaz likr gvði en engill *ok* maðr ýilldv eignaz nafnlikin[-][[**675:15**]]gar gvðs af þvi villdi sonr gvðs maðr goraz þvi at við hann var imæin gort gær[-]ðe hann *ok* miskýnnsamliga ýið er hann mat*t*i fýrir dęma ret*t*liga Allir hlvt*i*r ero gorf*i*r fýr son *ok* at*t*i af þvi lavsn at vera fýr son

«1.120» <Discipvlvs> Hvi villdi hann fra mæý lata bæraz
<Magister> Fiorom ættom skapaði gvð menn einvm hætte fýrir vtan foðvr *ok* moðor sem adam At oðrvm hæt*t*e af karlmanne einvm sem efo Þriðia hætte fra karlmanni *ok* kono sem altit er Fiorða hæt[-]ti fra mæýio einni saman sæm krist*r* var borinn Avk sva sem davði kom iheim fýrir mæý Sva kom lif *ok* fýrir mæý þat er vti býrgði davðann

«1.121-122» <Discipvlvs> Hvi kom gvð eigi fýr noa floð eða ðægar eft*i*r
<Magister> Ef hann kæme fýrir floðit þæ\i/rar tiðar þa mvndv menn mæla at eigi væri navðsýnleg qvama hans þaer menn hofðo nvmit marga goða hlvti af fæðrvm si[-]nom er nýkomn*i*r voro or paradis En hann qveme eft*i*r floðit þa mvndv men segia at gvð hæfði mælt ýið noa *ok* abraham *ok* segia hann nvmit hafa allt man vit af þæim E ef hann kæmi alaga tið þa mvndv gýðþingar þýki[-]az fvllvel vera lærðer at logom en hæiðn*i*r menn af spekingom

«1.123-124» <Discipvlvs> hvi dval[-]ði hann eigi allt til heims ænda at koma
<Magister> Fa er mvndv honom i spor stiga *ok*eigi fýllaz tala heilagra þa var navðsýn til at krist*r* kveimiða erhann kom þa er gýðingvm þot*t*i ðýngia logser en eigi læt*t*a en heiðn*i*r menn firir leto æl\i/f log *ok* lifðv i gegnn logom *ok* þa er eigi bvrgv kenni menn monn[-]nom æða spa menn þa var navðsýn at hinn sami lækn*i*r kveme sa er gręd[-]di með ýið smiorýi *ok* milldi sinnar halfdavðan lýð *ok* saran i sýnðvm

«1.125» <Discipvlvs> Hverso mat*t*i hann lata beraz sýnða lavs or sýnd gætno kýni
<Magister> <G>vð valde fra vpp hafve af fýrstom þioðvm þa er trvlegaz þionv[-]ðv hanom er or þeira kýni var sv mær er sýnða lavst gat *ok*

the Father or the Holy Ghost assume human shape?

Master: If the Father or the Holy Ghost had taken on human form, there would have been two sons in the Trinity: the Son of God and the son of man. The Son is said to be like God, but the angel and man also wanted to be like God. Therefore God's Son wanted to become a man, because it was against Him that the offence was committed. He also showed mercy to those He might have justly condemned. All things are done on behalf of the Son, and redemption should therefore be on behalf of the Son.

«1.120» Disciple: Why did He allow Himself to be born of a virgin?

Master: God created men in four ways: first, without father and mother, like Adam; second, out of a single man, like Eve; third, out of man and woman in the usual way; fourth, out of a virgin alone, as Christ was born. And just as death entered the world through a virgin, so also life came shutting out death through a virgin.

«1.121-122» Disciple: Why did God not come before Noah's flood or immediately thereafter?

Master: If He had come before the flood, men would have said that His coming was not necessary at that particular time. For men had then learned many good things from their fathers who had only recently left Paradise. If God had come immediately after the flood, men would have said that God had spoken to Noah and Abraham, and they would have maintained that He had gotten all His understanding from them. If He had come at the time of the laws, the Jews would have considered themselves to be fully learned in the laws, just as the heathens did because of their philosophers.

«1.123-124» Disciple: Why did He not wait with His coming until the end of the world?

Master: Few would have followed His path and the number of saints would not have been fulfilled. It was necessary for Christ to come when He did, for it seemed to the Jews that the law was a plague and not a relief, and the heathens had turned away from the eternal law and were living in defiance of the law. Since priests and prophets were unable to help humanity, it was necessary for the Healer to come who would heal with oil and with His mercy all of the people who were half dead and suffering because of their sins.

«1.125» Disciple: How could He Himself have been born without sin from a race begotten in sin?

Master: From the beginning God chose from among the first people who truly served Him. From their kin came the virgin who conceived

bar hei*m*s græðara Svasem fordv*m* bar þv*rr* ɣondr fagran bloma fẏrir vtan ɣok[-]va

«1.126» <D*iscipvlvs*> Hver*ss*o gat ho*n*n h*ann* æða bar

<M*agister*> Fẏr vtanalla sẏnð *ok* sot*t* eða sar[-]læik krist*r* ko*m* til hen*n*ar at loknv*m* dẏrv*m* at samtengia sem ma*nn*likt eð[-]li *ok* læt beraz af hen*n*i at loknv*m* qviði

«1.127» <D*iscipvlvs*> hvi var h*ann* niv manaðr iqviþi

<M*agister*> At h*ann* samtegndi niv engla sveitv*m* þaer bẏrgðir ɣoro iɣesolld þe*ss*a [[675:16]] hei*m*s

«1.128» <D*iscipvlvs*> Ahve*rr*i stvndv var h*ann* borin

<M*agister*> At miðri nott sem ritat er þaer not hafði miðia þa ko*m* mal gvðs af kono*n*gligv sæti

«1.129» <D*iscipvlvs*> Hvi anot*t*

<M*agister*> Þvi at h*ann* hvlði gvð do*m* si*nn* ok ko*m* at læiða þa til hins sa*nn*alios eradr ɣoro i ɣillo not

«1.130» <D*iscipvlvs*> Uissi h*ann* nakot erh*ann* var barn

<M*agister*> Allt vissi h*ann* þvi at i hono*m* er oll ɣitra *ok* speki

«1.131» <D*iscipvlvs*> Mat*t*e h*ann* þegar mæla eða gan[-]ga

<M*agister*> hvartveggia mat*t*i h*ann* en h*ann* likðiz ma*nn*ligv æðli at ollo fẏr[-]tan sẏnð

«1.132» <D*iscipvlvs*> Gęrðoz nokorar iartegn*ir* i bvrð h*ann*

<M*agister*> Siav agæti vr[-]ðv

«1.133» <D*iscipvlvs*> Hvær s\i/av

<M*agister*> Nẏ stiarna ɣitraðiz gvl lígr hringr varɣm sol Yiðs smiors brvnn*r* sprat vp or iarðv friðr en*n* mæsti varð Allr hei*m*r var skipaðr at mantalli Þrirtiger þvs hvnðra gvðs oɣina ɣaro drepnir aeino*m* degi kẏcɣende melto manz roddv

«1.134» <D*iscipvlvs*> Yita villda ek takn þessa lvta

<M*agister*> Stiornvr mærkia lif hæilagra lios stiarna sẏndiz þvi at heilagr heilagra ɣar borin Gvllegr hringr skei*nn* vm sol þvi at ræt læt*r*is sol ko*m* at lẏsa kri[-]stni*nn*i með gvlli gvðoms sins *ok* fægrð pinslar si*nn*ar Yiðr smiors brẏnn*r* sprat vp*p* or iarðv þvi at miscvn*n*ar brvnn*r* læt beraz fra meẏ Friðr mikẏll varðr þvi at hi*nn* sa*nn*i friðr vitraðez a iarðv Allr hei*m*r var ritaðr at mantali þviat allir ɣeralldar men*n* ɣaro v ɣallder af gvði *ok* er skarð a lifs bok Þeir voro drepn*ir*

without sin and who bore the Saviour of the world, just as once a dry twig bore a beautiful flower without receiving any water.

«1.126» Disciple: How did she conceive and deliver Him?

Master: Without any sin, disease or pain. Christ came to her through locked doors to join with her like a human being and let Himself be born by her through her locked womb.

«1.127» Disciple: Why was He in her womb for nine months?

Master: To be united with the nine hosts of angels who were caught in the misery of this world.

«1.128» Disciple: At what time was He born?

Master: At midnight, as is written: When the night was in the midst of her course, the word of God came from the royal throne (Wisd. 18:14-15).

«1.129» Disciple: Why at night?

Master: Because He hid His divinity and He came to lead those to the true light who before had been dwelling in the night of error.

«1.130» Disciple: Did God know anything when He was a child?

Master: He knew everything because in Him is all knowledge and wisdom (Col. 2:3).

«1.131» Disciple: Could He speak and walk immediately?

Master: He could do both, but He resembled human beings in everything except sin.

«1.132» Disciple: Did any miracles occur when He was born?

Master: Seven glorious miracles took place.

«1.133» Disciple: What seven miracles?

Master: A new star made its appearance (Matt. 2:2); a golden ring encompassed the sun; an oil well sprang up from the earth; there was great peace; the whole world was counted in a census (Luke 2:1); thirty thousand enemies of God were killed in one day; animals spoke with human voices.

«1.134» Disciple: I would like to know the meaning of these miracles.

Master: The stars symbolize the life of the saints. A bright star became visible because the Holiest of the Holy was born. The golden ring encompassed the sun because the Sun of Righteousness (Mal. 4:2) came to give light to Christianity with the gold of His Godliness and the beauty of His suffering. An oil well sprang up from the earth because the Spring of Mercy let Himself be born of a virgin. There was great peace because True Peace appeared on earth. The whole world was written down in a census (Luke 2:1), because not all men in the world were chosen by God and there is a gap in the book of

þ*eir* er gvði nittv þ*v*iat þ*eir* firir faraz er eigi *y*ilia gvðs riki *y*fir ser kvc qvende mælti þvi at qvic qvendlegr l*y*ðr heiðin*n*a þioða sneroz til sk*y*nsemi gvðs orða

«1.135» <D*i*sc*i*p*v*l*v*s> Hvi kallaði gvð til sin þria avstr *y*egs kono*n*nga meðr fornv*m*
<M*a*g*i*ster> Þvi at h*ann* villdi til sin leiða alla þriðivnga hei*m*s sins Asia*m* ok afrika*m ok* E*y*ropam *ok* goðverk

«1.136» <D*i*sc*i*p*v*l*v*s> Hvi fl*y*ði h*ann* helldr til eg*y*pta lan landz en ian*n*an stað
<M*a*g*i*ster> þvi at h*ann* s*y*ndi sik san*n*an mo[-]isen at sva sem mo*y*ses læ*y*sti l*y*ð gvðs or *y*ellgi pharao *ok* leid[-]di af egifta lande *ok* til f*y*rir heittin*n*ar iarðar Sva læ*y*sti kri[-]str vt þan*n* l*y*ð *ok* or *y*ellde fiandans *ok* leiddi fra helvitis pislv*m* [[675:17]] *ok* til eil\i*y*frar sælo Af þ*v*i hvarf h*ann* aft*r* eftir siav vet*r* tiliarða israel Þvi at siva giaf*i*r heilax anda leiðir oss or heimi þ*e*s*s*o*m* til hi*m*neska israel

«1.137» <D*i*sc*i*p*v*l*v*s> hvi ke*n*ndi \gvð/ eigi ne gerði iartegn*ir* in*n*an þratigi vet*t*ra
<M*a*g*i*ster> Dæmi gaf h*ann* mon*n*om ef h*ann* gerði f*y*r goð verk enh*ann* gen*n*di siðan at engi dir*y*iz f*y*rr at ke*n*na e*n* h*ann* hef*ir* logsæmlegan alldr *ok* sk*y*nsemi

«1.138» <D*i*sc*i*p*v*l*v*s> Hvi var i*esv*s kri[-]s*tr* skirðr er oll f*y*lling *y*ar gvð doms i hono*m ok* ma ekci avkaz krapt*r* h*ann*s
<M*a*g*i*ster> At h*ann* hælgaði oss *y*atn til skirnar

«1.139» <D*i*sc*i*p*v*l*v*s> ðvi *y*ar h*ann* i *y*atni skirðr
<M*a*g*i*ster> vatn er helldr gagnstaðlekt en h*y*at er s*y*nð nema elldr Sva sem ræiði er i hvg eða girnd losti i hollði af þ*v*i skal i *y*atni skira at s*y*nða ælldr slokne Yat\n/ þvær savr *ok* slǫkkvir þorsta *ok* s*y*nir sk*y*gga Sva þver miskv*n* heilaxanda s*y*nða savr i skir*n*n *ok* slǫckvir anda þorsta með or[-]ðe gvðs *ok* giallder likneiski gvðs þat er *y*ér t*y*ndv*m* f*y*rir s*y*nð [[674a:35]]

«1.140» D*i*sc*i*pulus Vas *christus* venn at lica*m* sem ritit es of h*ann* at h*ann* se fegre at alite an son*er* m*er*.
M*a*gister At oþle vas h*ann* skicr sem h*ann* uitraþesc lǫre sueino*m* sino*m* afialle; en h*ann* leýn-desc fvr m*onno*m. sua at h*ann* vas held*r* liotr angolegr at alite sua se*m* ritet es. Vér som h*ann* eige hafa fegrþ ne alit.

life.[4] Those were killed who denied God, because they are destroyed who do not want God's kingdom above them (Luke 19:14). Animals spoke, because the brutish flock of heathen people turned to the reason of God's Word.

«1.135» Disciple: Why did God call unto Him three Eastern kings bearing gifts?

Master: Because He wanted to lead to Himself the three separate parts of the world: Asia, Africa, and Europe, and likewise good deeds.

«1.136» Disciple: Why did He flee to Egypt rather than to some other place?

Master: So that He might show Himself as the True Moses. Just as Moses had freed God's people from the power of the Pharaoh and led them from Egypt to the promised land, so Christ also freed the people from the power of the devil and led them from hell's torment to eternal bliss. Therefore after seven years He returned to the land of Israel, because through the seven gifts of the Holy Spirit he leads us from this world to heavenly Israel.

«1.137» Disciple: Why did God not teach or perform miracles during His thirty years on earth?

Master: He gave men an example by performing good deeds, and later on He taught that nobody should venture to teach before reaching legal age and possessing reason.

«1.138» Disciple: Why was Jesus Christ baptized, when all the fullness of the Godhead dwelt in Him (Col. 2:9) and His grace could not be increased?

Master: So that He would sanctify the baptismal water for us.

«1.139» Disciple: Why was He baptized in water?

Master: Water is the opposite of fire. But what is sin if not fire? Just as anger is in the mind or lust lurks in the flesh, so shall we be baptized with water that the fire of sin may be extinguished. Water cleanses dirt, quenches thirst and reflects shadow. In the same way, the grace of the Holy Spirit cleanses the stains of sin in baptism, quenches the thirst of the soul with God's word, and restores the image of God, which we lost through sin.

«1.140» Disciple: Did Christ have a handsome body, since it is written of Him that He was fairer in appearance than the sons of men (Pss. 44:3/45:2)?

Master: He was such by nature as He revealed Himself to His disciples on the mountain; but He hid Himself from men, so that He was ugly rather than handsome in appearance, as is written: We, like Him, have no form nor comeliness (Isa. 53:2).

«1.141» D*iscipulus* Vas h*ann* pinelegr eþa dauþ[-]legr.

M*agister* Pisl *oc* dauþe es synþa vite. En h*ann* c*om* hi*n*gat ón sýnþ *oc* lifþe ón synþ. *oc* vas h*ann* af þui o[-]pinelegr at oþle *oc* odauþlegr en h*ann* matte *oc* uilde pinasc *oc* dey-ia.

«1.142» D*iscipulus* Fvr hui do h*ann*.
M*agister* Fvr hlyþne se*m* ritet es. *Christus* vas hlvþen alt til dauþa.

«1.143» D*iscipulus* Hei*m*te faþer dauþa at h*onom*.
M*agister* Ollunges e*i*ge.

«1.144» D*iscipulus* Hui vogo gvþi*n*gar [[674a:36]] h*ann*.
M*agister* Þui at h*ann* helt retlete ilive *oc* sanleic ikenni*n*go. Sia hlyþne es ma*n*ne scyld viþ Goþ *oc* hei*m*ter Goþ þat at al-re scynsa*m*legre scepno. en þa hlyþ-ne gofo gyþi*n*gar h*onom* at sok.

«1.145» D*iscipulus* Hu*err* mønde vega lata einga són sín goþan *oc* saclausan ef h*ann* mette ban[-]na.

M*agister* Þa es Goþ faþer sa son si*nn* vil*i*a sua gott v*er*c g*er*a. at stiga yu*er* diovol *oc* hialpa ma*nn*kvne. þa vette h*ann* h*onom* sua dvrlect v*er*c *oc* leyfþe h*onom* at deyia.

«1.146» D*iscipulus* Hu*e*rso vas þat ret fvr Goþe at h*ann* sende en batzta til bana fvr vondo*m*.

M*agister* Þui*a*t en v*e*rste sveic einfal-dan ma*nn* þa vas ret. at e*nn* batzte gi*n*gi ígisli*n*g fvr h*ann* *oc* stige vu*er* en v*e*rsta; e*nn* leidde afstr ein faldan til [[675:18]] frel[-]sis A þessa lýnd sýndi gvd oss ast sina er h*ann* sendi son at firalsa þrel

«1.147» <D*iscipvlus*> E*n*′ faðrer sældi son eða son*r* seldi sik sialf*r* tilbana fir*ir* ǫst hvat mis[-]gerðe ivdas er h*ann* sældi krist

<M*agister*> Faðer *ok* son*r* sælldi sialfa*nn* sik fir*ir* ǫst enivda selldi h*ann* fir*ir* fe girni

«1.148» <D*iscipvlus*> Hvi villdi kris*tr* dæýia atre

<M*agister*> At sa stigi ýfer þan atre er fýr tre ýar sigraðr *ok* h*ann* læýsti þa*nn* atre er misgorðe atre

«1.149» <D*iscipvlus*> Firir hvi akrossi

<M*agister*> At h*ann* grædde fio[-]rar ætt*ir* heim*s*ens

«1.150» <D*iscipvlus*> Matte davðe h*an*s allar sýnðer bæta

<M*agister*> Ytan iýan

«1.151» <D*iscipvlus*> Sanna þv þat

<M*agister*> Ef kris*tr* stæýðe fir*ir* þer *ok* vissir þv at ýære gvð allz

«1.141» Disciple: Did he experience pain and death?

Master: Pain and death are punishment for sins. But He came to earth without sin and lived without sin; and therefore by nature He did not experience pain but was immortal. But He wished and desired to be tortured and to die.

«1.142» Disciple: Why did He die?

Master: Because of His obedience, as is written: Christ was obedient even unto death (Phil. 2:8).

«1.143» Disciple: Did God, the Father, demand His death?

Master: No, definitely not.

«1.144» Disciple: Why did the Jews slay Him?

Master: Because He observed righteousness in life and truthfulness in teaching. Man owes his obedience to God and God claims it from all rational creatures; but the Jews made this obedience a charge against Him.

«1.145» Disciple: Who would have his only good and innocent son killed if he were able to prevent it?

Master: When God, the Father, saw that His Son wished to perform this good deed of overcoming the devil and helping mankind, He allowed Him to undertake this glorious deed and permitted Him to die.

«1.146» Disciple: How was it right before God to send the Best to His death on behalf of all evil?

Master: Because the worst deceived common man. So it was only right that the Best should be a hostage for man and overcome evil and lead him back to freedom. In this way did God show us His love when He sent His Son to free the slave.

«1.147» Disciple: And because of His love, the Father sacrificed His Son and the Son sacrificed Himself to death. What wrong did Judas do when he sacrificed Christ?

Master: Father and Son sacrificed Themselves because of Their love, but Judas sacrificed Him because of his avarice.

«1.148» Disciple: Why did Christ want to die on a tree?

Master: To vanquish him at a tree, who had been victorious through a tree; and to free him on a tree, who had sinned at a tree.

«1.149» Disciple: Why on a cross?

Master: To heal the four parts of the world.

«1.150» Disciple: Could His death atone for all sins?

Master: Without doubt.

«1.151» Disciple: Explain to me how.

Master: Let us say that Christ stood before you, and you knew that He

ɣalldandi ef nokorr mællte at þv skýllder ɣegahann æða ellegar mvndi allr heimr faraz mvnðer þv ɣega hann þa

«1.153» <Discipvlvs> Sem sizt þvi at lif hans er allvm heimmi æðre ok gærða ek þann glæp ef ek ɣega hann er eigi mætti bæta þo at allr heimr læitaði ɣiðr

<Magister> Ef ˋlifˊ hans er ollom heimi betˋrˊa þa er ðavði hans ollom heimi dýrra ok ɣinnr þorf til lavsnar

«1.154» <Discipvlvs> Hvat gaf faðer syni firir þenna ɣærðlæik

<Magister> Hvat gaf hann hanom þat er hann atti allt aðr sem ritat er Sonr sagðe feðr aller minir lvtir ero þiner

«1.155» <Discipvlvs> Matte hann sialfr geɣa ɣerk kavp davða sins þeim sem hann villdi

<Magister> Matti hann sialf ok gerðe sva ok gaf monnom þeim sem hann læýsti i pisl sinni ok gaf lif eilift firir davþa en himneska faðvr læifð firir þessa heims vtlegð

«1.156» <Discipvlvs> Hve mar[-]gar stvnder ɣar hann davðr

<Magister> Fiora tegv

«1.157» <Discipvlvs> Hvi sva

<Magister> At hann lif[-]gaðe fiorar ettir heims þær er davðar ɣoro af tiv laga brotom

«1.158» <Discipvlvs> Hverir krosfesto krist

<Magister> Gyðingar reðo hann en heinir menn drapo hann ok krossfesto þviat hann villdi dæýia firir hvarotvæggia

«1.159» <Discipvlvs> Hvi la hann tuer netr igrof ok einn dag

<Magister> Tvęr nætr merk[-]ia tvænnan davða annan likamns davða ɣarn en annan andar [[675:19]] En dagr merkir davða hans þvi at sa er lios ɣarsdavða annan davða ɣarnn tok hann abravt en annnan let hann eftir til ravnar heilagra ok mvn hann afta[-]ka er hann kemr i annat sinn

«1.160» <Discipvlvs> hvar kom ond hann eftir davða

<Magister> Jparadis sem hann melte ɣið þofenn a krossinvm idag skallðv með mer iparadis

«1.161» <Discipvlvs> Hve ner steig hann til helɣitis

<Magister> Amiðri dags nott ok ræn[-]te helɣite aþeiri stvndv sem engill drap frvmbvrði egipta laz ok for hann þaðan með sigri ok leiddi iparˋaˊdis þan er hann tok abrot or helviti ok ɣitiaðe hann likams igrof ok reisti hann af davða En svmir seg[-]ia at hann væri með

was God Almighty. Then if someone were to say that you should kill Him or else the whole world would perish, would you kill Him?

«1.153» Disciple: Certainly not, because His life is superior to the whole world. If I killed Him, I would commit a crime that could never be atoned for even by the whole world.

Master: If His life is more valuable than the whole world, then His death is more precious than the whole world and fulfills the need for redemption.

«1.154» Disciple: What reward did the Father give to His Son?

Master: What could He have given Him since He possessed everything from the beginning? As is written: The Son said to the Father: All that I have is thine (Luke 15:31).[5]

«1.155» Disciple: Could He Himself confer the reward of His death on whomever He chose?

Master: He Himself could and did so. He gave to those men whom He redeemed through His suffering eternal life in exchange for death; and He gave to them the inheritance of the Heavenly Father in exchange for the exile of this world.

«1.156» Disciple: How many hours was He dead?

Master: Forty hours.

«1.157» Disciple: Why is that?

Master: So that He could revive the four parts of the world which were dead because of the violations against the ten commandments.

«1.158» Disciple: Who crucified Christ?

Master: The Jews plotted against Him, and the heathens killed Him and crucified Him because He wanted to die for them both.

«1.159» Disciple: Why did He lie in His grave two nights and a day?

Master: The two nights symbolize double death: one night is the death of the body, the other the death of the soul. But the day signifies His death because it is the light of our death. One of our deaths He took away, but the other He left to test the saints, and He will take it away when He comes a second time.

«1.160» Disciple: Where did His soul go after His death?

Master: To Paradise, as He said to the thief on the cross: Today shalt thou be with me in Paradise (Luke 23:43).

«1.161» Disciple: When did He descend into hell?

Master: In the middle of the night of the day of resurrection. He despoiled hell at the same hour as the angel killed the first-born of Egypt. He emerged thence in victory and led them to Paradise whom He had taken away from hell; and He visited the Body in the grave and raised Him from death. But some say that He was in hell

vinvm ihelγiti fra davda sinvm ok til vprisv ti[-]ðar ok risi hann þaðan ⱽ⁄pmeð þeim

«1.162-163» <Discipvlvs> Hvi reis hann eigi brat vpp eftir dav[-]ða

<Magister> Ef hann risi brat vpp eftir davða þa mvndv gvðingar segia at hann hef[-]ði legið ivγiti en eigi andaz Avk ef hann risi vpp nokoro siðar þa mvndo menn iγaz hvart hannveri eða ann nar brat reis hann vpp þvi at hann γilldi braðla hvgga γini sina er greto davða hans

«1.164-165» <Discipvlvs> Hvi reis hann vpp a hinvm fýrsta degi γikv eða þriðia degi eftir pisl sina

<Magister> At hann endr bøtti a þeim degi sem hann skapaðe ok hann reisti vpp þa er davðer γa[-]ro a þeim tiðvm þat er fýr log ok vndir logom ok vnder miskvnn ok ⸌at⸍ ver ri[-]sim vpp i þrenningar trv er fellom isγnðer iorðvm ok iverkom ok hvgren[-]ningvm

«1.167-168» <Discipvlvs> Hveria asion hafðe kristr eftir vpp risv

<Magister> Siav hlv[-]tvm biartare en sol en γinir sa hann slikan sem hannvar með þeim firir pisl sina

«1.169» <Discipvlvs> Yittraðez hann klæðr

<Magister> Klæðe tok hann or lopte en þav eýdoz i lofte þa er hann steig vpp

«1.170» <Discipvlvs> Hve oft γitraðez hann

<Magister> Tolfsinnvm atta sinnvm γittraðez hann þegar hinn fýrsta dag fýr Joseph ab arimaðia er i mýkvastofo var settr fýr þat er hann iarðaþelikam iesv sem rit nikodemvs skýra Annat sinni vitraðez hann mæýðr sinni sem sedvlivs sæghir Þriðia sinni mariu magdalene sem markus skýrir Fiorða sinni tveim [[675:20]] konom er fra grof hans gengo sem matthevs vattar Fimta degi Jakobe er a pislar degi hans sór at hann mýndi eigi eta ne drekka aðr en hann sæi krist lifannda sem pal postole γattar Setta sinn γittraðiz hann petre postola sem lukas sýnir e skilðr var fra oðrvm lærisveinvm ok gret þat erhann nitti cristi Siavnda sinni γittraðiz tveim agætom monnom sem en segir lvkas þeim er foro i kastala emavs Atta sinni ollom lære sveinvm saman at app⸌t⸍ni at locnom dýrvm sem Johanness boðar Nivnda sinni þa er thomas þreifaðe vm sar hans

with His friends from the hour of His death until the time of His resurrection and that He rose thence in their company.

«1.162-163» Disciple: Why did He not rise again immediately after His death?

Master: If He had risen again immediately after His death, the Jews would have said that He had lain unconscious and had not died. Had He risen some time later, men would have wondered whether it was He or someone else. He rose again quickly because He wanted to comfort His friends right away who were lamenting His death.

«1.164-165» Disciple: Why did He rise on the first day of the week, that is on the third day after His suffering?

Master: To renew the world on the day on which He had created it. And He raised those who had died during the ages, that is before the law, under the law and by His mercy. He did this that we should rise in the belief of the Trinity, we who have fallen into sin in words, deeds and thoughts.

«1.167-168» Disciple: What did Christ look like after His resurrection?

Master: Seven times brighter than the sun, and His friends saw Him just as He had been with them before His suffering.

«1.169» Disciple: Did He appear dressed?

Master: He took His clothes from the air, but they vanished in the air when He ascended into heaven.

«1.170» Disciple: How often did He show Himself?

Master: Twelve times. On the first day He already appeared eight times, as the writings of Nicodemus explain: first to Joseph of Arimathaea,[6] who had been imprisoned because he had buried the Body of Jesus. The second time He appeared to His mother, as Sedulius says.[7] The third time to Mary Magdalene, as Mark (16:9) explains. The fourth time He appeared to two women who were leaving His grave, as Matthew (28:9) witnesses. On the fifth day He showed Himself to James who had sworn on the day of His suffering that he would neither eat nor drink until he had seen Christ alive again, as the Apostle Paul witnesses (1 Cor. 15:7). The sixth time He showed Himself to the Apostle Peter who was separated from the other disciples and who was lamenting his denial of Christ, as told by Luke (24:12). The seventh time He showed Himself to two excellent men who travelled to the castle of Emmaus, as Luke also recounts (24:13). The eighth time he appeared in the evening through locked doors to all His disciples, as John (20:19) relates. The ninth time He showed Himself a week

Yikv þo siðar Tiunda sinni siav lærisveinom við galilea sæ Ellefta sinni agalilea fialli ellifv postolvm þa er hann steig til him\i´ns

«1.171» <Discipvlvs> Hvi segia gvðspioll at gvð vitraðiz fyrst mar\i´v magda[-]lene
<Magister> Gvð spioll ero sva set at þat eit er i þeim ritat er ollom er kvn[-]nigt ok þegar matte eigi lavynaz Af þvi melte Johanness sva morg takn gerðe gvð þav er eigi ero skrifoð aþessi boc

«1.172» <Discipvlvs> Steig hann einn vpp til himins
<Magister> Með honom stigo vpp þeir er með honom risv vpp af davða

«1.173» <Discipvlvs> Með hverri asyn steig hann vpp
<Magister> Með slikv sem hann hafðe fyrir pisl sina ok hann hafðe a fialli þa er hann yitraðez postolom sinvm
«1.174» <Discipvlvs> Hvi steig hann eigi þegar vpp eftir vprisv sina
<Magister> At læirisveinar hans mette ræyna sanna upp risv hans er þeir sa \hann´ eta ok dreka siðan Eftir fiora[-]togo daga steig hann vpp ok syndi þviat at þeir mvnv stiga vpp til dyrðar at fylla tiv laga orð ok boðorðr fiogora gvðspialla manna

«1.175» <Discipvlvs> Hver[-]sso sittr gvð a hǫgre hond foðor sins
<Magister> Mandomr hviliz idyrð gvð[-]doms
«1.177» <Discipvlvs> Hvi sendi cristr hælgan anda eftir tiv daga hælldr en þegar er hann ste vpp
<Magister> At postolar gerðe sik allyerða hans til kvamo i fostvm ok ibønvm þat syndi hann enn iþvi at þeir mvndv taka hælgan anda at fylla tiv laga orð ahimni .l. degi fra vpp risv sinni sendi hann hælgan anda at sva tæyki kristnir menn astarlǫg afimtogonda degi eftir lavsn sina fra diǫfli sem forðvm tok gyðinga lyðr rezlo logh a .l. daga eftir lavsn aegypta lande ok tok sva cristinn lyðr aþeim dogom frelse ok erfð pa[-][[675:21]]radisar sem Gyðinga lyðr tok frelse ok ærfð firir heittennar Jar[-]ðar .a .l. yettre

«1.178» <Discipvlvs> Hefir cristr nv fyllan fagnað
<Magister> Fvllan fag[-]nað hefir hann sialfr i ser en liðer hans hafa eigi

later when Thomas felt His wounds (John 20:26-27). The tenth time He appeared before seven disciples at the sea of Galilee (John 21:1-2). The eleventh time, He showed himself to eleven apostles on the mountain of Galilee when He ascended into heaven (Acts 1:9-13).

«1.171» Disciple: Why do the Gospels say that God showed Himself first to Mary Magdalene?

Master: The Gospels are composed in such a way that only that is written in them which is known to everybody and which could no longer be hidden. Therefore John (20:30) said: God did so many signs which are not written in this book.

«1.172» Disciple: Did He ascend into heaven alone?

Master: No, those who rose with Him from the dead ascended along with Him.[8]

«1.173» Disciple: How did He look when He ascended?

Master: Just as He had looked before His suffering and when He showed Himself to His apostles on the mountain.

«1.174» Disciple: Why did He not ascend immediately after His resurrection?

Master: So that His disciples would be convinced that His resurrection was real since they saw Him eat and drink afterwards. After forty days He ascended, showing thereby that all shall ascend to glory who obey the ten commandments and the commands of the four evangelists.

«1.175» Disciple: Why does Christ sit at the right hand of His Father?

Master: Humanity rests in the glory of the divinity.

«1.177» Disciple: Why did Christ send the Holy Spirit ten days later rather than immediately after He ascended?

Master: To allow the apostles to make themselves worthy of His coming by fasting and praying, thus showing them that they were prepared to receive the Holy Spirit to fulfill the ten commandments from heaven. On the fiftieth day after His resurrection He sent the Holy Spirit so that Christians could receive the law of love on the fiftieth day after their redemption from the devil, just as earlier the Jews had received the law of fear within fifty days of their release from Egypt. And as in those days the Christians had received their freedom and their inheritance of Paradise, so in the fiftieth year the Jews had received their freedom and their inheritance of the promised land.

«1.178» Disciple: Is Christ's joy complete now?

Master: He has complete joy in Himself, but His members are not full of

fvllan fagnað þvi at gýðin[-]gar bolɣa honom en heiðnir menn hlæia at honom en ɣillv menn dreifa boðom hans en ɣander menn cristnir beria lioðom hans Slikar méin ger[-]þer þolir cristr hvernn dag i liðvm sinvm En ef hann kæmr ǫllvm hlvtvm til sin þa hefir hann fvllan fagnat

«1.179» <Discipvlvs> Hverso kallaz kristnir menn li[-]kamar gvðs en helger menn liðir hans

<Magister> Sva sem liðir ero afastír hofðe ok stýraz af þvi Sva samtengiz he'i'log kristni gvðs ok goriz einn likamr með honom fýrir holld tękiv hans Avk af honom stýraz aller rettlater i sinni skipan sem liðer af hofðe Þessa hofoz avgv ero spamenn er sa firir v orðna hlvte ok postolar eða aðrir ɣisvǫv retta gavtv til hins san[-]na lios Eýrv hans ero lýðnir menn en nasar skýnnsamir menn þeir er gora gott fra illv sva 's'em nasar ilma davn En hor er vt fer or navsvm ero villo menn þeir er domr skýnsamra manna rýðr vt or hofði krist sem horr ór navsom. Mvnnr hans ero kenni menn er telia ok skýra hæl[-]gar rittningar Hendr hans ero rikis menn þeir er beriaz firir cristnvm monnom igegn oɣinvm Fętr hann ero verk menn þeir er vpp halld ɣeita ol[-]lom lýð i sinv erɣaðe Savrr farande or quiði ero sýnðer ok sýndvger menn ok o hreinir þeir er þýngia qviði kristninnar þa gripa dioflar i dav[-]þa sva sem svin i vt gang en aller likamer kristz samtengiz i ei[-]nv astar bandi

«1.180» <Discipvlvs> Hvi gerðiz holld or bravði en bloð or ɣini

<Magister> Holld hans gorez af þvi or bravði at hann mællte sialfr ek em lifannda lif Bloð hans gerez or ɣini þviat hann mællte Ek em satt vín ber Avc sva sem lik[-]hamr fæýðiz af bravði sva fœðez ǫnd af bloðe krist Avc sva sem bravð ger'e'z af morgom kornvm sva samtennger likhamr krist afmǫr[-]gvm helgom monnom Avk sva sem bravð bacaz ɣið elld sva stæiktiz likhamr krist ipislar omne þetta kallaz holld þvíat cristtr er [[675:22]] søfðr fýrir oss sem lamb Sva sem ɣín gerez afmorgom ɣinberivm ok krestingvm sva sem tengiz likamr crist af morgom retlatvm monnom fýrir þrønginng manna

«1.181» <Discipvlvs> Hversso callaz holld ok bloð þat er bravðz ok vins asion hefir

<Magister> þat holld er maria okþat er hek a crosse ok vpp steig til himins hefir af þvi bravðz asion ok ɣins at engi þora at bergia af þvi

joy because the Jews curse Him, the heathens laugh at Him, the heretics disobey His commands, and evil Christians fight against His people. Christ endures such wrong every day in His members. But if He could get all things to follow Him, He would be filled with perfect joy.

«1.179» Disciple: Why are Christians called the bodies of God and the saints His members (1 Cor. 6:15,19)?

Master: Just as the members are fastened to the head and are controlled by it, so, too, God's holy Christianity unites and becomes one body in Him through His incarnation. He directs all the righteous in an orderly fashion just as the members are directed by the head. The eyes of His head are the prophets, who foresaw future things, and the apostles and others who showed the right way to the true light. His ears are the obedient and His nostrils are the reasonable, who distinguish good from bad just as the nostrils perceive a foul stench. The slime which comes out of the nostrils is the heretics, whom the judgment of righteous men drives out of Christ's head like slime out of nostrils. His mouth is the teachers who tell and explain the Holy Scriptures. His hands are the powerful men who fight for the Christians against their enemies. His feet are the workers who offer help to everyone in trouble. The excrements in the belly are the sins and the sinners, as well as the unclean who weigh down the belly of Christianity. The devils catch them like pigs at the exit when they die. But all the bodies of Christ are united by one bond of love.

«1.180» Disciple: Why did flesh become bread, and blood become wine?

Master: His flesh comes from bread because He said Himself: I am the living life (John 6:51). His blood comes from wine because He said: I am the true grape (John 15:1). And just as the body is fed by bread, so the soul is fed by the blood of Christ. And as bread is made from many grains, so is Christ's body composed of many saints. And as bread is baked by fire, so Christ's body is baked in the oven of suffering. It is called flesh because Christ is slaughtered for us like a lamb. Just as wine is made of many grapes and through many pressings, so the body of Christ is composed of many righteous men because of the oppression of men.

«1.181» Disciple: Why do we call that His flesh and blood which has the appearance of bread and wine?

Master: The flesh that Mary brought forth and which hung on the cross and ascended to heaven, now has the appearance of bread and wine so that nobody dares to eat from it if he sees it for what it is: true

ef sæ sva se*m* er þ*at* er sanlega holld *ok* bloð *ok* hef*ir* sa mæira
ɣerðlæik er trvir þ*vi* er h*ann* ser eigi

«1.182» <D*iscipvlvs*> Hver er hi`a´lp at þ*vi*

<M*agister*> Sva sem fæzla snvz i holld þess er ettr sva snẏz hvæ*rr* trvaðr
i holld kri[-]st er ah*ans* bloðe berger Firir trv krist krossfestimk ɣer
m*e*ð h*o*n*om* fra hei*m*s gir`n´dv*m* *ok* lavstv*m* En i skirn ero*m* ɣér
grafn*ir* m*e*ð hano*m* en i holld tækiv h*ans* ɣærð*om* ɣer licahamer
krist *ok* er af þ*vi* navðsẏn[-]likt at ɣér kome*m* þangat er kristr er

«1.183» <D*iscipvlvs*> Hafa þ*eir* mer`i´a ɣærð[-]læik er me`i´ra hafa af
þ*e*s*s*e andar fæzlv

<M*agister*> Sva er sagt fra hi*m*[-]na bravðe at sa hafe eigi meira er meira
skapnaðe ne sa mi*nn*a er mi*nn*a samnaðe Sva taka aller þessa fæzlv
ok ettr hve*rr* allt lamb þ*at* er þo liɣir allt i riki gvðs

«1.184» <D*iscipvlvs*> Hvert ɣerk kavp hafa þ*eir* er þ*at* hallda ma*nn*liga

<M*agister*> Tvefalldri ambvn dẏrkaz þ*eir* a*nn*ari þeiri er þ*eir* handla
corpvs d*o*m*i*ni með manligri gofgan *ok* a*nn*ari er þeir gera sik
makliga þeirar þionosto igoðom verkv*m*

«1.185-187» <D*iscipvlvs*> Hvat døm*ir* þv vm þa er þ*at* hallda v makliga
i gægn rettre sætningv

<M*agister*> þe`i´r er i hordome ɣefiaz *ok* igegn gvðs bodorðv*m* eða
log*om* eða þeir er fe kavpa ɣigslor eða kirkivr *ok* meiða gvðs lẏð
i rong*om* lvtv*m* *ok* gera þ*e*ssa hlvte alla diarflega Ðeir ero
sæl`i´arar gvðs *ok* crosfestenðr þ*vi* at ke*nn*i me*nn* skvlo mes[-]sor
sẏngia fẏr*ir* ǫst *ok* heilso andar si*nn*ar *ok* allrar cristni En ef þer
gøreð til fe fanga *ok* ma*nn*a lofs *ok* sælia takn pislar crist hvat er þa
nema þeir se selianðr gvðs En þa er þ*eir* hondla holld drot[-]tens
ɣars sẏndvgv*m* hondo*m* *ok* v hrienv*m* hvg hvat gera þ*eir* þa
ne[-][[**675:23**]]ma crostfesta kristr

«1.188» <D*iscipvlvs*> Ma lẏðr taka sẏnd af þeim

<M*agister*> Þa er sẏnir heli b*i*scop*s*s savrgvðo gvðs þionvsto þa fell mikill
lẏðr með þei*m* idav[-]ða af þeira sẏnda lvt tæking *ok* aller þeir er
eft*ir* likingv samten[-]giaz þei*m* *ok*falla þa hvarer tvæggiv igrof se*m*
blinðr leiði blin[-]dan

«1.189» <D*iscipvlvs*> Hava þeir sẏnd er samneɣttvz við þaoɣitande

<M*agister*> Savrgaz sa er gripr i tiav`r´n Sva savrgaz *ok* þ*eir* er san

flesh and blood. For he has greater merit who believes yet does not see (John 21:29).

«1.182» Disciple: How is one redeemed by it?

Master: Just as food turns into the flesh of the person who eats it, so every believer turns into the flesh of Christ who drinks of His blood. Because of our belief in Christ we are crucified with Him «and cleansed» of the world's lusts and vices; and through baptism we are buried with Him. By eating His flesh we become bodies of Christ and it is therefore necessary that we should come to where Christ is.

«1.183» Disciple: Do those have greater merit who have more of this food for the soul?

Master: It is said about the heavenly bread that he shall not have more who has gathered more, nor shall he have less who has gathered less (Exod. 16:18). So all take this food and everyone eats the whole lamb, which lives entirely in God's Kingdom.

«1.184» Disciple: What reward do those receive who do this in a human fashion?

Master: They are doubly rewarded. First, because they receive the *Corpus Domini* in human worship; second, because they make themselves worthy of this service through good deeds.

«1.185-187» Disciple: How do you judge those who act unworthily against the right order?

Master: Those who are involved in adultery and act against God's commands or laws, and those who buy offices or churches for money and harm God's people by doing wrong things, as well as those who do all things impudently, are the betrayers and crucifiers of God: for the priests shall sing masses for the sake of love and for the salvation of their own souls and of all Christianity. If they act only for money and for the praise of men, and if they sell the miracle of Christ's suffering, what else are they save the sellers of God (Acts 8:20)? When they handle the flesh of Our Lord with sinful hands and with an unclean mind, what else do they do but crucify Christ (Heb. 6:6)?

«1.188» Disciple: Can people become sinful through them?

Master: When the sons of Bishop Eli soiled divine service (1 Sam. 2:22-24), many people fell to death with them because they took part in their sins, just as all those who by imitation followed them. They will all fall into the grave, just as the blind leading the blind (Matt. 15:14).

«1.189» Disciple: Do they sin if they associate with them unknowingly?

Master: He who touches tar, will be defiled (Eccl. 13:1). So are those

ɣistaz þei*m* þo at þ*eir* se oɣitande en þei*m* grandar eigi villa sv er þeir ɣiðkaz

«1.190» <D*iscipvlvs*> Mego sɣndgir hælga korpvs

<M*agister*> Þo at hinir værstv se þa gerez corp*vs* d*om*ini fɣrir saker orða þeˋi⁄ra er þ*eir* svngia ɣfer þvi at crist helgar en eigi þeir *ok* ɣiner ha*n*s heˋi⁄lsa sono*m* sinv*m* fɣrir hendr oɣina sva sem solar geisli savrgaz eigi af savr *ok* lɣsiz eigi af altari

«1.191» <D*iscipvlvs*> Ef got*t* er þ*at* er firir þa geriz af kristi en eigi af þei*m* ma þ*at* eigi got*t* ɣer[-]ða þei*m* er af þeira hondo*m* taka þ*at* igegn set*t*ningv*m*

<M*agister*> Eigi stoðar helldr grand *ok* ɣerðr eigi gott þ*at* er tekit er igegn goðri set*t*nin[-]gv af þei*m* er þa skal taka

«1.192-193» <D*iscipvlvs*> San*n*a þv þ*at*

<M*agister*> Eki epli var illt i paradis þvi at gvð skop allt got*t* en maðr snere goðo til illz þa er ha*n*n tokþ*at* af hoggorme en en*n* helldr af diofli Sa er fɣrir retˋle⁄tis ost tekr corp*vs* d*om*ini af þei*m* *ok* trviz hvern dag sam tengiaz almen*n*ileg[-]re cristni firir bænir ken*n*i manz þan*n* ætla ek hialpaz me[-]ga af tru sin*n*i þo at ha*n*n døɣ En sa er tekr verk þeira er misge[-]ra *ok* gofgar corp*vs* d*om*ini *ok* tekr þionosto krist af þeim þan ætla ek hialpaz af þessi trv þvi at iosep tok lika*m* krist af pilato

«1.194» <D*iscipvlvs*> Mego þeir sætta lɣð ɣið gvð

<M*agister*> helldr gremia þeir gvd at ser þa er þ*eir* savrga helga staðe i sin*n*i gavngv *ok* spilla vigðv*m* klæðv*m* isin*n*i a tavkv Slika ken*n*i menn likaz englv*m* *ok* flɣia þa sialf*ir* sem ritat er Sɣnir gvðs *ok* dætr g[..]mðv ha*n*n at ser *ok* ero eigi ha*n*s sɣner fɣrir savrlifi af þvi mv*n* ek fela andlit mit*t* fra þei*m* qvað gvð Sono kallar ha*n*n þa fɣrir ken*n*i manz naf*n*n en eigi sono fɣrir savrlifi þeira forn ðiggr gvð eigi helldr [[675:24]] rękir ha*n*n sem sagt er forn ɣðra hatar ond min*n* kvˋe⁄ðr cristr þvi at þer føreð mer savrgat bravð holld gvðs ma eigi savrgaz en þ*eir* savrgaz er af þvi næɣta o skɣnsamliga sem bravðan*n*at bæn þeira hevrir egi gvd helldr ɣerð hverio*m* þeira at sɣnð *ok* snɣz blezan þeira i bolɣan

«1.195» <D*iscipvlvs*> Taka þ*eir* corpvs d*om*ini

<M*agister*> Sɣnir gvðs ein*ir* taka holld ha*n*s þeir er ha*n*s likamer skolo

defiled who live among them even if they are innocent. However, if they come to their senses, their error will not harm them.

«1.190» Disciple: Can the sinful consecrate the *Corpus Domini*?

Master: Yes, even if they are the lowliest, for the *Corpus Domini* is created for the words they sing over it. It is Christ who consecrates and not they. And His friends greet their sons through the hands of the enemies, just as a ray of sun is not soiled by dirt nor made more splendid by the altar.

«1.191» Disciple: If that which is done for them by Christ and not by themselves is good, can it not be good for them who receive it from their hands against the rules?

Master: No, it is not useful but harmful, and that will not be good which is taken against the just rules by him who shall receive it.

«1.192-193» Disciple: Explain this to me.

Master: The apple was not evil in Paradise, because God created everything good; but man turned good into evil when he took the apple from the snake, that is from the devil. He who takes from them the *Corpus Domini* for the love of righteousness and believes himself to be united with all of Christianity every day through the prayers of the priests, such a person, I think, can be helped by his faith even though he dies. And, whoever receives the deeds of those who sin and worships the *Corpus Domini* and takes Christ's service from them is, I think, helped by his faith, for Joseph received Christ's body from Pilate.

«1.194» Disciple: Can such priests reconcile the people with God?

Master: No, they provoke God's anger against them when they soil holy places by their coming and defile consecrated clothes by their touching. The angels abhor such priests and flee them, as is written: His sons and daughters provoked Him against them, and they are not His sons because of their indecent life. Therefore I will hide my face from them, said God (Deut. 32:5, 19-20). He calls them sons because they are priests in name, but not sons because of their indecent life. God does not accept their offering but rejects it, as is written: My soul hates your offering (Isa. 1:13-14), says Christ, because you bring me polluted bread (Mal. 1:7). God's flesh cannot be polluted but they are polluted who eat of it indiscriminately as of ordinary bread. God does not hear their prayers, but their prayers turn into sin for each of them and their blessing turns into a curse.[9]

«1.195» Disciple: Do they receive the *Corpus Domini*?

Master: Only the sons of God receive His flesh, those who shall be His

ɤera en þeir er eigi ero i gvði þo at þeir sýniz taka holld hans ok
bloð tilmvnz þa taka þeir þat eigi helldr eta þeir ser a fallz dom en
englar bera hollld crist til himna en dioflar casta eitri i mvnn hinvm
sem ciprianvs seger Avk þeir er blod crist taka sem vin annat þa
snýz þeim þat i orma gall ok o vm reðilikt eitr

«1.196» <Discipvlvs> Tok eigi ivdas slikt holld drottens sen petrar
<Magister> Uist eigi þvi at petr ælskaði gvð ok tok hann af þvi heilagt
taccn af gvði en ivdas hataði gvð ok tok hann af þvi eitr en kraptr
ok takn heilax hollz var eptir með gvði

«1.197» <Discipvlvs> Er slikvm hlýdanda
<Magister> Ðat er þeir bioða gott ða er skýllt at hlýða goðo eneigi
þeim þvi at þeir mæla ok gera ei[-]gi en ef þeir bioða illt þa ero þeir
firir litande þvi at gvði býriar hælldr at hlýða en monnom

«1.198-199» <Discipvlvs> Mego þeir læýsa eða binnda
<Magister> Ef þeir ero eigi iberlegvm domi skilðer fra cristninni þo at
þeir se sialfer fast bvnnir þa mego þeir þo hvartveggia þvi at cristr
binðr ok læýser fýrir þionosto þeira en eigi þeir sialfir en þeir fýrir
litendr sem heiðnir menn ef þeir ero fra cristi skilðir Meðan Jvdas
ɤar með postolvm þa sýndiz hann sem ɤin kenndi hann ok
ski`r´ði ok gerði iartegnir sem aðrir postolar en siðan hann hvarf
fra þeim þa sýndiz hann bærr fiandi sv`a´ ero ok þessir meðan þeir
ero isam[-]ɤellldi kr`i´stinnar þa er nýtandi holl sv er þeir gera En
ef þeir ero þa[-]ðan skilðir þa er o nýtt allt þat er þeir gera þeir ero
flýendr af krist sav[-]ðom þvi at þeir ero ɤargar sem ritit er Fareð
vt fra þeim lýðr minn at ei[-]gi takit ðer lvt með þeim ipislvm
flýanda er samlag þeira hellzt i gvðs embøtti at samnæýzlv sem
ritat er Eigi skoloð er mat eiga við þa ne svefn ne heilsa þeim Flýia
skal þa ihvg okollom ɤil[-]ia ok tæýgiaz eki eft[ir] ɤerkom þeira

«1.200» <Discipvlvs> Hversso geraz eftir lat [[675:25]] ɤærk þeira
<Magister> Ða er lofoð ero ill ɤerk þeira eða ellfdir tilsýn[-]ða með
raðom eða avðefvm af þvi ero eigi þeir einir davða ɤerðir er gera

bodies. But those who are not in God do not receive it, even though they seem to take His flesh and blood into their mouths. They eat their sentence of condemnation (1 Cor. 11:29), but, as Cyprian[10] says, the angels carry the flesh of Christ into the heavens and the devils cast poison into their mouths. To those who receive Christ's blood as ordinary wine, it turns into the venom of asps and unspeakable poison (Deut. 32:33).

«1.196» Disciple: Did not Judas partake of the same flesh of the Lord as Peter did?

Master: Certainly not, because Peter loved the Lord and therefore he received the holy Eucharist from God. Judas hated God and received poison instead, but the sacramental power of the holy flesh remained in God.

«1.197» Disciple: Should we obey them?

Master: When they command what is good, not they but God must be obeyed, for they say and do not (Matt. 23:3). If they command evil, then they must be despised because we ought to obey God rather than men (Acts 5:29).

«1.198-199» Disciple: Do they have the power to loosen or to bind (Matt. 18:18)?

Master: They can do both, if they have not been separated from Christianity by a public judgment even though they themselves are strongly bound, because it is Christ who binds and loosens through their service and not they themselves. But those who are separated from Christ shall be despised as heathens. While Judas was among the apostles, he appeared to be a friend. He taught and baptized and performed miracles as did the other apostles. But after he had turned away from them, he appeared as an open enemy. And so it is with the priests today: as long as they are under the rule of Christianity, the hall which they build is useful. But if they are separated from it, everything they do is useless. They are fugitives from Christ's sheep because they are wolves, as is written: Get away from them, my people, so that you must not partake in their torment with them (Rev. 18:4). Any kind of fellowship with them, especially in God's service, must be avoided, as is written: You shall not eat with them nor sleep with them nor greet them (1 Cor. 5:11). You shall flee them in your mind and in your will and you shall not be enticed by their deeds.

«1.200» Disciple: How do they get consent for their deeds?

Master: When their evil deeds are praised and they are assisted to sin by counsel and riches. Hence not only do they deserve death who do

helldr *ok* hinir er raðendr ero missgorðv*m* En eigi er fl*y*ianda fra illv*m* ken*n*imo*n*no*m* meðan þeir ero eigi fra cristi skilðir nema sva *y*er[-]ði sam satt*ir* a illzcv læiðir men*n* *ok* v lærðir at engi sake an*n*an ran[-]gin*n*da þ\a′ero þ*eir* fl*y*andi þ*vi* at þa skpilla þeir f*y*rir gvðs l*yð*

«1.201» <D*iscipvlvs*> Skal ke*n*[-]na illv*m* mo*n*nno*m* orð gvðs
<M*agister*> Eigi ero þei*m* gvðs orð kennandi er *y*isir ero gvðs o*y*inir þvi at sa er gvðs lav*y*nandi hl*y*ti se*gir* fiando*m* ha*n*s sem sagt er eigi skoloð þer heilagt tacn hvndv*m* gefa eða casta gimstei[-]nv*m* firir svin at eigi troði þav þa vnðir foto*m* En þ*at* er eigi vitat at þeir se fiandr gvðs þa er goðv*m* mo*n*nom at hallda gvðs vilia þei*m* sem snvaz *y*ilia fra illv þo at dalegr se ihia þei*m* Sva sem gvð kendi petre heilsv orð eða ollo*m* þei*m* er hialpaz matto þo at vissi Jvdas eða g*y*ðingar st*y*ggvaz *y*ið þ*at*

«1.202» <D*iscipvlvs*> Skal þei*m* ðola mein gerð sem cristr þolðe Jvdas
<M*agister*> Jllv*m* er þolanda i kristni en engv*m* eftir likende at ge[-]ra
«1.203» <D*iscipvlvs*> hve lengi ero þei*m* misgerðir þolandi
<M*agister*> Tilþes*s* er sa kemr er skilr korn fra agno*m* *ok* kastar halmi i elld en hirðir hv\e′iti i hirzlv*m* sinv*m*

it (Rom. 1:32), but also those who are their counselors in crime. But we need not flee from bad teachers as long as they are not separated from Christ, unless learned men and laymen turn to evil and charge one another with injustice. In this case we must flee from them because they destroy God's people.

«1.201» Disciple: Shall wicked men be taught the word of God?

Master: They shall not be taught the word of God who are God's certain enemies, because he is a traitor who tells God's secrets to His enemies, as is said: You shall not give the holy Eucharist unto the dogs nor cast pearls before swine lest they trample them under their feet (Matt. 7:6). If it is not known whether they are God's enemies, good men who want to turn away from evil should obey God's will even if evil is within them. In the same way the Lord taught Peter and all those who were to be saved the words of salvation even though He knew that Judas and the Jews were angered by it.

«1.202» Disciple: Must one endure wrong as Christ endured Judas?

Master: Evil must be endured by Christianity, but no one must imitate it.

«1.203» Disciple: How long must one endure wrong?

Master: Until He appears who separates the grain from the chaff and throws the stalks in the fire and gathers His wheat into the garner (Matt. 3:12; Luke 3:17).

«2.1» <Discipvlvs> Skili gvð þik fra ollom illvm lvtvm goðr lærifaðer ok
staðfesti þik i himneskv sæte Ond min fagnar gvði þvi at ek lýsvmk
af spec[-]tar geisla fýrir þik at bravt [re]kkene ýillo þoko En bið ek
þik goðr lærifaðer at mer se lofat at spý'r'ia framar
<Magister> Spýrðv þess er þ[v] villt ok mvnþv heýra þat er þv fýsiz

«2.2» <Discipvlvs> Sva er ritat at eki er illt en ef eki er illt þa vndra ek
hvi gvð firir dømir menn eða engla ef þeir gera eki illt En ef ýere
nokot illt skapat þa ýere þat af gvði þvi at af gvði ero allir hlvtir
Avk ýerðr þa sem gvð hæfði illt skapað eða hann dømi ranglega
þa er þat gera erhann skop
<Magister> Af gvði ero allir hlvtir ok oll skep[-]na hans goð En illt kallaz
af þvi ekki at þat er engi skepna þvi at gvð skopal[-]la hlvti goða ok
ekci illt En ekki er annat illt nema þat er eigi gott ok er þat spiall
skepnv en eigi eðli Annat er skepna en annat eðli ok annat ýerk
Skepna callaz allar hofoð skepnor en eðli þat er af þeim geriz ok
gøzsko [[675:26]] sem log verk þat er men gera Gera menn sýnðir
ok taka pislir firir þat en þat skapadi gvð eigi helldr leit hann verða
sem ritat er Eigi gerði gvð dav[-]ða en sýnð er ekki annnat en gera
eigi þat er boðit er eða gera annan ýeg en boðit er Sva sem ekki
er annat illt en missa goðs þat er eil'i'fs fagnaðr en þat geriz eigi
af gvði helldr af skepnv gvðs En gvð dømir ða makliga þat er hann
[gaf] þeim eigi fagnað er eigi ýilia til hans eða anan veg en boðet
er

«2.3» <Discipvlvs> Hver er gørýare sýndar
<Magister> Sialfr madr með tøýgingvm fiandans
«2.4» <Discipvlvs> Er þvngt at misgera
<Magister> Hinn minsta sýnd at ýitand gor er ǫllom h'e'imi þýngri En
hvatke er gort ýerðr sýnda eða illzkv þa snvz þat allt ilof gvðs

«2.5» <Discipvlvs> Hvat melir þv nv Er eigi mandrap illt eða hordomr
<Magister> Man drap er stvndom gott sva sem daýið ýa goliam eða
Jvdith Oloferne en þat er þa illt er af rongom hvg 'er framt' hiv

« Book 2 »

«2.1» Disciple: May God preserve you from all evil, dear teacher, and establish you in your heavenly seat! My soul rejoices in God because through you I have become enlightened by the rays of wisdom which you have brought me after the fog of ignorance was dispersed. I beg of you, dear teacher, that I may be allowed to ask further.

Master: Ask what you will and you shall hear what you request.

«2.2» Disciple: It is written that nothing is wicked, and if nothing is wicked, I wonder why God condemns men or angels if they do nothing wicked. But if something wicked was created, it was created by God because all things are from God. And in this case God created evil, otherwise He judges wrongly those who do what He created.

Master: From God are all things and all His creation is good, and no creature therefore is wicked. For God created all things good and nothing wicked (1 Tim. 4:4). But nothing is wicked except that which is not good and that is a flaw in the substance and not in its nature. First there is substance, then comes nature, and finally there is deed. All elements are called substance, and nature is that which is made out of them, and kindness and laws are deeds which men do. Men commit sins and undergo sufferings; however, God did not create this, He only allowed it to happen, as is written: God did not make death (Wisd. 1:13). Sin is no more than not doing what is ordered or acting differently from what is ordered, just as wickedness is nothing else than the loss of good. This is the joy of eternity and it is not done by God but by God's creatures. God judges them properly by not giving joy to those who do not wish to come to Him or who follow another path than was ordered.

«2.3» Disciple: Who is the perpetrator of sin?

Master: Man himself under the enticement of the devil.

«2.4» Disciple: Is it a serious matter to sin?

Master: The smallest sin consciously committed is more serious than anything in the whole world. But whatever is committed, be it sin or malice, it all turns into the praise of God.

«2.5» Disciple: What are you saying now? Are not homicide and adultery evil?

Master: Homicide can sometimes be justified: for instance, when David killed Goliath (1 Sam. 17:49), or Judith killed Holofernes (Judith 13:10), but it is evil if committed for a wrong reason.

skaprer goðr en hordomr illr ok ekki annat en olofaðr hivskapr ok af þvi illr at annan veg er framt en ɣera a eða loɣat se En þat snɣ[-]ðz allt ilof gvði þa er hann hefnir þess retliga þvi at sva sem konongr er lof[-]ligr þaer hann gefr mala riddarvm sinvm þa er hann firir dømir þioɣa ok ill menni ok ɣikinga ok sem gvð dɣrkaz af hialp retlatra Sva er hann ok lofaðr i hemd v milldra

«2.6» <Discipvlvs> Sva er ritat at gvð hattar ekki þat er hann gerði Hversv segiz hann þa hata illa en elska goða
<Magister> Alla skepno sina ælskar gvð en hann setti eigi alla i einn stað sva sem skriɣare æ\ l/ skar alla hlɣti a smið sinni ok ælskar þo svmar framar en svma ok settr hvern lit imak[-]ligan stað af þvi sægiz hann þa ælska er hann tekr til himins hallar en hina hatar hann er hann skolemr ihelɣitis divpi

«2.7» <Discipvlvs> Hvat er sialfrædi
<Magister> Jvelldi manz at vera eða ɣilia eða gera gott eða illt þat sialfræ[-]ði hafði maðr i paradis fr\ i/ alst en nɣer ɣfrialst þvi at hann ɣill eigi gott ne[-]ma gvðs miskvn fari fɣrir ok ma hann þat eigi nema gvðs miskvnn fɣl[-]gi

«2.8» <Discipvlvs> Hvat røðer þv vm þa er hafnaðo heimi ok toko siðan bv[-]ning en siðan casta þeir niðr þvi ok hverɣa aftr til sɣnða
<Magister> Um þa er sva mælt Slæger men eggia reiði gvðs ɣfir sik Oft dre[-]gr þręll villtan son til faðvr ok hæɣir aftr til þræls ɣerks Sva [[675:27]] læiða ok stɣndvm þessir men til gvðs ok hverɣa aftr til illzkv sinnar Sa sem diǫfvll þionar gvði sva þiona liðir hans liðvm gvðs

«2.9» <Discipvlvs> Hværs[-]so þionar fiande liðvm gvðs
<Magister> Þvi at hann firir leit at ɣera ængla hofðingi ahimni þa gerðe gvð hann starfsaman smið iheimi at hann þio[-]nadi navðigr með illv erɣiði þa er hann ɣilldi eigi ærɣiðis lavst þio[-]na gvði i himnvm vppi sem ritit er Gera man ek hann þer eilifan ðręl Þessar smiðs aflar ero qvalar heims Smið bælgir hans ablastar fræstni hamrar hans ok tænggr ero ofriðar menn ok qvęliaðrar þrælar hans ok sag[-]ðer ero bolvenðr ok bakmalogar tvngvr Jþesso afle ok með þessom to[-]lvm hræ\ i/ nsazc gvllker himna konongss þat ero hælgir menn en ɣanðer pinaz i dvflizɣ hans þeir er moti gera himna kononge aþessa lvnd þionkar diavɣvll gvði

Wedlock is good, but adultery or unlawful wedlock is evil. Therefore, everything is bad that it is not performed as it should be or is permitted. But all is transformed into the praise of God when He takes justified revenge for it. For just as a king is praiseworthy when he rewards his knights, condemns thieves, villains and vikings, so God is worshipped with the help of the righteous and He is also praised for taking revenge on the cruel.

«2.6» Disciple: It is written that God does not hate what He created (Wisd. 11:25). Why then is He said to despise the wicked and to love the good?

Master: God loves all of His creation, but He did not set all of them in one place, just as a painter loves all the colors in his work, but nevertheless loves some more than others, and puts each color in the appropriate place. Therefore God is said to love those whom He receives into the hall of heaven and to hate those whom He banishes into the depths of hell.

«2.7» Disciple: What is free will?

Master: It is in the power of man to be or to want or to do good or evil. Man possessed free will unconditionally while in Paradise; but now he is unfree because he does not wish to do good unless God's grace precedes that wish, and man cannot achieve that unless God's grace follows.

«2.8» Disciple: What is your opinion of those who turned away from the world and assumed the habit, but then cast it away and returned to sin?

Master: About them is said: Cunning men provoke the wrath of God upon them (Job 36:13). Often a slave drags a wayward son to his father and returns to his slave-work. In the same way such men sometimes lead others to God but then turn back to their evil ways. Just as the devil serves God, so his members serve God's members.

«2.9» Disciple: How does the devil serve God's members?

Master: Because the devil abandoned his leadership of the angels in heaven, God made him an industrious smith in the world. In that way he was able to serve with evil work, since he did not want to serve God in heaven without work, as is written: I shall make him your servant forever (Job 40:23/41:4). The torments of the world are this smith's forge. His bellows are the inspirations of temptation. His hammers and tongs are his enemies and his tormentors. His slaves and his saws[11] are the swearing and back-talking tongues. In this forge and with these tools the golden vessel of the King of Heaven is cleansed — that is the saints. The wicked — that is those

«2.10» <Discipvlvs> Hversso þiona liðer hans lidvm gvðs
<Magister> Þa er þeir leiða þa til rikis með fagrlego rettlęti eða
meingørðvm Með fallego rettlæti leiða þeir þa er þeir sýna vtan
goð verk þav er þeir ælska eigi innan ok taka sý[-]ner gvðs af þeim
dømvm goð verk þav er þeir elska af illv hiarta ok festaz þeir af
tekno godo þa er hinir firir lata þat er eigi ælskaðv sva sem gvðs
englar stý\r⁄ctvz forðvm þa er illir fello Með mein gørðvm draga
þeir þa til rikis gvðs þa er þeir taka fra þeim þessa heims avðęfi þav
er þeir ælskv[-]ðv aðr til miok eða þeir standa amott þeim at eigi
mege þeir fram kom\a⁄ likamligvm girndvm af þvi reýniz fianden
o nýtzsamligr at liðir hans enn helldr navzsýnilegr þvi at helger
menn dýrkaz af þeirra freistni ok hafaz til rikis himna

«2.11» <Discipvlvs> Firir hvi hafa her illir menn gno[685b r l g au]ðæγa
ok γelldi ok heillso en goðir γalað ok sottir ok taka o[685b r l ptt
meinger]ðer illvm
<Magister> Til þess illvm avðæfi sælld at goðer f[ý............] avð er þeir sia
hina γærstv menn mestan hafa Avðøγ[............] ok avmbon þæss er
þeir gøra gott þvi at γander menn [...............] iarðlega hlvti ok taka
þeir fýrir þvi her allt γerk k[....................] til þess at þeir mego sialfer
þa illk\d⁄v fræmia ok g[.......................] la þa til illz Yelldi hafa þeir
til þess at gvðs ý[....................] ok stilliz firir þa af illvm verkvm hafa
þeir ok [...................] [[675:28]] take þess at þýngri qvaler annars
heims er þeir γerða \eigi⁄ her bar[-]ðer með monnom En goðer
menn hafa af þvi γalað ok sottir ok meingerðir at eigi fýsizc þeir
illz eða bæti þat er þeir misgorðo i gægn gvði eða þeir dýrkaz i
þolen męði

«2.12» <Discipvlvs> Hvi hafa svmir goðer her avðeγi ok γelldi ok heilsv
en illir þrongiaz i γesolld ok meingerðvm ok sottom
<Magister> Svmvm goðvm mavnnvm geγaz til þess avðefi a\t⁄þeir
fremia ok ero þeir aþat minntir hýersso þekciligirr γera mvnv goðir
eil\i⁄fir hlv[-]tir ef þessa heims avðæγi þikcia fogr vera Uelldi hafa
þeir til þess at avka gøzko sinar ok til þess at þeir meghe æfla aðra

who work against the King of Heaven — are tormented in his dungeon. In this way the devil serves God.

«2.10» Disciple: How do the devil's members serve God's members?

Master: They lead them to the heavenly kingdom either in beautiful righteousness or by misdeeds. In beautiful righteousness[12] they lead those who outwardly perform good deeds which they do not love inwardly. And by such examples the sons of God adopt good deeds which they love in their wicked hearts.[13] They adhere to the good they have accepted which the others abandoned because they did not love it, just as God's angels were strengthened earlier when the wicked fell. By perpetrating misdeeds and at the same time taking from them the wealth of this world which they loved too much, the devils drag God's members to His kingdom or they stand in their way so that they cannot enjoy carnal pleasures. Thus the devil proves to be useless rather than useful to his members, because the saints are glorified by their temptation and taken into the kingdom of heaven.

«2.11» Disciple: Why do evil men possess «much wealth», power and health here on earth, while good men suffer poverty, diseases and «often» endure «injustice» from the wicked?

Master: The wicked are given riches so that the good «will forsake» those riches, which they see that the worst men have. «They are wealthy, first of all, so that with their money they can perform the evil deeds which God's righteous law expects of them; second, so that they can be rewarded if they do good, which they do only for the sake of this world that gives them their riches. These wicked men enjoy their power mostly for their own benefit, but also for the sake of the damned whom they assist with their evil deeds, and finally for the good whom they punish or chastise. They possess health so they can» suffer much more serious torment in the other world, for they were not punished here among men.[14] Good men therefore suffer poverty, disease, and injustice so as not to desire evil, but to make amends for their wrongdoing against God, or so that they are glorified for their patience.

«2.12» Disciple: Why then do some good men have wealth, power, and health here on earth while the wicked wallow in misery, injustice, and disease?

Master: Wealth is given to some good men so they may act «correctly». They are thereby reminded how agreeable eternity will be, since the wealth of this world is so desirable. They have it in their power to increase their goodness, they can strengthen others to do good or

til goðs eða stoðγa illa menn at eigi meghe þeir gøra illzkv heilsv hafa þeir til þess at eigi rýggviz retlatir af sottom þeirra helldr fagne þeir heilso þei[-]rra En svmir illir hafa her af þvi fatøkt ok likams mein at þeir me[-]ge þaðan af nema hversso til mýkilla illra hlvta þeir skýnda i illvm hlvtvm eða siðvm

«2.13» <Discipvlvs> Hvi liγa svmir illir lengi en svmir goðer andaz bratt eða hvi hafa svmir goðer langt lif en svmir illir døýia brat

<Magister> Illir liγa af þvi lengi at goðer dýrkaz fýrir þa ok birtiz fra illv en illvm γerðr þat at a fallz domi ok avki pinsla En goðir andaz af þvi bratt at þeir komi brat til eilifra fagnaða ok γære eigi lengi inavðvm heims En þeir igægnn hafa rettlatir langt lif at margir rettlatir leiðrettez af dømvm þeirra ok avkiz γerðleikr þeira En illir γerða skiott [....]nir til qvala at gvðs γattar ok o γalðer menn þeir er enn erv γil [.........] γið þat ok hverfa fra illv

«2.14» <Discipvlvs> Ero þeir sæler er her ero fa [...........]
<Magister> γesler er her liγa sælega ok hafa þat er þeir γilia ok ˋer´ þeim [...........] en siðan γerðr þeim castat iælld brennanda sem þýr [............] igægn ero þeir er her na eigi girndvm sinvm ok þrøn [...............]vm morgvm þvi at þeir læraz með bardogvm sem sýnir [...............] er Gvð berr hvern son sinn er hann tekr En þat er [...............]ro aγallt ó moðger þo at þeir hafe konongs rik[.] [[675:29]] ok ero þeir alldrigin ón qvalar En retlater ero jamnan vtan qˋv´ol ok ero þeir iamnan moðker ok alldrigin dýrðar lavsir þo at þeir se her ihattre eða i mýrkva stoγo sættir

«2.15» <Discipvlvs> Sýn þv þetta mer skýrra
<Magister> Jllir ero af þvi v moðker at þeir γilia eigi gott ne megho en þeir γilia illt ok megho þat en illt reýniz ekci ok af þvi sizt at þeir megho ekci Alldrigin ero þeir vtann qvol þvi at þeir qveliaz af grimleik ok ero vm allt rædder vm sik at þeir γerðe teknir eðaræntir eða drepnir sem ritat er eigi er friðr v milldr qvˋa´ð gvð En goðer ero moðker þvi at gvðs miskvnn æflir þa at γilia gott ok nema en hafna illv Alldriginn missa þeir dýrðar þvi at þeir ero mæddrir ok fagna avrvggleik eilifrar dýrðar ok sælo sem ritit er Ret lætte ero vttan ræzslo Þat γil ek ok segia at ekci bersk illvm got at hendi ne goðvm illt

they can stop evil men from doing harm. They have health so that the righteous will not be troubled by diseases but rejoice in their health. However, some wicked men experience poverty and bodily suffering on earth, so as to learn from that how they are hastening toward eternal damnation through evil deeds and actions.

«2.13» Disciple: Why do some wicked men live long and some good men die young? And why do some good men have a long life and wicked men die early?

Master: Wicked men live long to allow good men to be glorified by them and to stand out brightly against the wicked. But for the wicked this ends in a sentence of condemnation and in an increase of torment. Good men die soon so as to reach eternal joy quickly and no longer suffer the misery of this world. Also, good men often live a long life to allow many righteous people to be improved by their example and increase their merit. But the wicked are quickly «dragged» to their torment so that God's witnesses and the non-elect who continue «to err» are thus «struck by fear» and turn away from evil.

«2.14» Disciple: Are those blessed who do «not suffer misfortunes» here?

Master: Those who pass their lives in pleasure without being struck by adversity are miserable because they prepare themselves for the fire. Those who see their desires thwarted and who are tested by numerous trials are very happy because they are prepared for the kingdom of heaven like sons. God scourges every son of His whom He receives (Heb. 12:6). Those who are rejected even if they are kings are powerless and subject to eternal damnation.[15] But the righteous are always without torment and they are always powerful and never without glory, even if they are hated or put in prison here.

«2.15» Disciple: Explain that more clearly to me.

Master: The wicked are powerless because they do not want good nor can they, for they want evil and they can be evil; but the evil has been proved «to be» nothing. And from that it can be seen that they can do nothing. They are never without pain because they are tormented by cruelty and they are always and forever afraid that they will be captured or robbed or killed, as is written: There is no unrighteous peace, said God (Isa. 48:22). But the good are powerful because God's grace strengthens them to want and to learn to be good and to reject evil. They will not fail to achieve glory even though they are tired,[16] and they rejoice in the assurance of eternal glory and bliss, as is written: The righteous are without fear (Prov. 28:1).

«2.16» <Discipvlvs> Jgvðs nafni hvat mælir þv nv Eigi fag[-]na illir goðvm lvtvm *ok* liɣa at mvnvðvm *ok* glæðiaz i krasom *ok* skina idýrle[-]gom klæðom *ok* vna ɣið avðøɣi *ok* a*ll*a fegrd heims en goðer ero bvnir imýr[-]kvastoɣo *ok* mødder i bardogom *ok* qvalder i hvngri *ok* þorsta *ok* a*ll*zkýns pins[-]lvm

<Magister> Ða er hamingia lær ɣið illv *ok* fýser þa goða slikra lvta sem þv tal[-]der þa likiaz þ*eir* fiski þeim er fagnar litilli beitv *ok* ɣerðr h*ann* þa dreiginn vpp or ɣattni þvi at ðeir fýllaz bitr læix fýrir krasom *ok* brennosteis davn fýrir mvnvgð en ske*m*der fýrir fegrð klæða Av\c/ taka þ*eir* mýrkvar helɣitis graver fýrir fægrð hvsa *ok* eilifa fatøkt firir avðøɣe er þ*eir* toko Fram leiða þ*eir* dagha sina i goðom lvtvm en þ*eir* stiga á avgabragðe til pinnsla En þa er goðer taka slik meinn sem þv segir þa likiaz þ*eir* þeim er bergia a pipar eða avðrv rommo gra[-]si at h*ann* mege betr standaz ɣín drýkiv Sva taka *ok* pinslir eiliɣar tiallbvðer fýrir mýrkvastoɣo *ok* fagnað firir bardaga *ok* mvn þa eigi siðan þýrsta ne hvngra *ok* mvn a*ll*r sarlæikr flýia fra þeim Af þessom lvtvm reýniz at goðer ero iamnan sæler *ok*avðgir en illir ero iafnan ɣeslir *ok* avmir

«2.17» <Discipvlvs> Hvaðan com tign *ok* velldi

<Magister> Af gvði er o*ll* tign *ok* velldi goðra *ok* illra sem sagt er Ekci er ɣelldi annnat en af gvði

«2.18» <Discipvlvs> Hvat dømir þv vm þa er kav[-][[675:30]] pa eða selia tignar vellde

<Magister> Þeir er þat kavpa fara til davða með Simoni mago en þeir er selia þat ɣerða fýrir andar likðro

«2.19» <Discipvlvs> Hafa hofðingiar meira velldi firir gvði en aðrir

<Magister> Kennni manz þionosta er tignar ve*ll*di tior manni ekci ɣið gvð er ɣerðleiks misser En kircna hofðingiar þat ero bisko[-]par *ok* prestar en þeir geɣa goð dømi iorðvm eða ɣerkvm þa taka þeir sva mýklv framar dýrð sem margar ander hialpaz af þeira dømvm sem ritat er en ef þ*eir* spara heilso orð ɣið lýð sinn eða leiða þa i davða grof með illvm dø dømvm þa taka þeir þeimmvn fleiri pinslir

And I want to add that nothing good happens to the wicked nor anything bad to the good.

«2.16» Disciple: In the name of God, what are you saying now? Are not the wicked gladdened by good things? Do they not live for their desire, to delight in delicacies, and to dazzle in precious clothes? Are they not happy with the wealth and beauty of this world? And are the good not already in prison, fatigued by their struggle, plagued by hunger and thirst and all kinds of torments?

Master: When fortune smiles upon the wicked and the good desire such things as you have mentioned,[17] the wicked resemble the fish that is glad for a little bait as it is pulled out of the water. For the wicked are filled with bitterness (Lam. 3:15) for those delicacies; with the stench of brimstone for their lust; and with shamefulness for the beauty of their clothes. They receive the dark graves of hell for the beauty of their houses, and eternal poverty for the wealth they possessed. They may spend their days in pleasure, but in a moment go down into torment (Job 21:13). However, if the good contract such harm as you mention, they resemble those who eat pepper or some other bitter herb so as to savor the wine better. So the tormented receive everlasting habitations (Luke 16:9) instead of prison, joy instead of scourging, and they shall neither thirst nor hunger anymore (Isa. 49:10; Rev. 7:16), and all pain will flee from them (Isa. 35:10). From these facts it becomes obvious that the good are always blessed and wealthy, and that the wicked are always miserable and poor.

«2.17» Disciple: Where do honor and power come from?

Master: From God come all honor and power for the good and the wicked, as is written: There is no power but of God (Rom. 13:1).

«2.18» Disciple: How do you judge those who buy or sell honorable positions?

Master: Those that buy suffer death with Simon Magus (Acts 8:9-24). But those who sell contract spiritual leprosy.

«2.19» Disciple: Do leaders have more power before God than other men?

Master: The teacher's job is an honorable position, but it is of no use before God if there is no merit. If leaders of the churches, that is bishops and priests, provide good examples in words and deeds, then they receive as much glory as the number of souls that are redeemed by their example, as is written.[18] But if they hold back the words of salvation from their people, or lead them to the grave of death by their bad example, then they will suffer as many torments

en aðrer sem margar ander faraz af þeira dømvm eða sva margha sem þeir orøkto at grøða ikenningv sem ritat er Af þeim heimter gvð meira er hann leir meira ok taka amot qva[-]ler En þeir er ɣeralldrir tign hafa sem konongar eða domenðr ok kɣnna mil[-]lega ɣar kɣnna lɣð sinvm þa mvnv þeir meiri miskvn taka en aðrer menn af gvði rettlatom domanda þvi at þeir eignaz goðan sess af gvði er ɣel þiona ha[-]nom En þeir er fɣrir døma at grimleika þa taka þeir meiri kvaler en aðrer þvi at þeir hafa þvi at þeir hafa miskvnn lavsa doma

«2.23» <Discipvlvs> Ef gvð vissi allt fɣrir ok sagði firir spamen hvat verða mvndi ok ma hann eigi tælaz iforsio sinnni ok ef himin ok iorð liðr fɣr en orð gvðs meghe skiptaz þa sɣniz mer sem af navðsɣnvm ɣerðe allt þat er orðet hefir eða ɣerða mvn

<Magister> Tvennar ero navðsɣnir onnor eðlis navdsɣn sem sol er vpp or avstr\i/ eða dagr at koma iɣer nott en onnor ɣeralldar navðsɣn sem manne er at gan[-]ga eða sitia

«2.25» <Discipvlvs> Hvat ɣelldr ef kircivr brenna eða hvs manna

<Magister> Ekki ɣerðr at þarfleɣsv a Jorðv at þvi er sɣnt at engi kirkia iheimi eɣðiz eða bren[-]ne nema firir dømez af gvði En þat ɣerðr af þrimr lvtvm fɣrst er kirkivr eflaz af þeim avðøɣvm er með rangv er fengit en annat er sialfir savrga þeir af sɣnðvm sinvm en hit driðia ef men ælska þær meir enhimneska lvti Avk engi døɣr ne sɣkiz firir monnom eigi hinn minzsti fenaðr nema aðr dømiz af gvði

«2.26» <Discipvlvs> En sott eða davðe er sɣnða hefnnd firir hvi þola qvikcvende þat þav er eigi kvnna misgera

<Magister> Firir þat piniz maðr þa er hann rɣggviz ihvg af sot eða davða þeira

«2.27» <Discipvlvs> Hvat røðir ðv vm skogar dɣr

<Magister> Ef þav ɣerða sivc eða davð þa gørez þat af lopz vreinendvm

«2.33e» <Discipvlvs> Ekci er mer skɣlldra at vita en þetta

<Magister> Gvð hefdi sɣnda ifɣrsta kɣni þa er hann eɣddi sɣndvgv fol[-][[675:31]] ke með vaz of gang þeim er fɣrir leto eðlis log Annat sinni seɣkkti hann ni[-]ðr blot monnom i hafeno ravða Jhinv þriðia kɣni gallt hann sɣnðer þa er hann eɣd[-]di iorostom þeim er fɣrir leto ritoð logh Jhinv fiorða kɣni dømir hann sɣnðer þa er hinn æfsti alldr heims brenir sɣnðvga þa er fɣrir leto gvð spialla boð orð þo ɣerðr þat oft at sɣnir giallda feðra ef þeir lik\i/az þeim i illzkv fiogvr ero kɣn sɣnða þat er hvgreninng orð ok ɣerk ok

as souls were lost by their example or as many as they neglected to save by their teaching. As is written: God requires more from those to whom He gives more (Luke 12:48), and they will receive their torments. Those who possess worldly honor, like kings and judges, and who can nobly pardon their people will receive greater mercy from God, the Righteous Judge (2 Tim. 4:8), than other men, because they will be given a fitting seat by God who serve Him well. And those who cruelly condemn others will suffer more pain because they have «delivered» judgment without mercy (Jas. 2:13).

«2.23» Disciple: If God knew everything beforehand and told through the prophets what was to come, He cannot be deceived in his foresight. And if heaven and earth should vanish before God's word can be changed (Matt. 24:35; Mark 13:31; Luke 21:33), then it seems to me that everything happens of necessity that has or will come to be.

Master: There are two necessities: One is the necessity of nature, such as the sun rising in the east or day following night. The other is the necessity of earth for a man to walk or sit upon.

«2.25» Disciple: Why do churches or the houses of men burn?

Master: Nothing happens on earth needlessly (Job 5:6); therefore it is obvious that no church in the world is destroyed or burns unless it is condemned by God. That happens for three reasons: first, when churches are built with ill-gotten gains; second, when men pollute themselves with their sins; and third, if men love the churches more than divine things. For nobody dies or falls ill among men, not even the smallest creature, unless they have been first judged by God.

«2.26» Disciple: Illness or death is punishment for sins. Why then do animals suffer if they cannot sin?

Master: So that man will be tormented when he worries about their illness and death.

«2.27» Disciple: What do you think about wild animals?

Master: If they grow ill or die, it is because of unclean air.

«2.33e» Disciple: Nothing is more important for me than to know that.

Master: God avenged the sins of the first generation when He sent the flood to destroy sinful men who had abandoned the laws of nature (Gen. 7:1-24). In the second generation, He sank the idolaters in the Red Sea (Exod. 14:26-28). In the third generation, He retaliated by waging a war and destroying those who had abandoned the written law. In the fourth generation, He will judge the sins when the last age of the world burns those who neglected the commandments of the Gospel. It happens often, however, that the sons pay for their fathers if they resemble them in malice. For there are four types of

ɣenia illra lvta Gvd hefner sýnða i hit þriðia eða fiorða kýn þa er pinir stað fasta i illvm verkvm eða orðvm

«2.44» <Discipvlvs> En menn geta born frænðr með frenkonom eða reinliɣis monnom með nvnnvm
<Magister> Yist ekci ef þav fa skript Sva sem ekci spillir hɣeiti þo at þiofr stæli þvi ok sae
«2.51a» <Discipvlvs> Hvert er takn hivskapar
<Magister> Firir likamlegan hiv skap sva ɣerðr crist[-]ni eins likamns með kristi firir hollð tekiv hans ok er hann einn lichamr með cristi[-]nni þviat hann er manlegt eðli sem ritat er Yera mvnv tveir ieinv hollðe sva sem øðle þat er cristr samtengði ser ɣar annars kýns en gvðdomr sva skal ok kona sv er maðr fær at gvðs logom ɣera annare kindar en hann er En með gvðziɣivm er hivskapr bannaðr þvi at þat er andleg samtenging ok er o[-]maklegt at hverfa fra andlego ok til likamlega lvta

«2.51c» <Discipvlvs> Er loɣat at eiga meir en eina kono
<Magister> Sva sem kristr samtengdiz einn almennilegre krist[-]ni sva ero ok gvðs logh at maðr eigi eina kono sva sem hinir fýrstv alldar menn ɣarer gørðv En þat er eigi gvðs boðorð helldr løɣui postola igegn hor[-]dome at cristnir qvangaz annat sinn ef kona hans andaz En svmir kalla hordoms liking er optar qvangaz

«2.52» <Discipvlvs> Fagnar ond min þvi at ek nae at heɣra þat er ek fýsvmk <Y>eitðv mer goðr meistare sem þreli sinvm drýk heilax anda ok sva sem þv sagðer mer fra hofðinngiom cristinnar sva skýrðv nokor at qveðe fra hinvm lægrvm þionvm hennar
<Magister> kenni menn ero settir til goðra døma iheim ef þeir liɣa vel en þeir kallaz sallt iarðar ef þeir kæna ɣel En aðrer þionar ero glvggar a hvsi gvðs firir þa skin ɣit ɣizkv lios er i heimskv mýrkri ero Ef þeir liɣa ok fagna eigi þa ero þeir brennanda glæðr en eigi lýsandi En þeir kenna ɣel ok liɣa illa þa ero þeir sem loganda kertiþat er a aðrvm lý[-]sir en firir fersk sia`l´ft at brennanda ɣaxe eða klvcka sv er fagrt gefr hlioð oðrvm [[675:32]] en hon maz siolf af oftlegom ringinngvm En ef þeir liɣa eigi ɣel eða ken[..] ero þeir sem reýkr sa er dockvir elld ok me´i`ðer sýn avgna Stiavrnvr [....] eigi af þvi fello þær `a´f himni

sin: thoughts, words, deeds, and wicked habits. God avenges the sins in the third or fourth generation (Exod. 20:5) by tormenting the steadfast through wicked deeds and words.

«2.44» Disciple: But what if human beings beget children such as men with female relatives or celibate monks with nuns?[19]

Master: Certainly not if they receive penance. Just as wheat does not spoil even if a thief steals and sows it.

«2.51a» Disciple: What is the sacrament of marriage?

Master: In physical marriage Christians become one body in Christ by eating of His flesh, and He is one body with Christians because of His human nature, as is written: They two shall be one flesh (Eph. 5:31). Just as that nature with which Christ was united was of a different kind than the Godhead, so shall the woman whom a man marries according to God's Law be of another kin than he (Lev. 18:6). Likewise, marriage with a godfather is forbidden because of the existing spiritual unity, for it is not proper to turn from spiritual to carnal matters.

«2.51c» Disciple: Is it permitted to have more than one wife?

Master: Just as Christ is united with one common Christianity, so is it God's Law that a man shall have only one wife exactly as the men of the first generation did. It is, however, not God's command, but rather permission given by the apostles to prevent adultery, that a Christian may marry a second time if his wife dies. But there are some who consider a person who remarries an adulterer.

«2.52» Disciple: My soul rejoices because I hear what I want to hear. Good master, give to me as to one´s slave the drink of the Holy Spirit; and just as you told me about the leaders of Christianity, please explain the details regarding their humbler servants.

Master: Teachers are put into the world as good examples if they live justly, and they are called the salt of the earth (Matt. 5:13) if they teach well. The other servants are windows in the house of God. Through them shines the bright light of wisdom for those who live in the darkness of folly. If they live justly and do not rejoice, they are the embers of the fire, but do not shine. And if they teach well and live wickedly, they are like a burning candle which shines for others but disappears itself as its wax is burned; or they are like a bell which makes a beautiful sound to others, but is worn out by frequent ringing. And if they neither live nor «teach» well, they are like the smoke which darkens the fire and impairs the sight of the eyes. The stars «did» not «shine» (Joel 2:10), therefore they fell down from heaven (Matt. 24:29).

«2.53» <Discipvlvs> Hvat røðer þv vm heims hafnaðr
<Magister> Ef þeir hall[da...] ok siðliga firir ætlan sinni til hins øfsta dags þa ɣerða þeir dømdr með gvði en ef þeir firir dømaz þa ero þeir ollom monnom vesalle þvi at þeir røkto hvarke gvð [..] þenna heim

«2.54» <Discipvlvs> Hvat skilldv vm riddara
<Magister> Fat got þvi atþeir liɣa við ran ok avðg[a]z af hernaðe ok ɣeita þaðan af þat er þeir ɣeita Ym daga þeira er sva melt þ[...][-]noðo ander þeira ionɣtvm lvtvm ok stigr ɣɣer þa reði gvðs

«2.55-56» <Discipvlvs> Hveria ɣon ha[-]va kavp menn
<Magister> Lit goða þvi at þeir fa merr með lɣgðvm ok miseiðvm mikinn lɣta þess er þeir hafa ok miðla lit sinom avðøɣom ɣið þvrɣanda ok fara þeir þvi sem mẹlt er treɣstaz fiold avra til pinsla ok eɣðer þeim davði

«2.57» <Discipvlvs> Hvat røðer þv vm smiði alzkɣns
<Magister> Fle`i´ri firir dømaz en hialpaz þvi at þeir svikia miok ive[-]lvm sinvm
«2.58» <Discipvlvs> Haɣa leikarar nøkora ɣonn
<Magister> Enga þvi at þeir ero þionar fiandans ok taka þeir sem melt er haðvng er haðong ɣeita
«2.60» <Discipvlvs> Hɣeria ɣon hafa fifl
<Magister> Sli[-]ka sem born ok hialpaz þav af þvi at ðav kvnnv eigi betr

«2.61» <Discipvlvs> Hvat dømer þv vm verkmenn
<Magister> Mɣkill lvti þeira mvn hia`l´paz ef þeir liɣa vel ok retlega þvi at þeir neɣta ærɣeðe handa sinna ok gvðs lɣðr með sveita sinvm

«2.62» <Discipvlvs> Hvat skill þv vm born
<Magister> Hialpaz oll er skirð ero ok mego eigi mela þreɣetr eða ɣngri en þav er fim ɣetra ɣer[ða] hialpaz svm enn eigi oll

«2.63» <Discipvlvs> Sva sɣniz mer sem faer mvnv hialpaz
<Magister> Þrong er gata til gvðs sv er til lifs leiðer
«2.68-69» <Discipvlvs> Hve morgom hattom firir geɣaz sɣnðer
<Magister> Sv hin fɣrsta sɣnða lavsn er skirn Onnvr er pinsl Þriðia er at ganga i iðran Fiorða er bẹna halld ok tara fall Fimta er ọlmoso gørð Setta er at firir geɣa oɣinvm Sivnda er ost ok heilagr goðr ɣili

«2.53» Disciple: What do you think about those who forsake the world?

Master: If they keep their vows «well» and live decently until doomsday, they will be judges with God. If they are damned, they are more miserable than all other men because they cared neither for God «nor» for this world.

«2.54» Disciple: What do you know about knights?

Master: Very little that is good, because they live by robbery, become rich by warfare and what they give comes from their ill gains. About their lives it is said: Their souls «were consumed» in vanity, and, the wrath of God comes upon them (Pss. 77/78:31).

«2.55-56» Disciple: What hope is there for merchants?

Master: Not much, because they acquire a great part of what they have chiefly by lies and perjury; and they share little of their wealth with the poor. And therefore those, as is said, who trust in the multitude of their riches (Pss. 48:/49:6) will enter torment, and death will destroy them.

«2.57» Disciple: What do you think about the various craftsmen?

Master: More of them are damned than saved because they deceive a great deal in their crafts.

«2.58» Disciple: Is there any hope for actors?

Master: None, because they are servants of the devil, and, as is said, those who scorn will receive scorn.

«2.60» Disciple: What hope do fools have?

Master: The same as children. They are saved because they do not know any better.

«2.61» Disciple: What do you think of laborers?

Master: Many of them will be saved if they live decently and lawfully, because they eat the labor of their hands (Pss. 127/128:2) and they «nourish» God's people with their sweat.

«2.62» Disciple: What do you think about children?

Master: All who are baptized, cannot yet speak, and are three years old or younger will be saved. Of the five-year-olds, some will be saved, but not all.

«2.63» Disciple: It seems to me therefore that only very few will be saved.

Master: Narrow is the way to God which leads unto life (Matt. 7:14).

«2.68-69» Disciple: In how many ways are sins forgiven?

Master: Baptism is the first way of forgiving sins; the second is suffering; the third is repentance; the fourth is holding prayers and shedding tears; the fifth is giving alms; the sixth is forgiving one's enemies; the seventh is love and a saintly good will.

«2.75» <Discipvlvs> Ef aller gofgoðv einn gvð i vpp haγe hvaðan hofs blot skγ́rgvða
<Magister> Risar gørðo stapvl havan þan er babel γar kall[-]aðr en hann γar hor sextvgv skeiða ok fiogora skeiða en skeið er stvndvm at længð fimtan faðmar en stvnðvm xx istað þeim er nv er hin mikla ba[-]bilon istað þeim γar fγ́rstr konvngr Nemroð þar reð siðan firir Dinvs hann let gøra likneskiv eftir feðr sinvm davðvm ensa het belvs ok bavð hann alþγ́ð[γ́][-]rikis sins at gofga likneskivna Avk toko þar til døma aðrer vti fra Sva sem rvn γerir blotoðv Romolvm En kritar men þor ok [[238.XVIII:1r]] oden sem ritad er. Hræd[-]sla gerdi fýst goda fiolda j heime. En dioflar geingv inn j liknesken. og tældv lýdenn j svǫrvm sinvm.

«2.76» Discipvlvs. hvar var babel.
Magister. J stad þeim sem nv er en mýkla babilon. sv er símeramiss drotning let gera. En sv bórg var sextige milna lavng og breid slikt hit sama. J þeirre borg hofvst blot skvrgoda. og mvn j þeirre borg anda kristvr berast. sem ritad er. Ór babí[-]lon mvn vt fara ormvr sa er svelgia mvn allan heim.

«2.77» Discipvlvs. Stodar nockvd at fara til iórsala. eda sækia helga stadi.
Magister. betra er at gefa avmvm monnvm þat fe er til fararennar þarf at hafa. En þo ero þeir lofande er fyrer gvds saker og ast heilagra manna fara þangat med fe þvi er þeir taka at erfdvm. eda áá verkvm sinvm. og hafi þeir adr til skripta geingid. og feli sig áá hende helgvm monnvm. vm gavtv j borgvm og j munklifvm med bænvm og avlmvsv gæde. þviat he[-]lena drottning og eýdoxa gerdv svo. og ero lofadar. En ef þeir sækia helga stade til for[-]vítne eda áágætis. þa hafa þeir þat fyrer verd kavp er þeir sia fagra stade. og eignvdvst lof þat er þeir elskvdv. En þeir er fara med fe þvi er þeir eignvdvst med ravngvm avexte. eda med ve[-]lvm. eda tokv þeir þat at ravngv. eda áá savkvm. þeir ero svo ræker fyrer gvdi og helgvm monnvm hans. sem sa er son hefer vegit fýrer manni. og kemvr til hans med blodgar hendr.

«2.78» Discipvlvs. þvi veitti gvd eigi þat manni at hann þýrfti eigi optar mat. en vm sinn æa vikv.
Magister. hvngr er einn hlvtr af sýndahefndvm. Madr var svo fýst sk[a][-]padr. at hann matte lifa sæll. áán erfide ef hann villde. Enn er hann fell j sýnd. þa m[a]t[-]te hann eigi áán erfidi vpp risa. En hann mvndi eigi vilia vinna ef hann þýrfti eigi matar ne klæ[-]da. og være hann þa áá vallt fra gvdi. En gvd le[t] til þess mann kala og

«2.75» Disciple: If everybody worshipped one God in the beginning, how did idolatry arise?

Master: The giants built a high tower called Babel (Gen. 11:9), and it was 60 and 4 courses high. One course is sometimes 15 and sometimes 20 fathoms long. In this place Babylon the Great stands now. The first king was Nimrod (Gen. 10:8-10). Then Dinus ruled there. He had a statue made of his dead father, who was called Belus,[20] and he ordered all the people of his kingdom to worship this statue. Others from abroad copied this example, such as the Romans who worshipped Romulus, and the Cretans who worshipped Thor and Odin, as is written: Fear initially created the numerous gods in this world.[21] But the devils entered the statue and deceived the people with their answers.

«2.76» Disciple: Where was Babel?

Master: In the same place where Babylon the Great is now, and which Queen Semiramis[22] had built. This city was 60 miles long and equally wide. In that city the sacrifice to idols began, and the Antichrist will be born in that city, as is written: From Babylon will come the dragon which will swallow the whole world.

«2.77» Disciple: Does it help to go to Jerusalem or to visit holy places?

Master: It is better to give the money necessary for such a journey to the poor. But they are nevertheless praiseworthy who travel there for the sake of God and for the love of the saints, using money which they inherited or received for their work, having gone to confession before, and commending themselves into the hands of the saints through prayer and charity in towns and monasteries along the way. The queens Helena and Eudokia did this and are praised for it.[23] And if they visit holy places out of curiosity or for fame, their reward will be that they saw handsome places and gained praise as they had hoped to. But those who travel using money which they have earned by usury or deceit, or which they extorted legally or illegally, those people are as abominable before God and His saints as a man who has killed the son of another and comes to him with bloody hands.

«2.78» Disciple: Why did God not grant to man that he should need food only once a week?

Master: Hunger is one type of punishment for sin. Man was first created in such a way that he could live happily without work if he wished. But when he fell into sin, he could no longer live without work. However, he would not have wanted to work if he had not needed food or clothing and if he had not been separated from God

hvngra. at [sv] navdsẏn skẏlld[-]adi hann til erfidis. og mætte hann fyrer þat erfide hverfa aptvr til lifs. Svo er skilianda vm go[-]da menn. en il[l]vm er slikt allt til pisla.

«2.79» Discipvlvs. Er manne ende mark sett til lifs. eda ma hann leingr lifa eda skemvr.

Magister. hverivm manni er sett endi mark af gvdi. hversv leinge hann skal lifa her j heime og ma hann eigi eitt avga bragd lifa ẏfer þat fram. svo sem ritad er. Setter þv endi mork þav [er eigi] ma vm lida. En med morgvm hattvm ma fẏr deẏia. þat er ef madr hleẏpvr áá vatn [eda æ ell]d. eda áá vopn. eda at olmvm dẏrvm. eda heingist. eda deẏr af eitri. Svo sem leígv madr sa svo ma osidlega lifa at hann misse verd kavps. og se reken af vist fyrer fardaga.

«2.80» Discipvlvs. Sanna þv þat.

Magister. Gvd leiddi sonv israel af egipta lande at hann gæfi þeim fyrer heits iord. En þeir nadv henni eigi fyrer sẏndvm sinvm. og dov marger j eẏdi mork. adr þeir kæme til fẏrer heits iardar.

«2.81» Discipvlvs. Misgerer domande ef hann fyrer dæmer seka.

Magister. helldr misgerer hann ef hann fyrer dæmer þa eigi. þviat hann er settvr hefnande sẏnda af gvdi.

«2.82» Discipvlvs. Misgera þíonar ef þeir drepa illmenne þa er domendr fyrer dæma.

Magister. Eigi misgera þeir. helldr þvo þeir hendr sinar j blodi sẏndvgra.

«2.83» Discipvlvs. hafa þeir nockra von hialpar er fvndner verda j glæpvm. og dæmder til davda. en þeir idrast sẏnda æ sialfri davda stvndv.

Magister mẏkla von hafa þeir. þviat svmer hreinsast fyrer davda kvol. sem þi[-]ofvr æ krossi. En svmer leẏsast ór pislvm fyrer bæner heilagra.

«2.85» Discipvlvs. hvat vard ór vítnis avrk gvds.

Magister. þa er nalgadist avdn hiervsalem af babilons monnvm. þa fal heremias. hana j grof moẏsi at bod órde gvds. En hon mvn finnast áá hinne epstv tid af enoc og helia.

«2.85a» Discipvlvs. þvi megv hel[-][[238.XVIII:1v]]ger eigi takn gera nv sem fordvm.

Magister. Eíngi heilagra gerdi sialfvr takn. helldr gvd fyrer þa. sa er hvg þeirra ser. sem ritad er. þv ert j gvdi er takn gerer. Fordvm gerdi

forever. God made man endure cold and hunger so that necessity would force him to work and that through his work he might return to life. That is the arrangement for good men, but for the wicked everything turns into torment.

«2.79» Disciple: Has a definite end been set for man's life or can he live for a longer or shorter period?

Master: For every man there is definite end set by God how long he shall live here in this world. He may not live a single moment longer, as is written: You have appointed his bounds that he cannot pass (Job 14:5). But he can die earlier in many ways; for example, if a man jumps into water «or fire» or runs into weapons or wild animals, or if he hangs himself or dies of poison. Just as the hired man can live so irresponsibly that he loses his pay and is dismissed from his lodgings before the annual moving days.[24]

«2.80» Disciple: Prove this to me.

Master: God led the sons of Israel out of Egypt so that he might show them the promised land. But they did not reach it because of their sins (Deut. 1:35). Many of them died in the desert before they came to the promised land.

«2.81» Disciple: Does a judge commit a sin if he condemns culprits?

Master: On the contrary, he sins if he does not condemn them, because he is charged by God to avenge sins.

«2.82» Disciple: Do servants sin if they kill villains who were condemned by the judges?

Master: No, they do not. Rather, they wash their hands in the blood of sinners.

«2.83» Disciple: Do criminals have any hope of redemption if their crime is discovered and they are sentenced to death, but they repent their sins in the hour of their death?

Master: They have great hope because some of them are cleansed through the agony of death, like the thief on the cross (Luke 23:43). Others again are released from their torment because of the saints' prayers.

«2.85» Disciple: What happened to God's Ark of the Covenant?

Master: Jeremiah concealed it in the grave of Moses (2 Macc. 2:4-5), according to God's command, when the destruction of Jerusalem at the hands of the men of Babylon approached. It will be found again at the end of the world by Enoch and Elijah.

«2.85a» Disciple: Why can the saints not perform miracles now as before?

Master: None of the saints performed miracles by themselves, but God acted through them, He who sees their mind, as is written: You are in God who does wonders (Pss. 76:15/77:14). In earlier times, He

hann sÿnilig takn fyrer helga menn. at læ[-]gia otrv þa er græddi
sivka likame. En nv gerer hann meiri takn andlig fyrer þa er hann
græ[-]der sivkar ander af sÿndvm. þa gerer hann en stvndvm fyrer
sina menn en ÿtri takn ef navdsÿn verdvr. En af þvi takast avll takn
fra ecclesia æ hin[ne] epstv tid. at rettlater dÿrkast at meir er þeir
standast meire freistní.

«2.86» Discipvlvs. Sk[i]l[d]v spamenn allt þat er þeir ritvdv.
Magister. allt skil[-]dv þeir.
«2.87» Discipvlvs. þvi mæltv þeir svo mÿrkt.
Magister. Annat er at marka tott. en annad at smida og an[n]ad at skrifa.
    Alldar fedr morkvdv tott kristne. en spamenn settv grvndvoll. en
    postvlar s[m]idvdv veggi hennar med kenningvm. og spor gavngv
    menn þeirra skrifvdv med skÿringvm. En heilog r[i]tning er sonvm
    gv[d]s einvm riten. En heilog kristni moder lÿkvr þeim vpp oll bÿrgi
    med lÿkli david. þat er christvs. En þeir er eigi ero sÿner. sia hina ÿtri
    hlvti eína. og skilia eigi þviat þeir elska eigi ne trva.

«2.88» Discipvlvs. hafa menn vard halld eingla.
Magister. hverri borg og hverri þiodv rada einglar. og kenna þeim rett lavg.
    og retta sidv. hverri avnd fÿlger eingill sa er hana eggiar æ vallt til
    gods. og þæger oll verk hen[-]nar gvdi og einglvm æ himne.

«2.89» Discipvlvs. Ef gvd veit allt og einglar sia alla hlvti j honvm. hvat ma
    þeim segía þat er þeir viti e[igi].
Magister. Eingli er ecki annat at segia eda þægia verk vòr gvdi en at fagna
    batnade vorvm. sem ritad er. favgnvdr er einglvm. gvds ÿfer einvm
    sÿn[d]vg[v]m [er i]drvn gerir. Svo sem þeim er þat at hrÿggvast
    \er þeir reidast/ illvm verkvm vorvm.

«2.90» Discipvlvs. ero þeir æ vallt æ iordv m[ed] þeim er þeir vardveita.
Magister. koma þeir til fvlltings þa er þorf verdr. og þa hellst er þeir ero
    b[...]er. en eingi er [dvol] æ kvomv þeirra. þviat þeir [f]ara æ ein[v]
    avga bragde til iardar af himne [og] en af iordv til hi[min]s. En er
    þeir koma til vor þa missa þeir eigi hinnar minstv dÿrdar. þviat þeir
    sia áá vallt andlit gvds hvert sem þeir ero sender.
«2.91» Discipvlvs. hversv vitrast þeir monnvm.
Magister. j mans a[s]ionv. þviat likamligvr madr ma eigi sia andliga skepnv.
    Af þvi taka þeir likam or lopti. þan er [si]a ma og heÿra. en eigi

performed visible miracles through the saints to vitiate against unbelief when He healed sick bodies. But now He performs even greater spiritual miracles through those whose sick souls He heals of sin. Occasionally He also performs visible miracles through His men if it becomes necessary. Therefore all miracles are taken away from the church until the end of time, so that the more temptations the righteous endure, the more they will be glorified.

«2.86» Disciple: Did the prophets understand everything they wrote?

Master: They understood everything.

«2.87» Disciple: Why did they speak so obscurely?

Master: It is one thing to mark out a plot, another to build, and yet a third to paint. The patriarchs marked out the plot of Christianity; the prophets laid the foundation; and the apostles built the walls with their teaching. Those who followed their footsteps painted them with explanations. The Holy Scriptures are only written for the sons of God. But holy Christianity, the Mother, unlocks for them all enclosures with the key of David (Rev. 3:7) which is Christ. Those who are not sons see only the external things and do not understand because they neither love nor believe.

«2.88» Disciple: Do men have custody over angels?

Master: Angels rule over every city and nation and teach the right laws and customs. Every soul is followed by an angel who always urges it on to be good and makes all its deeds acceptable to God and to the angels in heaven.

«2.89» Disciple: If God knows everything and the angels see all things through Him, what can one say to them that they do not know?

Master: To an angel it makes no difference to talk about or make our deeds acceptable to God or to rejoice in our improvement, as is written: There is joy in the presence of the angels of God over one sinner that repents (Luke 15:10). Likewise, it is distressing to them when they become saddened about our wicked deeds.

«2.90» Disciple: Are they always on earth with those whom they guard?

Master: They come to their assistance if necessary and particularly when they are «asked». They arrive without delay because they move from heaven to earth in an instant and return again from earth to heaven. And if they come to us, they do not miss the slightest glory because they always see the countenance of God wherever they are sent.

«2.91» Disciple: How do they show themselves to men?

Master: In the shape of man, because a human being cannot see a spiritual creature. Therefore they take a body out of the air which one can see and hear but cannot touch. And this body is not visible

76   The Old Norse 'Elucidarius'

þreifa vm. En sa likamvr er eigi ollvm syneligr [he]lldr þeim [e]invm [er] þeir vilia syn[a]st.

«2.92» Discipvlvs. erv dioflar aa vallt áá velvm vm menn.

Magister. [fyrer] hv[er]ri synd [r]ada dio[-]flar. og teygía áá vallt ander manna at misgera. og segia ill verk þeirra hof[dingia sin]vm med myklvm hlatri. En ef nockvr þeirra verdr yfer stigin af godvm manni. þa kastar vard hallds ei[n]gill þess mans honvm j vnder dívp. og ma alldri sa sidan beriast j gegn helgvm monnvm. þviat svo sem madr yfer stigin af diofli. var þegar reken or paradis. svo verdr og diofvll þegar sendr j helviti sa er yfer stigst af helgvm manni. En þo sender hofdingi diofla. annan j stad þess er yfer var stigin[.] þat er og at dioflar taka opt þa likami or env þyckra lopte. er þreifa ma vm.

«2.93» Discipvlvs. Megv þeir tæla þa er þeir vilia.

Magister. Ef þeir mattv eigi gripa svina flock nema þeim væri lofad. þa megv þeir myklv sidr menn svikia. Stvndvm kvelia þeir likam rettlats mans honvm til dyrdar. en ser til pisla. En aa vallt kvelia þeir ander illra. og stvndvm likame þeirra. Likamvr mans helgast j skirn gvds og helgvm anda sem mvstere med krisma og vid smiore. sem ritad er. þer sialfer erod heilagt mvstere gvds. Enn j þessv mvstere bygger annat tveggia áá vallt spiritvs sanctvs. eda o hreinn ande.

«2.94» Discipvlvs. hvat stodar smvrning sivkvm.

Magister. fyrer þessa smvrning ....

to all, but only to those to whom the angels want to show themselves.

«2.92» Disciple: Are the devils always deceiving men?

Master: The devils are behind every sin and always tempt the souls of men to do wrong. And they tell their evil deeds to their chief with much laughter. And if one of them is overcome by a good man, then the guardian angel of this man throws him into the abyss so he can never again fight against the saints. For just as a man overcome by the devil was driven forthwith out of paradise, so the devil who is overcome by a saint will be sent to hell right away. But the chief of the devils sends another in place of the one who was overcome. It is also «said» that devils often take their bodies out of thicker air so that one can touch them.[25]

«2.93» Disciple: Can they betray whomever they want to?

Master: If they were unable to seize a flock of pigs unless they were allowed to do so (Matt. 8:30-32), they are even less able to deceive men. Occasionally they plague the body of a righteous man (Job 2:7) for his glory and their own torment. And they always plague the souls of the wicked and occasionally their bodies, too. The body of man is sanctified in baptism by God and the Holy Spirit, like a temple with chrism and oil, as is written: You are yourself the holy temple of God (1 Cor. 3:17). And either the Holy Spirit or an unclean spirit lives in this temple.

«2.94» Disciple: How does anointing the sick help?

Master: Through such anointing .....

«3.7» .... [[238.XVIII:2r]] kvm godgirndar áár. Tolf manvder þessa ars ero tolf postvlar. Solar ˋfar´ skiptist vm sinn áá ari. en tvngl æa manadi. Sol merker krist. en tvngl kristne. Jafnleingd er hallden at fyrer gefest þat er madr gerde j gegn rettlætis solo christo. og j gegn kenningv .xíí. postvla er manvder [e]ro ens sanna ars.

«3.8» Discipvlvs. hvat er hreinsanar elldr.
Magister. Svmum meingerder þær er þeir taka af illvm monnvm j heime. En svmvm mei[n]læte þav er þeir mæda likam sinn j fostvm og j vokvm eda j odrv erfide. Svmvm er hreinsvnar elldr manna misser. en svmvm fiar skade. svmvm sotter. en svmvm voladi. og svmvm sarligvr davdi. En epter davda er hreinsvnar pisl bitvr elldr eda micit frost. eda avnnvr pisl nockvr. En hin minsta pisl af þeim er meiri en her j heime hin mesta. J þeim pislvm vitrast monnvm stvndvm einglar eda þeir helger er þeir hofdv j nockrvminning gert j heime. og veita þeim nockra hvggan eda hvilld. vnz þeir leýsast af pis[l]vm og ganga inn j himna holl.

«3.9» Discipvlvs. med hverre áá siono ero ander j pislvm.
Magister. j asionv likams þess er þær hofdv her. svo og fra dioflvm sagt at þeir kvelist j likamligri æa sionv.

«3.10» Discipvlvs. Ef likamvr kenner sín eigi og ma ecki sialfvr gera. nema þat er avnd gerer fyrer hann. hversv er rett at hann fyrerdæmest.
Magister. þa er menn taka o vine sina. þa brenna þeir fýst eda briota hvs þeirra. en leida sidan sialfa til bana. at hvgvr o uina harme bæde af skada og af pislvm likams síns. Likamvr er h[.....]dar eda klædi þat er hvn elskade meir en skapara sinn. og brennvr þat af þvi [.........]t hon harmi brvna hvs sins þess er hvn elskadi Rettliga fyrer dæmist likamvr med [.........]v ero svo samteingd. at likamvr sýnist allt gera þat er ond gerer.

«3.11» Discipvlvs. hve margar ander koma til himirrikis.
Magister Svo margar sem þar ero einglar fyrer. og skvlv ander hverfa j allar [ein]gla sveiter. sem gvd veit verd leik þeirra.

«3.12» Discipvlvs. hvat seger þv fra andlati illra.
Magister. þa er nalgast andlat illra. þa koma dioflar med mýklvm þýs.

« Book 3 »

«3.7» Master: .... the year of good will. The twelve months of the year are the twelve apostles. The course of the sun changes once a year, but that of the moon each month. The sun signifies Christ and the moon Christianity. An anniversary is held so that the sin man committed against the Sun of Righteousness (Mal. 4:2), that is Christ, may be forgiven, along with the sin against the teaching of the twelve apostles who are the months of the true year.

«3.8» Disciple: What is purgatory?

Master: To some the wrongs which they endure from evil men in the world, but to some the castigations with which they plague their body by fasting, vigils, and other hardships. To some purgatory is the loss of men and to some the loss of property, to some disease or misery, and to some painful death. And after death the torment of purgatory is hot fire or severe frost or some other torture. And the smallest of these torments is more than the greatest here in this world. In these torments angels occasionally show themselves to those men or saints in whose memory they performed something on earth, and they give them some comfort or respite until they are released from their torment and they can enter the hall of heaven.

«3.9» Disciple: How do souls in torment look?

Master: They have the same physical appearance they had here, as is also said about the devils that they are tormented in their earthly shape.

«3.10» Disciple: If the body does not know itself and can do nothing on its own except what the soul does through it, how can it be right that it is damned?

Master: When men defeat their enemies, they first burn or demolish their houses and then put them to death, so that the mind of their enemies is grieved both by this loss and by the torment of their bodies. The body «is the house of the soul» or its clothes which it loved more than its Creator and therefore it burns «with the soul, so that» it grieves for its burned house which it loved. Justly is the body condemned with «the soul because they» are so united that the body seems to do everything the soul does.

«3.11» Disciple: How many souls enter the kingdom of heaven?

Master: As many as there have been angels before; and as God recognizes their merit, the souls shall enter all the hosts of angels.

«3.12» Disciple: What do you say about the death of the wicked?

Master: When the death of the wicked approaches, devils come with much

hrædiliger at áá[-]lite. og draga þeir ander fra likam med mẏklvm sarleik til helvitis kvala.

«3.13-14» Discipvlvs. hvat er hel[-]víte. eda hvar er þat.

Magister. Tvenn erv helviti annad et nedra. en annat et efra. Et efra heluíti er hin nedste hlvtr þessa heims. En sa stadr er fvllvr mẏr[-][k]ra og meína. ellz og frostz. hvngvrs og þorsta og annarra likams kvala. bardaga og ecka og hræslv. sem ritad er. Leid þv ond mina or dẏflizv. þat er at skilia fra helvite. Hit nedra helviti er anndlig kvol. þat er o slavckviligvr elldr sem ritad er. þv leẏster avnd mina fra helvite hinv nedra. Sa stadr er vnder iordv. at svo se ander sẏndvgar grafnar j pisler sem likamer j iord. j þeim stad ero .ix. hofvd pisler. En fẏsta er svo akafligvr elldr. at eigi mvnde slokna þott j felli avll votn og sior. Sa elldr brenner og lẏser eigi. og þeim mvn heitare en vor elldr. sem sia se likneske skrifad epter hinvm. Avnnvr er frost svo mikid. at elldligt fiall mvndi verda at svelli ef þangat felle. Vm þess[ar] písler er ritad. þar er gratvr og gnotrvn tanna. þviat reẏkvr af elldi giorer grat a[v.][-]na. En frost tannna gnotrvn. Þridía kvol erv hrædiliger ormar og drekar [o...][-]leger j sẏn og j roddv. þeir er svo lifa j ellde sem fiskar j vatne. Fiorda kvol er leidiligvr davn. Fimta grimlegr bardage. Setta mẏrkvr þat er þreifa ma vm. sem [[238.XVIII:2v]] ritad er. Mẏrkra iord og meina. þar er bẏgger margr híte og eilif hræsla. Siovnda er sẏnda skemd. þviat þar ma ecke liott verk leẏnast. Atta er hræsla ogvrligrar sẏnar diofla og dreka. þeirra er blasa elldi og brennv steine. og vesalig heẏrn grasz og diofla hlatvrs. Nivn[-]da kvol er elldlig bond er þravngva ollvm lidvm.

«3.15-16» Discipvlvs. þvi hafa þeir svo margar kvaler.

Magister þvi þeir ero verder niv kvala. at þeir oræktv samlag nív eingla sveita. þvi brenna þeir þar j pislar elldi. at þeir brvnnv her j girndar elldi. Svo sem þeir stirnvdv her j illskv frosti. svo og er ritad at þeir gnotri tonnvm þar j pislar frosti. Svo sem þeir gloa vtan af elldi. sem iarn j afle. svo gloa þeir og innan af frosti sem svell æ vetrvm. Þeir sem heratvst innan af avfvnd og hatri. þa er makligt at þeir etist af ormvm. og svo sem þeir vndv her vid sẏnda davn. svo er makligt at

noise, terrible to look at, and they drag the souls with great pains from the body into the torments of hell.

«3.13-14» Disciple: What is hell and where is it?

Master: There are two hells: One is the lower, the other is the upper. Upper hell is the lowest part in this world. That place is full of darkness and diseases, fire and frost, hunger and thirst, and other pains of the body, such as fighting, grief and fear, as is written: Bring my soul out of prison (Pss. 141:8/142:7), which is to be understood out of hell. Lower hell is spiritual torture, that is inextinguishable fire, as is written: You delivered my soul from the lower hell (Pss. 85/86:13). This place is below the earth so that sinful souls are buried in torment as bodies are buried in the earth. In this place there are nine main torments. The first is such extreme fire that it could not be extinguished even if all lakes and the ocean would cover it. That fire burns but does not shine, and it will be to the same extent hotter than regular fire as fire is hotter than a picture painted of it. The second is frost, so great that a mountain of fire would turn into ice if it covered it. About this torment is written: There is weeping and gnashing of teeth (Matt. 8:12; 24:51), because the smoke of the fire makes the «eyes» weep and the frost makes the teeth gnash. The third torment is terrible snakes and dragons, «horrible» in appearance and in voice, which live in fire just as fish live in water. The fourth torment is repulsive stench. The fifth is fierce battle. The sixth is darkness that can be touched, as is written: The earth of darkness and disease where much heat lives and eternal fear (Job 10:22). The seventh is the disgrace of sin, because no ugly deed can be hidden there. The eighth is fear of the dreadful sight of devils and dragons which spew fire and brimstone, and the miserable noise of weeping and the laughter of devils. The ninth torment is fiery fetters which bind all members.

«3.15-16» Disciple: Why do they have so many torments?

Master: They deserve nine torments because they neglected their fellowship with the nine hosts of angels. Therefore they burn there in the fire of torment, because here they burned in the fire of lust. Just as they grew stiff here in the frost of malice, so it is also written that they should gnash their teeth there in the frost of torment (Matt. 8:12; 24:51). Just as they glow outwardly like fire as iron does in a forge, so they glow also inwardly with frost like ice in winter. Those who here on earth were inwardly eaten up by envy and hatred, will there be fittingly devoured by dragons. Just as here they enjoyed the stench of their sins, so there will they be tormented

þeir pinist þar j grimmvm hnyk. þeir er her villdv eigi radningar bardaga med monnvm. þa er makligt at þeir taki þar eilifan bardaga med dioflvm. þeir er her elskvdv villv mýrkvr. og vil[-]ldv eigi koma til ens sanna lios. þa er makligt at þeir kvelist j eilifvm pislar mýr[-]krvm. þeir er her skommvdvst at segia til sýnda þeirra er þeir skommvdvst eigi at gera. þa er makligt at þeir skammist þar j allra avgliti. þeir er her villdv eigi sia ne heýra gott. þa er makligt at þeir kvelist þar af hrædiligri sýn og heýr[n.] þeir er her bvndv sig j synda bondvm. þa er makligt at þeir þravngvist þar [............][-]dvm. þeir æskia ser at deýia. en davden flýr þa. þviat þeim var bod[............][-]dv þeir eigi. Bavkvm horfast þeir til. og fotvm vpp en hofdvm nidr. og ero bvndn[....][-]lar pisler. þviat þeir snero her bake vid gvde. og hofv sic vpp j of metnade.

«3.17» Discipvlvs. Ve[-]sæll er sa madr er til slikra pisla er borenn.
Magister. hvat grætvr þv. eda hvat harmar þv. diofvll einn hefer þessar kvaler og hans lider.
«3.18» Discipvlvs hverer ero lider hans.
Magister. Ofmetnadar menn. og avfvndsam[er]. flærdar fvller menn. og otrver. of drýckiv menn og galavser eda grimmer. mandraps ˋmenn´ eda þiofar. vikingar og illvirkiar. ohreiner og agiarner. hor doms menn. blotendr. og meinsærendvr bavlvendr og lýgner menn. gvdlastendr fiolkvnniger og bakmalvger syndr þýcker. og helvisker rogberarar. þeir er j slikvm illvm hlvtvm deýia fara til þessa pisla. og koma alldri þadan.
«3.19» Discipvlvs. Sia rettlater menn þa.
Magister. Rett[-]later sia illa j pislvm at þeir fagni þvi er þeir fordvdvst slikar kvalar. Jller sia og goda j dýrd fyrer domsdag. at þeir harmi sig o rækt hafa þessa dýrd. En ep[-]ter dom sia æ vallt goder illa j pislvm. En iller sia alldri goda.

«3.20» Discipvlvs. harma eigi rettlater er þeir sia þa kveliast.
Magister. þott fader siai son. eda sonvr fodr. moder dottvr eda dotter modr. eda siae madr konv sina. eda konan bonda sinn j pislvm. [..] harma þeir eigi helldr en ver þa ver siavm fiska leika j hýl. sem ritad er. glediast mvn rettlatvr þa er hann ser sýnd hefnda.

appropriately with abominable odors. Those who avoided the chastisement of beating among men here, there fittingly endure eternal thrashing by the devils. Those who on earth loved the darkness of heresy and did not desire to come to the true light, are appropriately tormented in the eternal darkness of agony. Those who here were embarrassed to confess the sins they were not ashamed of committing, are appropriately shamed before everyone's eyes there. Those who on earth neither wanted to see nor to hear good, are appropriately tormented by fearful sights and sounds there. Those who here bound themselves in the fetters of sin, are fittingly «fettered» there. They desire to die, but death flees from them (Rev. 9:6), because they were ordered «but did» not «obey». They turn their backs on each other, and their feet up and their heads down and are bound «in all» torment, because they turned their backs on God here and raised themselves up in arrogance.

«3.17» Disciple: Miserable is the man who is born into such torment!

Master: Why do you weep or why do you lament? Only the devil and his members suffer these torments.

«3.18» Disciple: Who are his members?

Master: Arrogant and envious men; deceitful and faithless men; drunkards; careless and cruel men; murderers and thieves; vikings and criminals; unclean and greedy men; adulterers, idolaters, and perjurers; swearers and liars; blasphemers, sorcerers, back-talkers, sin-lovers, and hellish slanderers. Those who die in such a wicked state descend into these torments and shall never escape them.

«3.19» Disciple: Do the righteous see them?

Master: The righteous see the wicked in their torment and they rejoice because they themselves escaped such pain. The wicked also see the good in their glory before doomsday, so that they may deplore having missed such glory. But after the Last Judgment the good will see the wicked forever in their torment, but the wicked will never see the good.

«3.20» Disciple: Do the righteous not grieve when they see the wicked so tormented?

Master: Even if a father sees his son or a son his father in torment; a mother her daughter, or a daughter her mother; a man his wife, or a wife her husband, they are no more grieved than when we see fish playing in a pool. As is written: The righteous shall rejoice when he sees sin avenged (Pss. 57:11/58:10).

«3.21» D*iscipvlvs*. bidia þ*e*ir *eigi* fy*rer* þ*eim*.
M*agister*. j gegn g*v*di g*er*de þ*e*ir. ef þ*e*ir bæde fy*rer* rekni*n*gv*m* h*ans*. En þ*e*ir
  er*o* svo .... [[544:11r]] her segír fra draumum.
«3.32» <D*iscipulus*> Huaðan koma draumar.
M*agister*. Stundum af guði þa er o orðn*ir* lutír vitrast. Sua sem ioseph var
  vítrat fy*rir* stiornur oc korn bundín. at ha*n*n míndi verða hofðíngí
  brœðra sínna. Eða þa er nauðsýnleg*ir* lut*ir* ero kendir. sua sem
  engill míntí ioseph at flýa a egifta land oc þaðan. Stundum v*er*ða
  draumar af diofle þa er nokot vsiðlict drœýmír eða þat er fy*rir* goðo
  v*er*[-]ki stande. sem sagt er fra kono pilati j pínsl drottens vars.
  Stundum af siolfum ma*n*ne. þa er ha*n*n drœýmir þat er ha*n*n ser eða
  hœýrír. hýg[-]gr eða reðezt eða vett*ir*. her segir fra antí*ch*ri*s*to.

«3.33» <D*iscipulus*> Lofat se muns þíns oc orð guðs þat er mer sýndi
  lœýnda luti fy*rir* munn þi*n*n. en nu villda ec at þu segð*í*r mer fra antí
  *ch*risto ef ec þor[-]ða at bíðia.
M*agister*. Anti *ch*ristus man berast i babilon hínní miclu or kýni dan fra
  port kono. oc fýllist ha*n*n þegar af diofle i moðor quiði.
  Fiolkunnigír me*n*n mono ha*n*n fœða i corozaím. oc ýfir ollum
  hei[-]mi man ha*n*n riki hafa. oc leggia vndir sic alt ma*n*n kýn a fiora
  vega. fýst gofga me*n*n m*e*ð auðefum. þeim er ha*n*n gefr þeím gnott
  þ*ui* at ha*n*n veit oll folgen fe. An*n*an veg skelf*ir* ha*n*n ogofga me*n*n
  m*e*ð mikilli rezlu oc ogurlegom pínslum. þui at ha*n*n er hi*n*n
  grímnas[-]te m*e*ð guðs víní. þriðia veg suicr ha*n*n kenní me*n*n m*e*ð
  speki oc melsku. þui at ha*n*n allar iþrotter. oc veit allar ritningar.
  fiorða [[544:11v]] veg telír ha*n*n munca. ha*n*n gerir miclar iartegn*ir*
  oc morg vndr. ha*n*n letr fal[-]la ælld af hífní ýf*ir* ouiní sina. oc letr
  ha*n*n vpp risa dauða me*n*n. oc bera ser vítní.

«3.34» d*iscipulus*. Reisír ha*n*n vpp dauða at sonno.
M*agister*. m*e*ð ollu eígí. þui at diofull gengr i*n*n i licam híns dauða oc
  melír fy*rir* ha*n*n oc sýnist h*an*n þa sem ha*n*n lífí er ha*n*n rœrist. oll
  tacn hans ero lýgín. ha*n*n man endr nýa hína fornu iorsala borg. þat
  er iherusalem. oc lata sic þar gofga sem guð. Við honu*m* monu
  gýðíngar taka fegensamlega. oc koma til hans or ollum heímí. En
  þeír monu snuast til tru af kenníngum enocs oc elias. oc ta-ka mioc
  sua aller harðar píníngar fy*rir* guðs nafne.

«3.21» Disciple: Do they not pray for them?

Master: They would act against God if they prayed for His outcasts. But they are so .... Here dreams are discussed.

«3.32» Disciple: Where do dreams come from?

Master: Sometimes from God when future things are revealed, as was disclosed to Joseph through the stars and the sheaves that he would become the leader of his brothers (Gen. 37:7, 9). Or whenever necessary, things are disclosed, as when the angel reminded Joseph to flee thence to Egypt (Matt. 2:13). Occasionally dreams come from the devil, when something immoral is dreamt or something impedes a good deed, as is said of the wife of Pilate at the martyrdom of Our Lord (Matt. 27:19). Occasionally dreams come from man himself, as when he dreams about what he sees or hears, thinks, fears or hopes. Here the Antichrist is discussed.

«3.33» Disciple: Praised be your mouth and the Word of God which disclosed hidden things to me through your mouth. And now if I dare to make such a request, I would like you to tell me about the Antichrist.

Master: The Antichrist will be born in Babylon the Great by a harlot of the lineage of Dan.[26] And immediately he will be possessed by the devil in the womb of his mother. Sorcerers will bring him up in Chorazin (Matt. 11:21; Luke 10:13) and he will reign over the whole world and subdue all mankind in four ways: first, he will reward the noble with enough wealth because he knows where all money is hidden. Second, he will make the low tremble with great fear and terrible torments, because he is most cruel towards God's friends. Third, he will deceive the learned men with knowledge and eloquence, because he «possesses» all skills and knows all writings. Fourth, he will tell the monks that he can perform great miracles and work many wonders. He will have fire fall from heaven over his enemies and he will let the dead men rise and bear witness to him.

«3.34» Disciple: Will he truly raise the dead?

Master: Of course not, because the devil will go into the body of the dead and speak through it and it will seem as if he lives when he moves. For all his wonders are lies (2 Thes. 2:9). He will renew the old city of "Jorsala," that is Jerusalem, and let himself be venerated there like God. The Jews will receive him joyfully and come to him from all over the world; and they will turn to the faith by the teachings of Enoch and Elijah and almost all of them will endure great sufferings in the name of God.

«3.35» discipulus. Með hueríum alldre koma þeír enoc oc helias.
Magister. með þeím alldre sem þeir voro vpp numnír en þeir monu drepnír verða af anti christo. en hann man hafa veldi .vij. miserí. oc man hann siðan setia tiald buð sína i fiallenu olíueti oc ber[-]iast i gegn rett latum. En þar mann hann fínnast drepinn braðum dauða með anda muns guðs. þat er at boðorðe hans sem ritat er. drottenn man stœýpa hofðingia allrar iarðar j helgu fialle olíuetí.

«3.36» discipulus. Ero þa dag-ar skemri en nu. þuí at sua er sagt i bokum at dagar monu skemmast fyrir helga menn.
Magister. Iam langer ero þa dagar sem nu. Sua sem dauid melti. A þínní skipan halldast dagar. En dagar segiast af þuí skemmast at anti christus hefir litla stund velldi. þat er .iij. vetr. En þa monu menn mín-ní vera vextí en nu sua sem ver erum mínní en hínír fyrru menn.

«3.37» Discipulus. huat verðr þa siðan.
Magister. xl. daga ero veíttír til iðranar. þeim er viltír vr-ðu fyrir ogn anta crist. eða flerð. en siðan veit engi ahuerium degi eða stundu doma dagr verðr. vm uprisu kuícra oc dauða

«3.38» <Discipulus> Hvat er hit œfsta mot horn.
Magister. mot horns rodd var hœýrð forðom þa er guð drottenn gaf log i fialle. sua taka englar þa likame oc mot horn or lofte. oc veckia allann heim með ogorlegri mot horns roddu. til doms sem ritat er. Mot horn man sýngia oc risa upp dauðer. oc enn er sua melt. A miðri natt gerðist kall mikit.

«3.39» Discipulus. huer er hin fýsta upp risa
Magister. Sua sem dauðar ero .ij. sua ero upp risur tuer. onnor andar en onnor likams. þa dœýr ond er maðr misgerír. þui at hon fyrir lítr hit [[544:12r]] sanna lif guðs oc er hon grafen j likam. En er honhuerfr aftr til lifs fyrir ið[-]ran. þa ris hon vpp af dauða. En onnor er likams upp rísa a hínum œfsta degi.
«3.41» Discipulus. Ero nokorer menn þa i heímí.
Magister. sua er þa heímr manna fullr sem nu. oc ero menn þa at verki sínu sem nu. sumir eria en sumir fara a skípum eða gera aðra sýslu.

«3.35» Disciple: What age will Enoch and Elijah be when they come?

Master: They will be the same age in which they were translated (2 Kings 2:11; Heb. 11:5), and they will be killed by the Antichrist. He will possess power for seven seasons and then he will pitch his tent on Mount Olivet and fight against the righteous, and there he will be found slain suddenly by the breath from the mouth of God. That will be according to His command, as is written: The Lord will overthrow all chieftains on earth on Holy Mount Olivet.

«3.36» Disciple: Will the days be shorter then than now, because it is said in the books that the days will become shorter for the sake of the saints (Matt. 24:22)?

Master: The days will be just as long as they are now. As David said: They continue the days according to your ordinances (Pss. 118/119:91), and the days are said to become shorter because the Antichrist will possess power for a little time, that is for three years. And then men will be smaller than they are now, just as we are smaller than our ancestors.

«3.37» Disciple: What happens after that?

Master: Forty days will be granted for repentance to those who were led astray by the terror or deceit of the Antichrist. No one knows at what day or hour (Matt. 24:36) doomsday will come. About the resurrection of the living and the dead.

«3.38» Disciple: What is the last trumpet (1 Cor. 15:52)?

Master: The sound of the trumpet was heard before, when the Lord God gave forth His commandments on the mountain (Exod. 19:16). So the angels will take bodies and the trumpet from the air and awaken the whole world to the judgment with the terrible sound of the trumpet, as is written: The trumpet shall sound and the dead shall rise (1 Cor. 15:52). And it is also said: At midnight there was a great cry made (Matt. 25:6).

«3.39» Disciple: What is the first resurrection (Rev. 20:5)?

Master: Just as there are two deaths, there are also two resurrections: one of the soul and one of the body. The soul dies if man sins, because it despises the true life of God and is buried in the body. But if the soul turns back to life through repentance, then it rises from death. The other is the resurrection of the body on the Last Day.

«3.41» Disciple: Will there be any men in the world then?

Master: The world will be full of men then as now. And men will pursue their work as they do now. Some will plow and some will travel on ships or conduct other business.

«3.42» D*iscipulus*. huat verðr þa or þeím.

M*agister*. þa er rett lat[*ir*] risa upp þa tacast þeír þegar i loft af englum a mot cristi. En þeir er aðr lifðu dœyia i sialfre upp numníngu. oc endr lifna þegar. þessa upp risu hofðu þau maria oc joh*anne*s. Maria toc licam eftír dauða oc groft. oc va<r> upp nomín siðan i dýrð. En ioh*anne*s do i síalfre upp numnín-gu. oc endrlifnaðe. En vander dœyia af rezlu engla raddar. oc endr-lifna þegar. þetta er at dœma lifendr oc dauða.

«3.57» [[674a:37]] .... ma *oc* þvi trua at h*ann* site adomstole i lofste tecnom sem domande. þu*i*at h*ann* sv[-]nesc þar maþr.

«3.58» D*iscipulus* Hafa postolar þar sęte se*m* sagt es at þeir mono sita á tolf domstolo*m*.

M*agister* Hug scot þeira ero sęte þeira íþei*m* huilasc þeir sva se*m* í sęte at v*er*stigno*m* ollo*m* losto*m*. Þeir sv-nasc *oc* sitia at dome ádomstolom ór lofste tecno*m*.

«3.59» D*iscipulus* Huerso gøresc domr sa.

M*agister* Nu ero samblandn*er* goþ*er oc* iller *oc* svnasc marg*er* goþ*er*. Þéir es iller ero. e*nn* þeir sum*er* iller es goþ*er* ero. en þa skilia englar goþa fra illo*m* se*m* corn fra ogno*m*. *oc* scifsta þei*m* ifiorar suei-t*er*. Ein sveit es algorra [..] døma meþ drotne onnor retlatra þeira es hialpasc idome. En þriþia omil[-][[674a:38]]dra es fvr farasc ón dóm en fiorþa ilra es fyr farasc idome.

«3.60» D*iscipulus* Huer*er* scolo døma.

M*agister* Postolar *oc* pind*er oc* munkar *oc* meyiar.

«3.61» D*iscipulus* Huerso døma þeir retlata.

M*agister* Svna þeir þa dyrþar v*er*þa fvr þat es þeir botnoþo afken-ni*n*gom þeira *oc* dømo*m*.

«3.62» D*iscipulus* Huer*er* hial-pasc ídome.

M*agister* Þeir er g*er*þo miskun-nar v*er*k ílogsamlego*m* hiuscap *oc* þeir es svnþ*er* sinar botto meþ iþru*n*n *oc* olmoso gøþe. viþþa es sva melt. komeþ ér blezaþ*er* foþor mi*nn*s. þu*i*at mik hungraþe *oc* gofoþ ér m*er* at eta.

«3.63» D*iscipulus* Męler cristr þesse orþ viþ þa.

M*agister* Ret es at trua at h*ann* męle. þar es h*ann* vitrasc maþr mo*nn*om E*nn* fvr þvi at þat vito aller fvr huer*nn* verþleic [[674a:39]] hve*rr* scal hialpasc eþa fvr døma-sc þa es fvr mei*rr* íþessom orþom kent fvr huer*nn* verþleik v*er* scolom hialpasc.

«3.42» Disciple: What will become of them then?

Master: When the righteous arise, they will immediately be transported aloft by the angels to Christ; and those who are still alive then will die during the ascension, but awaken to life again immediately. Mary and John began this resurrection. Mary resumed her body after her death and burial, and then was assumed into glory. And John died during the ascension and returned to life. And the wicked die for fear of the voices of the angels and then immediately revive. This is the judgment of the living and the dead.

«3.57» «Master: .... one» can also believe that He sits in the judgment seat established on high as a judge, because He appears there as a man.

«3.58» Disciple: Do the apostles have seats there, as is written that they will sit upon the twelve thrones of judgment (Matt. 19:28)?

Master: Their consciences are their thrones. After having overcome all vices, they rest in them like in seats. They also seem to sit in court in judgment seats established on high (Pss. 121/122:5).

«3.59» Disciple: How will the judgment take place?

Master: Now the good and the wicked are blended together, and many seem good who are wicked and some seem wicked who are good. But at the time of judgment the angels will separate the good from the wicked like wheat from chaff, and they will divide them into four hosts. One host consists of the perfect «who» judge with the Lord; the second consists of the righteous who are saved in the judgment; the third consists of the ungodly who perish without judgment; and the fourth are the wicked who perish in the judgment.

«3.60» Disciple: Who will judge?

Master: The apostles and the martyrs, the monks and the virgins.

«3.61» Disciple: How do they judge the righteous?

Master: They show that they are worthy of glory because they have been improved by their teaching and examples.

«3.62» Disciple: Who will be saved in the judgment?

Master: Those who accomplished works of mercy in lawful marriage and those who atoned for their sins through repentance and charity. To them it is said: Come you blessed of my Father, for I was hungry and you gave me to eat (Matt. 25:34).

«3.63» Disciple: Does Christ say these words to them?

Master: It is right to believe that He says them when He reveals Himself as man to men. But because all will know for what deed each shall be saved or condemned, these words reveal more clearly the merit for which we shall be saved.

«3.65» D*iscipulus* Hver*er* farasc ǫn dome.
M*agister* Þeir es fvr utan log misgerþo s*em* heiþn*er* eþa gv-þingar es efst*er*
pisl c*ri*stz v*oro*. þu*i*at ef-st*er* pisl h*an*s. es eno*m* forno*m*logo*m* iafnat
viþ blót.

«3.66» D*iscipulus* Mono þeir sia c*ri*st.
M*agister* Sia þeir h*ann* til afalz doms sér s*em* rit*et* es. Sia mono þeir þa*nn*
es þeir þu*i*at aller omilld*er* urþo sa*m*raþa adauþa c*ri*stz.

«3.67» D*iscipulus* Hui es sua sagt fra þei*m* at omild*er* risa e*ige* up idome.
M*agister* Eige bersc þei*m* þat at he*n*nde at þeir døm*e* þar of aþra s*em* her.
Of þa es sva m*e*lt. S*e*t-ia mo*n*du þa í ofn eldz á tiþ reiþe þi*nn*ar.

«3.68» D*iscipulus* Huer*er* farasc ídome.
M*agister* Gy-[[674a:40]]þingar þeir es misgerþo ílogo*m* fvr*er* pisl c*hri*sti oc
vand*er* c*ri*stnir þeir es Goþs v*er*co*m* nitto viþ þa es melt fareþ ér fra
m*er* bolva-þ*er* ield eilifan. þu*i*at mic hungraþe oc gofoþ*er* m*er* e*ige*
at eta ne drecca. Iþesso*m* orþom svnesc at þeir fvr dø-masc afþui at
þeir villdo e*ige* bø-ta svnþ*er* sinar meþ olmoso geþe. E*ige* m*e*ler
h*ann* sua komeþ*er* bleza ec vþr. held*r* komeþ*er* þu*i*at er eroþ
blec-zaþ*er*. Oc e*ige* meler h*ann* sua fareþ braut ér bolva ec vþr. hel*d*r
þu*i*at er eroþ bol-uaþ*er*.

«3.69» D*iscipulus* Hv*err* bletzaþe þesso*m* eþa boluaþe hino*m*.
M*agister* A*nn*de heilagr bletzar huerndag goþa m*enn*. s*em* rit*et* es. Blezaþ*er*
eroþ er af Goþe oc er blezon Goþs vfer vþr. E*nn* h*ann* boluar
il-[[674a:41]]lo*m* fvr allra mu*nn* s*em* sagt es. Bol-vaþ*er* ero þeir es
h`n´eig`i´asc af boþor-þe Goþs.

«3.70» D*iscipulus* Hverso dø*m*a þa helg*er*.
M*agister* Sv-na þeir þa pisla verþa fvr þat es þeir lifþo e*ige* efst*er* orþom
þeira oc v*er*-co*m*. Goþ scelv*er* þa íreiþe sine oc mon eldr suelga þa.

«3.71» D*iscipulus* Heu*er* Goþ reiþe eþa breþe.
M*agister* Eige es slic hrøþe hugar i Goþe held*r* dø*m*er h*ann* alt ikv*rr*leic e*nn*
þei*m* svnesc h*ann* reiþr. es fvr dø*m*asc af hono*m*.

«3.72» D*iscipulus* Hvat es góþo*m* til varnar eþa illo*m* til socnar.
M*agister* Hugscot þeira sialfra. þu*i*at af scine cros Goþs verþa aller hug*er*
þar ia*m*n auþs*e*er ollo*m* s*em* hér sól.

«3.65» Disciple: Who will perish without judgment?

Master: Those who sinned outside the law (Rom. 2:12), like the heathens or the Jews who lived after the passion of Christ. For after His passion, observation of the old laws is tantamount to idolatry.

«3.66» Disciple: Will they see Christ?

Master: They will see Him at the Last Judgment, as is written: They shall look on Him Whom they pierced (John 19:37), for all the ungodly were of one mind regarding the death of Christ.

«3.67» Disciple: Why is it said that the ungodly shall not rise at the Last Judgment (Pss. 1:5)?

Master: It is not proper for them to judge others there as they did here. It is said of them: You will place them in a fiery oven in the time of your anger (Pss. 20:10/21:9).

«3.68» Disciple: Who will perish in the judgment?

Master: Those Jews who sinned under the law before the passion of Christ and those wicked Christians who denied God's works. To them will be said: Depart from me, you cursed, into everlasting fire. For I was hungry and you gave me neither to eat nor to drink (Matt. 25:41). It is apparent from these words that they are condemned because they did not atone for their sins through charity. He does not say: Come, I bless you; but rather: Come, for you are blessed. And He does not say: Go away, I curse you; but rather: Go away, for you are cursed (Matt. 25:34, 41).

«3.69» Disciple: Who blessed these and cursed the others?

Master: The Holy Ghost blesses good men every day. As is written: You are blessed of God (Pss. 113/115:15), and: The blessing of God is upon you (Pss. 128/129:8). And He curses the wicked through everybody's mouth, as is said: They are cursed who err from the commandments of God (Pss. 118/119:21).

«3.70» Disciple: How do the saints judge them?

Master: They show that they deserve tortures because they did not live up to their words and deeds. God frightens them in His wrath, and the fire will swallow them (Pss. 20:10/21:9).

«3.71» Disciple: Does God have wrath or passion?

Master: There is no such emotion in God. Rather He judges everything with tranquility (Wisd. 12:18). He appears angry only to those who are condemned by Him.

«3.72» Disciple: What warning is there for the good and what prosecution for the wicked?

Master: Their own consciences. Because by the brightness of God's cross

«3.73» D*iscipulus* Hvat es þat es sagt es at bǿcr ly-casc up *oc* lifs boc *oc* domasc dav-þ*er* m*enn* af þei*m* hluto*m* es ritn*er* ero ábocom.
[[674a:42]]
[M*agister*] [B]ǿcr ero spam*enn oc* posto*l*ar. *oc* alg*er*ver. Þes-sar bǿcr lucasc up þa es ollo*m* verþa svnd dǿme þeira *oc* ke*n*ning. Iþei*m* dǿmo*m* mego aller sia sua se*m* ábocom. huat þeir scolo g*er*a eþa viþ hui varna. Lifs bóc es lif i*esu*. þ*ui*at af hono*m* lesa aller se*m* af boc þat es þeir skilþo eþa g*er*þo íboþorþo*m* ha*n*s. Lifs boc es *oc* G<oþ>doms afl. e*nn* iþvi sia aller si*nn* hug-scot sua se*m* rit abok.

«3.74-75» D*iscipulus* Hvat verþr siþan.
M*agister* At locno*m* dome stevpesc diofoll ídvflizo eldz *oc* bre*n*noste-i*n*ns meþ ollo*m* liþo*m* sino*m* þat es illo*m* m*onn*o*m*. E*nn* cristr f*er*r meþ dvrþ *oc* sig*re* iborg foþor sins ena hi*m*nesco ier*usa*le*m* meþ bruþe sinne þat es ollo*m* helgo*m* m*onn*o*m*. þa mon h*a*nn svnas vino*m* sino*m* se*m* [[674a:43]] h*a*nn es at frateke*n*ne þrels asiono.

«3.76» D*iscipulus* Hverso scal þat scilia es sagt es at h*a*nn mon sęlia rike Goþe feþr *oc* mon Goþ vesa allr iollo*m*.
M*agister* Ma*n*ndomr christi *oc* oll cristne ri-ker igoþdome. *oc* es Goþ fognoþr allra sama*n oc* ser huerra. þ*ui*at hv*err* hefer ísér fognoþ *oc* fagna aller sa*m*an sýn Goþs.

«3.77» D*iscipulus* Hvat verþr siþan ór heime.
<M*agister*> Sva se*m* forþo*m* gek floþ vuer heim .xv. foþmo*m* hę-ra an fioll sva mon þa eldr bre*n*na fiollo*m* hęre.

«3.78» D*iscipulus* Mon heim*r* farasc til lox.
M*agister* Oll scifste*n*g *oc* svnþa hefnd *oc* hriþ*er* frost *oc* él. *oc* eldi*n*gar *oc* reiþar þrumor *oc* onnor mein mono fvr[-]farasc e*nn* hofoþ scepnor scapasc á bett*ra* veg *oc* hreinsasc. Svasem lica-mar or*er* skifstasc til meire dvrþar [[674a:44]] *oc* verþa ogliker þvi es nu ero sva fersc nvleg ásiona heim*s* e*nn* onnor kǿm*r* be[-]tre ístaþ se*m* ritet es. Goþ mon g*er*a nyian himi*n* *oc* nvia iorþ. Himi*nn* *oc* sol *oc* tungl *oc* stiornor *oc* votn es nu renna á valt sva sem þau scvnde til ennar

all minds become equally visible to everybody — just as the sun does here.

«3.73» Disciple: What does it mean when it is said that the books and the book of life are opened, and that the dead are judged concerning the things that are written in the books (Rev. 20:12)?

Master: The books are the prophets and the apostles and the perfect. These books are opened when all will be shown their example and their teaching. In these examples — just as in the books — all can see what they must do or what they must not do. The book of life is the life of Jesus because all can read in Him as in a book what they understood or did by His command. The book of life is also the power of the Godhead in which all see their minds as they see the writing in a book.

«3.74-75» Disciple: What happens then?

Master: At the end of the judgment the devil together with all of his followers — that is the wicked — will be cast into a dungeon of fire and brimstone. But Christ goes together with His brides, that is all of the saints, to the city of His Father, to heavenly Jerusalem, in glory and victory. There He will show Himself to His friends as He is when His appearance of a slave will be removed.

«3.76» Disciple: How can one understand when it is written that He will deliver the Kingdom up to God, the Father (1 Cor. 15:24), and that God will be all in all (1 Cor. 15:28)?

Master: The human nature of Christ and all Christendom reign in the Godhead, and God is the joy of each and every one of them. For everyone has joy in himself and all rejoice together in the sight of God.

«3.77» Disciple: What will the world be like afterwards?

Master: Just as in former times the flood went over the world fifteen fathoms higher than the mountains (Gen. 7:20), so a fire will burn then higher than the mountains.

«3.78» Disciple: Will the world come to an end?

Master: All change, vengeance of sins, snowstorms, frost and rain showers, lightening, claps of thunder and other perils will end. But the elements will be recreated in a better way and cleansed. Just as our bodies will be changed to greater glory and will be unlike what they are now (1 Cor. 15:51-52), so the present appearance of the world will perish and another better one will emerge in its place, as is written: God will make a new heaven and a new earth (Isa. 6 5:17). Heaven, sun, moon, stars, and the waters that now run all the time as if they were rushing to a better place, will then stand still and

betre stoþo. þa standa þau kyrr oc fost íoskifstelegre dvrþ. Himinn mon scryþasc biart leik solar. oc scinn sol siav hlutom liosare annu sem ritet es. Sol mon hafa siaudaga lios. Tungl oc stior-nor mono scrvþasc o umbrøþelego sci-ne. Vatn þat es þvo helga menn. í scirn verþr gimsteinom fegre. Iorþ su es tok viþ likam Goþs oc døgþ vas bloþe heilagra mon verþa sem paradisus oc vesa ei fogr meþ o hrørnoþom blomom. Sia es scifsting [[674a:45]] ennar høgre handar Goþs þuiat iorþ su es bolvoþ vas oc grødde þorna oc þistla þa verþr hon ev af Goþe blezzoþ oc þar es eige siþann harmr ne erveþe.

«3.79» Discipulus fvlder þu mic af himnescom fagnaþe. segþu mer huilica helgr hafa licame.
Magister Siau hlutom biartare án sol oc scio-tare anhugr.
«3.80» Discipulus Með hveriom aldre eþa vexte
Magister Ef her es vnaþsamlect at sia unga menn meþ gomlom eþa karla meþ konom hofa meþ logom. Þa ma of trua allra þeckelegast þar vesa at sia ser hueria meþ sinom vexte oc aldre sva sem þekkelect es at hev-ra sundrleit hlioþ horpo strengia. Af þvi es rett at trua at hverr rise up meþ þeim aldre oc vexte sem hann fór [[674a:46]] ór heime.

«3.81» Discipulus Ero þeir clęder eþa nokþer.
Magister Nøcþer ero þeir oc scryder allre fegrþ oc scamasc enskes liþar heldr an aug-na. Gleþe oc heilsa er cleþnoþr þeira Goþ scrvde licame þeira heilso cleþe enn ander þeira fagnaþar scrvþe. Oc sva sem her ero sundrleiter liter ífegrþ grasa. sua verþa oc þar sundrleiter liter ilicomom heilagra sua sem annan lit hafa pinder. enn annan meyiar oc ero þat þa clęþe þeira.

«3.82» Discipulus Mego þeir gera þat es þeir vilia.
Magister Etke vilia þeir nema gott. af þvi gera þeir alt þat es þeir vilia oc ero þar es þeir vilia ón dvol.
«3.83» Discipulus Hvat gera þeir.
Magister Sia þeir ávalt á Goþ oc lofa hann of alder.
«3.84» Discipulus Hvat es lof þeira.
Magister Fog[-][[674a:47]]noþr sa es þeir gleþiasc af ˋsvn´ Goþs.
«3.85» Discipulus. Mu[-]nu þeir þa mein þau es þeir hof-þo hann alicommom.
Magister Oll munu þeir.

constant in unchanging glory. Heaven will shine as bright as the sun, and the sun will shine seven times brighter than now, as is written: The sun will have the light of seven days (Isa. 30:26). The moon and the stars will appear in incredible brightness. The water which cleansed the saints in baptism will become more beautiful than jewels. The earth that received the body of God and was sprinkled with the blood of the saints will become like Paradise and will be beautiful always with unwithering flowers. This is a change of the right hand of God (Pss. 73/74:11), for the earth, which was cursed and grew thorns and thistles, will be blessed by God forever and there will be neither grief nor toil afterwards.

«3.79» Disciple: You have filled me with heavenly joy. Tell me, what kind of bodies do the saints have?

Master: Seven times brighter than the sun and quicker than the mind.

«3.80» Disciple: What is their age and size?

Master: If it is delightful here to see young men together with old; or men together with women; or tall together with short — we can well believe that it is most pleasant to be there and to see every individual in his shape and age, just as it is lovely to hear the varying sounds of harp strings. Therefore it is right to believe that each person will rise again at the same age and shape as he left the world.

«3.81» Disciple: Are the saints dressed or are they naked?

Master: They are naked but adorned with great beauty; and they are neither ashamed of their limbs nor of their eyes. Happiness and salvation are their garments. God embellished their bodies with garments of salvation (Isa. 61:10) and their souls with the vestments of joy. And just as here there are different colors in the beauty of plants, so there will be different colors in the bodies of the saints. Thus martyrs will have one color, and virgins another; and these colors will then be their garments.

«3.82» Disciple: Can they do as they like?

Master: They only want to do good. Therefore they do everything they like, and they are where they want to be without delay.

«3.83» Disciple: What do they do?

Master: They look at God forever and praise Him in eternity.

«3.84» Disciple: What is their praise?

Master: The joy with which they rejoice in the sight of God.

«3.85» Disciple: Do they remember the pains they suffered in their bodies here?

Master: They remember them all.

«3.86» D*iscipulus* Hrvgguer þat e*ige* þa.
M*agister* He*ld*r fagna þeir þvi es þeir stigo vu*er* oll mei*nn*. sua se*m* maþ*r* seger fagnande vino*m* sino*m* þat es h*ann* co*m*sc abraut forþo*m* ór miklo*m* hasca.

«3.87» D*iscipulus* Melsca þin hof mik up vu*er* iorþ. segþu m*er* oc þa fognoþ þeira.
M*agister* Fagnaþ*er* þeira ero slik*er* se*m* auga ma*n*z ma e*ige* sia ne hev-ra. ne hugr hygia þat es G*o*þ hétt astvino*m* sino*m*.

«3.88» D*iscipulus* Hvat es þat
M*agister* Lif eilift *oc* fvllsęla eilif *oc* gnot altz góþs.

«3.89» D*iscipulus* Segþu m*er* þat scvrra
M*agister* Siau hafa þeir lika*m*s dyrþ*er oc* vii. an-dar. Ilica*m* hafa þeir lica*m*s fegrþ *oc* fro[-][[674a:48]]leic stvrkþ *oc* frelse sęllife *oc* heil-so *oc* odauþleik. E*nn* íond hafa þeir. speke *oc* vinótto sa*m*þvkce *oc* velde veg *oc* ørvgleik *oc* fog-noþ.

«3.90» D*iscipulus* Þessa hl*u*te girnesc ond mín at hevra. matþu scv́rra g*er*a meþ nekq*ue*riom dømo*m*.
M*agister* Hverso lica-þe þér at vesa ia*m*n ve*nn* se*m* ab-salón. es e*nn*ge lvta flecr vas a lica*m* h*an*s. *oc* vas hár h*an*s golle kev-fst.

«3.91» D*iscipulus* Dýrþ es.
M*agister* E*nn* þa ef meþ þes[-]se fegrþ vęr*er* þu svá frór se*m* asael. es huerio dýre vas froførre.

«3.92» D*iscipulus* Miskv*nn* es.
M*agister* E*nn* ef meþ þesso*m* tven-no*m* hluto*m* vęr*er* þu sua sterkr se*m* sa*m*son es .i. barþe. þusund ma*n*na meþ asna kialka.

«3.93» D*iscipulus* Mikil prvþe [[674a:49]] es.
M*agister* E*nn* ef þv hefþ*er* þessa þ*er*nna hl*u*te *oc* vęr*er* sva sialfraþe se*m* augus-tus es allr hei*m*r þionaþe.

«3.94» D*iscipulus* Gofog-leicr es.
M*agister* E*nn* ef meþ þesso*m* f*er*no*m* hluto*m* vęr*er* þu sua sellifr se*m* salomo*n* es e-tke let ímei*nn* sér þat es h*ann* fystesc.

«3.95» D*iscipulus* Sęla es.
M*agister* E*nn* ef meþ þesso*m* fi*m*m hluto*m* ver*er* þu sua heilendr sem moýsés q*uo*þo at aldre losnaþe tęþ*r* h*an*s ne oscygndosc augo h*an*s.

«3.86» Disciple: Does that not trouble them?

Master: No, they rejoice because they have overcome all pain just as a man joyfully tells his friends that he once has escaped a great danger.

«3.87» Disciple: Your eloquence has lifted me above the earth. Tell me also about their joy.

Master: Their joys are such that the eye of man cannot see, nor can he hear, nor can his mind conceive that which God promised His dear friends (1 Cor. 2:9).

«3.88» Disciple: What is that?

Master: Eternal life, eternal bliss, and an abundance of everything good.

«3.89» Disciple: Explain this more clearly to me.

Master: They have seven bodily and seven spiritual glories. In their body they possess beauty and knowledge, strength and freedom, pleasure, health, and immortality. In their soul they have wisdom and friendship, concord and power, honor, security, and joy.

«3.90» Disciple: My soul desires to hear these tidings. Can you explain them further with some examples?

Master: How would you like to be just as handsome as Absalom (2 Sam. 14:25-26), whose body was without a single fault and whose hair was bought for gold?

«3.91» Disciple: This is glory.

Master: And if then, together with this beauty, you were as swift as Asahel (2 Sam. 2:18) who was faster than any animal?

«3.92» Disciple: This is grace.

Master: And if, in addition to these two attributes, you were as strong as Samson (Judg. 15:16) who single-handedly slew a thousand men with the jawbone of an ass?

«3.93» Disciple: This is great bravery.

Master: And if, in addition, you were as free as Augustus whom the whole world served?

«3.94» Disciple: This is exaltation.

Master: And if, in addition to these four attributes, you were living a life of enjoyment as Solomon did who denied nothing to himself that he desired?[27]

«3.95» Disciple: This is happiness.

Master: And if, in addition to these five attributes, you were as healthy as Moses, of whom it is said that his teeth never became loose nor his eye dim (Deut. 34:7)?

«3.96» Discipulus Vnaþ es.

Magister Enn ef meþ þessom vi. hlutum vr-þer þu sua langlifr sem matusalen es mioc sua lifþe þusund vetra.

«3.97-98» Discipulus Mikilleicr es. Sva svnesc mer sem hver-iom vęre heldr øskiande íhlutr af þesso ankonongdomr. Enn sa svnesc mér ollom dv́rre es þessa hlute hever alla. [[674a:50]]

Magister Hlvþþu þvi es enn es betra. Enn ef meþ þessom hlutom ollom vere aller þer sli-ker viner sem david vas ionathe es hvarr vnne oþrom sem siolfom sér.

«3.99-97» Discipulus Fvll sę-la es.

Magister Hvat dømer þu of þann es meþ þessom hlutom ollom vęre sva spakr sem salomón es vitraþer voro marger levn-der hluter.

«3.98-99» Discipulus Goþ es.

Magister Enn ef aller vęre sva samþvker viþ þic sem rumabor-gar hofþingiar voro tyeir lecius oc cippio es huarge vilde annat an annarr.

«3.100» Discipulus Oumbrøþelect es.

Magister Enn viþ þessa hlute alla verer þu sva rikr sem alexandr conongr es meþ riki sino lagþe vnder sic allan heim.

«3.101» Discipulus Tígn es.

Magister Enn ef þu hefþer alt þetta oc verer sva veg[s]amaþr af ollom sem ioseph af egip-[[674a:51]]ta lands monnom es þeir gofgoþo hann sem Goþ.

«3.102» Discipulus Aldr fremþ es.

Magister Enn ef ollom hlutum þessom verer þu sva ørvggr sem þeir enoch oc helias.

«3.104» Discipulus Hór vegr es

Magister Enn ef þu ętter vinn þann es þu. vnner sem siolfom þér. oc hefþe hann slika dvrþ alla sem þu. vere eige þer þat þa tuefaldr fognoþr.

«3.105» Discipulus Fyselect es.

Magister Enn ef þu etter marga vine islikre dýrþ vęre eige þer þat auke fagnaþar þins.

«3.106» Discipulus Sva fagna ec molom þinom sem morgom auþøuom. Ollom heime tignare svnesc mer sa vesa es necqueria þessa hlute hever þot eige ha-fe alla. Enn ef necquerr mette alla hafa þa vere sa heldr Goþ an maþr.

Magister Rett scilrþu miclo øþre dyrþ ha-fa þeir an þetta er alt. Venleikr [[674a:52]] absalons vęre þar fęrliki þuiat fegrþ þeira es sem sol. es

«3.96» Disciple: This is joy.

Master: And if, in addition to these six attributes, you became as old as Methuselah who lived for almost a thousand years (Gen. 5:27)?

«3.97-98» Disciple: This is greatness. It seems to me that everyone would prefer one of these glories to a kingdom. But he seems to me to be the worthiest of all who possesses all of these glories.

Master: Listen to even better tidings. What if with all these attributes everybody would be as good friends with you as David was with Jonathan, each of whom loved the other like himself (1 Sam. 18:1)?

«3.99-97» Disciple: This is bliss.

Master: What would you say about him who, in addition to all these attributes, was wise as Solomon (1 Kings 5:7; 2 Chron. 2:12) to whom many hidden things were revealed?

«3.98-99» Disciple: That he is God.

Master: And if we all agreed with you — just as the two Roman leaders Laelius and Scipio[28] agreed with each other, neither wanting anything different from the other?

«3.100» Disciple: This is beyond expression.

Master: And if, with all these attributes, you were as powerful as King Alexander who with his might conquered the whole world?

«3.101» Disciple: This is sublimity.

Master: And if you had all this and were as honored by everyone as Joseph was by the Egyptians who worshipped him like God?

«3.102» Disciple: This is everlasting honor.

Master: And if, in addition, you were as faithful as Enoch and Elijah?

«3.104» Disciple: This is great honor.

Master: And if you had a friend whom you loved like yourself and he possessed the same glory as you, would that not be a double joy for you?

«3.105» Disciple: Oh what joy!

Master: And if you had many friends possessing such glory, would that not increase your joy?

«3.106» Disciple: I rejoice in your words as I would in many treasures. That man seems to be more exalted than the whole world who possesses some of these attributes even if he does not possess them all. But if someone would possess them all, then he would be God rather than a man.

Master: You understand correctly. The saints possess greater glory than all this. The beauty of Absalom would be monstrous ugliness by comparison, because the saints' beauty resembles the sun which will

þa es siau hluto*m* biartare an nv s*em* rit*et* es. Goþ e*nn*dr [sc]apar lica*m* litell*ę*tes vars efst*er* gli-ki*n*go lica*m*s birte si*nn*ar. Iflaust es at licamr cristz es biartare ansol. þu*i*at li[-]ca*m*r scap*er*a es biartare anscepna. Me[*nn*] ero kallaþ*er* m*u*stere Goþs ensol kallasc e*i*ge sua. Ef licam*er* heilagra scapasc efst[*er*] lica*m*s birte cristz. es solo es biartare e*nn* Goþ bvggver íþei*m* se*m* í m*u*stere þa es nauþsvn at þeir se liosare an sol Slic es fegrþ heilagra. Froleikr a[-]saels vere þar sei*nn* ofroleikr. þu*i*at hel[-]g*er* fara ia*m* sciott ór austre i vestr s*em* son re*nn*r vpíaustre *oc* lyser þegar í vestre. *oc* mego þeir ia*m* sciot fara [[674a:53]]........ cleþe *oc* goþ hús *oc* at hevra fagran song *oc* harpslótt *oc* ke*nn*a revkel-ses hilm *oc* a*nn*arra dvrlegra urta. eþa bergia sø*t*om groso*m oc* eiga morg auþøve. Þessa hl*u*te alla eignasc hel-g*er* on enda. þeir hafa unaþs svn þu*i*at þeir sia ia*m*t lokno*m* augo*m* se*m* opno*m*. þeir es sia kono*n*g dvrþar ífegrþ si*nn*-ne *oc* sia utan *oc* i*nn*nan dv́rþ Goþs *oc* dvrþ allra heilagra yver feþra *oc* spa-ma*nn*a. dvrþ postola *oc* pindra munka *oc* mevia *oc* allra heilagra *oc* sia þeir fagra alla liþo sina utan *oc* i*nn*an *oc* sva a*nn*ara *oc* hugre*nn*ingar. *oc* sia þeir alt þat es geresc áhi*m*ne *oc* aiorþo. *oc* sia þeir ovine sina íq*u*olom þa es forþom riso igegn þei*m oc* fagna þeir ollo þvi-[[674a:54]]s[a.] hevrnar unaþ hafa þeir þu*i*at fvr þei*m* rev́sta fagr*er* lofsongvar engla *oc* allra heilagra *oc* allar hi*m*nescar rau-st*er*. Unaþs hilm hafa þeir þa*nn* es þeir taca af siolfo*m* Goþe søtleix bru*nn*e. *oc* af englo*m oc* ollo*m* helgo*m*. Bergingar sęlo hafa þeir. þu*i*at þeir b*er*gia af søtleik Goþs *oc* seþiasc þa es Goþs dv́rþ vitrasc *oc* þei*m* ero aller hlut*er* søt*er oc* bliþ*er*. Gnott au-þøfa hafa þeir. þu*i*at þeir ero sett*er* yver alla goþa hlute ífagnaþe Goþs sins. Þet-ta es sęllive *oc* unaþ heilagra. Hei-lende moýsi vęre þar sótt. þu*i*at heilsa retlatra es af Goþe sva at etke ma þei*m* granda held*r* an skera iorno*m* solar geisla. Slic es heilsa þeira. Langlife matusale*m* vere þar daúþa [[674a:55]] dvol. þu*i*at sarleicr *oc* dauþe flør fra þei*m* es ei lifa meþ Goþe *oc* taka at e[r]fþ sęlo oþrotnanda lifs. Þesser ero li-ca*m*s hlut*er* ein*er*.

shine seven time brighter then than now. As is written: God recreates our vile body that it may be fashioned like unto His glorious body (Phil. 3:21). It is beyond doubt that Christ's body is brighter than the sun, for the body of the Creator is brighter than creation. Men are called the temple of God, but the Son is not called thus. If the bodies of the saints are created according to the brightness of Christ's body, which is brighter than the sun; and if God lives in them like in a temple; then it is imperative that they shine more brightly than the sun. Such is the beauty of the saints. Asahel's swiftness would be mere idleness by comparison because the saints move as quickly from the East to the West as the sun rises in the East and immediately shines in the West. And they can move just as quickly .... garments and good houses and to hear a beautiful song and the sound of a harp and to perceive the smell of incense and other costly herbs or to taste sweet herbs and to possess many riches. All these things the saints possess without end. They possess the joy of sight because they can see equally well with closed as with open eyes. They can see the King of glory in His beauty, and they can see from without and within the glory of God and of all the saints over and above the patriarchs and prophets. They can also see the glory of the apostles and martyrs, monks and virgins, as well as of all the saints. They can also see all of their limbs as well as those of others, beautiful inside and out; and they can see their thoughts. And they can see everything that happens in heaven and on earth; they see the tortures their enemies endure who formerly rose up against them, and they rejoice in all that. They possess the joy of hearing because lovely hymns of praise are sung before them by the angels, all the saints and other heavenly voices. They possess a delightful scent which they receive from God Himself, the well of sweetness, and from the angels and all the saints. They possess the bliss of taste because they taste of the sweetness of God and they can eat their fill; and God's glory reveals itself in them for whom all things are sweet and pleasant. They possess an abundance of riches, for they have been set above all good things in the joy of their God. That is the saints' life of enjoyment and happiness. The health of Moses would be sickness by comparison, because the health of the righteous is given by God in such a way that nothing can injure them any more than one can cut sunbeams with iron. Such is their health. The longevity of Methuselah would be the distress of an extended death, because pain and death leave those who live in God and who receive as

«3.107» D*iscipulus* Sva se*m* þvrstan ma*nn* gleþr søtr bruþr sva nø*r*er ond mina hunang fliotanda mal ór mu*nn*[-]ne þino*m*. Þu*i*at þeir ero fulsęler er til sva goþs ero hugþ*er* af Goþe.
M*agister* San-lega ero seler þeir es bvggva íh*u*se Goþs *oc* lifa íþesso*m* hluto*m* ollo*m* of. old alda. Þei*m* mønde speke salomons þvkkia mikil hei*m*sca. þu*i*at þeir sci-na íalre speke *oc* hafa vitro af siol-vo*m* Goþe spekþar bru*n*ne þu*i*at þeir vito alla hl*u*te liþna *oc* nulega *oc* oorþna *oc* allra m*a*nna ahi*m*ne *oc* aiorþo *oc* ihel-vite nofn *oc* kvnnu þeir *oc* verk bę-[[674a:56]]þe goþ *oc* ill. Oc levnesc etke fvr þei*m* þu*i*at þeir sia alt íretletes so-lo Goþs.

«3.108» D*iscipulus* Bruþr mę*l*sco þinnar scvl-der mik at fella tór. Vito aller helg*er* þat es ec gerþa.
M*agister* Eige at eins þat es þu gerþ*er* held*r* *oc* alt þat es þu hugþ*er* *oc* mę*l*t*er* gott *oc* illt.
«3.109» D*iscipulus* Hvat stoþar þa scristaga*n*ga *oc* iþron ef þeir scolo vita liotar synþ*er* orar þę*r* es ver sco*mm*o*m*sc þot allar ko-me íhug at ei*nn*s.
M*agister* Hvat ręþesc þu eþa ugger at þar mon*er* þu sca*m*-masc v*er*ka þinna. E*nn*na liotosto svnþa þi*nn*a til sagþra *oc* fvr iþro*nn* botta. *oc* scalþu e*i*ge mei*rr* sca*m*masc an þa ef necqu*err* segþe. þer þat es þu gerþ*er* í voggo. oc e*i*ge meir an [[674a:57]] algroe*nn*a sara þeirra es þu fect i orrosto. Etke es annat at fvr ge-fa svnþ*er* an hefna þeira e*i*ge fvr iþ-ron *oc* iatni*n*g. fvr gefasc svnþ*er*. e*nn* takasc e*i*ge ór mi*nn*e Goþs ne heilagra.

«3.110-111» D*iscipulus* Sannaþu þat.
M*agister* Veiz þu at d*a*vid gerþe hordóm *oc* ma*nn*drap. e*nn* ma-ria magdalena vas svnþog *oc* pe-ta*rr* neitte *christo*.

«3.112» D*iscipulus* Veit ec.
M*agister* Truer þu at þau se áhi*m*no*m*.

their inheritance the bliss of never-ending life. These are the physical attributes only.

«3.107» Disciple: Just as a sweet well gladdens the thirsty man, so the speech of your mouth flowing like honey nourishes my soul. For they are blessed for whom God intends such goodness.

Master: Truly blessed are they that dwell in the house of God (Pss. 83:5, 84:4) and who live with all these blessings throughout the ages. To them the wisdom of Solomon would seem great stupidity, because they themselves excel in great wisdom and they know God Himself, the well of wisdom. They know all things past, present, and future, as well as the names of all men in heaven, on earth, and in hell. And they also know their deeds, both good and evil, and nothing is concealed from them, for they see everything in the sun of God's righteousness.

«3.108» Disciple: The well of your eloquence makes me shed tears. Do all the saints know what I did?

Master: Not only what you did but also what you thought and said, good as well as evil.

«3.109» Disciple: Then what good is confession and repentance if they know all our horrible sins of which we are ashamed even though they are only in our minds?

Master: Why do you speak of and fear the shame of the sins of your mind? You shall be no more ashamed of your most terrible sins when they will be made known and will be atoned for by repentance, than if someone said what deeds you had committed in your cradle; nor would you be ashamed for wounds received in battle which are now perfectly healed. To forgive sins means nothing else but not to avenge them. Sins are forgiven through repentance and confession but they are not erased from the memory of God or the saints.

«3.110-111» Disciple: Can you prove that?

Master: Do you know that David committed adultery and murder (2 Sam. 11:1-27), that Mary Magdalene was a sinner (Luke 8:2), and that Peter denied Christ (Matt. 26:69-75; Mark 14:66-72; Luke 22:54-62; John 18: 15-27)?

«3.112» Disciple: Yes, I know.

Master: Do you believe that they are in heaven?

«3.113» D*iscipulus* Trui ec.

M*agister* Ef þu veizt þetta iarþlegr *oc* ostv-rkþ allre. E*nn* þevge sca*m*masc þeir þess he*ld*r fagna þeir hiolp sinne í Go*þ*e.

«3.114» D*iscipulus* Þyckia *eige* englo*m* go*þ*s slik*er* v*ę*rre anþeir es fat misg*er*þo.

M*agister* Vist *eige*. þu*i*at sua s*em* vin*er* fagna þei*m* mest es braut koma ór scipsbrote eþa [[674a:58]] [ó]r oþro*m* miklo*m* haska sua fagna en[-]glar *oc* helgir þeira heilso m*ę*st es or svnþo*m* levsasc *oc* sva s*em* sa. l*ę*cn*er* es mest lovaþ*r* es torvelzt groþ*er* sua es *oc christus* mest dvrcaþ*r* af slicra m*ann*a hiolp.

«3.115» D*iscipulus* Mikil gleþe es þat.

M*agister* Uinatta d*a*vid *oc* ionathe sa*m*teng*er* þa þu*i*at Go*þ* a*n*n þei*m* s*em* sono*m* en þeir hono*m* meira an sioluo*m* ser *oc* elsca þa aller englar *oc* helg*er* s*em* sialfa sic. Sa*m*þvcke leli*us* *oc* scippi[-]ons monde þar þvckia sundrlyn-de þu*i*at þeira sa*m*þvcke es slict sem augna es þangat litr annat þegar es annat ser. þat es e*inn* þeira vill. þat vill þegar Go*þ* *oc* þat aller englar *oc* aller helg*er*.

«3.116» D*iscipulus* Ef Go*þ* vill s*em* ec *oc* al-ler helg*er* þa vil ec vesa glicr pet*r*o. [[674a:59]]

M*agister* Ef þu vilder þat þa v*ę*r*er* þu [s]ua þegar. E*ige* sege ec at þu ver*er* pet*rr*us he*ld*r glicr petro. Efþu girndesc at vesa pet*rr*us. þa ver*er* þu etke. þu*i*at þu girndesc annat at vesa an þu ert. E*nn* þar vill e*n*nge meire dvrþ hafa e*nn* ha*n*n es verþ[r] sua s*em* her vill *eige* fotr vesa hond ne aýra at vesa auga. E*n*n ef þeir girndesc nacq*u*at framar*r*. þa hefþe þeir *eige* fullan fognoþ. E*nn* þeir hafa fullan fog-noþ *oc* fvsasc enskes framar*r* an þeir hafa *oc* ma etke leggiasc viþ fognoþ þeira ne af takask. þu*i*at þvi fagnar hver*r* meþ oþrom es *eige* hev*er* sialfr meþ ser. Pet*rr*us fagnar hreinlife ioh*ann*is en ioh*ann*es fagnar pislar vette petri *oc* [[674a:60]] v[*er*]þ[r] sua eins hvers dyrþ. at þat es [....]a dv́rþ *oc* allra dvrþ einom at dýrþ. Eþa hvat mege þeir framar*r* girnasc an vesa glik*er* englo*m* *oc* ha[-]fa þessa goþa hl*u*te alla es nu tinda ek *oc* marga aþra. Velde alexan-d*r* kono*n*gs v*ę*re þar þrongt varþhald. þu*i*at velde þeira es sva mottogt at þeir mego gøra annan heim ef þeir vilia. þu*i*at þeir ero soner*r* Goþs *oc* sa*m*er[-]u*i*ngiar cristz s*em* ritet es. Ec sagþa Go*þ* eroþ ér. Ef þeir ero goþ þa megoþeir alt þat es þeir vilia.

«3.113» Disciple: Yes, I do.

Master: If you know that as a human being in all your infirmity, «you must realize that these sinners»[29] are not ashamed of their transgressions, but rather rejoice in God for their salvation.

«3.114» Disciple: Do such people not seem worse to God's angels than those who transgressed only a little?

Master: Certainly not, because just as friends rejoice most for those who manage to escape from a shipwreck or other great danger, so the angels and the saints rejoice most in the salvation of those freed of sins. And just as that physician is most praised who heals the most serious cases, in the same way is Christ most glorified by the salvation of such sinners.

«3.115» Disciple: This is great joy.

Master: Friendship unites David and Jonathan because God loves them like sons, but they love Him more than they love themselves, and all the angels and saints love them like themselves. The concord of Laelius and Scipio would seem discord by comparison, because their concord is like the eyes of one who immediately looks at the same place to which the other looks. What one of them wants, God, all angels, and saints immediately want also.

«3.116» Disciple: If God and all the saints want what I want, then I would prefer to be like Peter.

Master: If that were your wish, that wish would be immediately granted. I did not say that you would be Peter but rather that you would resemble Peter. If you wished to be Peter, you could not, because you would wish to be someone other than you really are. But no one will have more glory there than he deserves, just as a foot here on earth does not want to be a hand, nor does an ear want to be an eye. If anyone desired more, they would not possess perfect joy. But they possess perfect joy and they desire nothing further than they have, and nothing can be added to their joy nor taken away, because each rejoices in that which the other has but which he does not have himself. Peter rejoices in the purity of John and John rejoices in Peter's testimony as a martyr; and the glory of one will be the glory «of all», and the glory of all will be the glory of one. What can they desire more than to be like the angels and to possess all the good things which I have just recounted as well as many more? The empire of King Alexander would be a cramped prison by comparison, because their empire is so powerful that they could create another world if they wished. They are the sons of God and

«3.117» D*iscipulus* Hui g*er*a þeir *ei*ge annan him[*in*] ef þeir mego
M*agister* Goþ let etke efst*er* vanv*n*net. *oc* leyste alt af hende algort. Af
  þvi v*ę*re a*n*nna*rr* hei*m*r osømr *oc* to*m*r þot go*rr* vere. E*nn*
  [[674a:61]] helg*er* vilia etke oso[*m*]t g[..........] laust sua se*m* ver
  gero*m* *ei*ge alt [...] es vér mego*m* g*er*a.

«3.118» D*iscipulus* Þetta mon fra postolo*m* eino*m* sagt eþa eno*m* hesto*m*
  Goþs vino*m*. E*nn* viþ oss es vel scipat. þot v*er* se*m* þr*ę*lar þei*rr*a.
M*agister* y Fra ollo*m* retlo-to*m* es þetta sagt þ*ui*at aller v*er*þa ia*m*ner se*m*
  englar Goþs. Sva se*m* kon*o*ngr s*ę* siukan liggia ísaure *oc* lete þua
  ha*n*n *oc* lau-ga *oc* scrvþa cl*ę*þom sino*m* *oc* gefe ho*n*om nafn sitt *oc*
  g*er*þe sér at oscmege. *oc* gefe ho*n*om erfþ rikes sins. sva let Goþ oss
  liggia ísvnþa saure *oc* þo oss fvr tru íscírn. *oc* gaf oss c*r*istet nafn *oc*
  g*er*þe sér at oskmogo*m* se*m* ritet es. Al-ler þeir es viþ honom toko
  gaf ha*n*n þeim velde at v*er*þa sono*m* Goþs. Þott a*n*nna*rr* [[674a:62]]
  [........]om [h]*ę*[re] dyrþ þar efst[*er*] [........] sino*m* *oc* taka þo aller
  ieino hu*ss*e foþor e*in*n fagnaþar pe*nn*ing af svn Goþs *oc* samlage
  engla. Iosephs vegr v*ę*re þar otige*nn*. þ*ui*at þeir hafa san[-]nan veg
  es Goþ vegsamar þa se*m* sono *oc* vegsama þa aller englar. *oc* aller
  helg*er* sua se*m* hofþingia. Goþ es scvl[-]dar maþr þeirra þ*ui*at þeir
  g*er*þo sic v*er*þa þess es Goþ etlaþe þeim. Scvldar me*nn* þeirra ero
  englar *oc* aller helg*er* þ*ui*at þeir costg*ę*fþo se*m* þeir motto at fvlla
  tolo þeira *oc* auka fognoþ þeira. Him*inn* *oc* iorþ *oc* oll scepna
  gof[-]gar þa. þ*ui*at þeir scv́ndo til þess ísino*m* roþo*m* at oll scepna
  scifstesc til e*nn*s betra. Ørvgleikr enoch *oc*.....

co-heirs of Christ, as is written: I said you are gods (Pss. 81/82:6). If they are gods they can do anything they want.

«3.117» Disciple: Why do the saints not create another heaven if they are able to do so?

Master: God left nothing unfinished and performed everything perfectly. Therefore another world would be inappropriate and pointless, even if it were created. The saints do not want to «do» anything inappropriate or «superfluous» just as we do not always do everything we are capable of doing.

«3.118» Disciple: That can be said of the apostles only or of the greatest of God's friends. But we would be fortunate if we could live like their slaves.

Master: That is said of all the righteous because all will be equal unto God's angels (Luke 20:36). Just as if a king saw a sick man lie in the mud, had him washed, bathed, his garments adorned, gave him his own name, made him his beloved son and heir to his kingdom, so God saw us lie in the mud of our sins, washed us for our faith in baptism, gave us a Christian name and made us His beloved sons. As is written: To all who received Him, He gave the power to become the sons of God (John 1:12). Although one «has» greater glory there than another «according to» one's «merits», yet all receive one penny of joy in the only house of the Father from the sight of God and the community of angels. Joseph's honor would be nothing in comparison because the righteous possess true honor. For God glorifies them as sons and all angels and all saints glorify them as chiefs. God is their debtor because they are worthy of that which God intended for them. Their debtors are the angels and all the saints because they strove as much as they could to fill their number and so increased their joy. Heaven and earth and the whole creation honor them because they proclaim in their speeches that the whole of creation will change for the better. The security of Enoch[30].......

Notes

1 Virgil, *Aeneid* 2:708: *ipse subibo umeris, nec me labor iste gravabit.*
2 The medieval scribe copied the Old Norse (ON) sentence twice here.
3 See Jerome, *Liber de situ et nominibus locorum Hebraicorum*, PL 23, 862.
4 The ON text seems to be mistaken since Lefèvre's Latin text (Bibliography [9], p. 385) affirms rather than negates the election of all mankind.
5 Lefèvre's Latin text (p. 389) reads: *Fili, omnia mea tua sunt,* which is just the other way around.
6 See Matt. 27:57, Mark 15:43, Luke 23:50 for Joseph of Arimathaea and for Christ's burial with Nicodemus John 19:38-40. See also Nicodemus, *Gesta Pilati* (*Evangelia Apocrypha*, ed. C. de Tischendorf, 2nd ed. Leipzig 1876, repr. Hildesheim: Olms 1966, 15:4, p. 380).
7 Sedulius Caelius, *Carmen Paschale* (Corpvs Scriptorvm Ecclesiasti-corvm Latinorvm, vol. 10, 1885, 5:359–364; also PL 19, 743).
8 *Gesta Pilati* 17:1, p. 389.
9 According to Deut. 23:5 and Neh. 13:2 it is God who turns the curse into a blessing.
10 Thascius Caecilius Cyprianus (died 258 A.D.), *Liber de Lapsis* (Corpus Christianorum Ser. Lat., vol. 3, 1972, p. 235; also PL 4, 486).
11 Lefèvre's Latin text (p. 408) reads *limae et serrae* (files and saws) which is also the reading provided by AM 685b, 4to, fol. 1^r, 7-8.
12 Lefèvre (p. 408) uses *simulatione* which suggests that what is meant here is "false righteousness" rather than "beautiful righteousness."
13 Lefèvre's Latin text (p. 408) *toto corde* means "wholeheartedly" rather than "in their wicked heart."
14 According to Lefèvre's Latin text (pp. 408–9), the mutilated passage 2.11 reads as follows: *Propter electos mali his redundant, ut haec despiciant quibus florere etiam pessimos videant. Divitiis abundant primo, ut mala quae concupiscunt justo judicio Dei explere per pecuniam valeant; secundo, ut, si qua bona fecerint, per haec remunerentur; omnia enim quae faciunt pro terrenis agunt, unde et mercedem suam recipiunt. Potentia splendent primo propter se ipsos, ut mala quae amant potenter expleant; secundo propter reprobos, ut eos in malis defendant; tertio propter electos, ut eos castigent et a malis actibus emendent. Sospitate autem pollent nec cum hominibus flagella sentiunt, ut post eos gravior dolor excruciet. Boni autem ideo inedia, oppressione, languore afficiuntur, ne in malis delectentur aut, si aliqua contra Deum egerunt, deleantur, si non, pro patientia coronentur.* See also fragment AM 685b, 4to, fol. 1^r, 27-1^v, 8 where the Old Norse/Icelandic passage is preserved.
15 According to Lefèvre (p. 410), 2.14 reads: *Immo infelicissimi sunt quibus permittitur hic per omnia suaviter vivere et omnia desideria sua pro libitu suo implere, si adversitate non tanguntur, quia tali modo, ut arida ligna, ad ignem nutriuntur. Econtra sunt felicissimi qui hic a suis desideriis arcentur et multis asperitatitus exercentur, quia tali modo ad regnum, ut filii, flagellis erudiuntur, ut dicitur: 'Deus flagellat omnem filium quem recipit.' [Hebr., XII, 6] Volo te scire quod reprobi, quamvis corona regni potiantregnòmnino impotentes sunt et nunquam sine supplicio erunt.*
16 Lefèvre's Latin text (p. 411) reads *quia sine timore manent.*
17 Lefèvre's Latin text (p. 411) reads *Cum fortuna malis prospera arriserit et eos copia de suo cornu his bonis quae enumerasti repleverit.*
18 The reference is to Matt. 14:47.

19 Lefèvre's Latin text (p. 424) reads: *Nocet aliquid infantibus quod de illicite conjugio, scilicet de adulteris vel cognatis* [vel canonicis] *vel monachis vel monialibus* [vel caeteris incestis commixtionibus] *nascuntur?*
20 For Dinus and Belus see Jerome, *Hebraica qvaestiones in libro Geneseos* (Corpus Christianorum Ser. Lat., vol. 72, 1959, p. 13; also PL 23, 953).
21 Statius, *Thebaid* 3:661: *primus in orbe deos fecit timor.*
22 Semiramis was a legendary Babylonian queen mentioned by Herodotus 1: 184.
23 Flavia Julia Helena (257–337) was the mother of Emperor Constantine. Eudokia, Empress of Constantinople, died in 460.
24 "Moving days" were four consecutive days in spring when households could legally move from one place to another, debts and loans were paid, and servants were exchanged.
25 See Augustine, *De civitate Dei*, 21: 10 (Corpus Christianorum Ser. Lat., vol. 48, 1955, p. 776).
26 See *De Antichristo* by Abbot Adso Dervensis (910–992 A.D.) (Corpus Christianorum Continuatio Medieualis, vol. 45, 1976, p. 23 f; also PL 101, 1292–1293).
27 See Flavius Josephus, *Jewish Antiquities*, 18: 1–7.
28 C. Laelius (190–123 B.C.), legate of Aemilianus Scipio Africanus (185?–129 B.C.) during the third Punic War. He was made into an example of friendship in Cicero's *Laelius de amicitia.*
29 Part of the sentence is missing. Lefèvre's Latin text (p. 469) reads: *Si ergo tu adhuc corruptibilis et fragilis haec nosti, quanto magis illi norunt qui ab omni corruptione et fragilitate liberi erunt!*
30 From 3.118 to 3.120 the Old Norse/Icelandic text is legible only in part and so I decided to fix it by keeping the wolf from the door and omitting these fragmentary paragraphs. For the Old Norse/Icelandic text see Firchow/Grimstad (Bibliography [8], pp. 155–159) and for the Latin text see Lefèvre (pp. 474 ff).

Select Bibliography

Texteditions and Translations

[1] Werlauff, E.C., K. Gíslason, N.L. Westergaard, A.F. Krieger, and P.G. Thorsen, eds. *Det Arnamagnæanske Haandskrift, Nr. 674A, 4to, indeholdende det ældste Brudstykke af Elucidarius paa Islandsk udgivet i fotolitografisk Aftryk.* Copenhagen: Gyldendal, 1869.

[2] Eiríksson, Magnús, trans. "Brudstykker af den islandske Elucidarius." *Annaler for nordisk Oldkyndighed og Historie* (1857), 238–308.

[3] Gíslason, Konráð, ed. "Brudstykker af den islandske Elucidarius." *Annaler for nordisk Oldkyndighed og Historie* (1858), 51–172.

[4] Gíslason, Konráð. "Småbemærkninger til de tvende udgaver af den Arnamagnæanske membran Nr. 674A, 4to, nemlig I) den photolithographerede fra 1869, II) den i Annaler for nordisk Oldkyndighed for 1858 side 51–98." *Aarbøger for nordisk Oldkyndighed og Historie* (1870), 262–268.

[5] Jónsson, Finnur and Eiríkur Jónsson, eds. *Hauksbók.* Copenhagen: Det kongelige nordiske Oldskrift-Selskab, 1892–1896.

[6] Helgason, Jón, ed. *The Arna-Magnæan Manuscript 674A, 4to: Elucidarius.* Manuscripta Islandica, 4. Copenhagen: Munksgaard, 1957.

[7] Helgason, Jón, ed. *Hauksbók: The Arna-Magnæan Manuscripts 371, 4to, 544, 4to, and 675, 4to.* Manuscripta Islandica, 5. Copenhagen: Munksgaard, 1960.

[8] Firchow, Evelyn Scherabon and Kaaren Grimstad, eds. *Elucidarius in Old Norse Translation.* Reykjavík: Stofnun Árna Magnússonar, 1989.

[9] Lefèvre, Yves, ed. *L'Elucidarium et les Lucidaires. Contribution, par l'histoire d'un texte, par l'histoire des croyances religieuses en France au moyen âge.* Bibliothèque des Écoles françaises d'Athène et de Rome, 180. Paris: De Boccard, 1954.

Secondary Works

[10] Bauerreiss, Romuald. "Zur Herkunft des Honorius Augustodunensis." *Studien und Mitteilungen zur Geschichte des Benediktinerordens und seiner Zweige* 53 (1935), 28–36.

[11] Breiteig, Byrge. "Elucidarius og Kong Sverre." *Maal og Minne* (1966), 22–34.

[12] Endres, Josef Anton. "Honorius Augustodunensis und sein Elucidarium." *Historisch-politische Blätter* 130 (1902), 157–169.

[13] Endres, Josef Anton. *Honorius Augustodunensis: Beitrag zur Geschichte des geistigen Lebens im 12. Jahrhundert.* Kempten and Munich: Kösel, 1906.

[14] Firchow, Evelyn Scherabon, Kaaren Grimstad, and Stephen Gilmour. "The Old Icelandic *Elucidarius*: A Diplomatic Edition with the Help of the Computer." *ALLC-Bulletin* 6 (1978), 292–301 and 7 (1979), 60–65.

[15] Firchow, Evelyn Scherabon. "Editing Medieval Manuscripts with the Help of the Computer: The Case of the Old Icelandic *Elucidarius*." In: *Sprachen und Computer. Festschrift zum 75. Geburtstag von Hans Eggers 9. Juli 1982.* Eds. H. Fix et al. Sprachwissenschaft-Computerlinguistik, 9. Dudweiler: AQ-Verlag, 1982, 173–186.

[16] Firchow, Evelyn Scherabon. "On the Multiple Use of the Computer in Medieval Text Editing." *Amsterdamer Beiträge zur älteren Germanistik* 24 (1986), 99–105.

[17] Firchow, Evelyn Scherabon. "Anforderungsprofil an eine Edition mittelalterlicher Werke." In: *Historische Edition und Computer.* Eds. Anton Schwob et al. Graz: Leykam, 1988, 29–43. ("Diskussion" 44ff.)

[18] Firchow, Evelyn Scherabon. "Altisländische Textedition am *fin-de-siècle*: Die Ausgaben des *Möðruvallabók* (1987) und des *Elucidarius* (1989)." In: *Helden und Heldensage: Otto Gschwantler zum 60. Geburtstag.* Eds. H. Reichert and G. Zimmermann. Vienna: Fassbaender 1990, 75–86.

[19] Flint, Valerie I.J. "The Original Text of the Elucidarius of Honorius Augustodunensis from the Twelfth Century English Manu- scripts." *Scriptorium* 18 (1964), 91–94.

[20] Flint, Valerie I.J. "The Career of Honorius Augustodunensis. Some Fresh Evidence." *Revue Bénédictine* 82 (1972), 63–86.

Bibliography 113

[21] Flint, Valerie I.J. "The Chronology of the Works of Honorius Augustodunensis." *Revue Bénédictine* 82 (1972), 215–242.

[22] Flint, Valerie I.J. "The 'Elucidarius' of Honorius Augustodunensis and Reform in Late Eleventh Century England." *Revue Bénédictine* 85 (1975), 178–189.

[23] Flint, Valerie I.J. "The Sources of the 'Elucidarius' of Honorius Augustodunensis." *Revue Bénédictine* 85 (1975), 190–198.

[24] Flint, Valerie I.J. "The Place and Purpose of the Works of Honorius Augustodunensis." *Revue Bénédictine* 87 (1977), 97–127.

[25] Flint, Valerie I.J. "Heinricus of Augsburg and Honorius Augustodunensis: Are They the Same Person?" *Revue Bénédictine* 92 (1982), 148–158.

[26] Glogner, Günther. *Der mittelhochdeutsche Lucidarius, eine mittelalterliche Summa*. Forschungen zur deutschen Sprache und Dichtung, 8. Münster: Aschendorff, 1937.

[27] Grimstad, Kaaren. "Editing the OI 'Elucidarius' with the Aid of the Computer." *Amsterdamer Beiträge zur älteren Germanistik* 24 (1986), 91–97.

[28] Holtsmark, Anne. *En islandsk scholasticus fra det 12. århundre*. Skrifter utgitt av Det Norske Videnskaps-Akademi i Olso. II. Hist. -filos. klasse. Vol. 36, No. 3, Oslo, 1936.

[29] Kelle, Johann. "Über Honorius Augustodunensis und das Elucidarium sive Dialogus de summa totius Christianae theologiae." *Sitzungsberichte der kaiserlichen Akademie der Wissenschaften Wien*. Philosophisch-historische Klasse. Vol. 143, No. 13, Vienna, 1900.

[30] Kelle, Johann. "Untersuchungen über den nicht nachweisbaren Honorius Augustodunensis ecclesiae presbiter et scholasticus und die ihm zugeschriebenen Werke." *Sitzungsberichte der kaiserlichen Akademie der Wissenschaften Wien*. Philosophisch-historische Klasse. Vol. 152, No. 2, Vienna, 1905–1906, and vol. 153, No. 5, Vienna, 1906.

[31] Kinkade, R.P. "Elucidarius and Spanish Lucidarius." *Dictionary of the Middle Ages*. Vol. 4. New York: Scribners, 1984, 434–435.

[32] Kirby, Ian J. *Biblical Quotations in Old Icelandic-Norwegian Religious Literature*. 2 vols. Reykjavík: Stofnun Árna Magnússonar, 1976–1980.

[33] Kirby, Ian J. *Bible Translations in Old Norse*. Geneva: Librairie Droz, 1986.

[34] Larsson, Ludvig. *Ordförrådet i de älsta isländska handskrifterna*.

Leksikaliskt ock gramatiskt ordnat. Lund: Lindstedt, 1891.
[35] Menhardt, Hermann. "Der Nachlass des Honorius Augustodunensis." *Zeitschrift für deutsches Altertum und deutsche Literatur* 89 (1959), 23–69.
[36] Salvesen, Astrid. "Elucidarius." *Kulturhistoriskt lexikon für nordisk medeltid fran vikingatid till reformationstid.* Vol. 3. 2nd. ed. Copenhagen: Rosenkilde and Bagger, 1980, cols. 598-602.
[37] Salvesen, Astrid. *Studies in the Vocabulary of the Old Norse Elucidarium.* Oslo: Universitetsforlaget, 1968.
[38] Sanford, Eva Matthews. "Honorius, Presbyter and Scholasticus." *Speculum* 23 (1948), 397–425.
[39] Schorbach, Karl. *Studien über das deutsche Volksbuch Lucidarius.* Quellen und Forschungen zur Sprach- und Kulturgeschichte, 74. Strassburg: Trübner, 1894.
[40] Schultz, Janice. "Honorius Augustodunensis." *Dictionary of the Middle Ages.* Vol. 6. New York: Scribners, 1985, 285–286.
[41] Walter, Ernst. Review of: *Studies in the Vocabulary of the Old Norse Elucidarium* by Astrid Salvesen, in *Mediæval Scandinavia* 3 (1970), 205–209.

Slavery, Freedom and Conflict

A Story of Two Birminghams

SLAVERY, FREEDOM and CONFLICT

A Story of Two Birminghams

JANE L. BOWNAS

sussex
ACADEMIC
PRESS
Brighton • Chicago • Toronto

Copyright © Jane L. Bownas, 2020.

The right of Jane L. Bownas to be identified as Author of this work has been asserted in accordance with the Copyright, Designs and Patents Act 1988.

2 4 6 8 10 9 7 5 3 1

First published in 2020 by
SUSSEX ACADEMIC PRESS
PO Box 139
Eastbourne BN24 9BP

Distributed in North America by
SUSSEX ACADEMIC PRESS
Independent Publishers Group
814 N. Franklin Street
Chicago, IL 60610

All rights reserved. Except for the quotation of short passages for the purposes of criticism and review, no part of this publication may be reproduced, stored in a retrieval system or transmitted in any form or by any means, electronic, mechanical, photocopying, recording or otherwise, without the prior permission of the publisher.

British Library Cataloguing in Publication Data
A CIP catalogue record for this book is available from the British Library.

Library of Congress Cataloging-in-Publication Data
To be applied for.

Hardcover ISBN 978-1-78976-044-6

Paperback ISBN 978-1-78976-058-3

Typeset and designed by Sussex Academic Press, Brighton & Eastbourne.
Printed by TJ International, Padstow, Cornwall.

Contents

Introduction   1

1
Guns, Sugar and Cotton   4

2
Abolition   29

3
The Aftermath, Jamaica   59

4
The Aftermath, Alabama   81

5
The Twentieth Century, 1900–1960   101

6
The Twentieth Century, 1960–2000   126

7
Into the Twenty-First Century   161

Notes   174
Bibliography   189
Index   193

Introduction

This is a story of two cities which share a name, one in the West Midlands of England and the other in the state of Alabama in the USA. These two cities have more than a name in common for both Birminghams have close connections with the history of slavery and with the descendants of those people who were transported from their African homelands and taken into slavery in the West Indies and Southern states of America. The cities most usually associated with slavery in the UK are the port cities of Liverpool, Bristol and London from which the slave ships sailed, but large inland cities like Birmingham developed close links with slavery as a result of the trade in guns, steam engines and metal goods all essential to the slave trade and to the running of the sugar plantations in the West Indies. Cotton plantations dependent on slave labour made huge profits for plantation owners in Alabama and the sale of their land to developers after the Civil War was essential for the development of the city of Birmingham.

Many books have been written on the history of slavery and its abolition in both Britain and the United States but in the following pages the emphasis is not on national political and economic policies but on the role played by individuals and communities in two very different areas united by their connection to slavery and its aftermath. The people of Birmingham in the UK became closely involved with the Anti-Slavery movement in the eighteenth and nineteenth centuries but in Alabama anyone campaigning for abolition would have been ostracized and often physically attacked. Some however were willing to take the risk, people like James Birney who settled in Huntsville, Alabama and spent his life campaigning against slavery. In the UK Joseph Sturge, founder of the Birmingham Anti-Slavery Society, travelled to the West Indies to investigate the hardships experienced under the apprenticeship system following abolition, and published the story of a young former slave who accompanied him back to England.

In Alabama, the records of the Freedmen's Bureau provide a vivid account of the attacks and murders carried out by the Ku Klux Klan and others between 1865 and 1870 with details of the horrendous crimes committed against supposedly free former slaves. In the 1870s under Radical Reconstruction many black men became involved in politics, one notable example being James T. Rapier who was elected to represent Alabama in the United States Congress in 1872, and campaigned for voting rights. After so-called 'Redemption' in 1874, Rapier lost his seat to a Democrat, a former Confederate Army Major.

The growth of the industrial city of Birmingham, Alabama resulted in an increased demand for labour and black workers moved into the city in large numbers to work in the mines and iron foundries. Many of these were interviewed for the Federal Writers' Project in the 1930s, describing their experiences as young men. In the 1880s and 1890s increasingly severe segregation laws were introduced affecting every aspect of life, notably housing, schools, public transport, hotels and restaurants. The anti-miscegenation law which criminalised marriage between a white and black person was defended, when challenged in court by a mixed race couple, as being necessary to prevent 'a mongrel population and a degraded civilization'.

The people of the West Indies living under British colonial rule after abolition had little say in the governance of their country but volunteered to fight in Britain's armed forces during the two world wars in the first half of the twentieth century. In the 1950s and 1960s thousands of West Indians left their countries to find work in Britain and many settled in Birmingham and neighbouring industrial towns in the West Midlands. Unfortunately these newcomers who were British subjects were not universally welcomed and had to face racism when applying for jobs and renting accommodation. Henry Gunter, a Jamaican accountant, writer and political activist settled in Birmingham, trained to be a tool cutter and grinder and became the first black delegate to the Birmingham Trades Council. He recorded his experiences and that of other immigrants exposing the 'appalling housing conditions', the unwelcoming attitude of many residents and the racism often encountered in the workplace. In certain areas tension developed between the police and young unemployed black men and in the 1980s riots broke out in many British cities including Birmingham.

In Birmingham, Alabama, new 'Racial Segregation Ordinances' were introduced early in the twentieth century, and zoning laws in housing meant that a black person building a house next to a 'white zone' would be likely to find it damaged or destroyed by dynamite. In 1963 the Civil Rights campaign led to violent confrontations between the police and black demonstrators, events which were witnessed and written about by journalists and Civil Rights workers. Although an agreement was eventually reached to end segregation in Birmingham the activities of the Ku Klux Klan and other racist organisations meant that the Civil Rights Act did not bring an end to segregation particularly in education and employment. The Voting Rights Act of 1965 failed to eliminate the many devices introduced in order to frustrate the ability of African Americans to register their vote.

For the descendants of those who endured slavery in the British West Indies and the Southern United States, life in the twenty-first century still contains echoes of those years, whether it be the increased likelihood of being unemployed, detained in prison, excluded from school or, in states like Alabama, attending segregated schools or being disenfranchised as a result of racially biased voter suppression tactics. Their story needs to be heard.

1

Guns, Sugar and Cotton

Many starting points could have been chosen for this story, and some might question my choice of a date nearly two hundred years before the founding of the city of Birmingham, Alabama in 1871. Most cities have had small beginnings and can trace their origins in ancient settlements and favoured positions on well used paths or waterways. The city of Birmingham in England is recorded as a village in the Doomsday book of 1086 and in the following centuries grew to be a flourishing market town, becoming engaged in the cloth trade and then, in the fifteenth and sixteenth centuries in the production of metal goods. The land on which the city of Birmingham in Alabama now stands had been inhabited for thousands of years by members of the Muskogee people, Native Americans who lived in settled villages with thatched, wattle and daub houses built around central squares where, just as in English villages, people could meet and plan communal activities. In the sixteenth and seventeenth centuries Spanish and then French and British explorers entered these tribal lands. The first Spanish explorer was Hernando De Soto who travelled through Alabama in 1540 fighting with and killing many Native Americans who dared to oppose him. French colonization began in the sixteenth century but was mainly confined to the south of Alabama around the city of Mobile. In 1663 King Charles II granted a charter to an area of land on the coast of South Carolina which developed into a settlement for English traders, mainly from Barbados, and was given the name Charleston. From here the traders made their way through Georgia into Alabama, making contact and trading with the Creek Indians in Northern Alabama. In exchange for furs and animal skins the Creeks received metal goods such as tools and knives but also guns, and it is with the trade in guns that the first link is established between the land on which Birmingham, Alabama now stands and Birmingham in England.

Guns

Evidence that this trade was being carried out before the end of the seventeenth century has been found from Native American burial sites excavated in northern Alabama, and finds from one particular site have recently been described in detail by archaeologists. In 2016 an article published in the journal *Southeastern Archaeology* describes a seventeenth-century, flint lock trade gun which forms part of a collection of artifacts donated to the Yale Peabody Museum by John H. Gunter in1915.[1] The gun was found on Pine Island on the Tennessee River in the north of Alabama, an area about sixty miles north of the site now occupied by the city of Birmingham. The gun was accompanied by pottery fragments and hundreds of trade beads which date from the late seventeenth century when the land around Pine Island was inhabited by various native peoples often collectively referred to as Creek Indians. The gun has been identified as English dating from between 1680 and 1690, a period when English traders from Carolina are known to have been in the area exchanging guns and beads for animal skins and furs. The gun is virtually identical to one found at a site in central Alabama but no guns of a similar type have been found in the Northeast, Virginia or North Carolina, confirming the conclusion that these Alabama guns were traded out of Charleston in South Carolina.[2] The one question which remains unanswered is whether this gun was manufactured in London or in Birmingham, both cities being involved in gun manufacture during this period. Specialist metal workers in Birmingham produced engraved locks and brass components for guns such as the brass butt plate described in the Pine Island gun, and it is possible that these components would have been sold to London manufacturers. It is also known that Birmingham gunmakers sold many of their guns to London merchants for export, and these guns received London proof marks as there was no official proof house in Birmingham until much later. By the end of the seventeenth century the Company of

Gunmakers of Birmingham had acquired a considerable reputation and corporate organization and began to complain about competition from London gunmakers. The main problem was the relationship between the London manufacturers and the Royal African Company which was founded in 1672 and had a monopoly over trade with Africa. This trade was initially in products such as gold, ivory and animal hides but soon the company became involved in the trade in human beings and the production and export of guns became essential for the Trans-Atlantic slave trade. In 1698 the Royal African Company lost its trade monopoly and the London gunmakers consequently lost their favoured position, enabling Birmingham makers to sell to companies trading from other ports such as Bristol and Liverpool. By the middle of the eighteenth century Birmingham had replaced London as the major producer of guns carried by slave ships to the West coast of Africa, where they were traded for men and women taken to work as slaves on the sugar plantations of the Caribbean.

The importance of the Trans-Atlantic slave trade for the Birmingham gunmakers cannot be overestimated and a study of one firm closely involved with the trade serves to illustrate the extent to which Birmingham industrialists were able to accumulate huge profits from the sale of guns to slave traders.

James Farmer and Samuel Galton both came from Quaker families who had run successful hardware and ironmongery businesses in Bristol in the seventeenth century. The families were linked by marriage and moved to Birmingham in the early eighteenth century. Joseph Farmer, James' father founded the firm of Farmer and Galton which specialised in making 'gunlock springs, sword blades, tower musket barrels and the files and bits used to bore gun barrels'.[3] In 1741 James took over the business and was joined by his brother-in-law Samuel Galton whose investment in the firm enabled it to develop into a major manufacturer and supplier of guns. Galton remained in charge of the Birmingham branch of the business while Farmer moved to London to liaise with the London manufacturers and merchants who constituted the main market for their guns. From the 1740s until the end of the eighteenth century the firm of Farmer and Galton specialised in supplying guns for the African trade and in the 1750s became the chief supplier of arms to the Committee of the Company of Merchants Trading to Africa, a successor to the Royal African Company. The firm had strong connections with merchants trading from Bristol and Liverpool, employing agents and maintaining warehouses in both ports. W.A.Richards notes that Farmer and Galton supplied arms to 'some of the most successful slave traders of the eighteenth century' and that most of these placed annual orders with the firm. One of their most important customers in the 1750s was Joseph Manesty, 'a leading Liverpool slave trader' and during this decade the firm 'supplied guns to at least six slaving ships belonging to Manesty'. Richards concludes, 'assuming that Joseph Manesty sent out at least four of his slaving ships each year, and an average gun cargo of five hundred guns, Farmer and Galton were supplying Joseph Manesty with at least two thousand guns annually in the early 1750s'. Another prominent slave trader who bought guns from Farmer and Galton was a previous Mayor of Liverpool, Foster Cunliffe who together with his two sons 'had four ships capable of holding 1,120 slaves, the profits from which were sufficient to stock twelve vessels on the homeward journey with sugar and rum'.[4] Interestingly, Eric Williams points out that an inscription to Cunliffe in St. Peter's Church, Liverpool describes him as 'a Christian devout and exemplary in the exercise of every private and publick duty, friend to mercy patron to distress . . . '[5]

Trading for slaves on the West coast of Africa had been taking place since the fifteenth century, but this was mainly carried out by the Portuguese and Spanish. It was not until the end of the Civil War in England and the establishment of sugar plantations in the British Caribbean colonies that the demand for slave labour resulted in a massive increase in what became known as the Triangular Trade. Ships carried trade goods from ports such as Liverpool to the African coast where these goods were exchanged for human beings who were then traded on the plantations for products such as sugar and cotton. African chieftains and monarchs demanded the type of flintlock muskets that Farmer and Galton were producing and knew that the only way they could obtain them was by trading slaves. In his comprehensive account of the slave trade Hugh Thomas notes that 'Lord Shelburne, then secretary to Pitt the Elder even thought in 1765 that 150,000 guns had been sent to Africa from Birmingham alone, thus enriching such businesses as the Quaker firm of Farmer and Galton in Birmingham'. Thomas adds that 'it was often said then that a slave had the value of one Birmingham gun', however as the demand for slaves grew it was more likely that five or six guns would be demanded for each slave.[6] The result of this trade meant that the rulers and merchants in states on the West African coast possessed large numbers of guns which in addition to being used for defensive purposes were used in various ways to procure an ever increasing number of slaves for sale to European traders. No doubt the demand for increasing numbers of guns meant that they were not always of the best quality and Barbara Smith notes that in 1765, after visiting Farmer and Galton's factory in Birmingham, Lord Shelburne commented 'what is shocking to humanity, above half of them from the manner they are finished in are sure to burst in the first hand that fires them'. Smith comments that 'more recently, it has been suggested that this oft-repeated accusation of poor quality was untrue and that the African was not to be fooled by poor goods'.[7] What is true however is that there was no official proof house in Birmingham and guns had to be sent unproved to Africa or sent via London, obtaining a London proof certificate and involving considerable extra expense for the firm. Direct evidence for the inferior quality of many guns supplied for the African trade is found in letters written by Samuel Galton in 1756 in which he describes the trading guns as 'got up in the common way without proof', although proved guns could be provided on request at an extra cost.[8]

The interdependence between the supply of slaves to European traders and the supply of guns to African merchants might suggest that this trade resulted in an increase in warfare between various ethnic groups in order to obtain captives who would then be sold as slaves. Abolitionists often used this as an argument for ending the slave trade but as Thomas points out 'wars were frequent before the Europeans arrived in West Africa and were probably sometimes undertaken in order to obtain slaves even then'. However he adds that 'the kings of Dahomey more than once appealed to their European trading partners for arms to enable them to carry out the raids on their northern neighbours which alone could provide the slaves needed to fill the European boats'.[9] In addition to the taking of prisoners in warfare many slaves were obtained by kidnapping which often involved the use of firearms. A first-hand account of such a kidnap is provided by the freed slave, Olaudah Equiano, who wrote an account of his life from boyhood in a village in Africa, to capture by slave-traders when he was ten years old and subsequent life as a slave in the latter part of the eighteenth century.[10] He describes how his village was 'sometimes visited by stout mahogany-coloured men from the south-west of us . . . they generally bring us fire-arms, gunpowder, hats, beads, and dried fish'. He describes how 'when our people go out to till their land they . . . generally take their arms with them for fear of a surprise . . . from what I can recollect of these battles, they appear to have been irruptions of one little state or district on the other to obtain prisoners or booty. Perhaps they were incited to this by those traders who brought the European goods I mentioned amongst us. Such a mode of obtaining slaves in Africa is common and I believe more are procured this way and by kidnapping than any other'.[11] One day when their parents were away working in the fields Equiano and his sister were seized by kidnappers. They were soon separated and Equiano describes how 'after many days' travelling, during which I had often changed masters, I got into the hands of a chieftain in a very pleasant country'. He was treated well by the chieftain's family but never allowed to forget that he was a slave. He was sold again and 'travelled through many different countries' where the people spoke many different languages, and despite his misery at being torn away from his family he acknowledges that 'in honour of those sable destroyers of human rights, I never met with any ill treatment or saw any offered to their slaves except tying them, when necessary, to keep them from running away'.[12] After six or seven months of travelling Equiano arrived at the coast, was delivered into the hands of European slave traders and dragged aboard an English slave ship where the treatment meted out to the captured slaves was to involve far higher levels of brutality and violence than any treatment they had received from their African captors, however harsh that might sometimes have been. Equiano's somewhat uncritical attitude towards his African captors probably results from the fact that kidnapped slaves were usually treated more favourably than those captured as prisoners of war. The botanist and explorer, Mungo Park who travelled through central and western Africa at the end of the eighteenth century witnessed many examples of the cruel treatment meted out to slaves as they travelled in long caravans or 'coffles' from the interior to the coast. He describes how the slaves were kept 'constantly in irons' and 'are commonly secured by putting the right leg of one, and the left of another into the same pair of fetters ... Every four slaves are likewise fastened together by the necks with a strong rope of twisted thongs'.[13]

There is no doubt that warfare was engaged in by neighbouring African states long before the arrival of European traders, however it is clear that the increasing demand for slaves in the eighteenth century and the ready supply of firearms did increase the frequency and aggressive nature of inter-tribal warfare. The slaves sold to foreign traders were transported to far distant lands with no hope of ever seeing their families or homelands again, or in the words of Equiano addressing his captors, 'torn from our country and friends to toil for your luxury and lust of gain'.[14]

Ample evidence for the financial gain made from the slave trade by the firm of Farmer and Galton may be found in the Galton Papers which contain letters exchanged between Samuel Galton and James Farmer as well as letters to business associates and traders with whom they were involved.[15] Galton frequently complains about the small profit margins made on the cheapest guns for the African market and Richards notes that 'it would appear that Birmingham gunmakers either relied on making most of their profit out of the African trade from the sale of their more expensive African guns, or that they reduced the finishing of the cheapest guns to the minimum'.[16] However it is quite possible that Galton was underestimating the profits made by the firm as the most frequent complaints occur in letters sent to his Liverpool agents 'who would no doubt have wanted a bigger commission had they been told that the profits were higher'.[17] Although they were the main supplier of guns to the Committee of the Company of Merchants Trading to Africa, Farmer and Galton realised that greater profits could be made by partaking in direct trading deals. Richards writes that the firm 'often had agreements with the captains of slaving ships, whereby part of the gun cargoes were shipped and sold on behalf of Farmer and Galton, and the proceeds were remitted to the firm by the captains'.[18] Hugh Thomas notes that the Galton family actually owned a slaving ship called the *Perseverance* which took part in some African trading ventures.[19] Barbara Smith in her study of the Galton family identifies a reference in the Galton papers to 'Expenses attending the Ship *Perseverance* on a voyage from Liverpool to Africa, thence to the West Indies, and from the West Indies back to England' with a cargo of goods and 527 slaves. It details that '£6,430 nett gain was expected from the sale of the slaves at £50 each and from the freight on £7,000 of unspecified cargo'.[20] There is also evidence that the Farmer and Galton families were involved in the slave trade before the firm in Birmingham was formed, a reference in the Galton papers mentioning 'an assignment of shares by Joseph Farmer to Samuel Galton in two ships which were engaged in the trade with Africa and the West Indies'.[21]

In addition to the profits obtained from the sale of guns used in trading for slaves, Farmer and Galton had shares in the outfitting and cargoes of the trading ships and supplied weapons stored on board ship. It was important that strict control could be maintained over the captured slaves during the long journey to the West Indies, and for this purpose large guns called swivel blunderbusses were positioned around the ship to deter any attempt at insurrection. Richards writes that 'Samuel Galton was especially proud of his firm's swivel blunderbusses as Farmer and Galton made all the parts for this large gun, whereas other gunmakers supplied parts only'.[22] They also supplied guns, pistols and cutlasses for the ships' stores, ready to be used if any disturbance occurred.

The Galton papers provide evidence of the capital accumulated by the firm between 1747 and 1799. It increased from £10,000 to £36,143 between 1747 and 1766 when James Farmer died and in 1778 was recorded as being £91,404. In 1799 when Samuel Galton died, his son is recorded as possessing capital of £139,007.[23] It is no coincidence that the most rapid increase in capital occurred during the years when the trade in slaves from Africa was at its height.

The Farmer and Galton families were Quakers and had close connections, often as a result of marriage, with members of other Quaker families. Despite speaking out strongly for the abolition of slavery at the end of the century many Quaker families had connections with the slave trade throughout the eighteenth century and relied heavily on a strong supporting network of fellow Quakers engaged in the manufacture and trading of goods related to the slave trade. Finance was of prime importance and members of both the Farmer and Galton families were related by marriage to the main Quaker banking families, the names of two of which, Lloyds and Barclays, survive to this day. David Barclay, a member of the Quaker banking firm, Freame and Barclay was engaged in the slave trade and actually owned a plantation in Jamaica.[24] In a letter of March 1755 Samuel Galton acknowledged his deep gratitude to Freame and Barclay for advancing him enough money to keep the gun manufactory going in Birmingham.[25] A more local connection was with the Birmingham bank of Taylor and Lloyds, founded in 1765 by Sampson Lloyd, member of a Welsh Quaker family who moved to Birmingham in 1698. Lloyd was an iron manufacturer and trader before starting his banking business and had sold iron to Farmer and Galton. The link with Farmer and Galton's firm was further advanced by the marriage of Lloyd's son Charles to James Farmer's daughter. These strong family and business links enabled Farmer and Galton to survive financial crises and continue to gain financially from the trade in slaves well into the 1790s.

In the early 1790s questions started to be raised by members of the Society of Friends as to whether gun-making could be compatible with Quaker pacifist principles. In 1792, in a meeting at the Bull Street Meeting House in Birmingham, objections were raised to the making of guns by the Galtons and particularly to the inferior quality of some of the guns and the fact that they contributed to tribal warfare and slavery in Africa. Under pressure from fellow Quakers Galton retired from the gun trade in 1795 but his son Samuel Galton Junior continued in the firm, attempting to justify his decision in a letter presented at the Society of Friends monthly meeting in January 1796. It is worth quoting part of this letter in full:

> The censure, and the Laws of the Society, against Slavery, and Oppression, are as strict, and as decisive, as against War – Now, those who use the produce of the labour of Slaves, as Tobacco, Rum, Sugar, Rice, Indigo, and Cotton, are more intimately, and directly the Promoters of the Slave Trade, than the Vendor of Arms is the Promoter of War; -because the Consumption of these Articles, is the very Ground and Cause of Slavery; – but the Manufacture of Arms is not the cause, but only the consequence of War.[26]

Galton junior was prevented from attending any further business meetings of the Society, but his letter did make the important point that the majority of the population by demanding and consuming the goods produced as a result of slave labour, did contribute in some way to the slave trade. In addition to continuing the family gun business Samuel Galton junior became involved in many other business activities including becoming a partner in a bank. When he died in 1832 his sons inherited £300,000, a sum accumulated from profits made in the gun and banking businesses and from property investments. An interesting connection with the next part of this story is that in 1782 James Watt had suggested to Matthew Boulton that Galton junior who had just joined them as a member of the Lunar Society might be interested in investing in their steam engine project, although this never actually occurred.

Sugar

The Birmingham manufacturing company founded by Matthew Boulton and his partner James Watt made a significant contribution to one industry dependent on the use of African slave labour, when in the 1790s the stationary steam engine invented by Watt and financed by Boulton began to be exported in large numbers to the sugar plantations of the Caribbean.

Most of the men, women and children being carried across the Atlantic in slave ships were destined for the sugar plantations of Barbados, and later to other islands of the West Indies including Jamaica. Sugar cane had been grown for hundreds of years on the Atlantic coast of Brazil and in the mid seventeenth century as demand for sugar grew, Brazilian planters financed by the Dutch East India Company established sugar plantations in West Indian islands such as Barbados. English colonists developed the system of large plantations which depended on a continuous supply of cheap labour. This labour had previously been supplied by indentured white servants sent out from England but as the plantations increased in number and size their owners depended more and more on the African slave trade. The planting, harvesting and processing of sugar cane was extremely labour intensive, the slaves working long hours under horrendous conditions, the only interest of the plantation owners being the size of the profit they could make from the sale of the sugar produced by slaves who they considered as being less than human. It might be presumed that Boulton and Watt's steam engine which mechanised the cane crushing process would have improved the working conditions of the slaves but in fact it made little difference, the increase in production rate only resulting in increased profit for the plantation owners and of course providing huge profits for Boulton and Watt.

Before considering in more detail the financial gains made by Boulton and Watt from their involvement with the sugar plantations it is important to examine the conditions under which the slaves laboured in order that these profits might be achieved. In the planting season gangs of workers dug holes to receive the cane sugar cuttings, using as Williams notes 'Birmingham hoes' rather than spades. It was indeed the metal workers of Birmingham who supplied most of the tools used in the plantations.[27] Large quantities of manure had to be carried in baskets and deposited in the holes containing the young plants. The slaves were under constant surveillance by overseers with whips who did not hesitate to use them on anyone who failed to carry out the tasks assigned to them in the required amount of time. At harvest time gangs of slaves had to cut the thick stalks of sugar cane by hand with sharp, curved knives and then load them into wagons and transport them to the mill for grinding to extract the juice.[28] The efficient operation of the mill was pivotal to the success of the whole plantation and therefore to the profit made by the planter for as Watts writes 'the effective use of the mill is always a key factor in the manufacture of high quality sugar'.[29] In the seventeenth and for most of the eighteenth century the typical mill consisted of three vertical rollers in which the centre roller turned against the two outer ones. Jennifer Tann describes how the 'cane passed between the rolls twice, two slaves standing either side of the rolls, passing cane through first one way and then the other'.[30] This was extremely dangerous work as the exhausted slaves sometimes failed to release their hold on the sugar cane in time and their arm would be drawn into the rollers, the crushed arm then being chopped off with an axe by a supervisor. Dunn quotes Edward Littleton, a late seventeenth-century planter as writing 'if a Mill-feeder be catch't by the finger, his whole body is drawn in and he is squeez'd to pieces'.[31]

The mills used various sources of power depending largely on their location. In Barbados windmills were favoured in the larger plantations but as Tann points out 'a lull in the trade winds during the harvesting season could stop milling with heavy losses'.[32] Water mills were common in Jamaica where there was a plentiful supply of water from mountain streams, but in all locations the most widely used power source for driving the mills was that provided by animals such as cattle, horses, donkeys or mules, or even occasionally human slaves. Satchell points out that for various reasons the use of animals in the mills was highly inefficient. The speed generated in turning the mills was not constant leading to unevenness in wear of the mill rollers and a decrease in efficiency. One set of animals could not be used for prolonged periods, the animals becoming exhausted after a shift of about two hours. Most mills used four teams of livestock each with eight animals and much time was wasted replacing the animals after each shift. In addition to the animals up to eighteen slaves were needed to feed the cane into the mill and collect the juice into copper pans.[33] It is not surprising that most plantation owners were constantly searching for new techniques which would enable them to remain competitive in the sugar market, and from the middle of the eighteenth century news began to reach them of the new steam engines which were being developed in Britain.

It had long been known that the expansion of steam could be used to provide power, but it was only at the beginning of the eighteenth century that the Englishman, Thomas Newcomen, designed a steam engine that was capable of pumping water out of mines, the first engine being installed at a colliery in Staffordshire. The Newcomen engine, however was not highly efficient and used a large amount of fuel, making it unsuitable for powering machines in the rapidly expanding manufacturing industries of the eighteenth century. The person who was to solve this problem was the Scotsman James Watt who had made several improvements to the Newcomen engine when working as an instrument maker at Glasgow University. He introduced a separate condenser into the engine which improved its efficiency and in 1769 he took out a patent for his invention but unfortunately could not find a manufacturer in Glasgow willing to invest in its development. He had heard of Matthew Boulton who had developed a highly successful engineering business known as the Soho Works in Handsworth, Birmingham, and in 1774 he left Scotland to join Boulton, entering into a partnership with him a year later. Boulton was able to manufacture and market Watt's inventions which in the 1780s included a rotary motion and double-acting engine in which the steam acts on both sides of the piston increasing its efficiency.

Watt continued to make improvements to his engine and its efficiency and fuel economy meant that Boulton and Watt received increasing orders from the growing number of industries now becoming dependent on steam power to operate their machinery. Their interest in possible trade with the West Indies was no doubt stimulated by the number of enquiries they received from West Indian plantation owners and slave traders. In 1776 William Pulteney, a wealthy politician who had invested in land in the West Indies and was aware of the need for developments which might increase the efficient running of the sugar mills, had written to Boulton and Watt saying 'I can hardly conceive anything which is more likely to bring you a great return'.[34]

In 1786 and again a year later Lord Penryhn wrote to Boulton and Watt drawing their attention to the need for steam engines in Jamaica.[35] Penryhn was a wealthy merchant and Member of Parliament for Liverpool who owned six sugar plantations in Jamaica and hundreds of African slaves. In a debate on the slave trade in May 1788 Penryhn, who was an anti-abolitionist, was one of only two Members who spoke in support of a continuation of the African slave trade. In 1790 John Dawson, one of Liverpool's leading slave merchants and captain of a slave trading vessel, wrote to Boulton and Watt about the possibility of obtaining an engine for a Trinidadian mill. It was Samuel Galton junior, who knew Matthew Boulton through membership of the Lunar Society in Birmingham, who had suggested to Dawson that he should contact Boulton and Watt about supplying steam engines for the sugar works he was erecting in Trinidad. Dawson explains that 'the want of wind and water the principle on which they are at present work'd, retards the progress so very much, particularly in crop time', and he asks if 'an engine could be invented with a certainty of answering the purpose, the rollers so contriv'd that if possible to have a greater effect in the pressing of the cane than what is at present used'. Dawson adds that the engine should be able to use wood as a fuel as coal would be too expensive.[36]

The first genuine Boulton and Watt engine was exported to the Caribbean in 1803, although less efficient versions of the Newcomen engine had been installed in some plantations before that. Between 1803 and 1825 the firm exported one hundred and nineteen engines and then a further forty eight between 1826 and emancipation in 1833, the majority of these being to Jamaica. This exceeded any other overseas market for British engines and in fact was 'only exceeded in the British domestic market during the same period by engines supplied to the cotton industry'.[37] Tann notes that the demand in the Caribbean was for 'small, cheap, reliable engines' which could substitute for water or wind power when this was inadequate. An eight horse-power Boulton and Watt engine could cost around nine hundred pounds and the cost of transport, erection and housing had to be added to the purchase price. However the fuel cost was low as the engine was able to burn dried cane vegetation and refuse from the milling process.[38] Between 1818 and 1830 the number of engines exported by Boulton and Watt gradually declined partly due to competition from other manufacturers who unlike Boulton and Watt had locally appointed agents with expertise in installing and running the engines. James Watt maintained that their engines were 'made with best materials and by finest workmanship',[39] but the prices they demanded were certainly higher than many smaller planters were willing to pay.

Towards the end of the eighteenth century many people in public life in Britain began to support the anti-slavery movement and spoke out against those industries which made large profits out of partaking in the slave trade. In 1789 Samuel Whitbread, a Member of Parliament and strong supporter of abolition questioned Boulton and Watt over the export of steam engines to the West Indies.[40] Some abolitionists however, believed that steam power might contribute to the abolition of slavery as it would diminish the need for slaves to operate the sugar mills. This did not in fact occur as an efficient steam-powered mill still required four or five slaves and the majority of slaves in a plantation were employed in tasks related to growing and harvesting the sugar cane. After the defeat of a bill to abolish slavery in 1791 some abolitionists started to campaign for a voluntary ban on sugar from the West Indies. Mary Anne Galton, the daughter of Samuel Galton junior wrote of her visits with her father to the palatial houses of West India merchants in Liverpool where she saw 'the table laden with West India produce, in its various forms of fruit and sweetmeats, and saw the black servants looking on at the produce of a land, their native home, which they had left for us, and of which they might not partake, my heart often ached; and it is no wonder that my resolution was confirmed never to taste anything made with sugar . . . '[41] It is possible that she might also have been influenced by her father's view that 'those who use the produce of the labour of slaves' are also promoters of the slave trade. Under her and others influence thousands of people stopped consuming sugar from the West Indies, one Birmingham grocer finding that his sugar sales were cut by 50 percent in four months. Unfortunately these campaigns were unable to influence Parliament to vote for abolition until 1807 when the trade in slaves eventually came to an end.

Little is known about the views of either Matthew Boulton or James Watt on the morality of slavery although both were members of the Lunar Society, many of whose members including Erasmus Darwin, Josiah Wedgwood and Joseph Priestley did campaign against slavery. They shared an interest in scientific subjects and met every month, usually at Soho House, Boulton's home in Handsworth, Birmingham to share opinions and discuss the latest developments in science and technology. There is some evidence that James Watt was a critic of slavery. In October 1791 he wrote to a client informing him that Boulton and Watt would have to suspend the production of an engine he had ordered, due to the crushing of a campaign to claim voting rights for black people in St Domingo now Haiti. He ended the letter with the words 'we heartily pray that the system of slavery so disgraceful to humanity were abolished by prudent though progressive measures'.[42] In a letter to Watt in February 1788, Josiah Wedgwood had written, 'I take it for granted that you and I are on the same side of the question respecting the slave trade. I have joined my brethren here in a petition from the pottery for the abolition of it, as I do not like a half measure in this black business'.[43] Wedgwood's reference to 'you and I' being 'on the same side' might suggest that he was doubtful that Boulton would also be on his side, maybe due to their differing views on the American fight for independence which Wedgwood had wholeheartedly supported. Boulton, however, had been 'unashamedly self-interested', worrying about the threat of American competition.[44] Wedgwood must have guessed that this self-interest would influence Boulton in the anti-slavery debate and indeed in 1783 Boulton 'had been happy to dine with three plantation owners . . . including the notorious Pennant, owner of the largest plantation in Jamaica'.[45] In a letter to Watt, Boulton described Pennant as a 'very amiable man with 10 or 12 thousand pounds a year' who wished to see steam engines replace horses on his plantation'.[46] Despite this Boulton joined with Galton and Priestley to welcome Olaudah Equiano, the anti-slavery campaigner when he came to speak in Birmingham in 1789. As Jenny Uglow observes 'Boulton was not above slippery thinking'.[47]

Matthew Boulton died in 1809 and his son Matthew Robinson Boulton took over the running of the firm in partnership with James Watt's son. The firm continued to export engines to Jamaica but sales gradually declined due to increased competition and the growing importance of Cuba in the production and export of sugar. The decline in overseas sales was more than compensated for by the supply of steam engines to the rapidly expanding cotton industry in Lancashire, an expansion which was a direct result of the huge increase in cotton exported from the plantations in the southern states of America.

Cotton

For the story of cotton it is necessary to move from Birmingham in the West Midlands of England to Alabama and the land on which Birmingham, the capital of that state now stands, land on which for much of the nineteenth century African slaves laboured in the cotton plantations and when slavery officially ended continued to labour in the formation of the new industrial city.

Cotton had been cultivated by Native Americans and was grown by English colonists in Virginia from the early seventeenth century. However for most of the eighteenth century the main crops grown in the South were tobacco in Virginia and rice in South Carolina and Georgia. The problem with large scale cotton production was the difficulty of separating the cotton fibres from the seeds but in 1793 a young inventor from Georgia called Eli Whitney solved the problem with his invention of the cotton gin. The gin, short for engine, consisted of a wooden cylinder embedded with a series of spikes which caught the cotton fibres as they were fed into the machine and pulled them through a comb-like grid. The cotton fibres could pass through the spaces in the grid which were too fine to allow the seeds to pass through. Before the introduction of the cotton gin the separation of the cotton fibres from the seeds had been an extremely labour intensive business, taking about ten hours for a single slave to separate a pound of fibre from the seeds. Using a cotton gin, two or three slaves could produce about fifty pounds of cotton in a day.[48] The result of this huge increase in productivity meant that cotton became the most important American export for most of the nineteenth century and although the use of the cotton gin meant that fewer slaves were required in processing the cotton, it still needed to be picked by hand resulting in an increased demand for slave labour on the plantations.

Before the Trans-Atlantic slave trade was abolished in 1807, African slaves had been transported to mainland America but in far smaller numbers than those taken to labour in the sugar plantations of the Caribbean. There is a record of a slave ship arriving in Mobile on the south coast of Alabama in 1721 with '120 surviving slaves',[49] but most slaves would have been taken to the East coast states of Virginia and North Carolina to work in the tobacco plantations and to South Carolina and Georgia to work in the rice fields. For most of the eighteenth century there had been a movement of colonists westward from these coastal states in search of trading opportunities with the Native American population and also of new land in which to settle. In the early years of the nineteenth century this movement rapidly increased, partly due to the expansion of the cotton industry after the introduction of the cotton gin, but also due to the increased availability of land after the gradual removal of Native American tribes, culminating in the passing of the Indian Removal Act of 1830.

Many of the Muskogee or Creek Indians sided with the British in 1812 when the Americans declared war on the British. They believed that the British would help them to push the Americans out of the land that was rightly theirs, and the Southern Creeks also relied on trade with the white settlers. However one group of young Creek braves who became known as the Red Sticks were determined to fight for their land and in 1813 when American frontiersmen had attacked them in a fierce battle they stormed the garrison at Fort Mims killing many of the militia, settlers and Creek Indians loyal to the Americans. Andrew Jackson, colonel of the Tennessee militia, was ordered to crush the rebel Indians and was supported by Cherokee Indians from north Georgia and the Carolinas who 'believed that in the Red Sticks they were fighting renegade outlaws and that Jackson cherished their loyalty and would reward them well'.[50] In March, 1814 Jackson with his army of Tennessee volunteers and Cherokee Indians encountered the Upper Creek warriors or Red Sticks at a bend of the Tallapoosa River where the Red Sticks had their village of Tohopeka, a position just seventy miles south-east of where the city of Birmingham now stands. Jackson supported by Cherokee and Lower Creek warriors crossed the river and after a fierce battle which became known as the Battle of Horseshoe Bend the Red Sticks leader, Red Eagle surrendered to Jackson. Only 200 of the 1,000 Red Sticks who took part in the battle survived, whereas Jackson only lost 49 men. This defeat resulted in the Treaty of Fort Jackson in which 23 million acres of Indian land was ceded to the United States, and in 1819 Alabama itself was declared to be one of these states. Jackson became President of the United States in 1828 and two years later signed the Indian Removal Bill which forced the Native Americans in Alabama to move West, a journey which became known as 'The Trail of Tears'.

White land speculators and farmers moved in large numbers into the Indian lands of Alabama where a warm, humid, relatively frost-free climate provided the ideal conditions for cotton cultivation. Many of these settlers were accompanied by their African slaves but after the cessation of the Trans-Atlantic slave trade, the increasing demand for slave labourers on the cotton plantations had to be met by a natural increase in the slave population. However, as Thomas makes clear 'the United States Slave Trade Act of 1807 only prohibited the international slave trade. It condemned neither the internal nor the coastal traffic. There was no limit to the number of slaves who could be so traded, nor any regulations as to the way they should be carried'.[51] Kolchin adds that 'during the half century preceding the Civil War, slave owners moved hundreds of thousands of "surplus" slaves west, mostly from non-cotton-producing to cotton-producing states'.[52] This forced relocation resulted in the break-up of families, most of those being sold to the west being young men and women. This can partly be accounted for by the need for strong, fit workers, but also by the hope that these men and women would marry and produce the next generation of cotton plantation labourers.

Many of the new planters entering Alabama made their way to the central Black Belt region which contained the richest and most fertile soil. However, as the demand for cotton increased planters moved further north to Tuscaloosa, the Appalachian valleys region and to the area where the city of Birmingham now stands. A closer look at the lives of some of the plantation owners who settled on land between present day Birmingham and the nearby city of Bessemer, gives some indication of the large profits made from the sale of cotton produced by slave labour and how these profits made a significant contribution to the development of the city of Birmingham after the Civil War.

Williamson Hawkins was born in South Carolina in 1790 and as an adventurous young man joined Jackson's Tennessee Volunteers in the war of 1812. In 1815 he decided to move West with his wife and family into land vacated by the Upper Creek Indians, and settled in Jonesboro, now in the South West of the Birmingham Metropolitan area. This was one of the first pioneer settlements and was named after the first settler John Jones who had arrived in 1813. Hawkins started to cultivate and sell cotton and with the profits was able to buy more land and build a large family house. Increasing numbers of slaves were needed to work on his plantation and as Hawkins had not brought his own slaves into Alabama it was necessary to purchase slaves from traders who bought surplus slaves from slave owners in states to the east and the north of Alabama. Kolchin notes that 'between 1828 and 1836, partners Isaac Franklin and John Armfield, headquartered in Alexandria, Virginia, purchased and resold more than one thousand slaves annually'.[53] Hawkins would probably have obtained his slaves from the large slave market in Montgomery, about eighty miles to the south, from where they would be transported in wagons or even marched in chained coffles. By 1860 Hawkins owned

150 slaves and produced one hundred bales of cotton a year from his 3,000-acre plantation. His assets of 159,975 dollars made him the richest man in the county and his plantation continued to operate until the end of the Civil War. In 1865 Union soldiers entered and encamped in the plantation and Hawkins suffered a considerable reduction in the value of his assets. Fortunately the land on which the plantation was situated contained valuable limestone, iron ore and coal deposits and after the war it was purchased by the Thomas Iron Company of Pennsylvania who later developed the Thomas Furnaces complex on the land. By the end of the century this was the largest iron and steel company in the Birmingham District.[54]

Several other planters settled in the Jones Valley, notably Isaac Sadler who, between 1830 and 1860 established a large 2,800-acre plantation on land which had been taken from the Creek Nation at the Treaty of Fort Jackson in 1814. The Sadler Plantation House was spared by the Union troops during their advance through Alabama and is now one of the main attractions on the tourist route in the Birmingham area. Another planter, Thomas McAdory, developed a 2,000 acre cotton plantation near Bessemer and one of his descendants, Robert McAdory, became the first mayor of the City of Bessemer in 1887.

Fourteen miles to the north of the Hawkins plantation in the Elyton district, which is now part of the modern city of Birmingham, another plantation was established by William Mudd whose family came from Kentucky but had moved to Alabama when William was a child. Mudd was a lawyer and a circuit judge and later became a business man and member of the Elyton Land Company which helped to found the city of Birmingham in 1871. In 1842 he bought what was then a small property and proceeded to establish a five-hundred acre estate together with a large Greek Revival style mansion. Little reference is made to the nature of the estate but it is obviously no coincidence that it is situated on Cotton Avenue and that the house was built 'with the help of his slaves'. Some indication of Mudd's wealth is that in 1861 his investment in the Alabama Arms Manufacturing Company, together with additional investment from the Confederate Government, enabled it to construct the Oxmoor iron furnaces which supplied iron needed for arms manufacture in the Civil War. The furnace was destroyed by Union soldiers in 1865, the same year in which Hawkins's estate was commandeered to be used as temporary headquarters for the advancing Union soldiers. After the war Mudd became a major share holder in the Elyton Land Company, many of his fellow shareholders also being cotton plantation owners. The company bought up land and then sold land lots to developers involved in the construction of the new city. After Mudd died in 1884 the house passed through various owners, one of whom, Robert Munger, a wealthy cotton gin manufacturer, gave it the name of 'Arlington', the name of Robert E Lee's estate in Virginia. In the 1950s the City of Birmingham bought the house and it was restored and furnished by the Arlington Historical Association. It is now a major tourist attraction and publicity material describes in detail the 'eight-room mansion in the Greek Revival style . . . the rooms furnished with antiques from the Antebellum period, many of them original to the house . . . the notable collection of 19th century decorative arts and paintings' and of course 'the restored tea-room'.[55] No mention is made of the fact that this house was at the centre of a cotton plantation in which black slaves laboured to produce the cotton which would provide Mudd with much of his wealth. It is true that compared with many others this was a fairly small estate and there is no evidence that Mudd's slaves were treated badly but it does appear to be an anomaly that this aspect of the estate's history is ignored. The Arlington Director, Stephen Moode, does make a passing reference to this history when he says in an interview, 'despite the home's antebellum heritage, despite the fact that Judge Mudd had slaves, despite the picture of Confederate General Robert E. Lee on the wall in the main house – many of the site's loyal patrons are African-Americans'.[56]

James Oakes in his study of American slaveholders comments on their obsession with the pursuit of wealth and quotes a British traveller as saying 'this passion for the acquisition of money is much stronger and more universal in this country than in any under the sun, at least that I have visited'.[57] Another commentator in 1835 says 'to sell cotton in order to buy negroes -to make more cotton to buy more negroes, 'ad infinitum,' is the aim and direct tendency of all the operations of the thorough-going cotton planter'.[58] Oakes adds 'land and slaves became the two great vehicles through which slaveholders realised their ambitions of fortune',[59] and at the start of the Civil War in 1861 slaves made up forty five percent of the population of Alabama. At large slave auctions in Montgomery slaves could be bought for a few hundred dollars but young strong men capable of working long hours in the fields could fetch more than a thousand dollars. On the whole the slaves received better treatment in the Southern States than had been meted out to those in the Caribbean before the abolition of the Trans-Atlantic slave trade, but this was purely due to financial considerations, for if slaves could not be replaced from overseas they had to be fit and healthy enough to reproduce their numbers internally. On the larger plantations slaves worked in large groups called gangs under the supervision of white overseers and were responsible for ploughing the land, planting, harvesting and weeding. They worked in the fields from sunrise to sunset and at harvest time often worked for fourteen or more hours a day. Some of the women worked as domestic servants responsible for cooking, cleaning and sometimes acting as nursemaids for the young children of the planter family. Slaves were often beaten if they worked too slowly or did not meet the exact requirements of their overseers, and of course female slaves were often sexually abused or raped by their white masters.

In the 1930s a large project was initiated by the Works Progress Administration, an agency designed by the Roosevelt administration to provide jobs for the unemployed during the Great Depression.[60] This project, called the Federal Writers' Project, aimed to interview men and women who had been slaves on Southern plantations prior to the Civil War and record their recollections. The accuracy of these 'Slave Narratives' has been questioned by some historians who suggest that the age and failing memories of the interviewees and the fact that most interviewers were white and untrained might have resulted in a too positive view of the past. Most of those interviewed in Birmingham were suffering from the hardships of the Depression and some might have had a somewhat rosy view of a life in which they had sufficient food and somewhere to live even though that was a life without freedom. Despite this, comments made by many of those interviewed throw light on the extent to which slaves were controlled and abused by their masters in their desire to acquire wealth from the trade in cotton. Eighty-nine year-old Walter Calloway, living on the southside of Birmingham explains how he was born in Richmond,

Virginia and how when he was ten years old he was taken from his home with his mother and brother and sold in Montgomery, Alabama to a plantation owner. His job was to plough the fields and he describes how he was regularly whipped by one of the overseers who made an older black boy take part in the whipping using a 'rawhide lash'. This boy whipped a black girl about thirteen years old 'so hard she nearly died' and ever afterwards 'had spells of fits'. Fortunately the master discovered what had happened and dismissed the overseer.[61]

Simon Phillips, a ninety year-old ex-slave, was the Birmingham organizer of the union of ex-slaves and president of the society which was 'composed of 1,500 Negroes scattered throughout Alabama'. He belonged to a planter in Greensboro, Alabama and seemed happy enough with his occupation as a house man. He explains the procedure for obtaining a wife, how the slave would have to go to his master and tell him that there was a girl on a neighbouring plantation who he would like for a wife. The master would go to the neighbouring planter and offer to buy the girl but she would have to be 'strong and healthy' and often her owner would refuse to sell her. Phillips comments how the slaves were 'bought mostly like horses'. He describes how 'sometimes slaves were parted from their families, because when one planter bought a Negro from another planter, he did not necessarily buy his wife or children, or husband, as the case might be. The slaves were advertised around and put on a block to stand while they were auctioned'.[62]

Most of the ill treatment meted out to plantation slaves came from the overseers rather than the planters who were aware of the cost of replacing slaves injured or even killed by over-zealous subordinates. In 1852 the state legislature passed the Alabama slave code which, as Kolchin points out, 'consisted of provisions designed to ensure the slaves' subordination' but 'also contained measures setting guidelines for their treatment and limits to their mistreatment'.[63] Someone killing a slave 'through excessive punishment' would be found guilty of murder, but because slaves were not allowed to testify against whites it was difficult to obtain sufficient evidence for a prosecution. In addition to wielding extreme power over their slave workers, most plantation owners occupied positions of power in local and state government, about three quarters of state legislators in Alabama being slave holders, William Mudd, the Elyton lawyer, circuit judge, slave owner, and later land speculator being an example.

From 1820 to 1860 cotton production expanded rapidly throughout Alabama, bales of cotton being taken by river to the ports of Mobile, Appalachicola and New Orleans and then shipped to New England, Europe and Britain. In the 1830s the United States was producing the majority of the world's cotton and by the outbreak of the Civil War the value of cotton exports exceeded that of all other exports combined, 88 per cent of the total cotton crop being exported to Britain. Abolitionists in Britain who had welcomed the end of the trade in slave grown sugar must have been disheartened by the fact 'that the crop's successor as the prime import was cotton . . . another slave-made product'.[64]

The increase in demand for cotton in Britain was a direct result of the rapid expansion in the number of cotton mills following James Watt's invention of the rotative steam engine in 1781. Earlier cotton mills had been powered by water wheels and in fact a textile worker from England who had emigrated to America assisted with the design of the first water powered mill in New England. The new steam powered mills in England were concentrated in Lancashire, in the small mill towns around Manchester, and by 1860 nearly three thousand mills were operating in this area. Manchester was linked to the port of Liverpool by the Bridgewater Canal which was constructed in 1772 and enabled imported raw cotton to be transported directly to the cotton mills and cotton goods to be exported. By 1779 Manchester was exporting £300,000 worth of cotton goods annually, a third of which was taken to Africa and traded in exchange for slaves, most of the remainder being traded in the West Indies and in North America. Eighty year later on the eve of the Civil War, the total value of cotton goods exported through Liverpool was thirty two million pounds and accounted for nearly half of all exports. The wealth generated in Britain by the sale of cotton goods and the even greater wealth generated in the United States by the export of raw cotton was dependent on a continuing supply of free slave labour. Sven Beckert quotes Herman Merivale, a 'British colonial bureaucrat' as saying that Manchester's and Liverpool's 'opulence is as really owing to the toil and suffering of the negro, as if his hands had excavated their docks and fabricated their steam-engines'.[65] In the 1850s a certain disquiet began to arise on both sides of the Atlantic about this connection between the large profits obtained from the cotton industry and its reliance on an unpaid, slave workforce who could at any time rise up against its owners. In the words of Sven Beckert, 'American slavery had begun to threaten the very prosperity it produced, as the distinctive political economy of the cotton South collided with the incipient political economy of free labor and domestic industrialization of the North . . . ample supplies of fertile land and bonded labor had made the South into Lancashire's plantation, but by 1860 large numbers of Americans . . . protested such semicolonial dependence'.[66] Many southern planters believed that Britain would intervene in their dispute with the North in order to protect their profitable cotton industry, but despite the economic loss, Britain was not prepared to continue supporting a system of slave labour which they had legislated against thirty years previously. As a result the Confederate government banned all cotton exports from the South and ports were blockaded, thousands of bales of cotton being burned as they piled up on the docks. The blockade obviously affected the Lancashire cotton mills but not as drastically as might have been expected as the larger mills had accumulated large stockpiles of cotton bales, and as Dattel makes clear 'England did manage to import considerable cotton from India during the war, but afterward the American South resumed its dominant position as the leading exporter of cotton until the 1930s'.[67] How the wealthy Southern planters managed to survive defeat in the Civil War resuming cotton production and investing in industrial development will be examined in later chapters. The liberated slaves were not so fortunate, encountering hostility from most of the white Southern population who considered black servitude to be the natural state of mankind. It was in the development of the new city of Birmingham that much of this hostility became evident.

2

Abolition

The first third of the nineteenth century saw a rapid expansion of plantation slavery in the Southern states of America due to the westward migration of cotton planters into territory previously occupied by Native Americans, During the same period in Britain the movement against slavery was gaining increasing support, which despite the defeat of an anti-slavery bill in 1791, eventually resulted in the bill to abolish the Trans-Atlantic slave trade in 1807. It would however be another twenty six years before slavery in the British Territories was finally abolished by an Act of Parliament. In the United States it would take a further thirty two years, a lengthy war and the deaths of thousands before the Thirteenth Amendment to the Constitution was passed by Congress in January 1865 and slavery was officially barred anywhere in the United States. Despite these victories for the abolitionists the people of both the West Indies and the Southern States of America did not escape from the legacy of slavery for many years, and in some respects are still suffering from the failed attempts to reconstruct their societies.

In this chapter I examine the important but often overlooked role played by abolitionists in Birmingham, England and in the Southern States of America where arguments based on moral and economic considerations were used by both sides in the debate. Events occurring after abolition in the West Indies and the Southern States reveal the extent to which the governments of Britain and the United States failed to fully realise their responsibilities in atoning for more than two hundred years of black African slavery.

The Birmingham Abolitionists

In 1870, J.A. Langford, a Birmingham newspaper editor, used back copies of the newspaper, 'Aris's Gazette', to build up a chronicle of events occurring during its first one hundred years. These were published in a book entitled *A Century of Birmingham Life: 1741–1841*, which includes many references to the activities of abolitionists in Birmingham. Langford states that 'Every Birmingham man will rejoice to learn that this town took an active part in the noblest philanthropic labour of the age – the Abolition of the Slave Trade'.[1] He maintains that the contribution made by these Birmingham abolitionists was as great as that made by the more familiar national campaigners such as Granville Sharp, Thomas Clarkson and William Wilberforce. Most of these Birmingham anti-slavery campaigners were Non-conformists – Quakers, Unitarians and Baptists, and as such were forbidden from standing for Parliament. They produced anti-slavery literature, organised meetings, gave speeches, delivered petitions and formed societies, including the first Ladies' Anti-Slavery Society. Many of these abolitionists were members of the Lunar Society although not all members were enthusiastic supporters of the abolitionist cause. Wealthy industrialists like Matthew Boulton were only too aware of the extent to which their wealth was dependent on the use of slave labour in the sugar plantations of the West Indies. In 1789 some Birmingham manufacturers actually signed a petition to Parliament against abolition, declaring that the town was dependent on the African slave trade and without the money from that trade the local economy would collapse.[2]

Joseph Priestley, perhaps best known for the discovery of oxygen, moved to Birmingham in 1780 to take up the position of minister at the Unitarian Meeting House and was welcomed into the Lunar Society whose members shared his wide range of interests which included science, theology, philosophy and politics. In 1788 he published his *Sermon on the Slave Trade* which he had delivered to 'a society of Protestant Dissenters, at the New Meeting in Birmingham'.[3] Near the beginning of his sermon Priestley states that 'it must give every good man an unspeakable pleasure to see the general interest that is now taken in behalf of the Negro slaves', and it soon becomes clear that he sees Christianity as being the main influence in the fight for equal rights for all men. He sees a time when 'all Christian masters will respect and love their servants . . . considering them as *brothers* and *equals*', and believes that these 'noble and elevating sentiments' are 'peculiar to believers in revealed religion'. Priestly takes things further by saying that however well slaves might be treated by their masters they are still slaves 'subject to the wills . . . of others', and should be protected by law.

A large part of the sermon is taken up by a detailed description of the African slave trade, and the 'numberless miseries' suffered by the African Negroes whose 'oppressors are our countrymen'. He reminds his congregation of their complicity in the trade by their demand for West Indian sugar and other commodities and how in satisfying this demand 'perhaps half a million of persons are annually destroyed' either in the plantations or as a result of the terrible conditions on the slave ships. He admits that 'hitherto the nation in general has been but little apprized of the enormity and extent of this evil, and those who have been interested in the continuance and extension of it have likewise been interested to conceal the horrid circumstances attending it'. He believes that 'now that the eyes of the nation in general' have been opened to this evil the ensuing national guilt will be sufficient to put an end to this iniquity. He hopes that 'this guilt will lie the heaviest . . . upon ministers of state, and all those who have the greatest influence in public measures', but the guilt will be shared by all those who do not exert whatever influence they may have to put an end to the evil of slavery.

Priestley recommends to his congregation that they should join with those from other parts of the country in sending a petition to the present session of parliament demanding an end to the slave trade. The year before delivering his sermon Priestley had met Thomas Clarkson, who together with Granville Sharp, Josiah Wedgwood and others had formed the London Committee for the Abolition of the Slave Trade. Clarkson travelled throughout the country, organising anti-slavery committees and offering advice to local activists. On his visit to Birmingham in 1787 he had encouraged Priestley to start an anti-slavery petition for as Priestley notes in his sermon, 'a general application from all parts of the country, and especially from towns of note like this, will tend to promote it, and almost ensure its success'. Altogether more than one hundred petitions were presented to the House of Commons in 1788 but unfortunately on this occasion opposition from Members of Parliament who had a financial interest in the continuation of the slave trade meant that no action was taken.

Priestley was familiar with the writings of Adam Smith whose *The Wealth of Nations* had been published in 1776, twelve years before Priestley delivered his sermon on slavery. Unlike Priestley, Smith's arguments for the abolition of slavery were based on economic rather than humanitarian considerations but it is clear that Priestley also understood the importance of economic arguments if slavery was to be abolished. He says 'it is demonstrable that we may have sugar, and every other commodity that we now raise by means of slaves, even cheaper without slaves', for it is found that when labourers are paid wages they 'labour so much more cheerfully, and do so much more work, when freemen than when slaves'.[4]

Barry Weingast in writing about Adam Smith's Theory of Slavery, points out that the 'net product under freedom is twelve times larger than under slavery', and therefore questions have to be asked as to why slavery persists and why slaves are not freed by the slave owning elites.[5] Smith suggested two answers to these questions, the first being the desire elites possess to dominate others and the second, which Smith favoured, being the fact that freeing slaves would deprive slaveholders of their property. They would demand compensation for this loss and as the legal processes involved would be lengthy they could not be certain that they would benefit financially. Despite this fear Smith emphasises the immediate economic gain to be made when slave labour is replaced by a system of tenant farmers. The slave labours 'entirely for his master' and there is no incentive to work harder or take extra trouble in cultivating the land. The free tenant, however, pays rent to his master and can keep any profit for himself, providing a greater incentive to cultivate and improve the land.[6]

Despite the existence of both humanitarian and economic reasons for the abolition of slavery, Priestley realised that it might take a long time for a change to occur in what was accepted by many to be a natural state of affairs. He even suggested that 'the immediate emancipation of all slaves would be an improper, because in fact no humane measure. Those who have been long slaves would not know how to make a proper use of freedom'. However he suggests that 'if a stop was put to the further importation of slaves, it would immediately become the interest of the masters to make the most of their present stock, and consequently to treat their slaves with more humanity'.[7] It is important to realise that most abolitionists of the time were not campaigning for an end to slave ownership but rather for an end to the trade in slaves. Michael Jordan points out that 'the London Committee for the Abolition of the Slave Trade was not about freeing slaves' and that 'the slave trade and slave emancipation were wholly discrete issues'.[8] The Committee were also aware that most members of the public saw slavery as a normal part of life and considered that 'the use of slaves on the sugar plantations was right and proper both economically and morally'.[9] There was however a growing feeling that the trade in slaves from Africa was ceasing to be economically advantageous and therefore petitioning for an end to the trade was more likely to meet with success than total abolition.

Priestley's hope that all Christian masters would come to consider their Negro slaves as 'brothers and equals' rather than 'a species of men greatly inferior to themselves', would take many years to be fulfilled, and very few of his fellow Christians at the time would have agreed with his view that 'were Europeans treated in the same manner for a sufficient length of time, it is demonstrable that the most intelligent of them all would be no better. Those who see Negroes in their native country, or in circumstances of better treatment among ourselves, are satisfied that they are by no means inferior to Europeans in point of understanding'.[10] It is worth noting that seventy years after Priestley's sermon, Abraham Lincoln, speaking in the Lincoln-Douglas debates of 1858, was not ready to acknowledge the existence of complete equality between 'white and black races'. He says,

> There is a physical difference between the two which in my judgement, will probably forbid their ever living together upon the footing of perfect equality; and inasmuch as it becomes a necessity that there must be a difference I, as well as Judge Douglas, am in favour of the race to which I belong having the superior position.[11]

One other member of the Lunar Society who travelled frequently from his home in Lichfield to attend meetings of the society at

Matthew Boulton's home in Handsworth, Birmingham, was Erasmus Darwin, a medical practitioner, poet, botanist, philosopher, religious sceptic and supporter of the French Revolution. He also proposed a theory of evolution by natural selection long before his more famous grandson, Charles, wrote *The Origin of Species*. He strongly believed that industrial progress would improve the lot of mankind and he condemned slavery, supporting fellow anti-slavery campaigners in Birmingham. He considered that just as progress in science and technology has occurred in response to man's changing needs so animals and plants have evolved from simpler past forms, gradually acquiring new structures and functions which enable them to survive in changing environments. In 1791 Darwin published *The Botanic Garden* which consisted of two lengthy poems in which he put forward his ideas on scientific progress, evolution and revolutionary politics. Both poems include sections in which Darwin criticises the practice of slavery. In *The Economy of Vegetation* he writes,

> Hear, Oh Britannia! Potent Queen of isles,
> On whom fair Art, and meek Religion smiles,
> Now Afric's coasts thy craftier sons invade,
> And Theft and Murder take the garb of Trade!
> — The Slave, in chains, on supplicating knee,
> Spreads his wide arms, and lifts his eyes to Thee;
> With hunger pale, with wounds and toil oppress'd,
> 'Are we not Brethren?' sorrow choaks the rest;
> — Air! Bear to heaven upon thy azure flood
> Their innocent cries! — Earth! Cover not their blood![12]

In *The Loves of the Plants* he again appeals to those who rule Britain to put an end to the suffering of the African slaves,

> E'en now, e'en now, on yonder Western shores
> Weeps pale Despair, and writhing Anguish roars:
> E'en now in Afric's groves with hideous yell
> Fierce Slavery stalks, and slips the dogs of hell;
> From vale to vale the gathering cries rebound,
> And sable nations tremble at the sound!
> — Ye bands of Senators! Whose suffrage sways

Britannia's realms, whom either Ind obeys;
Who right the injured and reward the brave,
Stretch your strong arm, for ye have power to save! . . .
Hear him, ye Senates! hear this truth sublime,
"He, who allows oppression, shares the crime."[13]

Unlike Priestley, Darwin does not see Christianity as being the main driving force in the fight against slavery and as Patricia Fara, the biographer of Darwin points out he actually 'questioned the Christian concept of a beneficent God, concluding that evil arises as a consequence of the struggle for existence'.[14] His argument that caring for the wellbeing and happiness of others is essential for the survival of the human race is very much in keeping with humanist thought. Few members of the established Church of England were active in the anti-slavery movement, Thomas Clarkson being a notable exception, and indeed the Society for the Propagation of the Gospel which was the missionary arm of the Church of England actually owned sugar plantations in the West Indies. Hochschild notes how on noticing the high death rate on one of the plantations in 1760, the Archbishop of Canterbury wrote 'I have long wondered and lamented that the Negroes in our plantations decrease, and new Supplies become necessary continually. Surely this proceeds from some Defect, both of Humanity, and even of good policy. But we must take things as they are at present'.[15] Unfortunately this attitude, arising from a reluctance to challenge the prevailing position on slavery was adopted by many who actually had sympathy with the abolitionist cause.

The extract from Darwin's poem *The Economy of Vegetation* quoted above refers to 'the Slave in chains, on supplicating knee', a direct reference to an image produced by Darwin's friend and fellow member of the Lunar Society, Josiah Wedgwood, an industrialist and potter who shared Darwin's interest in science and the arts. Like Joseph Priestley he was a committed member of the Unitarian church and was also a friend of Thomas Clarkson who had invited him to join the London Committee for the Abolition of the Slave Trade. Wedgwood's skills at advertising and marketing prompted him to suggest to Clarkson that an emblem already used by the society should be attached to leaflets and pamphlets they produced. This image of a kneeling slave in chains with hands lifted up to heaven surrounded by the words 'Am I not a man and a brother?' became more widely known when designers in Wedgwood's factory produced a porcelain cameo of the emblem. Thousands of these were produced and distributed at Wedgwood's expense and became fashionable accessories, worn as brooches and hair pieces. Wedgwood also sent hundreds of the cameos to Benjamin Franklin, writer, scientist, inventor and politician who was a prominent abolitionist in America and had visited Wedgwood, Darwin and other members of the Lunar Society in Birmingham during his long stay in Britain.

Despite increasing popular support for the abolition of the slave trade, petitions such as those raised by the people of Birmingham continued to be ignored by Parliament and in April 1791 an Abolitionist bill was defeated in the House of Commons even though the London Committee had enlisted the support of a few parliamentarians, notably William Wilberforce who considered it his duty as a devout Christian to support the abolitionist cause. Realising that lobbying and petitioning were having little effect large numbers of abolitionists decided to put economic pressure on the government by campaigning for a sugar boycott which, as described in the previous chapter met with considerable success in towns like Birmingham where women such as Mary Anne Galton played an important role in the campaign. Wilberforce however was 'wary of anything that smacked of stirring up popular feeling',[16] at a time when a vast popular revolution was taking place across the Channel in France. Members of the London Committee were accused of being in sympathy with the republican revolutionaries and of course many abolitionists such as the Birmingham members of the Lunar Society did support the aims of the revolution in France. Foremost among these was Joseph Priestley who was to suffer personally and financially because of his beliefs and outspoken views. In July 1791 he arranged to have a dinner with his friends to celebrate the anniversary of the storming of the Bastille on July 14, 1789. Being warned that there might be violence from protesting rioters Priestley was persuaded not to attend the celebration but other attendees were attacked and Priestley's New Meeting House was set alight and destroyed. The rioters made their way to Priestley's house in Sparkbrook, he and his wife just managing to escape before the house was set alight destroying all their belongings including Priestley's laboratory and scientific equipment. Two more churches and several houses were destroyed but the authorities took no immediate action the suggestion being that the local magistrates and even the Anglican clergy had encouraged and supported the riot. Priestley had many followers in Birmingham but there were also many who supported the established church and the monarchy and were afraid of revolution. George III himself commented, 'I cannot but feel pleased that Priestley is the sufferer for the doctrines he and his party have instilled, and that the people see them in their true light'.[17] Priestley escaped with his family to London and became a Minister in Hackney but after declaration of war with France in 1793 and the arrest of many of those suspected of supporting the French revolution he left with his family for America in 1794 and spent the rest of his life in Pennsylvania.

The connection between radical politics and anti-slavery campaigners meant that for the next decade very little progress was made in Parliament towards the abolition of the slave trade. In April 1792 an abolition bill was presented to Parliament demanding immediate cessation of the African slave trade but defenders of the trade demanded that the word 'gradually' should be inserted into the bill. The amended bill was passed by 230 votes to 85 and 1796 was agreed upon as the cut-off point. However, in the words of Michael Jordan '1796 would come and go without change, when fears of social upheaval grew on the home front along with concerns about events unfolding across the English Channel'.[18] Repeated attempts were made to reintroduce an abolition bill over the next ten years but without success and even the London Committee seemed to lose enthusiasm for the cause. At last in 1807 Lord Howick presented a bill to Parliament using mainly economic arguments to persuade the members to vote for abolition of the trade. He argued that little profit was now made out of the trade and that in most parts of the West Indies the population of slaves was increasing without the need for further importation. The bill to abolish the slave trade was finally passed on 23 March 1807. It would be another twenty six years before the bill to abolish slavery was passed, and this time it was not the members of the London Committee who dominated the campaign but 'local campaigners in the newly industrialised Midlands and North'.[19] It was now time for a new generation of Birmingham abolitionists to take over from Priestley, Darwin and Wedgwood in the fight for emancipation.

Although the Act of 1807 was welcomed by those who had fought for abolition of the slave trade it soon became clear that actual enforcement of the Act was not going to be easy with many clandestine trading operations being carried out in the years after the Act was passed. The wording of the Act also allowed for Africans to be taken to serve as soldiers or seamen or to work as indentured apprentices which meant that they were not paid and were subject to often lengthy contracts. Slaves were also imported to Jamaica from Cuba or the Spanish mainland despite the fact that many sugar plantations had been abandoned due to decline in the West Indian sugar industry. Some of those who had campaigned for abolition travelled to the West Indies and returned with shocking accounts of the continuing ill treatment of African slaves. Eventually in 1823, some of those who had been involved with the original London Committee for the Abolition of the Slave Trade, including Thomas Clarkson, formed a new Anti-Slavery Society [20] which provided the stimulus for similar societies to be formed in other parts of the country, most notably in Birmingham.

Many of these societies were organised and run by women and the first and undoubtedly most successful of these was the Birmingham Ladies' Negro's Friend Society for the Relief of Negro Slaves which later became known as the Female Society for Birmingham. Women's groups in Birmingham had been very active in campaigning for the boycott of slave produced sugar and some of the daughters of Lunar Society members such as Sarah Wedgwood and Mary Ann Galton became active members of the new abolition society. The founder of the society, Lucy Townsend, the wife of an Anglican clergyman from West Bromwich, had met Thomas Clarkson on one of his visits to Birmingham and wrote to him asking for advice on the setting up of a women's abolitionists group. He sent her information and pamphlets from his own society and also suggested that she contact Samuel Lloyd, the Quaker campaigner who had been involved in setting up the men's Birmingham Anti-Slavery Society.[21] It was actually Lloyd's wife Mary who worked with Townsend in setting up the women's society and became joint secretary. Clare Midgley notes that 'The Female Society for Birmingham was the first, the largest, the most influential and the longest lasting of the associations' and 'acted more like a *national* than a local society, actively promoting the foundation of local women's societies throughout England, and in Wales and Ireland, and supplying them with information and advice'.[22]

Not all male abolitionists were supportive of the new active role played by women in the fight against slavery and foremost amongst these were evangelical Anglicans like William Wilberforce. In a letter in 1826 he writes,

> I own I cannot relish the plan. All private exertions for such an object become their character, but for ladies to meet, to publish, to go from house to house stirring up petitions – these appear to me proceedings unsuited to the female character as delineated in Scripture. I fear its tendency would be to mix them in all the multiform warfare of political life.[23]

The petitioning of Parliament and the signing of petitions was considered to be an exclusively male prerogative, but in July 1825 a petition for gradual abolition, organised by some members of the Birmingham Ladies Society and signed by two thousand women from Birmingham was presented to the House of Commons. However, petitioning was not supported by all women's groups and it was not until 1833 that a national female petition was presented to Parliament. The support of local Parliamentary candidates was obviously important for the successful passing of the Emancipation Act, but as Midgley points out 'it can be seen that petitioning by women contributed to creating a climate of public opinion in favour of emancipation' and 'the efforts of the Female Society for Birmingham 'were particularly important in establishing a network of women's anti-slavery associations.[24]

The men's Birmingham Anti-Slavery Society which had been set up by Samuel Lloyd in 1823 had become largely inactive but in 1826 was refounded with Charles Lloyd as Chairman and Joseph Sturge as Secretary. The inaugural meeting on 29 November 1826 'for the purpose of forming an Association in Birmingham and its Vicinity for Promoting the Abolition of Slavery', passed various resolutions. The overall purpose of the society was for 'meliorating the conditions of the slaves in the British colonies and ultimately effecting the total and entire Abolition of Slavery and the Slave Trade'. To achieve this aim the association was to 'diffuse information on the evils of slavery and condition of slaves in our colonies'. Further resolutions aimed to 'promote petitions to Parliament' and 'aid the efforts of the London Society'.[25] Initially meetings were held monthly but attendance was usually low and at a special meeting on 21 May 1827 a request was made to increase the subscription. In September of that year it was noted that most of the money collected from subscriptions was paid to the London Anti-Slavery Society. Joseph Sturge, a Quaker and abolitionist, had moved from Gloucestershire to Birmingham in 1822 to join his brother's manufacturing business, and had also met with founder members of the London Society. According to his memoirs he found the London Anti-Slavery Society 'greatly addicted to moderation, compromise and delay' and that it 'shrank from placing the great issue of total and immediate abolition fairly before the country'.[26] Sturge's comments reveal the controversy that existed over the question of immediate versus gradual emancipation and at a General Meeting of the Birmingham Society on 16 August 1830 a resolution was unanimously agreed that 'the present state of the great and important question of the Abolition of Slavery requires the adoption of a more decided plan of operations than has yet been pursued'.[27] One prominent supporter of immediate abolition was the District Treasurer of the Birmingham Ladies Society, Elizabeth Heyrick, a Quaker from the Leicester Society who in 1824 had published a pamphlet entitled 'Immediate, not Gradual Abolition'. Like Joseph Sturge she criticises mainstream antislavery figures such as Clarkson and Wilberforce for their 'slow, cautious, accommodating measures' pointing out that 'the West Indian planters, have occupied much too prominent a place in the discussion of this great question. The abolitionists have shown a great deal too much politeness and accommodation towards these gentlemen'.[28] One of the reasons put forward by more conservative abolitionists for favouring gradual emancipation was that sudden freedom would result in insurrection by the slaves and murder of their white masters. One Member of Parliament, Fowell Buxton, although in favour of eventual abolition, speaking in the House of Commons in May 1823 said 'we are far from meaning to attempt to cut down slavery in the full maturity of its vigour. We shall rather leave it to decay – slowly, silently, almost imperceptibly, to die away and to be forgotten'.[29] Rather than fearing insurrection, Elizabeth Heyrick was in complete sympathy with the small number of insurrections that had taken place in the West Indies, saying 'was it not in the cause of self-defence from the most degrading, intolerable oppression'.[30] Despite concerns about the possible consequences for the white planters, in October 1830 the men's Anti-Slavery Society proposed that 'the principle of immediate emancipation of the slaves' must be adopted, but added that the Meeting was 'willing to recognise the principle of compensation' for losses incurred by the slave owners. They considered the 'propriety of petitioning parliament for the immediate abolition of slavery in the British colonies' and in the following year it becomes clear from the Society minutes that the London Society had conveyed their intention of pressing for immediate emancipation. This decision was partly due to the actions of Joseph Sturge who had helped to form a sub-committee of the Anti-Slavery Society referred to as the Agency Committee which campaigned vigorously for the passage of the Slavery Abolition Act.

While the men continued with their meetings and discussions members of the Ladies Society were out canvassing throughout Birmingham and the surrounding areas, collecting signatures for petitions and encouraging support for immediate emancipation. Joseph Sturge's sister Sophia 'personally called on three thousand households' and delivered reworked images of Josiah Wedgwood's kneeling slave bearing the image of a female slave and the words 'Am I Not a Woman and a Sister?'[31] Petitions signed by both men and women were presented to Parliament in the two years prior to the final passage of the Slavery Abolition Act which received Royal assent on 28 August 1833 and made the purchase or ownership of slaves illegal within the British Empire.

The work of Joseph Sturge and his fellow abolitionists was by no means over with the passage of the Emancipation Act and in 1834 he sailed for the West Indies where he was to discover that the systems put into place to deal with the aftermath of slavery had much in common with the system they were intended to replace. The consequences of abolition and its effect on the lives of the emancipated slaves will be the subject of my next chapter, but first I examine events leading up to the abolition of slavery in the Southern states of

America and the role played by abolitionists in Alabama and neighbouring states.

Southern State Abolitionists

The abolition of slavery in the British West Indies was achieved after many years of arguing, campaigning, petitioning and persuasion based on religious, philosophical, humanitarian, economic and even scientific reasoning. Very few ordinary members of the public were against abolition, the main opposition coming from those who had an economic interest in the West Indian sugar plantations, many of whom were Members of Parliament whose votes would be necessary to achieve abolition. David Brion Davis notes that 'by 1833 the ratio of British signatures calling for immediate emancipation, when compared to those in opposition, was more than 250 to 1, and he acknowledges the importance of 'the local activists who organised meetings, disseminated tracts and solicited petition signatures'.[32] The situation in America was very different, for although most slaves of African origin were working on plantations in the Southern states, the majority of states had at least some slaves at the beginning of the nineteenth century, and the system of slavery was seen by many as a necessary part of life and essential for the economy.[33]

Since the beginning of the seventeenth century the Trans-Atlantic slave traders had carried slaves from Africa to the West Indies and many of these were then transported to the north-eastern states of America where the demand for labour was rapidly increasing. Throughout the eighteenth century many Americans in the North began to question the practice of slavery and foremost amongst these were members of the Society of Friends, or Quakers, who like the Quakers in Britain believed that to enslave fellow human beings was incompatible with their Christian faith. After the American War of Independence various anti-slavery societies were set up in the north but these were state based organisations mainly concerned with promoting gradual abolition. The subsequent decline in support for the anti-slavery movement was partly due to the fact that many slave owners in the north began to sell their slaves to cotton plantation owners in the south obtaining large prices as demand for labour on the plantations increased. In the 1820s and 1830s growing concern developed over the conditions experienced by black slaves in the South and abolitionists began to call for an immediate end to slavery, echoing the debate taking place in Britain at this time between gradualists and immediatists.

Relatively few abolitionists actually lived or worked in the South for any length of time and most of these originated from upper South states such as Kentucky. Cultural and economic factors meant that southern slave holders were determined to maintain their way of life and those campaigning for emancipation were ostracized and often subjected to verbal and physical abuse. One of the better known of these southern abolitionists was James G. Birney who spent all his life campaigning for abolition and moved from Kentucky to Alabama in 1818 at the age of twenty six. Birney's father had arrived in America with other immigrants from Dublin in 1783. From the beginning he was opposed to slavery but this did not prevent him from using free slave labour to advance his business interests and within five years he had accumulated sufficient wealth to buy land and establish a plantation in Kentucky. Despite owning slaves Birney senior opposed the adoption of the 1792 Kentucky constitution which perpetuated slavery, for in common with many other Kentuckians he did not wish to see the state enter the Union 'with the curse of slavery perpetuated within her borders'.[34] An important influence in the life of the young James Birney was his friendship with a young slave, Michael, which had started when they were both children and continued for the rest of their lives. The slaves on the Birney plantation were well treated, never whipped or forced to work excessively long hours, but the young James became increasingly aware of the differences which existed between his way of life and the opportunities it presented compared with the life of slavery which lay ahead for his young playmate. James Birney went on to study law at Princeton University where he came into contact with abolitionists many of whom were Quakers. In 1814 at the age of twenty two he returned to his home town in Kentucky to practice as a lawyer and two years later was elected to the state legislature. However as his abolitionist views became more widely known he started to receive death threats from pro-slavery members of the public whose livelihoods depended on an increasing supply of slave labour to the rapidly expanding cotton plantations. Things came to a head in 1818 when he opposed a fugitive slave law which prevented slaves from gaining their freedom by escaping into states where slavery was illegal and fearing for the safety of his wife and young child he decided to leave Kentucky.

By 1804 slavery had virtually been abolished in the northern states but the situation was very different in the South. Slave holders argued that their slaves had been legally purchased and therefore according to the law were their property, an argument which a lawyer like Birney found difficult to refute. They also maintained that slavery was sanctioned by the Bible and was therefore the will of God. As the words of the 1776 Declaration of Independence obviously contradicted these beliefs, various theories were adopted which proposed that the statement 'all men are created equal' referred to white people only. The theory of polygenesis put forward the idea that black and white people were actually separate branches of the human race with black people belonging to an inferior race.[35] The 'unalienable Rights' of 'Life, Liberty and the pursuit of Happiness' were consequently only to be enjoyed by members of the white race who saw it as their right to enslave their fellow human beings. While at Princeton University James Birney was exposed to the ideas of the president, Rev. Samuel Stanhope Smith, a strong believer in monogenesis who believed that 'men are of one blood, and that slavery is wrong morally and an evil politically'. However Smith was himself a slaveholder and believed that slavery could not be ended by law because the law protected an individual's property rights and if slaves were regarded as property they could not be removed from their owner without consent.

When Birney left Kentucky in 1818 he did not move northwards but travelled south into Alabama together with thousands of other immigrants who had learned of the large profits to be made from growing cotton on land previously occupied by Native Americans. He was accompanied by his boyhood friend Michael and his family and about 'two dozen family slaves of all ages ... who Birney intended would be the foundation of a successful cotton plantation'.[36] They settled in Madison County near the town of Huntsville, Alabama, about ninety miles north of present day Birmingham but Birney soon discovered that running a cotton plantation was not as easy as he had imagined. The slaves he had brought with him had no experience in growing cotton and were not used to the heavy manual work involved so Birney was forced to buy more experienced slaves. He was not however prepared to employ the methods used by more successful plantation owners who relied on overseers with whips to ensure the slaves kept working even when they were exhausted or sick. His humanitarian approach meant that he made little profit from his plantation and his increasing conviction that slavery should be abolished led to a growing involvement with Alabama politics. Alabama joined the Union in 1819 as a slave state and in the same year Birney became a member of the first state legislature making no secret of his antislavery views. In the words of Rogers 'frontier Alabama eventually would be where Birney's dramatic transformation from traditional Southern slaveholding planter to antislavery activist took shape'.[37] One of his first actions was to persuade the state legislature to pass a law preventing the importation of slaves to be sold and allowing slaves to obtain their freedom if their owners agreed or if they received compensation. It was also under his influence that the Alabama constitution contained a clause asserting that 'For any crime more serious than petit larceny a slave was entitled to a trial by jury. Any person dismembering or killing a slave was to be subject to the same punishment as that which would be meted out if the crime were committed against a white man. The only exception was in case of a slave insurrection'.[38] Unfortunately this provision was never enforced as very few white people would have been willing to report such a crime even though many slaves died as a result of physical punishment. In 1824 Birney left his plantation in the hands of an overseer and moved with his family to the town of Huntsville so that he could devote more time to his legal career. In his position as state prosecutor he successfully sued a lynch club based in Jackson County and also 'won an indictment against a white man who had slain an escaping Negro'.[39] This was an important victory as it was one of the few occasions when a white man was found guilty of killing a slave. Unfortunately public support for the culprit prevented his extradition from the neighbouring state of Tennessee to which he had fled.

A particular friend of Birney on the state legislature was Clement Comer Clay, a fellow lawyer and planter as well as a politician who shared Birney's antislavery views. He did not however agree with Birney's opposition to the actions of Andrew Jackson who had been responsible for the removal of Creek Indians from Alabama in the war of 1812. Birney spoke out in support of Native American property rights in Alabama, a position which lost him the backing of the many Jackson supporters in northern Alabama. Clay later became a governor of Alabama and a US senator.

In Huntsville Birney joined the Presbyterian Church and became involved with various religious, social and educational reform initiatives including the setting up of the Huntsville Female Seminary where the education of women was based on the latest ideas put forward by Catherine Beecher, a renowned educator and sister of Harriet Beecher Stowe the abolitionist and author. Catherine Beecher shared Birney's strong feelings concerning Native American rights and in 1829 led a women's movement to protest against Andrew Jackson's Indian Removal Bill which was eventually passed in May 1830. From then on Birney devoted himself to the cause of the abolition of black slavery, increasing his unpopularity with the slaveholders of northern Alabama. He became a trustee of the new University of Alabama which was being established in Tuscaloosa in an area where many wealthy cotton growers were establishing large plantations. As discussed in the previous chapter it was the profits from these plantations which helped to establish the new city of Birmingham after the Civil War and the University in Tuscaloosa is now a major part of the University of Birmingham. Rogers describes how Birney travelled north in order to recruit faculty members and officers for the new university and during these visits attended anti-slavery meetings in Philadelphia, New York and Boston. At these meetings he met members of the American Colonization Society which supported the migration of freed slaves to Africa and actually founded a colony in West Africa which became known as Liberia. Many African Americans opposed this scheme as they wished to stay in America and saw colonization as a racist strategy for removing black people from America. Birney did initially believe that slaves should have the opportunity of returning to Africa but soon realised that he should instead be fighting for emancipation within America. He actually organised a gradual emancipation society in his home state of Kentucky on his way back to Alabama after one of his visits to the North. Birney's journey from a supporter of colonization to an advocate of gradual and then immediate emancipation was no doubt partly influenced by the Boston abolitionist and journalist William

Lloyd Garrison who in 1830 started publication of the anti-slavery newspaper, *The Liberator*. Garrison was also one of the founders of the American Anti-Slavery Society which was formed in 1833 and with which Birney would later become closely involved. When copies of *The Liberator* started to filter into the southern states the slave holders and indeed the majority of the white population were incensed and anti-abolitionist feelings reached a new high. Anger was further increased by the Virginia slave revolt in August 1831 during which more than fifty white people were killed. The revolt was led by Nat Turner a literate and deeply religious slave who believed that God had called him to rebel against his white masters. He gathered more than seventy slaves and free blacks and went from house to house killing white people and freeing slaves. In reprisal fifty six slaves were executed by the state and more than a hundred by militias and mobs, many of them being beheaded. The state legislature passed laws forbidding slaves from learning to read and write, similar laws having been passed in North Carolina in 1830. An unfortunate consequence of these laws was that at the end of the Civil War most freed slaves were illiterate.

Two anti-slavery activists from South Carolina where anti-literacy laws were already in place were sisters Sarah and Angelina Grimké, who were to become acquainted with Birney later in the 1830s when he and Angelina's husband, Rev. Theodore Weld were working with the American Anti-Slavery Society. The Grimké family owned hundreds of slaves who worked on their plantation near Charleston. Just as the young James Birney had made friends with Michael, Sarah and a young house servant, Hetty became firm friends and playmates. One day Sarah's father discovered her teaching Hetty to read and consequently the two girls were separated and Hetty was threatened with a beating if she was ever found reading again. Sarah defied her father and continued to teach Hetty and the other slaves in secret. Mark Perry describes how years later Sarah identified this event as 'planting the seeds of her antislavery activism', and he quotes her as saying 'I took an almost malicious satisfaction in teaching my little waiting-maid at night, when she was supposed to be occupied in combing and brushing my locks . . . the light was put out, the keyhole screened, and flat on our stomachs before the fire, with the spelling-book under our eyes, we defied the law of South Carolina'.[40] Sarah and her younger sister Angelina were later to move north to Philadelphia to remove themselves from 'the stench of slavery' and become active in the antislavery cause.

In Alabama Birney and his fellow abolitionists were feeling the consequences of the Virginia slave revolt and the increase in anger and hatred directed towards the black slaves and those who supported emancipation. The 1833 Alabama slave codes included several sections concerned with anti-literacy legislation. Section 31 states:

> Any person or persons who attempt to teach any free person of color, or slave, to spell, read, or write, shall, upon conviction thereof by indictment, be fined in a sum not less than two hundred and fifty dollars, nor more than five hundred dollars.

Section 32 states:

> Any free person of color who shall write for any slave a pass or free paper, on conviction therof, shall receive for every such offense, thirty-nine lashes on the bare back, and leave the state of Alabama within thirty days thereafter . . .[41]

It is only too clear that the state legislators realised the importance of literacy in enabling enslaved people to learn about their rights and communicate with those in other parts of the country. Birney's position in Huntsville gradually became more untenable as he made no secret of the fact that he supported immediate emancipation. He wrote letters to churches and ministers in an attempt to persuade them that slavery was incompatible with Christian principles saying 'If then slavery be characterised by *violence, oppression, injustice* – by tendencies to the ruin of the souls of both master and slave – why should you hesitate to say *it ought to cease* AT ONCE?'[42] His words had no effect on an increasingly militant population in Madison County and in 1834 he decided to move with his family back to his father's home in Danville, Kentucky. One of his first actions was to free his own slaves and then to devote his life to the cause of abolition.

Soon after arriving in Kentucky Birney set about publishing an abolitionist newspaper, *The Philanthropist* in the mistaken belief that the residents of Kentucky would be more sympathetic to the abolitionist cause than those in Alabama. He was soon to be disillusioned when he was forced to confront pro-slavery mobs and even received death threats. In desperation he went to visit his old friend and fellow lawyer Henry Clay, who now represented Kentucky in the United States Senate and House of Representatives. Birney remembered words from one of Clay's early speeches; 'We must have freedom for all men. Slavery is an evil which must be ended', but the man he now met held very different views and was certainly not prepared to support his old friend in his abolitionist activities. With an obvious eye on his own political future Clay asserted that only a mild form of slavery was present in Kentucky and that the question of the property rights of slave holders was an 'insurmountable barrier' to emancipation. A disappointed Birney decided to move his printing press to Cincinnati just across the border into Ohio where slavery had officially been banned, but Cincinnati still had strong ties with the south and his anti-slavery newspaper was not welcomed by many of the citizens. Birney was told that only five years before his arrival 'the outright murder of black men and women by mob violence was accepted practice', many freed slaves from the south having settled in Cincinnati.[43] These freed and escaped slaves were competing with poor white people for jobs and in 1836 riots broke out during which black people and the white abolitionists who supported them were threatened and attacked. Rioters broke into the premises where *The Philanthropist* was printed and vandalised the printing press, moving on to demonstrate outside Birney's house and the house of his printer, Achilles Pugh, a Quaker who shared Birney's anti-slavery views. The press was dumped into the Ohio River and the rioters moved on to vandalise the areas of the city where most black people lived. Although Birney did have the support of the local anti-slavery society and many of the residents, he decided in 1837 to move with his family to New York, leaving Pugh to continue publication of *The Philanthropist*. In New York he joined with members of the American Anti-Slavery Society and became its corresponding secretary.

Birney's work with the AASS brought him into contact with Theodore Dwight Weld, an abolitionist and preacher who was the editor of books and pamphlets for the association. Birney had first met Weld when he visited Huntsville in 1832 to lecture on the subject of colonization. Like Birney, Weld thought that colonization might serve as a first step towards emancipation but both men soon realised that it would do nothing to bring about abolition within the United States. In 1834 when Birney had moved to Kentucky, Weld helped him to distribute his 'Letter on Colonization' in which he strongly denounced the practice. Thousands of copies were distributed to antislavery societies in the South and West with the result that Birney became nationally known for his antislavery views. Weld worked closely with Birney during his time in Cincinnati and as a member of the Lane Theological Seminary he organised a series of debates on slavery in 1834 which resulted in a decision to support abolitionism. The board of directors of the seminary showed their disapproval by prohibiting the students from discussing slavery, resulting in 80 percent of the students leaving the seminary. Perhaps the most important collaboration between Weld and Birney while they were both associated with the AASS was the publication in 1839 of Weld's book *American Slavery As It Is: Testimony of a Thousand Witnesses*, co-written with his wife Angelina Grimké and her sister Sarah. Weld had made a detailed search of thousands of southern newspapers containing documented accounts of cases involving mistreatment and murder of slaves. He collected first-hand testimonials from those still in the South and those who had moved north where they could reveal what they had witnessed without fear of persecution. One of those providing testimony was the Rev. William T. Allan of Alabama who was the son of a slaveholder and pastor of the Presbyterian Church in Huntsville. He describes incidents on a plantation opposite his father's house in the suburbs of Huntsville belonging to Judge Smith. He says of the overseer, Tune,

> I have often seen him flogging the slaves in the field, and have often heard their cries. Sometimes, too, I have met them with the tears streaming down their faces, and the marks of the whip on their bare necks and shoulders... Tune became displeased with one of the women who was pregnant, he made her lay down over a log, with her face towards the ground, and beat her so unmercifully, that she was soon after delivered of a dead child.[44]

The Rev. Allan describes several incidents reported to him that occurred in the neighbourhood of Courtland in Lawrence County, Alabama, about eighty miles north of present day Birmingham.

> A man near Courtland, of the name of Thompson, recently shot a negro woman through the head, and put the pistol so close that her hair was singed. He did it in consequence of some difficulty in his dealings with her as a concubine. He buried her in a log heap; she was discovered by the buzzards gathering around it.[45]

A Mrs. Barr, wife of Rev. H. Barr from Courtland, Alabama told Rev. Allan

> she has very often stopped her ears that she might not hear the screams of slaves who were under the lash, and that sometimes she has left her house, and retired to a place more distant, in order to get away from their agonizing cries.[46]

Mr. L. Turner, a regular member of the Presbyterian Church, mentioned the case of one slaveholder

> Whom he had seen lay his slaves on a large log, which he kept for the purpose, strip them, tie them with the face downward, then have a kettle of hot water brought – take the paddle, made of hard wood, and perforated with holes, dip it into the hot water and strike – before every blow dipping it into the water – every hole at every blow would raise a 'whelk'.[47]

He adds that this was the usual punishment for attempting to run away.

Weld's book published with Birney's assistance contained, as the name suggests, about a thousand such statements from most of the southern slave states. The historian, J.C. Furnas called Weld's book 'a hair-raising compilation of atrocities . . . that remained the keystone of antislavery propaganda for the duration'.[48] It was widely distributed, selling about one hundred thousand copies in the first year and played a vital role in the growth of the political abolitionist movement in the 1840s.

When the Grimké sisters moved from South Carolina to Philadelphia they soon came to realise that although slavery had been abolished in the northern states prejudice against free black people was still widespread. In 1835 William Lloyd Garrison the publisher of *The Liberator* was attacked by a mob in Boston and in response Angelina Grimké wrote in a letter to the newspaper,

> If persecution is the means which God has ordained for the accomplishment of this great end, EMANCIPATION, I feel as if I could say, LET IT COME; for it is my deep, solemn, deliberate conviction that *this is a cause worth dying for*.[49]

As a result of this letter Angelina and her sister were expelled from Philadelphia's Quaker community which had forbidden its members from taking part in political activities. The sisters however were not deterred, Angelina writing 'An Appeal to the Christian Women of the South', described by Mark Perry as 'perhaps the most eloquent and emotional argument against slavery made by any abolitionist'.[50] In 1836 Sarah wrote 'An Epistle to the Clergy of the Southern States' which 'was meant to undermine and embarrass Southern ministers who used the Bible to defend the indefensible'.[51] Copies of the Epistle were confiscated at the Charleston customs house and many others were burned. In February 1838, a year before the publication of *American Slavery As It Is*, Angelina Grimké addressed a committee of the State Legislature in Boston on the subject of slavery. She said,

> I stand before you as a southerner, exiled from the land of my birth by the sound of the lash, and the piteous cry of the slave . . . I stand before you as a moral being . . . and as a moral being I feel that I owe it to the suffering slave, and to the deluded master, to my country and the world, to do all that I can to overturn a system of complicated crimes, built up upon the broken hearts and prostrate bodies of my countrymen in chains, and cemented by the blood and sweat and tears of my sisters in bonds.[52]

The legislators listening responded with thunderous applause and in the words of Mark Perry the speech 'was a turning point for the abolitionist movement'.[53]

Although support for emancipation was increasing in the northern states ambitious politicians like Henry Clay were reluctant to come out as abolitionists fearing that to adopt such a position would adversely affect their chances of progressing to high office. In 1840 the Liberty Party was formed with James Birney as leader, the sole purpose of the new party being to advance the abolitionist cause. Birney had by then fallen out with William Lloyd Garrison, leader of the AASS, partly due to his support for female suffrage but also due to his unwillingness to work within the current political system, maintaining that the Constitution was a pro-slavery document. In the 1844 presidential elections the Liberty Party nominated Birney as their candidate for President, Henry Clay being the Whig party candidate. Birney only received 2.3 percent of the popular vote, but this was enough to prevent Clay from winning New York and he consequently lost the election which was won by James Polk a member of the Democratic Party. Rogers in his biography of Birney suggests that his role in the 1844 election which resulted in the election of a pro-slavery, expansionist president, has meant that Birney's huge contribution to the abolitionist cause has been underplayed by many politicians and historians. However, Clay's Whig Party was itself divided on the question of slavery and in 1848 anti-slavery Whigs joined with the Liberal Party which had failed to attract a large membership and New York Democrats who had split with the rest of the Democratic Party because of its pro-slavery position. The new party was called the Free Soil Party and in 1854 joined with the remnants of the Whig party to form the new anti-slavery Republican Party.

In the years following the formation of the Republican Party its members became increasingly aware of the strong abolitionist sentiments held by people in the northern states, but also of the seemingly insurmountable differences between the policies of the Republican Party and the Democratic Party which had a majority in the Southern states. In 1858, one year after the death of James Birney, Abraham Lincoln was adopted as the Republican candidate for the United States Senate and delivered what became known as the 'House Divided Speech'. In this speech he said,

> A house divided against itself cannot stand.
> I believe this government cannot endure, permanently half slave and half free.
> I do not expect the Union to be dissolved – I do not expect the house to fail – but I do expect it
> will cease to be divided.
> It will become all one thing or all the other.
>
> Either the opponents of slavery will arrest the further spread of it, and place it where the public mind shall rest in the belief that it is in the course of ultimate extinction, or its advocates will push it forward, till it shall become alike lawful in all the States, old as well as new – North as well as South.
> Have we no tendency to the latter condition?[54]

Lincoln made it clear where his own sympathies lay, saying in Cincinnati, Ohio in 1859, 'I think slavery is wrong, morally and politically', and on another occasion saying that America could not be seen 'fostering human slavery and proclaiming ourselves, at the same time, the sole friends of human freedom'.[55] However, as the Lincoln-Douglas debates revealed he was not prepared to accept that the freed slaves would be 'politically and socially our equals', adding that 'my own feelings will not admit of this, and if mine would, we all know that those of the great mass of whites will not'.[56] Lincoln was elected as President in 1860, a decision which was totally unacceptable to the Southern Democrats and which set in motion the chain of events which led to the Civil War.

The abolition of slavery which Birney and many others had worked for throughout their lives was not of course the only factor which plunged the country into four years of horrendous warfare. The southern states considered that the central, federal government was taking away the rights of individual states and that the agrarian interests of southern planters were being ignored by an increasingly industrialised North. The southern Democrats supported expansion into new territories in the south west in which the planters would establish new plantations dependent on slave labour, a policy which Lincoln and the Republicans opposed. Leading politicians in the southern states threatened to withdraw from the Federal Union and at a convention held on January 7, 1861 Alabama became one of the first states to declare its independence from the Union. Representatives from six other states joined with Alabama in Montgomery and declared the formation of a new government of the Confederate States of America, under a new President, Jefferson Davis. On April 12, 1861 Confederate troops opened fire on Union occupied Fort Sumter in Charleston harbour and the war had begun.

Thousands of young men in Alabama joined local military units which were grouped into regiments and dispatched to the battlefields of the eastern and western fronts. Southerners were afraid that with the departure of so many white men black slaves might take the opportunity to rise up against their masters, and several wrote to Jefferson Davis suggesting that black men should either be imprisoned or compelled to enrol in the Confederate army. This suggestion was rejected, but as the war proceeded many slaves were drafted into auxiliary roles such as stretcher bearers and labourers.[57] In February 1862 gunboats carrying Union troops entered Alabama for the first time, steaming up the Tennessee River to the town of Florence, about seventy miles west of Huntsville which was occupied a few months later. From this time Northern Alabama with its important rail and river transportation routes was under the control of Union troops and some districts which had opposed secession actually sent troops to fight with the Union army. Many escaped slaves assisted the Union soldiers as they advanced through Alabama, one General reporting from Huntsville to the Secretary of War writes 'I have promised protection to the slaves who have given me valuable assistance and information . . . with the assistance of the Negroes in watching the River I feel myself sufficiently strong to defy the enemy'.[58] Unfortunately when these freed slaves returned to their homes in the South after the war they and their families were often subjected to persecution and violent physical attacks because of their association with the Union army.[59]

As the war progressed the Confederate army began to suffer from a shortage of weaponry and by 1863 iron furnaces and weapon making factories were set up in central and northern Alabama. By 1865 Union troops had made their way south to Jefferson County and here, as described in the previous chapter, they commandeered the estates of wealthy cotton planters such as William Hawkins and William Mudd. Mudd had invested in the Alabama Arms Manufacturing Company whose furnaces supplied iron needed by the Confederate Government for arms manufacture. Although these furnaces were destroyed by Union soldiers the wealthy plantation owners found that when the war came to an end fortunes were to be made from the sale of land rich in iron ore and limestone to developers of the new industrial city.

Despite early Confederate successes their defeat at the Battle of Antietam in 1862 prompted Lincoln to issue a Preliminary Emancipation Proclamation in which he warned the Confederate states that he would order emancipation if they did not return to the Union. In 1863 the Confederate army led by General Robert E. Lee invaded Pennsylvania but was defeated by the Union army at Gettysburg and forced back to the South. The following year Atlanta was captured by Union forces and in November 1864 Lincoln was re-elected. On 31 January 1865 the 13th Amendment to the U.S. Constitution on the Abolition of Slavery was passed by Congress and on 10 April General Robert E. Lee surrendered to General Ulysses S. Grant. Just five days later Abraham Lincoln was assassinated. The 13th Amendment, which was ratified on 6 December 1865 states,

> Neither slavery nor involuntary servitude, except as a punishment for crime whereof the party shall have been duly convicted, shall exist within the United States, or any other place subject to their jurisdiction.[60]

In July 1868 Alabama was restored to the Union and 440,000 black Alabamian slaves were freed and granted citizenship. In reality the lives of the majority of these freed slaves were not to improve appreciably for many years to come.

In this chapter, I have emphasised the roles played by abolitionists in Birmingham England, and in the regions of the Southern States where the city of Birmingham, Alabama was to develop and expand after the Civil War. Before examining the after effects of abolition I conclude by looking briefly at the links between abolitionists in England and those in America during the years between British abolition and emancipation in the United States.

In 1839, six years after the passing of the Slavery Abolition Act in Britain, Joseph Sturge of Birmingham set up the British and Foreign Anti-Slavery Society (BFASS), the objectives of which were 'the universal extinction of slavery and the slave trade, and the protection of the rights and interests of the enfranchised populations in the British possessions, and of all persons captured as slaves'. The society organised a World Anti-Slavery Convention held in London in June 1840 which attracted delegates from many countries, the majority coming from North America. This convention and those that followed encouraged British campaigners to support fellow abolitionists in America and as Clare Midgley points out,

> American abolitionists, lacking widespread public support in their own country, weakened by ideological divisions, and admiring British abolitionists' successes, attached great importance to gaining financial and moral support in Britain and Ireland.[61]

Throughout the 1840s and 1850s much of this support came from women's societies and in 1859 the BFASS singled out the Birmingham Ladies' Negro's Friend Society as one of the main organisations supporting its work. This organisation had met with particular success in fund-raising during the British campaign and they were eager to help fellow campaigners in America. The British women made and collected items which were shipped out to America to be sold in fund-raising bazaars and financial support was given to groups in America and Canada who were aiding runaway slaves. Women writers and poets contributed items to the *Liberty Bell* an annual abolitionist gift book, one of the contributors being Elizabeth Barrett Browning who in a poem published in 1850 gives voice to a runaway black slave describing her life of servitude, abuse and rape:

> O pilgrim – souls, I speak to you!
> I see you come out proud and slow
> From the land of the spirits pale as dew . . .
> And round me and round me ye go!
> O pilgrims, I have gasped and run
> All night long from the whips of one
> Who in your names works sin and woe.[62]

Members of the Birmingham Ladies' Society made a particular contribution during the 1850s by raising money in tribute to the abolitionist writer Harriet Beecher Stowe from the many British readers of her novel, *Uncle Tom's Cabin*. A total of £1,800 was raised which was used by Stowe to promote abolition but also black Christian education. Although the novel did much to increase people's awareness of the evils of slavery it has more recently been criticised for promoting sentimentalised, stereotypes of black people and the belief in the necessity of converting all black people to Christianity. It has to be remembered that most southern slave owners were fervent Christians many of whom believed that black people were created by God as an inferior race.

A further link between the Birmingham Ladies' Society and American abolitionists was the popularity of the society's treasurer, Elizabeth Heyrick, whose *Immediate, not Gradual Emancipation* was republished by the Philadelphia Ladies' Society in 1836. William Lloyd Garrison particularly praised Heyrick's work seeing it as providing inspiration for American women to become involved in the anti-slavery movement.

In 1846 a campaign was started to boycott the import of slave grown cotton from America and the women of Birmingham who had previously carried out a successful campaign to boycott the import of sugar, presented a petition to Queen Victoria in 1850 urging her not to use slave grown cotton but instead to encourage the import of free grown cotton from British India.

After 1865 and the passage of the 13th Amendment British abolitionists continued to provide support and aid for the freed slaves in America, just as in the 1830s and 1840s they had attempted to provide education for those freed in the West Indies. Unfortunately perhaps this was mainly left to missionaries who felt their main duty was to train and instruct the freed slaves in the principles and practice of Christianity.

In the following two chapters I examine the aftermath of abolition in the West Indies and the southern states of America revealing how emancipation failed in many ways to meet the dreams and expectations of those liberated from slavery.

3

The Aftermath
Jamaica

In 1831 when the British Parliament was preoccupied with drawing up the first Reform Bill a slave uprising took place around Montego Bay in Jamaica. The slaves were well aware of the abolitionist movement in Britain and in December 1831 rumours spread that the King had granted emancipation, rumours that were immediately denied by the governor of Jamaica. The rebel slaves led by the Baptist preacher, Samuel Sharpe called a strike to demand better conditions which soon developed into a full scale rebellion involving damage to plantation property. Mary Reckord summarizes the causes of the rebellion as being 'political excitement stirred by rumours of emancipation, economic stress, a revolutionary philosophy circulating among the slaves and the presence of a group of whites whom the slaves could identify as their allies'.[1] The rebellion was quickly suppressed by British forces and the Jamaican government carried our brutal reprisals, killing about five hundred slaves during the rebellion and executing over three hundred when it was over. Fear of further rebellions in the Caribbean together with the increasing number of petitions being presented to Parliament accelerated the processes leading to the passage of the Slave Emancipation Act in August 1833. A year later after much debate over the exact terms to be included the Emancipation Act came into effect. To the dismay of many who had fought for abolition the act did not immediately transform slaves into free workers but stipulated that slavery was to be replaced by a period of apprenticeship originally planned to last for six years. During this period ex-slaves would be required to work for their former owners for up to forty-five hours a week in return for an allowance to cover food, clothing and housing and in their 'free time' would be expected to work for wages. Magistrates were sent out from England to ensure that these terms were enforced and a plantation police force of free blacks was employed to maintain discipline. Although many in Britain welcomed the Emancipation Act it was evident to the majority of active abolitionists that slavery had merely been replaced by another form of servitude based on a belief that the released slaves would be incapable of dealing with the demands of immediate freedom. Henry Taylor, a member of the Colonial Office and active in the role of drawing up the terms of the act described the slaves as being volatile and shallow, possessing 'the intelligence, in short, of minds which had neither discipline nor cultivation, and nothing but natural vivacity to enlighten them', and who would relapse 'into a barbarous indolence' if suddenly emancipated.[2]

Joseph Sturge, who had played a prominent role in the Birmingham Anti-Slavery Society took a leading role in protesting against the apprenticeship system and to the proposed payment of twenty million pounds in compensation to the plantation owners. In August 1835 Sturge and other members of the Birmingham Anti-Slavery Society signed a resolution presented to Lord Glenelg, the Colonial Secretary, attacking the apprenticeship system and in November of that year an anti-slavery meeting was held in Birmingham Town Hall at which it was resolved that 'apprenticeship be abolished' and that Birmingham should play a large part in this. In February 1836 Sturge led another public meeting in Birmingham at which he read letters he had received from the West Indies describing the hardships of apprenticeship. These reports were mainly from missionaries and residents in Jamaica, one of the most outspoken of these being William Knibb, a Baptist missionary and a close friend of Sturge. In March 1836 a Parliamentary Select Committee was set up to enquire into the working of the apprenticeship system and its report contained seven major objections. These included the observations that the local planters retained excessive influence, that the corporal punishment of females was contrary to the law and that there was a lack of educational provision for children who had been freed under the 1833 Act. Despite these objections the British Government still considered that voluntary local action would be sufficient to remedy any abuses associated with apprenticeship.

Exasperated by the lack of Government response to the findings of the Select Committee, Sturge decided to travel to the West Indies to discover the true facts of the situation for himself and in November 1836 accompanied by three fellow Birmingham Quakers, he sailed for the West Indies. On arriving in Barbados the four men split into two groups enabling visits to be made to different colonies.[3] Sturge and Thomas Harvey spent about three months in Jamaica where they found the apprenticeship system more harshly controlled and the punishments meted out to the supposedly freed slaves more severe than in any of the other islands. After arriving in Kingston they travelled to Browns Town in the north of the island where they stayed with a Baptist missionary, John Clark. It was here that they were introduced to James Williams, a young former slave who now worked as an apprentice on a nearby plantation. Sturge was impressed by the eighteen-year-old's 'intelligence, articulateness and prodigious memory',[4] and realized that if he could persuade Williams to relate his story it would be the most effective way of conveying to the British public the conditions still endured by thousands of ex slaves. Sturge provided the money to purchase Williams' freedom and arranged to take him to Britain where they arrived in May, 1837. His story was written down by Dr Archibald Palmer, a magistrate who had tried to help Williams in Jamaica but was in England after being persecuted by the Jamaican authorities for his anti-slavery views. The 'Narrative of Events' relating in Williams' own words the brutality of his life as an apprentice was published as a pamphlet in June 1837. The narrative records events occurring in Williams' life during the three years following the implementation of the apprenticeship system. He describes how he was previously a slave belonging to a Mr. Senior and continues,

> I have been very ill treated by Mr Senior and the magistrates since the new law come in. Apprentices get a deal more punishment now than they did when they was slaves; the master takes spite, and do all he can to hurt them before the free come; – I have heard my master say, "Those English devils say we to be free, but if we is to be free, he will pretty well weaken us, before the six and the four years done; we shall be no use to ourselves afterwards".[5]

He explains how since the new law began he has 'been flogged seven times, and put in the house of correction four times'. He describes how Senior constantly made up false charges against him and the other apprentices, both young and old being flogged 'for trifling, foolish thing, just to please the massa'. On one occasion Williams and another apprentice, Adam Brown, were accused of being late in carrying out their task of turning the sheep out in the morning. For this they were sentenced by the magistrate to be locked up in the dungeon of a neighbouring estate for ten days and nights with very little food. When they were released they could hardly stand but were sent straight back to work. They complained to another magistrate about their treatment but were accused of insolence and sentenced to get 'twenty lashes apiece'. In Williams' words 'the punishment was very severe – both of us fainted after it – we lie down on the ground for an hour after it, not able to move ... we back all sore, quite raw, and we not able to stoop'. Ten days after the flogging Williams was again accused by Senior of not turning out the horses and cows on time and was sentenced by the magistrate to a further twenty-five lashes. He says 'I was flogged with lancewood switches upon the old flogging – it tear off all the old scabs, and I was not able to lie down on my back for two or three weeks after – was made to work with my back all sore'.[6]

The Emancipation Act stipulated that apprentices should be allowed some time outside their work hours to cultivate their own piece of ground and grow their own food, but Williams was only allowed to have every other Sunday off, hardly sufficient to provide himself with food. Despite working from early morning until late at night Williams was constantly accused of not performing his allotted tasks and eventually when Senior threatened to take him to the magistrate to receive punishment he decided to run away. He walked fifty miles to Spanish Town hoping 'to present his case to a higher authority' but no one would see him. He was taken back to Brown's Town by policemen and put into a dungeon for ten days before being tried by the magistrate, Mr. Rawlinson. Williams records 'he sentence me to St. Ann's Bay workhouse for nine days, to get fifteen lashes in going in – to dance the treadmill morning and evening, and work in the penal gang ... and I have to pay fifty days out of my own time for the time I been runaway'.[7] Williams' account of his own experiences in the workhouse, and those of the other prisoners including many women, is truly horrific, and the incidents described were confirmed by many witnesses and recorded at the time by Sturge and Harvey in their account of their visit to Jamaica.[8]

Many new workhouses were built after the introduction of the apprenticeship scheme and most of them contained a treadmill, described simply by Henrice Altink as 'a giant wheel with a series of steps propelled by the inmates' climbing motion'. [9] A bar above the steps had straps attached to it which secured the wrists of the prisoners. Williams describing his first experience of the treadmill says,

> At first, not knowing how to dance it, I cut all my shin with the steps; they did not flog me then . . . but them flog all the rest that could not step the mill, flogged them most dreadful. There was one old woman with grey head . . . and she could not dance the mill at all: she hang by the two wrists which was strapped to the bar, and the driver kept on flogging her; – she get more than all the rest, her clothes cut off with the Cat . . . but all the flogging couldn't make she dance the mill, and when she come down all her back covered with blood.[10]

Sturge and Harvey visited the same workhouse in St Ann's Bay, in February 1837 and were informed that most of the prisoners were 'incorrigible runaways' from slavery, an indication that the planters and magistrates recognized no difference between slavery and apprenticeship. On viewing the treadmill Sturge noticed that 'every step is stained with blood both recent and old . . . it had been shed so profusely, that even the sand on the floor was thickly sprinkled with it'.[11] As well as from floggings, as described by Williams, Sturge noticed that injuries were caused by the sharp projecting steps of the mill hitting against the bodies and legs of the prisoners if they lost their step and hung on by their wrists. On returning early the following morning, Sturge and Harvey witnessed 'two mixed gangs of men and women' being put on the treadmill, the women having 'no suitable dress, and were therefore liable to be indecently exposed'.[12] After their time on the treadmill the prisoners were immediately chained together and sent to work in a penal gang. Recalling his own experience Williams describes how these gangs were sent to different estates to work 'to dig cane-hole, make fence, clean pasture, and dig up heavy roots, and sometimes to drag cart to bring stone from mountain side'. In the late afternoon they were taken back to the workhouse and again put on the treadmill, after which they were re-chained and shackled together 'to sleep so till morning'. It is important to remember that like Williams these prisoners had not committed serious crimes, one prisoner telling Sturge that 'he was sent because a cattle (a steer), died under his charge'. In a similar case an old woman was imprisoned for running away through fear of punishment because one of the sheep she had been sent to mind had died.[13]

After nine days Williams was released from the workhouse and returned to the plantation. He recounts how 'when I got there, Mr. Senior put me in the dungeon, and keep me there for four days and nights; he give me four little bananas and a piece of pumpkin with a little dry salt, and a pint of water. Magistrate didn't order me to be locked up in the day, only at night, but massa do it of his own will'.[14] Under the terms of apprenticeship it was actually illegal for an apprentice to be imprisoned for more than twenty four hours without an order from a magistrate, but it is clear that many planters had no qualms about ignoring these regulations. It becomes obvious throughout Williams' narrative that any apprentice who dared to question the treatment they received was subject to harsher punishment, carried out with the willing cooperation of local magistrates. Williams recounts many occasions on which he and other apprentices were sentenced to be flogged, to be imprisoned in the workhouse with its feared treadmill and to labour in chains in penal gangs. He notes that 'there was a great many woman in the workhouse, and several have sucking child; and there was one woman quite big with child, and them make her dance the mill too morning and evening; she not able to dance good, and them flog her'.[15]

Henrice Altink in her study of apprenticed women in Jamaican workhouses during this period makes the point that Clause 17 of the 1833 Abolition Act stated that no 'court, judge or justice could punish any female apprentice by whipping or beating her person'.[16] They could however be sentenced by a stipendiary magistrate to time and labour in a workhouse where the rules were devised and controlled by local magistrates and use of the treadmill and flogging were common punishments. It is clear that these magistrates were carrying out the demands of influential planters who pressed for more severe punishments even for the most trivial offences. Abolitionist pamphlets repeatedly pointed out this violation of the 1833 Act but the Governor was reluctant to override the autonomy of the Jamaican legislature or challenge the power of the planters. Sturge's own account of the abuses he had witnessed on his travels around Jamaica was submitted to Lord Glenelg and also to the Governor, Sir Lionel Smith, who realized that Sturge's account would be strongly disputed by the planters but nevertheless agreed to set up an inquiry to investigate the claims. It was, however, James Williams' story published in June 1837 that had the greatest effect on the British public and which accelerated the move towards the abolition of the apprenticeship system. The *Narrative of Events* was reprinted in newspapers in both Britain and Jamaica and encouraged many other apprentices to relate their own stories. It is natural that some of those who read the *Narrative* would question the validity of the events described by Williams and it was therefore important that Sir Lionel Smith's inquiry should receive and report on evidence from those who had known Williams or who had suffered similar treatment in the St Ann's workhouse or on the plantation. Several of the apprentices who worked on the Penshurst estate at the same time as Williams described the harsh sentences they had received from the magistrate, Mr Rawlinson. Mary Ann Bell remembered 'being sent to the workhouse and treadmill by Mr. Rawlinson when I was quite heavy in the family way', and how he had told her mistress that the apprentices 'were not entitled to half a day in each week' without work. William Dalling, a constable on the Penshurst estate corroborated the account Williams had given of how Rawlinson had ordered for him to receive twenty lashes on his back which was still covered with scabs from old wounds which had not healed and how they bled profusely. Dalling comments that Williams was 'a very brave boy' and that 'he went to work immediately to cut grass'. Many other witnesses commented on the bravery and resilience shown by Williams and revealed how the magistrate Rawlinson had collaborated with Senior the planter to ensure that excessively severe punishments were meted out for the most trivial of offences.[17] After returning to England Joseph Sturge corresponded frequently with the Rev. John Clark in Browns Town and in a letter of 30 December, 1837 after the completion of the enquiry in Jamaica he comments 'I think I understand by the papers Rawlinson is suspended'.[18] Rawlinson was indeed suspended as a stipendiary magistrate in November 1837 and was later dismissed.

Sturge had arrived back in England accompanied by James Williams in May 1837, but it was not long before he began to have doubts about his decision to transport the young former apprentice to a strange country where he would attract a great deal of attention. In a letter to Clark written only three months after his return he writes 'the comparatively idle life and luxurious living but probably above all the attention James Williams has attracted and his introduction to persons and situations so different to what he was accustomed has ... produced an unfavorable effect upon him an ... I find him going on so very far from satisfactorily that I believe it will be the kindest thing to him ... to send him back as soon as I can'.[19] Sturge, who many considered had done more than anyone else to promote the abolitionists' cause, could not bring himself to see that black people were just the same as other human beings. As Catherine Hall observes, the planters had represented their black slaves as being 'lazy, mendacious, incapable of working without the whip, mentally inferior and sexually depraved'. In response the abolitionists produced their own stereotypical image of 'the new black Christian subject – meek victim of white oppression, grateful to his or her saviours, ready to be transformed, the kneeling figure of the enslaved man in the famous Wedgewood cameo'.[20] When James Williams did not conform to the docile, respectable, hardworking image which Sturge expected, and actually seemed to enjoy the good life and company which he encountered in England, Sturge decided that he should be sent back to 'labour for his bread' in Jamaica. He made arrangements with Clark that Williams should live and work in Kingston rather than in Browns Town where he may 'fall into the hands of those from whom he suffered so much'.[21] At the end of December 1837 in a letter to Clark, Sturge expressed his hope that 'James Williams may again settle down comfortably in Jamaica', but after that he makes no further mention of him.[22] In July 1838 a report in the *British Emancipator* recorded how in February of that year Williams together with other Penshurst apprentices had given evidence to the Middlesex Grand Jury in an attempt to charge Senior, the planter with false imprisonment, providing insufficient food and assault of a female apprentice. 'However, the jury, made up of white male property owners and apprentice holders, decided that there was insufficient evidence to pursue the prosecution'.[23] Although James Williams is largely forgotten his *Narrative of Events* played a large part in making the British public aware of the cruelties and injustices involved in the apprenticeship system and particularly in the Jamaican prison system.

After his return from the West Indies Sturge was welcomed back by members of the Birmingham Anti-Slavery Society and thanked for his 'unwearied attempts for the release and ultimate welfare, of the captive, the desolate and the oppressed'.[24] In December 1837 a meeting was held in the Town Hall after which petitions were organized pressurizing Members of Parliament to demand action from the Government to bring about an end to apprenticeship. Unfortunately, Lord Glenelg, the Colonial Secretary, in his reply to the petitioners said that 'after a careful consideration of the subject he was not of the opinion that there were sufficient grounds to justify the government in proposing for Parliament to make an alteration in the Act of 1833'.[25] Further petitions followed but all were opposed by Glenelg who considered that 'sudden emancipation would be a disaster to all parties'. Eventually on 1 August 1838 the planters in the Jamaican House of Assembly, realizing that the British government would soon have to give in to the pressure being exerted on them by abolitionists, acted to abolish apprenticeship themselves rather than being seen to be obeying instructions from the imperial power. The people of Birmingham who had campaigned tirelessly for this outcome held celebrations in the Town Hall where Sturge, responding to the cheers of the crowd told them 'through the mighty moral influence of the people of England the sun had risen for the first time upon the freedom of a large majority of their sable brethren in the British islands of the West'. Catherine Hall notes that 'other speakers were more concerned with emphasizing the docile, obedient, peaceful nature of the negro and celebrating achievements rather than looking to problems that remained'. A speaker from Leeds said that 'the people of the spirited and independent town of Birmingham would always be in the forefront of philanthropy in the West Indies'.[26] Hall's concluding comment on this self-congratulatory occasion is important,

This was Birmingham's celebration for the end of apprenticeship, one in which the men of their town, particularly Joseph Sturge, and the town itself, were seen as endowed with great moral stature and power. It was a vision that had little place for black or female agency, which assumed that 'poor negroes' were grateful, and that England and Birmingham must continue to watch over them from on high.[27]

Any celebration of the end of apprenticeship was soon seen to be premature for as Holt makes clear 'if the planters thought that abolition of apprenticeship would free them from British government interference ... they were wrong. It had become all too obvious that the former slaveholders were not apt pupils of a free labor ideology and liberal democratic statecraft'.[28] It was in fact the prison system with its continued use of flogging and the treadmill which initially led to conflict between the Assembly and the British government, and in September 1838 when Parliament introduced an 'Act for the Better Government of Prisons of the West Indies' the Assembly members were infuriated, declaring the Act to be a violation of their rights and refusing to implement it. This conflict was to continue for a further twenty five years during which the white minority continued to ensure that their own interests were paramount and that little improvement was made to the living and working conditions of the black majority population. In October 1838 Henry Taylor of the Colonial Office wrote:

> ... assuming the objects of the government to be necessary to the establishment of the liberty and promotion of the industry of the negroes, and that the habits and prejudices, if not the interests of the planters, are strongly opposed to them, then the only method of accomplishing them effectually and completely ... will be by exerting at once and conclusively, a power which will override all opposition and set the question at rest.[29]

Despite continuous efforts by the Colonial Office to bring about changes which would enable a 'smooth transition from a slave to a free society', the Jamaican legislature failed to carry out any changes which would reform the court system, reduce the power of the local magistrates, or result in the setting up of an effective police force. One of the main areas of concern for both the Colonial Office and the planters was the distribution of land. Even before the end of the apprenticeship system Lord Glenelg had maintained that ex-slaves should be prevented from obtaining land by raising the price of Crown lands so that they were 'out of the reach of persons without capital'.[30] The rationale for this was that if the freed apprentices left the plantations to work their own land there would be insufficient labour to maintain the cultivation of sugar and coffee for export. There was indeed a rapid decline in the production and export of sugar from Jamaica in the twenty or so years following abolition but this was mainly due to the introduction of free trade arrangements whereby the duties on produce from British colonies became the same as that from countries such as Cuba and Brazil.

Instead of encouraging their freed slaves to remain on the plantations and work as waged employees the planters introduced measures that would ultimately result in workers moving out of the estates to settle on land in other parts of the island. Most slaves had built their own simple houses and lived in these rent free. When apprenticeship ended the planters decided to collect rents for these homes and surrounding land, and if rents were not paid the money was deducted from the already low wages of the occupants. As a result workers who had managed to save sufficient money left the estates and rented or bought small plots of land on which they could grow their own produce. This migration out of the estates led to what some consider was the 'development of two competing cultures in Jamaica, a European-oriented plantation sector and an African-oriented peasant sector'.[31] The planters whose racial stereotype of their black workers as being lazy and unable to work without the threat of the whip envisaged that those who left the estates would be leading a subsistence-level existence, barely able to survive on the produce they were able to grow. This was far from reality, the freed apprentices grouping together to buy plots of land with a house for each family, usually in or near a previously developed area with a church and school and a market for selling their produce. Some of them did continue to work at least part of the week on the estates but the wages paid were very low and travelling long distances was often necessary. Most found that working their own land and controlling their own labour was considerably preferable to working for their old masters.

The establishment of free villages where ex-apprentices could live and work was in large part due to the efforts of the prominent Birmingham Baptist and lawyer, William Morgan who was secretary of the Birmingham Anti-Slavery Society. Morgan joined with Joseph Sturge to establish the West India Land Investment Company which provided capital to assist freed slaves to buy their own land. One of the villages established under this scheme was named Birmingham, later becoming known as New Birmingham, another being given the name Sturgetown. Sturge and his fellow abolitionists from Birmingham also backed the establishment of the Jamaica Education Society, raising money to set up schools and working to protect the legal rights of the freed slaves. In 1852 Sturge's missionary friend, John Clark wrote a review of the state of the free villages which was published as a pamphlet and reported in the *Anti-Slavery Reporter*. He says 'the settlement of emancipated negroes in these free villages has been productive of great good; they have become more industrious, thoughtful and frugal, and generally are desirous of occupying respectable stations in society'.[32]

The Birmingham Ladies' Negro's Friend Society directed their attention to 'the education of the African race to undo as much as possible the miserable and demoralizing effects of slavery' and to 'assist in training them to the principles and practice of our holy religion'. Clare Midgley points out that the Society's project of civilization and Christianization was also intended to 'eradicate aspects of African societies which they found objectionable', and although they had 'a firm belief in Africans' innate humanity' this was combined with a 'conviction of the inferiority of African culture to European'.[33]

The entrenched racist and paternalistic views of the planter class together with the fact that they continued to be supported by the magistrates and the court system and dominated the Jamaican Assembly meant that the interests of the black majority failed to be considered. The view that freed black people were inherently lazy and would 'relapse into barbarous indolence' in the Jamaican hills was blatantly untrue. Holt notes that honest observers 'conceded that the freed people were hard workers . . . when they worked for their own benefit rather than the planters . . . they prepared for market on Friday, went to market on Saturday, and attended church on Sunday.'

On the remaining four days they worked on their own land or for wages on neighbouring estates. They often walked ten to fifteen miles to the nearest market with their produce, mainly bananas, coffee or chickens in a basket on their heads. As Holt comments, 'these were not a lazy people'.[34] The prejudices held by the planters against their former slaves were upheld by the magistrates who abided by laws set by the Assembly, and although the Colonial Office under Glenelg attempted to introduce new laws to reflect the new free situation of former slaves the 'colonial systems of justice became increasingly biased in favor of planter interests and against the freed people'.[35] One example was the misuse of the Vagrancy Act which gave local magistrates the power to arrest and imprison anyone they considered to be a 'vagrant', interpreted as anyone walking in the countryside without apparent employment.

The anticipation of many in the Colonial Office that black and white residents of Jamaica would have equal voting rights after the end of apprenticeship remained unfulfilled for many years. The Assembly was made up of two parties, the Town Party consisting mainly of mixed race people, non planter whites and eventually a few black people, and the Planter Party consisting of white planters and their associates. In 1840 changes in voting qualifications were made which enabled black men to vote but the planters managed to restrict the franchise by including a clause which required farm tenants to be tax payers and own a certain amount of property. It was later suggested that a literacy qualification should be included but this was defeated in the Assembly. The main interest of the planters was to retain political power and any move towards a black majority in the Assembly was seen as a direct threat to the interests of the white planter elite. Even though some black freeholders were eligible to vote very few of them actually went to the polls. One reason for this was that to become a member of the Assembly an annual income from property and rents of at least three thousand pounds was required meaning that the black majority had no other choice than to elect their representatives from the white elite. Various attempts were made by the Colonial Office to bring about reforms in the Assembly during the 1840s and 1850s but its different sections with their contrasting interests and priorities made it almost impossible for any decisions to be made and even the members of the white planter party found it increasingly difficult to agree amongst themselves. In1855 the Assembly was dissolved and new elections were held with the result that the Assembly now contained eleven white, fifteen mixed race and three black members. Some of the mixed race members supported the white Planter party meaning that it was difficult for any legislation favoring black interests to be passed. Shortly after the elections a new Governor, Charles Darling was appointed under whose administration much needed educational and health reforms were neglected in favour of law and order issues aimed mainly at the black population. Conflict between Darling and the Colonial Office continued into the 1860s with Darling attempting to loosen the authority of the British Government and, after elections in 1860, forming an Executive Committee of the Assembly consisting only of members of the Planter party and with no Afro-Jamaicans.

In the years leading up to 1865 Jamaica suffered various calamities including disease outbreaks, severe droughts and a rapid decline in sugar exports together with increasing discontent amongst the black population. This discontent was fuelled by high taxes, very low wages for those still employed on the estates and the fact that the British government had forbidden black people from growing their own crops on Crown lands or abandoned plantations. In 1862 Darling was replaced by Governor Eyre who continued with the racist policies of his predecessor, insisting that it was 'the low moral character of blacks' that was responsible for the situation in which they found themselves. In a letter to the Colonial Secretary in August 1864 Eyre revealed his total lack of understanding of the situation which was in fact the result of measures introduced by his own Assembly. He writes that the people must improve 'in social habits and in domestic comfort, as well as in material prosperity', they must 'improve in civilization' and 'educate their children in religion, industry and respectability'.[36] There were a few Assembly members who opposed Eyre and warned of the dangers of imposing such high taxes on everyday items such as food and clothing but they were largely ignored and the majority seemed blind to the fact that if the black population were encouraged to buy land and produce and sell crops it would help to alleviate the economic situation of the country. The presumption was that the only way to improve the economy was to increase production from the plantations using hired labour despite the fact that the freed slaves were no longer willing to provide that labour.

In October 1865 the grievances that had been building up in the population came to a head when a disturbance occurred at the Morant Bay courthouse over the imposition of excessive court charges for the trying of petty crimes and the charging of a man with trespass for entering estate land without permission. A local black preacher Paul Bogle disputed the court decisions and when police arrived to arrest him they were met by a large group of local men who attacked and overcame them. Governor Eyre called out the troops and the next day hundreds of men and women marched to Morant Bay to confront them. The militia opened fire on the crowd and some individuals responded by setting fire to the courthouse and surrounding buildings. The rebellion continued for several days, involving up to two thousand people, mostly small freeholders but also estate workers protesting against low wages and high rents and taxes. Eyre's retribution was severe with over four hundred rebels killed, their houses burned down and many severely flogged. When news of the rebellion reached Britain the reaction was mixed depending on the allegiances of those receiving the news and their personal knowledge of the situation in Jamaica. Reports of the events appeared in the Birmingham newspapers enabling the people of Birmingham who had fought for emancipation and an end to aprenticeship to read the facts as interpreted by those journals. It took some weeks for news to arrive from Jamaica and full reports did not appear until early in November, however reports of the rebellion were sent to newspapers in America soon after it occurred and these were later reprinted in newspapers such as the *Birmingham Daily Gazette*. On 13 November 1865 the *Gazette* printed a letter dated 22 October which had been sent to the *New York Daily News* from a correspondent in Jamaica. The writer of the letter sees a connection between the rebellion and recent events in America, the passing of the Thirteenth Amendment on the Abolition of Slavery, the surrender of the Confederate states and the assassination of Abraham Lincoln. He writes,

> The cloud has passed over your country to lour upon ours. The result of giving rein to the savageism of the negro is felt in our beautiful but desolated island. It commences with us; it may end with you . . .

> For some time past symptoms of insubordination have been apparent among the freedmen of this island. Released from the discipline of compulsory labor, the black population have, from the hour of emancipation, exhibited a disposition to relapse into their native barbarism. Their natural disinclination to work, their ignorance and improvidence, have long since disordered the industrial system that depended upon them for its physical efficiency...
>
> Then came your civil war, and the consummation of the grand project of 'universal freedom' that has cost you so fearful a sacrifice ... The stories of indulgence and support afforded by your Government to the freedmen of the South have reached, with the inevitable exaggerations, the ears of our shiftless, depraved, and irresponsible black population. They regard the result of the struggle in the United States as an invitation to them to assert the privileges of an equal, if not a superior race.[37]

The correspondent admits that from his position in Kingston he cannot provide details of the rebellion and hopes that reports of atrocities may prove to be untrue. However, he refers to 'atrocities revolting to human nature' and to the slaughter and torture of men, women and children. On 17 November an article in *The Gazette* included the remarkable statement that the rebels were 'determined to seize the land from all the landowners, white and coloured, and after killing all the males and children, to share the land and women amongst themselves'.[38]

A letter written by a 'gentleman resident in Jamaica' on 13 November was published by the *Birmingham Post* and reprinted in *The Globe* on 13 December. It demonstrates that not all white residents believed the horrendous stories of atrocities carried out by the rebels. He writes,

> Today we are able to record the cessation of 'martial law', which for a month has allowed the shooting and hanging and flogging of its victims. The evil spirit engendered by slavery is not got rid of in less perhaps than a hundred years. In this late outbreak they have revelled in blood, and sported with life; and when the truth dare be told it will appear.
>
> No one attempts to do anything but condemn the savage outbreak; yet none of us can believe there was a widespread intention to murder

the white and coloured people at Christmas, form a republic, burn Kingston, etc., etc. These are the false and foolish assertions of men who are alarmed, and conjure up to themselves the most dreadful things.[39]

Initially those reading reports of atrocities committed by the rebels were inclined to believe that their aim was to totally rid the island of its white population. There were many however who were familiar with accounts brought back by abolitionists such as Joseph Sturge and by missionaries who witnessed the sufferings endured by former slaves. They realized that the pressures and indignities inflicted by the planters on the black population would eventually be met with resistance. An article in the *Birmingham Journal* of 18 November criticizes the Colonial Office for not taking measures to prevent the uprising, writing that,

> For a longtime past there have been in Jamaica abundant signs of approaching difficulty between the white and coloured races. While increasing in numbers, the latter have steadily declined in prosperity, and, partly through poverty, partly through the course taken by legislation, have lost the hold they partially acquired upon the Government of the island. Their grievances, it appears have been known to the Colonial Office for months past ... At last, the discontent in the island had risen to such a pitch, that for nearly two months past the Colonial Office has been in daily expectation of receiving news of an outbreak.[40]

The writer of the article continues to refute reports made in some journals regarding the aims and actions of the rebels. He writes,

> Judging from the official despatches which have come to hand, it may be doubted whether the conspiracy had any such aims as those attributed to it; or that its extent was at all so formidable as is represented. One thing is very clear. Not only was the outbreak confined to the district round Morant Bay, but it was promptly and seemingly effectually put down within a few days after its occurrence ... We hope we do not underrate the difficulties of the task undertaken by the Government of the island; but while we are fully conscious that it was their first duty to restore order, we must confess that the accounts of the vengeance inflicted upon the unhappy negroes are such as to strike

with horror the mind of an English reader. Wholesale slaughter appears to have been the first thought of both civil and military authorities.

The writer describes how men and women were executed by order of Court Martial rather than being tried before a civil court, the trials usually lasting just a few minutes with no credible witnesses. He concludes,

> The bare recital of these lamentable stories is enough to demonstrate the necessity of immediate action on the part of the Home Government, if a rising of the whole negro population of Jamaica is to be prevented. And there is no question that immediate action must be followed by close enquiry into the causes of the recent outbreak, and the conduct of those who undertook to suppress and to punish it.

The Colonial Office under the leadership of Henry Taylor had indeed shown no enthusiasm for interfering in Jamaican affairs but as more reports arrived revealing the savage treatment of the black population under Eyre's command Taylor found himself under considerable pressure from abolitionists throughout Britain. He reluctantly set up an enquiry into Eyre's conduct which resulted in a decision to replace Eyre as Governor and eventually led to the abolition of the Jamaican Assembly and the imposition of Crown Colony government in April 1866. Those expecting that the situation of the black population would improve under the new governing body were soon to be disappointed. With the introduction of property qualifications for members the planters were actually given a greater share in government with black people having very little influence on decision making. Most members of the Colonial Office believed that the planters were best qualified to govern and used racist arguments to justify the exclusion of black Jamaicans.

Members of the Birmingham Anti-Slavery Society had joined with other abolitionists throughout the country to criticize the actions of Eyre and at a meeting in the city in the first week of December 1865 a majority voted to condemn the atrocities committed after the Morant Bay rebellion. William Morgan, the secretary of the society who had worked closely with Joseph Sturge started to collect signatures for a petition but found that many influential citizens had been influenced by newspaper reports of the rebellion and were not willing to criticize Eyre. A correspondent in the *Birmingham Journal* of 6 January wrote 'the unguided instincts of the mass in this country are undeniably in favour of the white in prejudice to the black population' and considered it 'better for fifty blacks to die than one white'.[41] After the establishment of the Crown Colony interest in the affairs of Jamaica gradually declined with matters closer to home, such as electoral reform, claiming the attention of public minded citizens in Birmingham and other cities. A Jamaica Committee was set up in Britain demanding that Eyre should be tried for his actions, but only a few representatives from Birmingham attended the inaugural meeting. A meeting of the Birmingham Jamaica Committee was held in the Town Hall at the end of 1866 but it was soon evident that there was insufficient support in the country for the trial and hoped for prosecution of Eyre.

The Ladies' Negro's Friend Society did condemn Eyre's actions but did not excuse 'negro misdeeds'. They reported that 'the events of the last few months solemnly instruct us, that when a nation emancipates its bondsmen, after ages of degradation and wrongs, its obligations are but half discharged; and that unless the freedmen are instructed and educated, emancipation . . . will never produce its most beneficent results'.[42] By this time the Ladies' Society was devoting most of its resources to providing aid for the freed slaves in America and obviously hoped that the white people of America would learn from the mistakes of those in Jamaica.

One Birmingham man who continued to campaign on behalf of the black population of Jamaica was William Morgan. In February 1866 he was sent by the British and Foreign Anti-Slavery Society, which had been founded by his friend Joseph Sturge, to carry out an investigation into the administrative and legal systems in Jamaica and their contribution to the unrest which had resulted in the uprising. He was accompanied by two Quakers, Thomas Harvey and William Brewin who later wrote an account of their experiences and what they had learned of the possible causes of unrest in the island. They talked to people who had witnessed events and visited prisons where men were still being held under martial law. On a visit to the overcrowded Kingston Penitentiary they saw 'about sixty prisoners with the word 'Rebel' conspicuously printed on the front of their dress: these had been sentenced by Court Martial to penal labour for various periods from three to ten years. William Morgan, the representative of the Anti-Slavery Society . . . felt great doubts, as a lawyer, of the validity of these sentences, now that martial law had ceased: he took an early opportunity of stating the case to the Governor . . . The decision of the Chief Justice set these prisoners free, and as a consequence about one hundred prisoners in this and other prisons of the island were gradually set at liberty'.[43]

Later in the year a correspondent wrote to Morgan 'I am glad to say that after making all enquiries respecting the conduct of the people who were released from prison through your kind interposition, not one of them has misbehaved himself in any way. They have all returned to their work'.[44] Morgan himself sent regular reports on his visit to the Anti-Slavery Reporter in London. He recalls talking to some white women who admitted hearing the cries and screams of men and women as they were beaten and flogged with 'wire cats', and yet 'not one expression of pity dropped from their lips when they recounted the horrors of the scene'. Morgan comments that 'their ideas were derived from the old times of slavery, and I was much pained by their apparent insensibility to the sufferings of the 'black creatures', as they call them'.[45] Despite his obvious concern for the black people of Jamaica, Morgan retained the view common amongst abolitionists and missionaries that it was only by imposing English values and Christian education upon the people that progress would be made. Observing how more land was being cultivated by small producers while land previously occupied by sugar plantations was uncultivated and abandoned he commented 'if the remainder of the land could be brought into cultivation under European auspices, then perhaps a higher type of civilization might be introduced, and the world would be the gainer'.[46] In the light of developments which occurred in the remaining years of the nineteenth century his words appear somewhat unfortunate, for sugar plantations were taken over by large firms such as Tate and Lyle but there was very little improvement in the lives of the peasant farmers most of whom still preferred to be independent freeholders. Holt notes that by the end of the century 'half the population lived on peasant-sized freeholds' which formed the 'backbone of the economy', and yet peasant farmers were given little financial support to acquire and maintain land. It was not until 1895 that legislation was passed for the sale of Crown lands but even then preference was given to those able to buy large areas of land which in effect meant members of the planter class. One important development which temporarily improved the financial situation of many peasant farmers was the introduction of the fruit industry and by 1890 bananas had replaced sugar as the principal export. However, as was the case with sugar, large companies, this time mainly American, stepped in with full support from the Colonial Office. As the main interest of companies such as the United Fruit Company was the accumulation of large profits the peasant fruit growers were paid the minimum for the fruit they supplied and in many cases had to resort to selling their land. Towards the end of the century limited self-rule was gradually introduced together with a new constabulary force and improved county courts. However, governing officials were still British and black Jamaicans had little influence in politics due to the high property qualifications needed for election to the House of Assembly. The country was run by and in the interests of the white elite and the Colonial Office seemed perfectly happy to go along with their racist policies. The American consul in Kingston wrote 'the prisons and penitentiaries of this island are conducted on the ideas prevailing fifty years ago – the treadmill, the stocks, and the whipping triangle being in full swing'.[47] In May 1897, Sir H. Hocking, a resident of Jamaica, wrote in a letter to the Colonial Office 'It must be remembered that the negro stands very low in the scale of humanity. The present black population is only a few generations removed from wild cannibal savages'. Holt adds the note that 'the Colonial Office merely praised Hocking's memo as a valuable minute'.[48]

Evidence that such views were common even amongst those who had supported abolition is not difficult to find. In 1896 William Adlington Cadbury, a Quaker and member of the Cadbury family of Birmingham, well known for their anti-slavery views, voyaged to the West Indies to visit the Cadbury cocoa estates in Jamaica, which had recently expanded to satisfy the demand for chocolate in Britain. Cadbury notes that one eighth of the population was British with French, German, Portuguese and 'Hindus' working on the estates. He estimates that half the population are coloured descendants of

African slaves whose 'lazy habits, drawling talk and uncontrollable mirth betray descent and must for ever place a natural barrier between them and races of Europe and America'.[49] In other words these proud people of African descent do not conform with Western ideas of civilized behavior.

Joseph Sturge, William Morgan and other members of the Birmingham Anti-Slavery Society who had worked tirelessly for emancipation and an end to apprenticeship also believed that they had a duty to bring Western modes of behavior and Christianity to the people they had helped to release from slavery. It was inevitable that the white elite who had the power to impose taxes and high land prices would continue to place financial restrictions on the black majority depriving them of the opportunity to demonstrate that they could achieve economic success on their own terms.

4

The Aftermath
Alabama

The black people of Jamaica suffered for many years after abolition as a result of racist policies imposed by the Jamaican Assembly and the British Colonial Office. However, although their suffering was great it cannot be compared in either severity or duration with the indignities and injustices imposed upon the freed slaves and their descendants in the Southern States of America.

After the momentous events of 1865, the surrender of the Confederate army, the assassination of Lincoln and the ratification of the 13th Amendment, the population of Alabama whether black or white, free or slave were left bewildered and uncertain about the direction their lives would take. One of the last slaves to be brought to Alabama through the port of Mobile in the South was Cudjo Lewis who related his story to the writer and anthropologist Zora Hurston in 1931.[1] He describes how on April 12,1865, 'Yankee' soldiers came to the boat where he was living and told him and the other slaves that they were now free and didn't belong to anyone. When he asked the soldiers where they should go the reply was that they could go wherever they felt like going. Without a house or land on which to build one Cudjo and his friends sought employment in the local sawmill or on the railroad but this possibility was not open to the thousands of freed slaves further north whose lives had been spent on the large cotton plantations of Alabama. After the initial celebrations on learning of their freedom many decided to test this freedom by leaving their homes and walking through the countryside to the nearest town. Many planters refused to acknowledge that their slaves were actually free, one resident of Alabama saying 'there is a kind of innate feeling, a lingering hope ... that slavery will be regalvanized in some shape or other'.[2] They warned the freed slaves not to give up 'the friendly, comfortable life on the old plantation for the illusory benefits of an unknown freedom', and when this method of persuasion was unsuccessful they resorted to more forceful methods. Kolchin quotes an army officer reporting that in Alabama 'whipping and the most severe modes of punishment are being resorted to to compel the Freedmen to remain at the old plantations and the negro kept in ignorance of his real condition, his freedom'.[3]

One initiative of Presidential Reconstruction was the setting up of the Freedmen's Bureau by Lincoln's successor, President Andrew Johnson in 1865. This was intended to oversee the transition from slavery to freedom and was staffed mainly by Union Army officers who had returned from the war. Its remit was to distribute food to those in need, provide the finance necessary for the setting up of schools and medical facilities and to oversee the provision of waged labour on the estates. The fact that the Bureau was set up to provide assistance to the planters as well as to the freed slaves meant that neither group had confidence in its ability to represent their own particular interests. In Alabama there were only twenty agents in the entire state led by Assistant Commissioner, Wager Swayne who undertook the difficult task of meeting the needs of the Freedmen while at the same time liaising with the planters. There were some abolitionists including Frederick Douglas who believed that the freed slaves should be left to take control of their own lives rather than being guided into particular courses of action laid down by the Bureau. Before Reconstruction he had said of the ex-slaves 'Let them alone ... our duty is done better by not hindering than by helping our fellow-men ... and the best way to help them is just to let them help themselves'.[4] Whether this strategy would have provided a better outcome for the freed slaves is a matter of conjecture for one of the first actions of Wager Swayne was to persuade them to stay on the plantations working for their former masters. In the words of Kolchin 'everywhere blacks were urged to 'behave' themselves and prove that they were worthy of their freedom by continuing to toil in the cotton fields'.[5] This labour was to be carried out under a contract system which specified the work to be carried out and the wages to be received and the labourers worked in gangs as they had done under slavery. Wages were often withheld if the labourer did not abide by the strict and often petty demands of the contract, a situation reminiscent of that imposed upon the freed slaves in Jamaica under the apprenticeship system. The dominance of the planter class in the State legislature enabled a series of laws known as the 'Black Codes' to be passed which placed considerable restrictions on the freedom and rights of the ex-slaves. In Alabama this included a vagrancy law which like the similar law in Jamaica enabled any black person found wandering in the countryside without apparent employment to be taken into forced labour on a plantation. The possibility that such a person might in fact be out searching for work would not be considered as the enactment of this law provided the planters with a supply of free labour. Another law included in the Black Codes was that forbidding the enticement of labourers which made it a crime to 'hire, entice away, or induce to leave the service of another, any laborer who had already contracted to work for another'.[6] This law aimed to reduce conflict between the planters but also served to reduce the freedom of labourers to make their own decisions as to where and for whom they should work. It was also an attempt to prevent planters from neighbouring Mississippi, which was suffering from a labour shortage, sending agents into Alabama to entice black labourers with promises of higher wages.

Despite laws aimed at enabling planters to maintain an adequate labouring force the aim of most freed slaves was to acquire their own plot of land and grow and sell their own crops. For most freedmen this was an impossible dream but there was an alternative to low-paid gang labour and that was some form of sharecropping. This involved an individual family signing a contract with the planter for a piece of land which all members of the family worked on and felt responsible for. Ideally they could retain and sell up to half the crop but the landowner was still able to dictate the terms of the contract and many planters were reluctant to relinquish the control they had exerted over their former slaves.

The introduction of the Black Codes designed to keep the freed slaves on the plantations failed to meet the planters' demand for labour as an increasing number of freedmen either moved to neighbouring towns to find employment or, despite laws restricting land ownership, managed to acquire their own plots of land. In 1867 the

United States Congress now dominated by Radicals in the Republican Party took control of the Reconstruction process and proceeded to introduce legislation which would protect the rights of the freed slaves threatening even further the dominant position of the planter class. The consequence, according to Jonathan Wiener, was that 'some planters, increasingly desperate to preserve the large-scale plantation organization based on wage labor, turned to terror, to the Ku Klux Klan'.[7] The Klan was a white supremacist group which had developed out of smaller groups of white men who assisted planters to retain their black workers by using threats of physical violence and often actual violent attacks to achieve their compliance. They were widespread in the black belt region of Alabama but also in the north of the state where poor white farmers feared competition from black workers moving north after emancipation. In some of the northern hill counties Klan members used threats of violence to prevent black people from entering the county and forcing those already there to leave. Circuit Judge, William S. Mudd[8] declared to a congressional investigating committee, 'In some portions of my circuit they will not let a negro live, that is, it is a white population, and they do not want to come in contact with a negro. They want to cultivate the lands themselves, and they want to have an exclusively white society'.[9] The Klan did not just target black people but also any white people who supported them which might include members of the Republican Party, missionaries and teachers in black schools. They usually operated at night, forcing their way into houses, violently attacking the occupants and whipping women and children. Many black churches and schools were regularly burned down.

 The Freedmen's Bureau in Alabama kept a record of all the beatings and murders carried out by members of the Ku Klux Klan and similar groups or individuals between 1865 and 1870. At a hearing in May 1865, Louisa Jeffries, a slave belonging to planter John Jeffries, testified that on the night of 11th of May their master with two other men broke into their cabin, each carrying a shot gun. They forced her husband Albert out of his bed, tied his hands and pointed a gun at his head. They took him out of the cabin and rode off and she had not seen him since. Later the same day Jeffries called all his labourers, who were now officially free, together and told them that their freedom would only last for 60 days. Brandishing his pistol he warned them 'that they had to be more obedient and humble if they did not want to go the way Albert went'. Another ex-slave testified that on 17th of May in a nearby field he saw 'the body of a colored man hanging by the neck which he recognized to be that of Albert Jeffries formerly slave of John Jeffries'.[10] Undoubtedly this murder was carried out as a warning to the remaining labourers of what might happen to them if they left the plantation.

The records of the Freedmen's Bureau contain a list of the murders and attacks carried out in Alabama in 1866, the following being those recorded in Tuscaloosa County adjacent to Jefferson County and present day Birmingham in the months between May and September.

May 7 – Moore taken to woods and hung till nearly dead to make him tell who robbed a store at Tuscaloosa.
May 30 – Freedman found hung by a grapevine in woods near Tuscaloosa.
July 16 – Black girl beaten to death by Washington and Greene McKinney, 18 miles west of Tuscaloosa.
July 18 – One Yerby set fire to colored church near Tuscaloosa. Threatened to kill black man who saw him do it
September 14 – Black man picking fodder in a field shot dead – and another who had difficulty with a white man abducted and supposed to have been murdered near Tuscaloosa.
September – Freedman shot dead while at his usual work near Tuscaloosa.[11]

Needless to say no one was brought to trial or punished for these crimes as anyone who might give evidence against a Klansman would be sure to receive retribution. In addition all the most prominent citizens including the district judges supported the Klan, one judge maintaining that Klan members were 'gentlemen of education and intelligence'. Wiener notes that 'when a black registrar of voters was murdered in Greensboro in 1867, and the murderer's accomplice was captured, his bond was signed by fifteen of the wealthiest citizens of Greensboro'.[12] The editor of the Tuscaloosa newspaper, the *Independent Monitor*, Ryland Randolph was actually a prominent Klan leader who declared he would 'thank God for another war if it re-established slavery' arguing that 'negroes as bondsmen were happier, more sleek and greasy-looking and better clothed, than they are now. We never hear the ringing horse-laughs . . . that formerly marked their *sans souci* existence'. Wiener comments 'for the boldness and clarity of his justification of Klan terror, Randolph was elected to the state legislature'.[13]

After Congressional, or what became known as Radical Reconstruction in 1867 the work of the Freedmen's Bureau continued, but under the Reconstruction Act the Southern States came under Federal control ensuring that laws protecting black rights were enforced. In July 1868 the Fourteenth Amendment to the Constitution was passed stating that all United States citizens should have equal protection under the law, including for male citizens, the right to vote. It also prevented Southern states from using property and literacy tests to bar blacks from voting by ensuring that the number of representatives they could send to Congress would be reduced in proportion to the number of male citizens denied the vote. Not surprisingly the Democrat supporting planter class, the poor whites and their violent accomplices in the Ku Klux Klan were not prepared to accept the new regime imposed by the Republicans under their new President Ulysses S. Grant, and during the following eight years any hope that a fairer and just society would emerge was gradually crushed as the aims of Radical Reconstruction failed to be accomplished.

Initially there was considerable optimism amongst the black population and in Alabama freedmen enthusiastically attended political meetings eager to learn more about their new won rights. The most important political organization was the Union League which supported the Republican Party and encouraged the freedmen to vote and to question their employment rights. They met in black churches and schools and were subject to frequent attacks by the Ku Klux Klan. The following statement was made at an Alabama convention in 1868:

> We claim exactly *the same rights, privileges and immunities as are enjoyed by white men* – we ask nothing more and will be content with nothing less . . . The law no longer knows white nor black, but simply men, and consequently we are entitled to ride in public conveyances, hold office,

sit on juries and do everything else which we have in the past been prevented from doing solely on the ground of color.[14]

Despite the large number of blacks going to the polls Alabama was one of five states where none were elected to high office during Reconstruction, all major positions being taken by white Republicans suggesting that black votes were being used to advance the careers of white politicians. A large number of black men were however employed in public services particularly the police force and also served as magistrates and justices of the peace. Most juries were racially mixed, Foner quoting one white lawyer as saying 'that being compelled to address blacks as gentlemen of the jury was the severest blow I have felt'.[15] Planters who were accustomed to controlling the court system were obviously unhappy to find their powers curtailed, and this particularly applied to the non-enforcement of the vagrancy laws which had provided them with a supply of free labour.

One of the most important tasks of Reconstruction was to establish an effective school system providing education for both black and white children. The Freedmen's Bureau assisted by the American Missionary Association had been successful in setting up some schools for black children in Northern Alabama, mainly in and around Huntsville, which due to early occupation had been less affected by the war. By 1866 there were still only 35 schools for black children in the state of Alabama mainly in towns and cities.[16] The situation did gradually improve, mainly due to the demand from the freedmen for education, and at the end of 1866 Wager Swayne declared 'too much cannot be said of the desire to learn among this people ... everywhere, to open a school has been to have it filled'.[17] Racist attitudes were still common even amongst well-meaning white teachers, one teacher commenting that 'it is not always the lightest ... skinned ones that are the best scholars,' and another that 'the very dark ones learn as rapidly as the light colored'.[18] It was important that more black teachers should be recruited and several training colleges were set up for that purpose, the largest being in Talladega just south of present day Birmingham. The American Missionary Association appointed Rev. Henry E. Brown to work with local black groups to appoint their own teachers and recruit students. Very few of the new schools were racially mixed, most white parents refusing to allow their children to mix with black children in the classroom and many black families believing that their children would be more fairly treated in an all black school. The Republicans realized that it would be impossible to legislate against this segregated system and as with many other measures found that they were unable to effectively confront the long-held and extreme racist views of most Southern Whites. Many Civil Rights laws were not enforced, an example being the promise of equal treatment on public transport. Even middle-class black people were not allowed to travel in first-class carriages on the railways and were relegated to lower deck smoking carriages. Many restaurants and hotels either excluded blacks or provided separate usually inferior accommodation.

From the beginning of Radical Reconstruction and into the 1870s an increasing number of black men became involved in politics. One of the most important was James T Rapier, a free-born African-American who was elected to represent Alabama in the United States Congress in 1872, and whose career is closely linked with events in Alabama during the late 1860s and 1870s. Rapier was born in Florence in the north of Alabama to parents who had been freed early in the century and his father, a successful barber made sure that James went to school and learned to read and write. When he was sixteen years old he went with his uncle to Ontario in Canada to live in a community of former slaves who had escaped from the South. He attended a Mission School and learned Latin, Greek and Mathematics as well as undergoing a religious conversion which made him determined to devote his life to fighting for civil rights. He trained as a teacher in Toronto and then studied Law before eventually returning to Florence in 1866 to care for his sick father. He became a successful cotton planter in the Tennessee Valley and after Congressional Reconstruction in 1867 was selected as a delegate to the first Republican State Convention in Montgomery, Alabama where a new state constitution was to be drafted. Feldman notes that,

> 'this was the first time in Alabama's history that whites and Negroes had met together. Rapier took an active part in these proceedings. On the opening day of the convention, he made a speech in favor of universal suffrage as a provision in the new constitution. Further, Rapier told the convention that the poor whites needed the protection of a constitu-

tion granting all the right to vote because during slavery they had few voting rights'.[19]

Some white Democrats objected strongly to a black man being involved in state politics and in 1868, despite his support for poor whites, Rapier was driven from his home by the Ku Klux Klan and was forced to live in hiding in Montgomery for nearly a year. On returning to the North of the state Rapier campaigned to organize people into Unions and started the Alabama Labor Movement to ensure the rights of black labourers. Feldman notes that Rapier 'rode horseback with literature in his saddle-bags, visited workers in cities and sharecroppers in the country in an effort to organize unions for the social and economic betterment of these people'.[20]

In 1872 Rapier won the Republican nomination to represent Alabama (2nd District) in Congress, beating the Confederate veteran, William C. Oates. He served on the Committee on Education and Labor and in1874 worked on the Civil Rights Bill which 'guaranteed equal access to public accommodation for all individuals'. In discussions on the Bill in Congress several black Congressmen spoke of the 'outrages and indignities' they had suffered and Rapier recalled how he had been 'denied service by inns at every stopping point between Montgomery and Washington'.[21] Although passed in 1875 this Bill was declared unconstitutional by the Supreme Court in 1883. As a result of their involvement with the Civil Rights Bill, Rapier and the four white Congressmen from Alabama who had supported him were threatened by the Ku Klux Klan and an attempt was made on the life of one of them. Feldman notes that 'after this attack, the Klansmen rode after Congressman Rapier, but his friends came to his defense and drove them off'.[22] In the year leading up to Rapier's campaign for re-election to Congress in1874 the country suffered a massive financial crisis and entered a period of Depression which lasted well into the 1880s. Racial violence and intimidation by the Ku Klux Klan together with loss of faith in the Republican government of Alabama meant that Rapier lost his seat in Congress to a Democrat, a former Confederate Army Major. Commenting on this election Feldman writes 'the white man was beaten and intimidated. The Negro was killed and denied the vote. This is the gangster way in which the glorious democratic unity which Rapier and others helped build was broken'.[23] In 1878 Rapier was appointed as a collector for the Internal Revenue service in Alabama's Second District and continued to work with the Labor Movement, but his health declined and he 'died penniless in 1883, having dispersed his wealth among black schools, churches, and emigration organizations'.[24]

Rapier's personal story is strongly linked with national and state affairs which in 1874 led to Alabama becoming the first Southern state to abandon the process of Reconstruction. From the beginning of Congressional Reconstruction in 1867 the Radical Republicans had realized that economic development was the most important factor in ensuring their success. They aimed to build new towns and encourage the development of industries which would make use of the vast mineral resources known to exist in the north of Alabama, particularly in Jefferson County and the area now occupied by the industrial city of Birmingham. This industrial development would necessarily involve the construction of new railroads which would provide employment for many of the freedmen. The Republicans' enthusiasm for development was not shared by the planter class who could see their dominant position in the state being usurped by the Northern industrialists. Wiener points out that 'the planters never opposed industry *per se*' but 'favored limited industrial development to the extent that it served their own interests and occurred under their own auspices', and 'took place strictly within the confines of a planter dominated agrarian society'.[25] Similarly they did not oppose all railroad development as they were dependent on rail to transport their cotton to the ports and receive manufactured goods from the north. A certain amount of industrial development had taken place during the Civil War when the Confederate army's increasing demand for weapons had resulted in the development of iron furnaces and weapon making factories in the north of the state, most of which were destroyed by the advancing Union army. The Shelby iron works, now a historical site just south of Birmingham, depended almost entirely on black slave labour which was 'leased' from plantation owners in central Alabama.

The immediate cause of the economic crisis in the North which occurred towards the end of 1873 was the collapse of banks which had made huge speculative investments in railroad construction only to find that the railroad industry failed to deliver on its building programme. The Republicans in Alabama could no longer borrow money from Northern investors and railroad construction came to a halt together with iron and steel production. The Democrats seized on these events to stress that Republican investment in the railroads was an economic failure and that the crisis would result in unrest amongst unemployed Southern blacks.

Nicolas Barreyre notes that 'the Civil Rights Bill then moving through Congress made things even worse politically' as it 'would ban all kinds of racial segregation', a move that would be totally unacceptable to the Democrats. Barreyre concludes, 'their idea that it was time to finish Reconstruction and give the direction of the country to its natural elite furthered northern acquiescence to the violent conquest of power by Democratic planters in the South'.[26] In the lead up to the 1874 elections in Alabama former members of the Ku Klux Klan formed a new paramilitary organization called the White League, 'openly dedicated to the violent restoration of white supremacy. It targeted local Republican officeholders for assassination, disrupted court sessions, and drove black laborers from their homes'.[27] In an attempt to avoid defeat the Republicans had nominated an all-white list of candidates but despite this many blacks turned out to vote, facing intimidation and violence as they did so. In one county hundreds of blacks on their way to cast their votes were fired on by armed whites, killing seven and wounding many more. As a result of the election the Democrats regained full control of the state legislature and proceeded to rewrite the state constitution undoing most of the reforms introduced by the Radical Republicans and bringing an end to Congressional Reconstruction.

Before considering the long-term effects on the black population of what came to be referred to by the victorious Democrats as 'Redemption', it is necessary to examine the developments occurring in Jefferson County which led in 1871 to the foundation of the city of Birmingham. In the 1850s geological surveys revealed the potential of the area for industrial development when large deposits of iron ore, limestone and coal were found in the Jones Valley region of the county where Birmingham now stands. The state legislature decided to put money into planning a route for a railroad which would connect the iron and coalfields with Selma and work began on the railroad in 1859. The planters actually supported the railroad but only so that coal and iron ore could be transported to Mobile in the South for foreign export. They were not interested in the possibility of industrial development in the Birmingham area and the local manufacture of pig iron and in fact sought to obtain finance from the North to construct another railroad which would run from Alabama to Chattanooga in Tennessee. Their idea was that iron ore would be transported to Chattanooga where it would be converted to pig iron thus avoiding the development of the labor intensive refining and smelting industry in Alabama. The Civil War prevented any further development of these proposed railroads but after 1868 sufficient investment was procured and, despite considerable conflict with the planters as to the routes to be taken, work began. Fortunately for the development of Birmingham the route to Chattanooga which would bypass the mineral rich area was abandoned and after investment by the Kentucky based Louisville and Nashville railroad the important route connecting Birmingham to the North was established. The end of the war and emancipation meant that many freedmen made their way northwards to find work on the railroads and as early as 1864 advertisements such as the following appeared in Montgomery, with instructions to apply to the Chief Engineer.

> Wanted to Hire 600 Negroes to work on the South and North Alabama and Central Railroads, between Montgomery and Elyton, at Bridging, Track laying, Grading, getting ties, timbers etc. for the year 1864.[28]

The demand for black labour on the railroads led to conflict between the industrialists and the planters who needed large numbers of labourers to work on the cotton plantations. One former slave interviewed for the Federal Writers' Project in the 1930s describes how after emancipation he left the cotton plantation and 'came to Birmingham ... to work on the railroad they were putting through ... lifting ties and sweating with the rails'. He describes how the foreman was always shouting at them 'about being lazy when we was working ourselves nearly to death'. He says that one day he saw a foreman hit a black man for taking a drink of water and how the man picked up a shovel, hit the foreman on the head and then ran away. He says 'Back in slavery days they didn't do something and run, they run before they do it cos they knew that if they struck a white man there wasn't goin to be no nigger'.[29]

The expansion of the railroads and reopening of iron furnaces in Jefferson County led to an increase in demand for land from developers and in 1871 a group of businessmen and financiers, realizing the potential of the iron ore producing region set up the Elyton Land Company with the aim of building a city based on the merger of three pre-existing towns, the largest of which was Elyton. They bought land and sold lots to developers, and as construction commenced had to find a name for the new city. The first president of the Company, James R Powell had recently visited Birmingham in England and recognizing the importance of this city in the Industrial Revolution suggested that the new industrial city in Alabama should be given the same name. Powell was a wealthy cotton planter who had supported the Confederate cause and during the Civil War purchased extensive cotton plantations in Mississippi. Together with other planters he was responsible for sending agents into neighbouring Alabama in order to hire labour from established plantations in contravention of the enticement law contained in the Black Codes. The banker, Josiah Morris, who was the founder of the Elyton Land Company, had advanced large sums of money to cotton planters before the war and several other shareholders including Benjamin P. Worthington and William S Mudd had been plantation owners. It may be said that the city of Birmingham, Alabama was founded on money made from the labour of slaves in the same way as much of the reputation and wealth of the city of Birmingham in England was founded on guns and machinery used to maintain the Atlantic slave trade.

The financial crisis of 1873 put a temporary break on further industrial development in Birmingham and the real estate boom came to an end. However with the end of Reconstruction some of the new Democrat members of the legislature realized that some industrial development was essential if the state was to prosper and in 1878 persuaded the Alabama based Pratt Coal and Coke Company to open the Pratt mines in Birmingham. The new President of the Elyton Land Company, Henry Caldwell, agreed to donate land for the development of the mines and it was fortuitous that around the same time new methods were being developed for the production of iron from iron ore in blast furnaces using locally produced coke. The resulting combination of the iron ore and coal industries meant that by the early 1880s Birmingham was on the way to becoming one of the largest iron producing areas in America. This rapid industrial growth was dependent on an increasing supply of manual labour, much of this labour being provided by black workers who had moved north in search of work and settled in Birmingham. The reversal of desegregation policies which had been introduced by the Radical Republicans before their defeat in 1874 meant that the black workers were forced to live in segregated areas of the city with inferior housing and few amenities. As can be seen from the account of the black railway worker previously described, the treatment of black workers by their bosses had much in common with the treatment received by slaves on the plantations before emancipation, a new industrial slavery replacing the old plantation slavery. It might be argued that unlike slaves, workers in the coal and iron ore mines were paid and were free to leave their work if they wished. However this did not apply to the large number of mainly black prisoners who were forced to work in the mines under the 'Convict-Lease System'. Unfortunately the 13th Amendment which brought an end to slavery in 1865 allowed this system of enforced labour to continue. The wording 'Neither slavery nor involuntary servitude, except as a punishment for crime whereof the party shall have been duly convicted, shall exist within the United States', contained no precise definition of what constituted a crime and presumed the existence of a just and fair legal system. Post-Civil War 'Black Codes' which had been abolished under Radical Reconstruction were re-introduced, particularly the laws relating to vagrancy and petty offences. People could be arrested and imprisoned if they were found moving around in search of work or for minor misdemeanors like gambling or petty thieving. Convicts would then be leased to private companies like the Pratt Mining Company providing them with a continuous supply of cheap labour and at the same time generating revenue for the state. Conditions in the mines were horrendous, far worse than most had experienced as slaves on the cotton plantations. A report in *The New York Times* in December 1882 described the living conditions of

> 'black prisoners packed into a single cramped cabin like slaves on the Atlantic passage. The building had no windows. Vermin-ridden bunks

stacked three high were covered with straw . . . food was served cold from unwashed coal buckets, and all 150 black convicts shared three half-barrel tubs for washing. All convicts were forced to wear shackles consisting of an iron hoop fastened around the ankle to which is attached a chain two feet long and terminating in a ring'.[30]

Frederick Douglass, the abolitionist leader, statesman and orator wrote,

'The vice of this proceeding is that the County Officials and Corporations are mutually interested in increasing the Convict class for selfish and pecuniary purposes, and that, instead of lessening the number of convicts, it is their interest to increase the number. Alabama has been very cruel to her convicts. At the meeting of the National Prison Association in 1880, Mr Dawson, President of Alabama Board of Inspectors of Convicts, said that, at one time, the prison mortality had been 41 per 100 annually . . . In 1882 a warden wrote of the state of affairs in Alabama, that the prisons were as filthy as dirt could make them, and both prisons and prisoners infected with vermin; that the convicts were excessively and sometimes cruelly punished; that they were poorly clothed and fed . . . that there was no adequate water supply, and that the men were so intimidated that it was next to impossible to get from them anything touching their treatment; adding 'Our system is a better training school for criminals than are the dens of our great cities. The system is a disgrace to the state, a reproach to civilization and the Christian sentiment of the age, and ought to be speedily abandoned'.[31]

Officially there were regulations governing the work and living conditions of prisoners, stating that they should 'receive adequate food, be provided with clean living quarters, and be protected from "cruel" or "excessive punishment"', but these laws were never enforced.[32] Whipping was frequently used as a punishment if the expected quota for each man of five tons of coal every day was not met. More than forty lashes were delivered with a leather whip sometimes spiked with metal. The only official requirement that did seem to be obeyed was that black men who made up 90 percent of the prison population were to be completely segregated from the small number of white convicts, segregation laws now being applied to all aspects of life.

W.E.B. Du Bois saw the convict-lease system as being 'a return to another form of slavery', adding 'in no part of the modern world has there been so open and conscious a traffic in crime for deliberate social degradation and private profit as in the South since slavery'. He quotes a Southern white woman describing the actions of a 'whipping boss' as 'he stands over his pinioned victim and applies the lash on the naked, quivering flesh of a fellowman . . . and just think of the mercilessness, the inhumanity, the bestiality of the sentiment that can drive the lash deeper and deeper through the cuts and gashes on the body of a human being'.[33] The convict lease system continued well into the twentieth century with little improvement in conditions. In 1923 a group of women from the Alabama Federation of Women's Clubs issued a report on a visit they had made to a mine in the Birmingham area. They noted that although lashes or whips were no longer used, 'stout staffs' were used as clubs to beat the prisoners if they did not complete their allocated tasks on time. There was also a new method of punishment in which prisoners were confined in 'punishment cells known as dog-houses . . . coffin-like boxes standing on end, dark, narrow, and ventilated only by air holes at the top'. Men could be confined in these cells, unable to move, for up to forty-eight hours.[34]

The treatment of black men, and a small number of women, under the convict leasing system was just one way in which the white supremacists in the Southern states strove to exert their authority and regain control over a group of people they considered to be innately inferior, lazy, irresponsible and fit only to serve them as slaves and then as labourers in agriculture and industry. In the 1880s and 1890s the State legislature in Alabama, in common with other Southern states proceeded to introduce laws which discriminated against black people in every aspect of their lives, laws which in the 1890s came to receive the racist appellation of 'Jim Crow laws'. The choice of the term 'Redemption' for this process reflects the belief possessed by the white supremacist Democrats that they were saving the South from the errors of the past just as Christ the Redeemer was supposed to have saved people from their sins. In consequence the process became closely associated with white Protestant Christianity. To use the words of Eric Foner the new Redeemers shared 'a commitment to dismantling the Reconstruction state, reducing the political power of blacks, and reshaping the South's legal system in the interests of labor control and racial subordination'. As in Jamaica the taxation system was designed to adversely affect labourers, tenants and small farmers who 'paid taxes on virtually everything they owned – tools, mules, even furniture – while many planters had thousands of dollars in property excluded'.[35] In Alabama public hospitals were closed and state funding for schools was reduced, with the large number of newly established white schools receiving most of the funds. In order to avoid violation of the Fourteenth Amendment which included the statement that no state could 'deny to any person within its jurisdiction the equal protection of the laws' a policy of 'separate but equal' was adopted by which services such as public transportation, housing, medical care, schools and even facilities such as hotels and restaurants would be segregated by race. Although abhorrent, this policy might have been more acceptable to black people if the separate facilities were in fact equal, but from inadequate, poorly equipped schools to uncomfortable and crowded railcar accommodation, the black population was continually made aware that they were not considered to be equal members of the society in which they lived and worked.

Perhaps one of the most egregious laws introduced by the Alabama state legislature was the anti-miscegenation law which had been in existence since 1867 but was updated in 1876 and again in 1886 and 1896. Originally designed to prevent 'dilution' of white southern society after emancipation, the law stated,

> If any white person and any negro, or the descendant of any negro, to the third generation inclusive, though one ancestor of each generation was a white person, intermarry, or live in adultery or fornication with each other, each of them must, on conviction, be imprisoned in the penitentiary, or sentenced to hard labor for the county, for not less than two, nor more than seven years.[36]

In 1883 a case was brought before the United States Supreme Court in an attempt to show that Alabama's anti-miscegenation ruling was unconstitutional. The case referred to as *Pace v. Alabama*, was brought by an African-American man, Tony Pace and a white woman, Mary Cox, who were residents of Alabama. The couple were forbidden from marrying under existing Alabama law but under anti-miscegenation legislation they were charged with co-habiting and sentenced to two years imprisonment. Pace cited the Fourteenth Amendment in his defense arguing that as he was being treated differently to a white person he was not receiving equal protection under the law. The convictions were upheld by the court on the grounds that it was not the colour of the defendants that was important but the fact that their relationship could lead to 'a mongrel population and a degraded civilization' by producing a mixed-race child. This ruling remained part of Alabama's state constitution for the next eighty years.

The policy of 'separate but equal' enabled the Southern State legislatures to manipulate the terms of the Fourteenth Amendment to accommodate their own racist policies, aided and abetted by sympathetic members of the Supreme Court. However the state legislature found themselves to be more constrained by the wording of the Fifteenth Amendment of 1870 which reinforced the requirement that all male citizens of the United States had the right to vote. The statement that 'The right of citizens of the United States to vote shall not be denied or abridged by the United States or by any State on account of race, color, or previous condition of servitude', meant that the state legislature were legally unable to introduce laws restricting the voting rights of black people. They were however able to introduce legislation which made it almost impossible for the majority of black men to cast their votes. Commencing in the early 1890s state constitutions contained clauses which introduced poll taxes, literacy tests, residency requirements, complex voter registration rules and even tests to demonstrate understanding of the Constitution. These clauses eventually had the effect of disenfranchising most black people but also a large number of poor whites. Legislation passed in the 1890s culminated in the Alabama Constitution of 1901 which effectively deprived all black people of the right to vote and established Alabama as a 'white supremacist' state for the next sixty years, the implications of which will be examined in the next chapter.

It now remains to consider developments in the city of Birmingham in the last twenty years of the nineteenth century as it struggled to progress as a major industrial city. From the early 1880s when the Birmingham iron industry started to expand, the planter press in the cotton growing areas around Montgomery increased their campaign against further industrial development. They stressed that 'agriculture was the true basis of Alabama's economy' and that iron production was susceptible to fluctuations in the market and economic downturns. The planters were concerned about the increasing number of black workers who were leaving the plantations to find work in the new industries in and around Birmingham and made frequent reference to the poor living conditions and low wages endured by those who moved to find work in the new city. In the mid 1880s an economic decline in the North might have provided Birmingham with the opportunity to compete successfully with the large steel producing industry in Pittsburgh, Pennsylvania, but unfortunately Birmingham was still depending on exporting pig iron and had not yet developed its own steel industry. In 1889 the first steel was produced in Birmingham using local iron but due to a lack of capital investment the steel plant was forced to close. By the end of the century Birmingham did succeed in producing commercially successful steel but was never able to fully compete with the steel producing areas in the North.

One development which, if it had been successful, would have profoundly affected the lives of black people in Alabama, was the formation of the Populist Party in 1891. In the 1880s poor white farmers and black labourers grouped together to oppose the Democrats and formed groups such as the Farmers' Alliance and the Colored Alliance with the aim of improving pay and conditions of work. In 1891 these groups joined together as the Populist Party which held its first state convention in Birmingham in 1892. White leaders said they would work to protect the rights of blacks and proposed to abolish the convict-lease system. Their leader Reuben F. Kolb ran for Governor but by manipulating the votes the Democrats gained a majority. The Populist Party did win two Congressional elections in 1894 but two years later when they joined with the Republicans in state and Congress elections they lost to the Democrats who remained in power in the Southern states until the second half of the twentieth century.

For the first few years after emancipation the freed slaves experienced little improvement in their lives and working conditions, mainly due to the imposition of the 'Black Codes'. W.E.B. Du Bois quotes from the Congressional Globe reporting on a convention of 'colored people of Alabama in 1866',

> They also state that many of their people daily suffer almost every form of outrage and violence at the hands of whites; that in many parts of the state their people cannot safely leave the vicinity of their homes; they are knocked down and beaten by their white fellow-citizens without having offered any injury or insult as a cause; they are arrested and imprisoned upon false accusations; their money is extorted for their release, or they are condemned to imprisonment at hard labor.[37]

After Radical Reconstruction in 1867 black people experienced a little of what a life of freedom and equality might mean. To quote Eric Foner, 'Black participation in Southern public life after 1867 was the most radical development of the Reconstruction years, a massive experiment in interracial democracy without precedent in the history of this or any other country that abolished slavery in the nineteenth century',[38] but this experiment was short-lived. In the words of Du Bois, 'the slave went free; stood a brief moment in the sun; then moved back toward slavery'.[39]

During the last twenty years of the nineteenth century the foundation was laid in the Southern states of America for a system of segregation and disenfranchisement that would last for a further sixty years, a system based on the idea of white supremacy, the enforcement of Jim Crow laws and the return of the Ku Klux Klan.

5

The Twentieth Century
1900–1960

From Jamaica to Birmingham, England

At the beginning of the twentieth century Jamaica was still a colony under the control of an Imperial power, a power which was intent on expanding its influence throughout the world. Changes had been made in an attempt to improve the lives of the peasant class but there was no intention on Britain's part of introducing changes which would give Afro-Jamaicans more political influence in the running of their country. The post of Colonial Secretary between 1895 and 1903 was held by Joseph Chamberlain, the Member of Parliament for Birmingham who had arrived in the city at the age of eighteen in 1854, five years before the death of Joseph Sturge. Chamberlain had come to Birmingham from London to join his uncle's screw making business, rapidly rising to the top in the business and in 1873 being appointed mayor of the city. He was responsible for initiating massive improvements to the infrastructure of the city, including the construction of roads, water and sewage works and a programme of slum clearance. He served as Member of Parliament for Birmingham from 1876 until his death in 1914. Chamberlain started his political career as a radical Liberal but because of his opposition to Home Rule in Ireland he became a member of the Liberal Unionist Party. In 1895 when the Conservatives gained power they formed a coalition with the Liberal Unionists and Chamberlain was now the member of a party which was in favour of expanding the British Empire and in his role as Colonial Secretary was able to implement imperialistic policies. Chamberlain's views with regard to the colonies was very much in line with late nineteenth century racist ideology which while admitting that the ex-slaves were perfectly capable of labouring on their own pieces of land producing fruit and vegetables to support the economy, they were certainly not capable of taking part in the government of their own country. In 1897 the report of a Royal Commission on Jamaica was published which was endorsed by Chamberlain and formed the basis of official policy. Its recommendations moved away from the widely held view that Jamaica would only flourish under a system in which large numbers of poorly paid labourers worked on large estates under the control of the planter class. Instead the report stated,

> . . . it seems to us that no reform affords so good a prospect for the permanent welfare in the future of the West Indies as the settlement of the labouring population on the land as small peasant proprietors, and in many places this is the only means by which the population can in future be supported.[1]

This system could only be profitable if small landowners were able to make a living from produce such as bananas which they were able to grow and sell, however by the end of the century the expansion of large international companies had made this increasingly impossible. Joseph Chamberlain and the Royal Commissioners may have supported peasant agriculture and reforms in land tenure but still considered that 'black economic and moral progress depended on white guidance and control'.[2] In a Parliamentary debate in March 1898 during which the allocation of funds to the Crown Colonies was discussed, Chamberlain did demonstrate an awareness of the 'special obligation which rests upon this country' in the case of the West Indies. He refers to the conclusion of the Report of the Royal Commission which stated that 'the population, which is chiefly a population of negroes, has been placed in the islands by force, either by compulsion employed by this country in the old days of the slave trade or by compulsion employed by other countries'. He quotes the Commissioners as saying, 'We have placed the labouring population where it is, and created the conditions, moral and material, under which it exists, and we cannot divert from ourselves responsibility for its future'. Chamberlain says that he associates himself entirely with that observation and believes 'it constitutes an additional claim upon this country, in consequence of the distress which now overhangs the islands'.³

The people of Birmingham, particularly the members of the Ladies' Negro's Friend Society and the Birmingham and Midland Freedmen's Aid Association had done much to support the black people of Jamaica and the freed slaves in America, but partly as a consequence of the Morant Bay rebellion and the often distorted reports carried by local newspapers, interest in the welfare of the emancipated slaves gradually declined, with many women devoting themselves instead to the struggle for full suffrage in their own country. In Chamberlain's time as Mayor and Member of Parliament the people of Birmingham, as in many other cities, became more concerned with improvements that were taking place in their own environment, and the feeling of pride in their own city led them to believe that they occupied a higher position in 'the hierarchy of races, peoples and nations'. As Hall rightly concludes, 'this was the formative myth for Joseph Chamberlain, on which late nineteenth century imperialism was built'.⁴

Despite promises of reform from the Colonial Government the black people of Jamaica entered the twentieth century having little or no say in determining the policies which controlled their lives. They continued to be regarded by many as members of an inferior race, they suffered from a prejudicial court system and when convicted suffered horrendous conditions in prison, and as in America voting rights were severely restricted by the imposition of property, tax and literacy requirements which made it impossible for most black men to vote. Despite the recommendations of the Royal Commission peasant farmers continued to lose land to large fruit companies as land prices increased to a point beyond the reach of small farmers. The result was that thousands of Jamaicans migrated to America in search of work, many being employed in the construction of the Panama Canal where they worked under horrendous conditions, many dying from disease or injury. Oswald Deniston, a Jamaican who sailed to Britain on the *Windrush* in 1948 when he was thirty-five years old, recalls in an interview the problems encountered by Jamaicans in search of employment in the 1920s. Denniston was born in St James, Montego Bay and left school when he was fourteen to work on a sugar estate, sixty miles from his home. The work was only for six months in the year and so like many others Denniston went to Panama 'when they were recruiting people for the Panama Canal'. He explains ' . . . people going away – that's the only way you see people. Most Jamaicans who have, at that time, had anything, they had travelled. They didn't make it at home because very few people could work and get well-off, you know, with the wages they earned in Jamaica'.[5]

The outbreak of the First World War in 1914 provided many Jamaicans with the opportunity to find employment fighting for Britain in the armed services. A small West India Regiment had existed in Jamaica since 1795 when men had been liberated from slave ships to fight in the wars against the French, but towards the end of 1915 as the First World War expanded beyond Europe and the casualty rate increased, the need for more troops led to the formation of the British West Indies Regiment (BWIR), the majority of the recruits coming from Jamaica. David Olusoga notes that those expecting that volunteers would be treated equally, irrespective of race were soon disillusioned, the War Office having no intention of permitting black volunteers 'to fight in France alongside white soldiers and against a white enemy'. The first four battalions were sent to Egypt and the Middle East and when the first West Indian troops were sent to France in 1916 expecting to fight alongside British troops they became instead a 'labour battalion', digging trenches, building roads and working in the munitions depots and as stretcher bearers. The men 'were subjected to racial taunts from white troops', one soldier complaining that he and his comrades from the BWIR were 'treated neither as Christians nor as British citizens, but as West Indian "Niggers", without anybody to be interested in or look after us'.[6] Instead of joining the BWIR some men managed to travel to Britain as individuals and enlist in British army units which were desperate for recruits. One notable Jamaican, Norman Manley, who was studying in Britain in 1915, was accepted into the Royal Field Artillery and fought in the Battle of the Somme. Olusoga notes that Manley was 'appalled by the routine racism and prejudice' that was directed towards him. His brother, Roy, who enlisted with him was killed near Ypres in 1917. The men who survived the war returned to Jamaica when it came to an end, many to face hardship and unemployment for the next twenty years before the outbreak of the Second World War.

During the 1930s the sugar industry in Jamaica, which had been in decline for many years started to revive, partly due to increased demand worldwide but also due to modernization in the industry and the amalgamation of many smaller estates into larger corporations. WISCO, the West Indian Sugar Company which was controlled by Tate and Lyle introduced policies which although aimed at improving the living and working conditions of their employees, actually resulted in lower wages and a reluctance to take on new workers from outlying areas. They built new housing which was provided free to their permanent workers, together with free health care, a clean water supply and sewage disposal, all designed to improve the economic value of their workforce. As one of the company doctors observed human life has 'a direct money value' and 'health must be regarded from an economic as well as a humanitarian point of view'.[7] WISCO's managing director R.L.M. Kirkwood admitted that 'expenditures on general welfare were in lieu of any significant wage increases'.[8] This system may have benefited the small number of employees who lived and worked on the estate throughout the year but it did not benefit the larger number of peasant farmers who worked on their own or rented land for most of the year and came down to the estates during harvest time. In 1937 WISCO started the construction of a new central sugar mill at Frome Estate employing increasing numbers of workers and there were reports that high wages were being offered. These reports attracted hundreds of unemployed workers but as Holt observes 'there were neither jobs enough nor housing enough to accommodate this influx. The disappointed aspirants simply camped out, their sullen despair barely softened by hope'.[9] On 29 April 1938 the stage was set for the first of many riots that were to take place at Frome and other estates. Workers were made to queue for up to seven hours to receive their pay which was lower than they expected due to unexplained deductions. Some threw stones at the pay office causing the clerk to retaliate by shooting a pistol into the crowd. On the following Monday the workers accompanied by unemployed job-seekers were met by a force of armed police, but undeterred they surrounded the estate hurling stones and metal bars towards the company's offices. The incident at Frome was followed by riots and demonstrations in other parts of the island resulting in death, injury and many arrests. As a result, another Royal Commission led by Lord Moyne was set up by the Colonial Office, which due to the outbreak of war was not fully published until 1945. Although the report recognized the bad social and economic conditions under which the majority of the population lived its tone seemed to imply that the reason for this lay with the people themselves rather than with those in government. In concluding their report the commissioners commented,

> One of the strongest and most discouraging impressions carried away ... is that of a prevailing absence of a spirit of independence and self help, the lack of a tradition of craftsmanship and pride and good work, and a tendency on all matters to appeal to government for assistance with little or no attempt to explore what can be done by individual self help.[10]

This statement demonstrates a complete lack of understanding of the situation in Jamaica. Ample evidence existed of the determination of the Afro-Jamaicans to become independent and earn a sufficient income to support their families without having to rely on the low wages offered by the large estate owners. However, an over-reliance on agriculture with insufficient investment in the development of small industries, together with the absence of technical training which would equip people with the skills needed to work in these industries, meant that for many there was little alternative to a subsistence existence growing and selling small quantities of fruit and vegetables. Sam King, a Jamaican who served in the RAF during the war and later returned to Britain on the *Windrush*, describes how it felt to be living in Jamaica before the war:

> From my point of view, if you did not know better, it was alright, as long as you had law and order. It didn't matter whether you had education, welfare, food or not, as long as you did not disturb the peace. Only about two per cent of the population had higher education, if your parents had money, result in that the opportunities were very limited. And to the best of my knowledge, I would say ninety per cent of the people were farming or farming industry. And in farming in the

colonies you do not control the market. The outlook was limited. Life was totally dictated by Britain . . . The schoolbooks, the missionaries and everything was the British mentality. You could not be good on your own. Your good was not good. Your good had to be British.[11]

One member of the Royal Commission, Sir Walter Citrine, was appalled by the living conditions of the people they visited, commenting 'the present generation in the West Indies seems to be . . . carrying a burden of decades if not centuries of neglect'.[12] Citrine, who was President of the International Federation of Trade Unions, worked with the newly formed trade unions in Jamaica which had been set up by Alexander Bustamante after the riots and strikes in 1938, an initiative which was not supported by other members of the Commission.

As had occurred in 1915 any further improvement in the lives of the people of Jamaica was interrupted by the outbreak of war in 1939. The British West Indies Regiment had been disbanded in 1919 and on the outbreak of World War Two men and women from the West Indies were encouraged to leave their homes and join the British armed forces. Many served with the Merchant Navy and large numbers were recruited by the Royal Air Force as both air crew and ground staff. In 1941 Allan Wilmot from Jamaica was only fifteen when he volunteered to join the Royal Navy. Like his compatriots in the First World War he had to endure racial prejudice. He says, 'being British you feel like you are coming home but when we came here it was like we dropped out of the sky. Nobody knew anything about us'.[13] Most British people, however, welcomed the West Indian servicemen who had come to help save them from Hitler, and it was the American troops stationed in Britain that subjected the black soldiers and airmen to the most severe physical and verbal racial abuse. The United States army was segregated according to Jim Crow laws and large numbers of black soldiers had arrived in Britain to carry out the labouring work of building barracks and preparing airstrips. Like the West Indian soldiers they were largely welcomed by the local communities and mixed socially in dance halls and public houses, a situation which was totally unacceptable to the white American servicemen who were used to 'whites-only' bars. US military authorities in some areas demanded that pubs should impose a colour bar and when they refused one US officer commented, 'One thing I noticed here and which I don't like is the fact that the English don't draw any colour line. The English must be pretty ignorant. I can't see how a white girl could associate with a negro'.[14] One Jamaican serviceman Lloyd King who joined the RAF in 1944 describes how he was based at a Butlins camp in Yorkshire. He says, 'My new West Indian friends and I could not begin to believe the very bad way that the black American soldiers were being treated both by their own people and by the English . . . We Caribbeans are resourceful people. The Americans may have been running their own kind of apartheid at the time but we all made sure that we would stand no nonsense from them, or the English'.[15] Lloyd King went back to Jamaica after the war but returned a few years later and settled in Birmingham.

The publication of the Moyne Report in 1945 did lead to some changes in the way Jamaica was run, most notably to an extension of the franchise and an increase in black representation on the legislative council, but despite a gradual move towards self-government power still remained in the hands of the Colonial Office and the white dominated Jamaican legislature. The majority of the black population continued to lead a subsistence existence, struggling to make a living by growing and selling crops or working for low wages on the industrial estates. Although not actively encouraged to migrate to Britain many West Indians, realizing that a large number of jobs were available as the country recovered from six years of war, decided to leave their homes and travel to the country that had encouraged and welcomed their contribution to that war. These people held British passports and under the British Nationality Act of 1948 had a legal right to reside in Britain. The first large post-war group of immigrants from the Caribbean arrived at Tilbury Docks in Essex on the SS *Empire Windrush* on 22 June 1948. Many of the passengers were men who had fought in the war and aimed to find employment before being joined by their families. The *Windrush*, a troop ship, had called in at Kingston in Jamaica on its way back to England and prior to its arrival advertisements had appeared in the local newspaper that spare berths would be available for twenty-eight pounds. Tickets were rapidly sold and the ship departed for England on 24 May. The Colonial Office and Civil Service in England were not fully informed of the arrival of the Jamaicans until the ship had departed and a report in the *Daily Express* of 8 June indicates the concern expressed in the House of Commons on the lack of preparedness for the arrival. It reports the Minister of Labour, Mr George Isaacs as saying that he did not know who sent the men, adding 'All I know is that they are in a ship and are coming here. They are British citizens and we shall do our best for them when they arrive'. Some members expressed concern over whether there would be sufficient housing for these new citizens and whether they would be able to find employment.[16] Correspondence exchanged between the Colonial Office in London and the Colonial Secretary's Office in Jamaica as the *Windrush* steamed towards Britain suggests that news of the imminent arrival of the Jamaicans would certainly not be welcomed by the Colonial Office. In a letter of 29 May 1948 the Colonial Secretary wrote in a letter to London,

> We are very sorry indeed that you and your staff will be put to all the trouble which the arrival of this large number, who are mostly unskilled and who have little money with them, will involve. It is an appalling thing with which to be saddled, but, as you know it has been quite impossible to prevent their going, which is symptomatic of the conditions here. I hope that you will be able to cope with them without too much trouble.[17]

In its reply of 15 June the main concern of the Colonial Office seems to be to determine 'why these 417 Jamaicans decided to come to this country and who instigated and organized the movement'. The hope was expressed that measures would be taken to ensure that 'further similar movements... are detected and checked before they can reach such an embarrassing stage. Otherwise there might be a real danger that successful efforts to secure adequate conditions for these men on arrival might actually encourage a further influx'.[18] On the arrival of the *Windrush* eleven Labour Members of Parliament wrote to the Prime Minister, Clement Attlee, complaining about excessive immigration, and others considered that people should only be allowed into the country if they had accommodation and work already arranged. In his reply Attlee reminded them that the Jamaicans were British subjects and that whatever their race or colour 'should be freely admissible to the United Kingdom'.[19] Despite this it is evident that initial reaction to the new immigrants was not entirely favorable, partly due to the impression given by the Colonial Secretary in Jamaica that the immigrants were mainly unskilled laborers. In fact, as Linda McDowell points out, about half of the men who came from the Caribbean in the late 1940s and in the 1950s 'had previously worked in skilled positions or possessed excellent employment credentials' but found themselves having to accept jobs 'with a lower status than their skills and experience qualified them for'.[20]

Most of the early immigrants settled in the London area, but many moved further north to industrial cities like Birmingham where there was a demand for semi-skilled workers in the expanding manufacturing industries. The contrast between life in a large industrial city like Birmingham and the rural environment in which most West Indians had so far spent their lives could not have been greater and the newcomers did not in general receive a friendly welcome from the local inhabitants. Peter Edmead, in his study of Caribbean immigration to Birmingham, comments that 'unfortunately, cultural and social differences, together with prejudice and misunderstandings contributed to a complexity of inter-communal relationships . . . many West Indians felt that they were being treated like colonial inferiors' instead of British subjects.[21] One of the main problems was the lack of suitable housing, most of the newcomers being forced to live in multi-occupied houses in poor inner city areas. Peter Edmead recalls the experiences of his parents when they arrived in Birmingham in the early 1950s. His father, Edgar Edmead recalls,

> A Jamaican man, William Grant, had a house at number twenty eight Morden Road, Stechford, in Birmingham. Eight of us slept in one bedroom there on my first night in England. Apart from the very few West Indians, only Polish people and Asians would even talk to you about a room. I am not sure about how Grant purchased the house, maybe he was part of a 'pardner hand' but I never asked him. I trusted Grant, he helped us out, he charged me one pound two shillings and sixpence for the bed a week.[22]

Ena Edmead, Peter's mother, adds that in Edgar's room there was no heating or lighting and that 'they had to get cardboard and wooden boxes from the greengrocer to build a fire with'.

The 'pardner hand' mentioned by Edmead refers to a scheme whereby groups of West Indians would contribute a certain amount of money into a kitty each week which could then be used to purchase houses. The scheme was not entirely successful as vendors inflated the house prices to prevent the devaluation of properties occupied by West Indian tenants.

In order to be able to afford even the lowest rent for their accommodation it was essential for the new arrivals to obtain employment. Many found low-skilled, poorly paid jobs in factories, work not wanted by the majority of the white population. In 1954 *The Times* newspaper reported that,

> Officials of the TGWU in Birmingham have invited a Colonial Office spokesman, who is a Jamaican to meet Birmingham Corporation bus workers in an attempt to persuade them to accept coloured workers for platform duties... The services of coloured men and women had been neglected although there were 860 vacancies for conductors, it is probably the worst case of the colour bar in the country.[23]

Opportunities were far better in the new National Health Service which was eager to employ women who had trained as nurses. However, when interviewed more recently many of these women admitted that they had not been given the same opportunities as their white colleagues for promotion and progression to higher paid jobs, and experienced harassment and often verbal abuse from some of the patients.

One Jamaican who moved to Birmingham in 1949 was Henry Gunter who was born in Portland, Jamaica in 1920. He trained as an accountant, was active in the Peoples National Party, and wrote frequently for the local press on social and political issues. During the war he spent time working in America where he became involved with the trade union movement in an attempt to improve working conditions for the black employees and end racial discrimination. Not surprisingly he was consequently banned from the United States and returned to Jamaica where he continued with his political activities. In 1949, hearing from friends that jobs were available, he decided to emigrate to Britain. Despite his training as an accountant he was sent to work at a brass rolling mill in Deritend in Birmingham but after challenging the shop steward there for using racist verbal abuse he was moved to another factory in Erdington as a machine operator. Shortly after his arrival in Birmingham Gunter wrote an article for *Jamaica Arise*, the magazine of the Peoples National Party entitled 'Impressions of Britain and its Workers'. He explains how six months ago he had come to Great Britain to work and 'study the attitude and action of the English workers towards their brother Colonial workers' and adds 'I have placed myself in the industrial heart of the country so as to meet more of the workers'. He describes the 'little knowledge (and even less interest) that the average English worker has about colonial conditions'.[24] He moved again to the Larches Tool Factory 'where he trained to be a tool cutter and grinder and joined the AUEW'. He was elected to be a delegate to the Birmingham Trades Council, being the first black delegate and also became Chairman of the Afro-Caribbean Organization in Birmingham. In February 1953 Gunter wrote an article for the *Caribbean News* with the title 'End Colour Bar in Britain – Say Workers in Birmingham'. He writes,

> Recognising the terrible conditions facing coloured workers in this city, the Birmingham Trades Council unanimously adopted a resolution moved by this correspondent at its meeting on Saturday 13th December which reads: "In view of the appalling conditions which immigrant workers have to live under in Birmingham, and the failure to meet this problem, we ask that the Government provide accommodation for these workers".

Gunter proceeds to describe the 'appalling' housing conditions in which most workers live,

> In Bordesley, Aston and Small Heath I found 3 or 4 sharing a small room, and paying one pound each a week. They had no bedding or proper facilities and the furniture consisted of a table and a chair. Most landladies refuse to let their vacant rooms to coloured people and those who do usually charge them far higher rents than they would white tenants. Where coloured workers ban together to try to solve the problem by buying their own houses there develops acute overcrowding.[25]

In 1954 Gunter published a booklet entitled, 'A Man's a Man: A Study of the Colour Bar in Birmingham – and an Answer' in which he describes in greater detail the conditions faced by black people in Birmingham. He covers areas such as employment, housing, social activities and hotels and suggests actions that should be taken, appealing to his readers to 'Take a stand against the colour-bar and the spreading of racial prejudice wherever you find it'. Gunter describes, with obvious anger, how many West Indians

> 'have been obliged to leave their own countries by the economic effects of the colonial system. The backwardness of industry, the exploitation of natural wealth by companies from the United Kingdom leaves poverty and primitive work as the lot of the colonial people. Education and health services are so limited, the chance of skilled work and a career is so negligible, wages are so low ... that thousands find themselves forced to emigrate in search of work. Here in Britain because they are black, they get labouring jobs because they are not thought capable of anything else and the value of their qualifications is either not known or not appreciated'.[26]

Gunter maintains that 'one of the most disheartening colour bars' was the refusal of the City Transport Department to employ coloured drivers or conductors despite having 'no facts, no logical grounds on which to stand'. He reveals that some public figures in the city believed that 'white workers would refuse to work with coloured, that parents and husbands of conductresses would object to their working late nights with coloured people, and that coloured workers are too stupid to issue tickets properly', views that Gunter describes as 'ignorant, race-superiority, hysteria'.[27] He does, however, make it clear that most Trade Union leaders did not agree with these views and supported the employment of black workers in Birmingham's transport system. As seen in his article of the previous year Gunter was particularly concerned about the housing conditions of the new immigrants and believed that the main problem lay in the fact that they were obliged to take accommodation in a few of the inner city wards leading to overcrowding and intolerable conditions. He says 'a great many white people refuse to have coloured men and their families as neighbours, although these coloured colonials would be only too willing to live in other parts of the city if they had the chance. Several times coloured men have found themselves in a position to buy a house in a better class area, but rarely does the purchase go through before a snag arising from the man's colour occurs', mainly, he explains due to protests from prospective neighbours who believe that property values will be lowered.[28]

Another example of racism revealed by Gunter is reminiscent of the situation endured by black people in the Southern United States under Jim Crow laws. He describes how some people, recently arrived from the West Indies, and seeking temporary accommodation, had been refused rooms in several leading Birmingham hotels. On one occasion,

> A coloured doctor, who did his post-graduate training in a Birmingham hospital, returned to visit his friends. One of his white friends booked hotel accommodation for him. The doctor had an English name and the booking was accepted, but when he arrived and they saw he was coloured he was told 'Sorry, but we haven't a room for you'.[29]

Gunter also notes that some hotels with public bars and restaurants refused to serve black people with meals and drinks. The unwelcoming attitude of many public houses, dance halls and clubs meant that there was little social contact between black and white people, although Gunter notes that some social contacts were made through Trade Union and Labour Party organizations. Some people started their own social clubs where black and white people met for activities such as dancing, billiards, dominoes and darts and they 'forwarded a petition to the City Council, asking for assistance to secure suitable buildings for the running of similar organisations', and also for the setting up of an inter-racial council 'to try to find ways of promoting good relationships between white and coloured people – relationships that simply do not exist at present'.[30] Some efforts were made by social and welfare organizations but at the time Gunter was writing very little had been done to ensure that those British citizens who had travelled from the West Indies to help the country to which they belonged recover from a war in which they had participated, were accepted by and integrated into that country. The consequences of this failure were to be seen throughout the rest of the century and beyond.

It was not until the nineteen eighties that Birmingham suffered from violent race riots such as those which took place in Notting Hill, London in 1958, but as Peter Edmead makes clear this does not mean that black people were not subjected to 'hostility and violence' from the moment of their arrival.[31] Much of this hostility came from poor, white, working class people who were understandably concerned about immigrants competing with them for the limited supply of affordable accommodation in the inner city. In poor areas of West London competition for housing was exploited by landlords such as Peter Rachman who built a property empire by converting large mansion blocks into flats and rooms which he filled with recent immigrants from the West Indies who were charged high rents and had no access to legal representation. White people in need of housing resented the fact that these newcomers were being provided with accommodation and this resentment was exploited by far right groups such as the 'White Defence League' and Oswald Mosley's 'British Union of Fascists'. On 30 August a group of three to four hundred white youths attacked houses occupied by West Indians and after five days of rioting many white and black youths had been arrested. A report on the London riots in the *Birmingham Mail* quoted the city's Housing Manager, Mr. John Macey, as saying, 'Birmingham Corporation made no colour discrimination in the housing of families', adding that 'housing coloured families had not, until recently, been a problem, as the coloured people had mainly been single. Where Jamaican families had bought houses, property values in those streets had depreciated'.[32]

The problems arising from lack of suitable housing for the new immigrants might have been alleviated if the country had been prepared for their arrival and Edmead notes that 'the lack of a government policy in relation to immigration... contributed to the violence which occurred'.[33] This is backed up by Layton-Henry who writes that 'the failure of central government to provide local authorities with additional funds to alleviate the shortage of housing and accommodation in areas of immigrant settlement was a contributing factor to inter-racial hostility'.[34] However, as Edmead points out 'had this taken place there would have been a risk of white residents arguing that the newcomers were attaining preferential treatment'.[35] An important factor which throws light on the antagonism shown by many white residents towards the new immigrants is that where these newcomers were white, for example Polish or Irish, they were more readily accepted. It might be concluded that the dominant factor giving rise to hostility towards black people from the West Indies was the colour of their skin rather than their need for housing, or at least a combination of both. Edmead quotes an Irish former soldier, John 'Jack' White saying 'It was easy for us. All we had to do was keep our mouths shut. When you think about it the black people had no chance as the English took them at face value a lot of the time, without even trying to get to know them'.[36] This racism was encouraged and exacerbated by right wing racists such as Oswald Mosley whose aim was to drive black people out of Britain and whose 'brown-shirt' fascists held rallies in Handsworth park in Birmingham at the beginning of the 1960s. The consequences of and possible reasons for this increase in violent racism in the second half of the twentieth century will be examined in more detail in the next chapter.

Birmingham, Alabama

The Alabama Constitution of 1901 set out in great detail the ordinances and laws which would control the way in which citizens lived their lives for the next sixty years and nowhere were these laws more rigorously enforced than in the city of Birmingham where increasingly restrictive Racial Segregation Ordinances were introduced throughout the first half of the century. The President of the 1901 Constitutional Convention was John B. Knox who made no attempt to hide the fact that one of the aims of the new Constitution was to establish white supremacy in the state. Shortly before the Convention Booker T. Washington, the black activist and founder of the Tuskegee Institute, wrote a letter to Knox in which he outlined 'the feelings and wishes of the colored people of the State of Alabama', requesting that the letter should be read out to the Convention. Washington points out that despite there being about 800,000 black people in the state they have no representation on the Convention even though it is 'to frame the fundamental law under which both races are to be governed'. He maintains that they are 'hard working, tax paying, law abiding citizens' and reminds Knox that 'as a race, we did not force ourselves upon you, but were brought here in most cases against our will . . . to render valuable service to the white man in clearing the forests, building the railroads, cultivating the lands, working the mines, as well as in many forms of domestic service and in other activities'. He reminds Knox that the actions of the Convention 'will not be directed or restricted by any pressure from the Federal government', as the North has agreed that 'the future of the Negro in a large degree rests with the South'. The tone of the letter becomes somewhat more emotional as Washington anticipates the discouragement and anger that would result if the rights of black people were not respected by the Convention. He cites fears held by many that 'the Negro's citizenship will be taken from him and that his schools will be virtually blotted out', and he appeals to the Convention members to ensure that the Negro has 'a share in choosing those who shall rule over him'.[37]

When the Constitution was published it became clear that Washington's fears were fully justified. Although Federal law stated that all male citizens of the United States had a right to vote, the wording of the new Constitution and its consequent interpretation made it almost impossible for the majority of black men to do so. Sections 181 and 182 of the Constitution set out the requirements necessary in order for a person to be entered on the register of electors. The first of these was a literacy test which required the applicant to 'read and write any article of the Constitution of the United States in the English language', the test being administered by white registrars intent on ensuring that most black applicants were rejected. Carol Anderson describes how 'while whites might have had a one-sentence section of the Alabama or US Constitution as their litmus test for worthiness to vote, African Americans would get difficult, complex passages in order to prove their literacy, and then they would have to interpret that legal treatise to gauge how well they could actually understand what they had just read'.[38] She describes how black men were usually ignored when they came to register, while whites were frequently registered without any tests taking place. Needless to say there was no opportunity to appeal the decision. A further opportunity for registrars to deprive black men of their right to vote was contained in Section 182 of the Constitution. This listed numerous crimes and misdemeanors which would disqualify a person from registering, which in addition to obvious serious crimes included living in adultery and miscegenation or any 'crime involving moral turpitude', or even living as a vagrant or tramp. It seems likely that an applicant might be accused of a minor crime without any proof of their guilt being required.

In an attempt to avoid discrimination against poor white men, a so-called 'grandfather clause' was introduced in Section 180 which created an exemption from the literacy test for all 'who have honorably served in the land or naval forces of the United States' in the wars of the nineteenth century or who 'are lawful descendants' of such persons. As most freed slaves and their ancestors would not have served in the military they could not take advantage of this clause. The requirement that all inhabitants of the state had by law to pay a poll tax in order to be eligible to vote also disenfranchised many voters as failure to pay resulted in a charge of vagrancy and criminal charges. Booker T. Washington's fear that the new constitution would not give priority to the education of black children was confirmed, as most of the funds allocated for education went to white schools. Section 256 of the 1901 Constitution stated that 'separate schools shall be provided for white and colored children, and no child of either race shall be permitted to attend a school of the other race'. The schools for black children were badly maintained and poorly equipped and the salaries of white teachers were twice that of black teachers. Officially segregation in public schools came to an end in 1954 but continued long after this due to the establishment of private schools which maintained segregation.

The terms of the Alabama Constitution were readily adopted by the leaders of Birmingham City Council, and a closer examination of the development of the city from the beginning of the century reveals the extent to which it came to epitomize the extreme implementation of racial segregation, culminating in the violence of the 1960s. During the first thirty years of the century the city of Birmingham expanded rapidly, steel production increased and there was an influx of capital from the North. In 1910, under the 'Greater Birmingham Plan' the city annexed many surrounding communities leading to large suburban areas on the edge of the city with skyscrapers and expensive housing for the industrialists and financiers who came to work in the city. Brownell writes how the city became 'dedicated to capitalist prosperity' and that 'real estate fortunes were made overnight'. He describes how 'rising middle-class' whites from the South found homes in pleasant residential areas in the south of the city whereas unskilled rural blacks who came to work in the iron and steel plants and coal mines lived mainly in company towns in dingy industrial suburbs on the fringe of the city with 'barely adequate ' housing. These black neighborhoods were mainly situated along creekbeds, railroad lines or alleys and had no basic amenities such as street lights, paved streets or sewers.[39] In 1917 the Supreme Court had declared residential segregation codes to be unconstitutional but local zoning laws were introduced in Birmingham as part of a series of Segregation Ordinances introduced between 1926 and the 1950s. The 1926 Birmingham Zoning Ordinance 'provided for rigid separation of white and Negro areas' and white residents had a right to object to the construction of housing for black people next to white neighborhoods.

An early case which illustrates how racist segregation was supported by the courts is that of *Wyatt v. Adair*, which was heard before the Supreme Court of Alabama on December 16, 1926. A white landlord, W. P. Wyatt had rented out the first floor of a large two-story house in Birmingham to a white man, J. E. Adair, together with his wife and thirteen-year-old daughter. Wyatt subsequently rented the second floor of the house to a black family, a seemingly important factor in the case being that the occupants of both floors had to share a single bathroom and toilet situated on the second floor. Adair pleaded that the fact that he and his family would be 'caused to use the toilet in common with negro men and women' would be humiliating and cause him 'to suffer physical pain and mental anguish, and to suffer mental anguish by seeing his wife and thirteen-year-old daughter humiliated'. Adair won his case and was awarded damages, the judge referring to the 'known and well-established custom in what may be termed a negro district to the effect that, if premises are leased to white persons, negroes shall not be put in connected premises with a common toilet for both tenants and their families. Twould be strange and deplorable if such custom did not exist, however humble the habitation'.[40] This case was important, not just for approving the principle of segregation but also for highlighting the extreme prejudice and animosity directed by many white people towards those with a black skin.

A proposed segregation ordinance for the separation of white and black people on the city's streetcars was voted for unanimously by the City Commission in 1923 but opposed by the Chamber of Commerce because of the expense that would be incurred. However in 1930 *The General Code of the City of Birmingham, Alabama, of 1930* was published which required 'the races to be kept separate in public places' and in 1944 this was replaced with a more detailed series of Racial Segregation Ordinances. It is important to quote from some of these Codes in order to reveal the lengths to which the city's leaders were prepared to go in order to ensure that white people would not have to come into contact with Birmingham citizens of a different skin colour.

Section 1002 of the Separation of Races Code stated,

> Every common carrier engaged in operating streetcars in the city for the carriage of passengers shall provide equal but separate accommodations for the white and colored races by providing separate cars or by clearly indicating or designating by physical visible marks the area to be occupied by each race in any streetcar in which the two races are permitted to be carried together and by confining each race to occupancy of the area of each streetcar so set apart for it.

In addition separate entrances and exits had to be provided for each car used for white and colored passengers 'in such manner as to prevent intermingling of the white and colored passengers when entering or leaving such car'.[41]

Section 369 of the Code declared,

> It shall be unlawful to conduct a restaurant or other place for the serving of food in the city, at which white and colored people are served in the same room, unless such white and colored persons are effectually separated by a solid partition extending from the floor upward to a distance of seven feet or higher, and unless a separate entrance from the street is provided for each compartment.

Several Sections referred to the playing of games, Section 597 stating that 'it shall be unlawful for a negro and a white person to play together or in company with each other in any game of cards or dice, dominoes or checkers', and later in Section 859 pool and billiards were added to the list. In 1950 a new Ordinance was adopted adding several team sports to the list, namely baseball, softball, football and basketball. This ruling effectively barred Major League teams from playing in Birmingham.

Sections 1110 and 1111 referred to the provision of Toilet Facilities for Males and Females, stating that 'every employer of white or negro males/females shall provide . . . reasonably accessible and separate toilet facilities. Such separate white and negro toilet facilities shall be clearly marked to distinguish each from the other and it shall be unlawful for any person to use any facility not designated for such person's comfort'.

The wording of these Ordinances, as in the case of *Wyatt v. Adair*, suggests that those responsible for producing them actually believed that some sort of contamination might result if white people came into contact with fellow citizens who happened to have darker skins than themselves. Many Southerners still believed that black and white people were separate branches of the human race with black people belonging to a separate and less advanced branch. There was also a fear amongst some that once freed from the bondage of slavery, the people they once owned would rise up against them and consequently their lives had to be subject to strict controls. The Alabama Constitution had already made interracial marriage and miscegenation unlawful in an attempt to prevent what they saw as the 'dilution' of the white race and the segregation laws certainly contributed to this aim by preventing black and white people from meeting socially or in the workplace.

The issue of residential segregation which had been introduced in 1926 assumed a far greater importance in the 1940s when a postwar economic boom led to an increased demand for housing. Land allocated for black housing became more and more congested and many black families were unable to find somewhere to live. Birmingham's new black middle class refused to accept the situation and started to build houses on the edges of white residential zones. In 1946 one group of black property owners who had built houses in the area of

North Smithfield, found that as a result of zoning laws they were denied access to their houses and land. They appealed to the Birmingham branch of the National Association for the Advancement of Colored People (NAACP) whose black attorney, Arthur Shores, took on their case, as he did for many others in similar situations, not always meeting with success. Glenn T. Eskew describes in detail a case in which Shores was involved which demonstrates how many of these disputes ended in extreme violence carried out by white vigilantes, usually members of the local branch of the Ku Klux Klan.[42]

In 1946, Sam Matthews, a black drill operator at a local ore mine, bought a vacant lot on the outskirts of North Smithfield on the edge of a black community. The white agent who sold the land had presumed that it was about to be rezoned and had sold fifty lots to black buyers. However, when the local white community found out about the sale they held a protest meeting declaring that 'if black people moved into the neighborhood, property values would decline and school districts might be integrated'. Meanwhile Matthews applied for and received a building permit from the city building inspector and proceeded to construct a six-room house, however when he applied for an occupancy permit his request was denied. Matthews contacted Arthur Shores who filed a suit against Birmingham's zoning law and the District Court Judge ruled the denial to be unconstitutional. On 18 August 1947, in the middle of the night vigilantes detonated six sticks of dynamite in the unoccupied house completely destroying it. Eskew notes that 'police did not investigate the bombing until after Shores and Matthews filed a report of the crime the following morning, and even then detectives delayed taking statements for several days'.[43] A report in the 'Birmingham World' newspaper on 22 August noted how Police Chief Eddins had assigned two of his 'topflight' detectives to 'rundown every clue and leave nothing undone to bring about the arrest of the dynamiters'. Three days later 'the detectives had not been able to turn up any evidence that would throw any light on the crime'. The FBI's special agent in Birmingham 'declined to say whether his office would look into the dynamiting' and Sheriff Holt McDowell 'discounted the suggestion that it might be the work of the K.K.K'. He added that the Ku Klux Klan has only a skeleton organization of

15 or 20 members and is not strong and never was'. In fact as Brownell records the K.K.K. had grown rapidly in Jefferson County and Birmingham since the formation of the Robert E. Lee Klan No.1 in 1916. It was estimated that by 1924 15,000 of Birmingham's 32,000 voters, at least two local judges, many city and county officials and 'most of the city's policemen, if not all of them' were members of the Klan. It was said that the Klan had more influence in Birmingham than in any other Southern city.[44] The Matthews case was closed with the words 'failed to reveal sufficient evidence to make an arrest', even though one suspect lived only two blocks from Matthew's house and was known to have told the police to discontinue the investigation. Eskew notes that 'for three decades similar words appeared at the bottom of Birmingham police department case reports on bombings in the city', and there were even rumours that police were actually involved in some of the bombings.[45] Altogether about fifty racially motivated bombings occurred in Birmingham between 1947 and 1965 earning the city the name 'Bombingham'.

One case of particular interest was that of the bombing, in March 1949, of two houses bought by Bishop S. L. Green of the African Episcopal Church, both having been previously occupied by white families who had been informed that the area was being rezoned as 'colored'. Several nearby houses had recently been bombed after being bought by black families and in May 1949 a prospective black purchaser, William German, was warned not to occupy the house he had bought. The person delivering the warning was Robert E. Chambliss a motor mechanic and a member of the Ku Klux Klan who 'pointing to the shattered remains of Bishop Green's property said to German: "If you move in, that is liable to happen to you"'. Eskew adds the note, 'Chambliss, known as "Dynamite Bob", was later convicted for the September 1963 bombing of the Sixteenth Street Baptist Church that killed four black girls'.[46]

In response to the large number of bombings in the North Smithfield area the city commissioners 'proposed the creation of a buffer zone to separate the black and white neighborhoods of Smithfield'. Arthur Shores, in his role as legal representative of the local NAACP branch declared that such a move would be unconstitutional as it legalized enforced residential segregation. James W. Morgan, the Commissioner of Public Improvements agreed, asking

'Where are those Negroes going to live and build? Almost fifty percent of our people are colored. So much of our area is zoned for white'. The 1950 Census of the United States recorded that 'Birmingham's black population . . . lived in the poorest quality housing of any metropolitan area in the southeast'. Those who had drafted Birmingham's Racial Segregation Ordinances consistently maintained that they conformed with the policy of 'separate but equal', but their policy of residential zoning clearly resulted in a situation where most African Americans lived in poor quality housing in badly maintained areas far inferior to those lived in by most whites.

The black population of Birmingham, particularly those living in the Smithfield area, were not prepared to passively accept the new ordinance which enabled the police to enforce racial zoning and in August 1949 when a new round of bombings occurred they grouped together to keep watch on houses bought by black purchasers. On some occasions members of these groups were armed and when the vigilantes arrived shots were fired into their cars. Bombs were still thrown, shattering windows and creating huge craters in the road but the city commissioners refused to provide police protection for the black home owners. Various black organizations including the NAACP called a mass meeting for August 17, 1949 to protest at the failure of the police department to find those responsible for the dynamite blasts. They particularly criticized the head of the Birmingham Police Department, Eugene 'Bull' Connor, who had said that he 'could not protect the lives and property' of African Americans who had chosen to live in the disputed area, even though no new land for black housing was approved by the city commissioners.[47] Protests by black groups continued to increase throughout the 1950s and formed the basis of the new Civil Rights movement.

On December 1, 1955 Rosa Parks, the secretary of the Montgomery branch of the NAACP, boarded a bus in the city and refused to give up her seat to a white passenger, leading to her arrest and precipitating the start of the Montgomery bus boycott to challenge the bus segregation laws. In November 1956 the U.S. Supreme Court ruled that bus segregation was unconstitutional and the following month the Montgomery buses were desegregated. In Birmingham the Reverend Fred L. Shuttlesworth and the Alabama

Christian Movement for Human Rights, were inspired by events in Montgomery and by the rise in activism amongst local black groups, and a protest against segregation on buses in Birmingham was planned for Christmas Day. The night before, members of the Ku Klux Klan dynamited Shuttlesworth's church and parsonage, injuring but not killing the minister. When recovered from his injuries his response to the attack was to follow the example of Rosa Parks by boarding a bus in Birmingham with the intention of being arrested. The following year Shuttlesworth was again attacked by Klansmen when he tried to enroll his children in an all-white school in Birmingham. As with bus segregation the US Supreme Court in the *Brown v. Board of Education* ruling of 1954 had ruled that state laws establishing racial segregation in public schools were unconstitutional. Although this was a victory for the Civil Rights Movement, states like Alabama with strict segregation laws refused to implement the Court ruling and introduced further laws to ensure that school segregation would continue. In 1955 a 'pupil placement law' gave school boards the power to determine where students would attend school and in 1956 further laws enabled them to resist desegregation and even to close a school if it faced integration. A 'freedom of choice law' allowed parents to decide which schools their children would attend and allowed separate schools for blacks and whites. Despite increasing integration after the Civil Rights Act of 1964, the Alabama laws of 1956 were still exerting an influence on the education of black children well into the next century.

6

The Twentieth Century
1960–2000

Part One Birmingham, England

During the 1950s and 1960s increasing numbers of people from the West Indies came to settle in Handsworth an area just to the north of the centre of Birmingham. Maybe few of these new residents would have realised that the large house surrounded by trees at the top of Soho Hill had links with their ancestors who had worked as slaves on the sugar plantations in the Caribbean. The house was built in the late eighteenth century by Matthew Boulton, close to where he had established the Soho Manufactory on Handsworth Heath. It was here, in partnership with James Watt, that he manufactured the steam engines which were exported to the West Indian plantations to power the sugar mills used for cane crushing and operated by slaves.[1] At the beginning of the nineteenth century Handsworth had been a fairly prosperous rural residential area for the Birmingham middle class but as a result of increasing industrialisation throughout the nineteenth century houses were needed for the factory owners and managers and also for the large number of workers employed by these industries. These small usually overcrowded houses were owned by landlords who provided few amenities for their tenants. By the 1950s most wealthy people had moved further north leaving many large houses which were suitable for multi-occupancy. The difficulty that new West Indian immigrants encountered in finding suitable housing in Birmingham has been described in the previous chapter and the antagonism shown towards them by many of the poor white residents of inner city areas meant that newcomers were anxious to live in an area where they might be able to form a more settled community. Unfortunately the poor quality of the housing, the lack of amenities for the increasing number of young people and the usual suspicion shown by the white residents towards those of a different skin colour meant that the next few decades saw an increase in racial tension in Handsworth and, as happened in other inner city areas, outbreaks of violence, usually between the police and young black men. Aware of the increasing number of immigrants coming from Commonwealth countries in the 1950s and 60s, the Government passed a Race Relations Act in 1965 which banned racial discrimination in public places and made the 'promotion of hatred on the grounds of colour, race or ethnic or national origins' an offence. This act failed to cover discrimination in employment and housing, areas where discrimination was most prevalent, and consequently in 1968 the Act was updated to make discrimination in these two areas unlawful.

Towards the end of the 1960s the Runnymede Trust decided to finance a study of the situation in Handsworth and commissioned a young, West Indian born youth worker, Augustine John to carry out a detailed three month study of the area. John interviewed many residents, both black and white, and investigated important areas such as education, housing, crime, youth facilities, work and the police.[2]

One white woman interviewed said,

> I have lived in Handsworth for fifty years, I was born here. Handsworth is no longer a place to be proud of . . . I used to spend many hours in the park but now with all these darkies running around there you never know what they would do to you . . . there seems to be so many young men about day and night with nothing to do . . . And of course there's all this talk about crime. I am afraid to walk the streets.[3]

Marcus, a nineteen-year-old Jamaican said,

> This place is a dump. There is nothing for a young fellow like me to do . . . It's hell to be young in Handsworth. No matter how good you try to be people still think you're bad. You can't walk the streets in peace without some bloody cop trying to pry and search you, or some white

guys trying to do you, especially at night when you're alone... Because some black guys get into trouble the cops and everyone else seem to think that all young blacks are criminals.[4]

A West Indian father of four describes how Handsworth is a difficult place to live in, saying,

> Man, all you seem to do in this place is work, work, and no matter how hard you work you never seem to have anything to show for it. It's hell to bring up children in Handsworth. As things are today you have to keep your eyes open all the time to make sure they don't get into trouble ... There are some white boys living near us. I know they don't like my big boy and I don't want them ganging up on him.[5]

John realised that the housing situation was 'one of the root causes of the social tensions and individual problems in the area'.[6] Although some West Indians had managed to buy their own homes, low wages and high mortgage payments meant that they had little money left to maintain and furnish their houses. Many lived in multi-occupancy houses which were often in a bad state of repair with shared amenities and often with whole families living in one room. John quotes a report from the *Birmingham Evening Mail* describing how 'a group of black children on their first day at school were seen huddling together in one corner of the playground, unable to make use of the open space'. It seems that they did not understand the concept of 'play' as they came from homes where there was no space for such activities. Another child 'lived with his parents in an attic room up three flights of stairs in a multi-occupied house. He was not allowed to play on the stairs or the landing. The room was at once bedroom, kitchen, living room and his father's radio and television repair shop', and there was no space to play.[7] John makes the comment that it is no wonder that as the children grow older they prefer to hang around in the street than to stay in their overcrowded homes. Another important cause of many of the problems encountered in Handsworth was the lack of adequate, suitable education for the children of immigrant families, particularly the absence of pre-school facilities. Most mothers of young children needed to work long hours, many having to support children who had remained behind in the West Indies. Although there were day nurseries in the area these were usually too far from their homes and were mainly used by white people. As a consequence most young children were sent to unofficial child minders, most of whom provided no play facilities and certainly no books. John writes, 'to stand on Grove Lane or Rookery Road around 6.30 in the morning and to watch streams of West Indian mothers taking toddlers by the hand into child-minding establishments – dingy front rooms in which anything from half-a-dozen to a dozen children will be herded for the rest of the day, a paraffin oil-heater in a corner in the winter – is to observe a very different world from the one inhabited by social scientists, teachers and officials'. He adds that 'it would hardly be surprising if these children did not become 'problems' during their first year at school'.[8] Whether the children did become 'problems' or not depended very much on the attitude of the teachers they encountered, and although there must have been some good teachers who understood the particular problems of children from West Indian families there were certainly many who underestimated the abilities of black children. One boy said 'Man, those teachers just don't care ... teachers not only think you stupid but ... make you yourself believe that you're stupid. I think some of them are just born racialist'. Another said 'I think they deliberately send second-rate teachers into Handsworth, and then they turn round and say because there are so many black kids in the school the standard of education is being lowered'. Another boy said 'All these teachers are trying to do is to keep us down. When the time comes for us to think of choosing jobs they always say we aim too high ... and tell some of us we're going to end up on the factory floor or on the buses'.[9] The problem was worse for those children who came from Jamaica when they were nearing the age of eleven and had to sit the feared 11 Plus selection exam which more or less decided their future career prospects. Many children 'expressed concern about the fact that their achievements were not very great by English standards', and that they were expected to answer questions on British history and other topics not covered by their schools in Jamaica. One girl who had to take her 11 Plus three months after arriving from Jamaica explained that she did well in everything except history and so failed and had to go to a 'lousy secondary modern' school. She says 'few black children get into grammar schools in Handsworth – I could only think of about three.

Are black people so stupid that of the hundreds of kids in school in this dump you could count those in grammar schools on the fingers of one hand'.[10]

This feeling of resentment against a system which many young black people felt undervalued them, which deprived them of a good education and which saw them as only being fit for entering low-paid, menial occupations, meant that some became involved in petty crime, possibly as a way of rebelling against a society which they felt had done little for them. However, John observes, 'that of the men and youths in Handsworth who find themselves existing under a mountain of odds, relatively few resort to violence or crime'. He quotes one nineteen-year-old West Indian saying they 'struggle courageously, hating the bloody system and hoping that that they ain't going to get broken by it'.[11] John makes the point that the police themselves estimated that the number of 'hard core' criminals in the community was no more than forty to fifty, a relatively small number compared with the total black male population. However, as shown in the response of the white woman quoted above, many residents were afraid to go to the local park or walk the streets at night, fears which increased racial tension in the community.

The relationship between the local police and the black population certainly deteriorated throughout the 1960s. In the early 60s the police concentrated on trying to stamp out 'petty pilfering, car-breaking, shoplifting and similar offences' as distinct from what they referred to as 'big jobs', in other words organised crime engaged in by gangs of black men who lived on the proceeds of this crime. This led them to 'scrutinise the activities of every black man whom they knew to be out of work, or whom they saw hanging around clubs, coffee bars, betting offices etc'.[12] The majority of the men questioned were completely innocent citizens who had never been involved in crime and resented the fact that the police regarded them as criminals even though they had no evidence of wrong-doing. Things became worse at the end of the decade when in the summer of 1969 a West Indian youth was accidentally stabbed in Handsworth Park and subsequently died of his wounds. The teenagers had been playing with knives and due to the general concern about the number of young men carrying knives the police introduced a policy of 'stop and search' which meant that black men and youths were indiscriminately stopped and searched for weapons, especially late at night. This policy resulted in few actual prosecutions and resulted in a feeling of resentment against the police by young black men who felt they were being unfairly persecuted because of their colour. John records the comments made by one West Indian man comparing the situation in Britain with that in America. He responds to those who say that race relations in Britain are nothing like those in America by saying that if the police in Handsworth were armed with guns, 'then people would realise just how like America this place really is'.[13] John admits that despite general hostility towards the police there were senior police officers who were well aware of the unfair treatment that many young black young men were receiving and he considers that they should be more ready to exert their influence on the 'men on the beat'. John concludes,

> Violence of a sporadic and unpredictable kind is the most immediately visible feature of urban decay both in America and Britain. But when this happens in an area which is racially mixed, then the concern and the fears acquire an extra racial dimension, so that the mere fact – or even the rumour – of one street assault by a black man instantly gives rise to local panic about 'black criminals' amongst the whites, which in turn leads to resentment from the blacks.[14]

Handsworth was not of course the only area in the West Midlands where new immigrants were faced with problems similar to those described by Augustine John. The town of Smethwick lies just two miles South of Handsworth and four miles to the West of Birmingham city centre, and since the Industrial Revolution had been a centre for the metal industry which employed many of the new immigrant workers. These were originally mainly from the West Indies but throughout the 1960s increasing numbers came from India and Pakistan. Most of the immigrants lived in the north of the town where the factories were situated and as in Handsworth the houses were old and poorly maintained. The South of the town was where most of the middle-class white people lived and amongst these was Peter Griffiths, a primary school headmaster and local councillor, who in the 1964 election was the Conservative Party candidate chosen to stand against the Labour Member of Parliament, Patrick Gordon

Walker. Griffiths's campaign was based almost entirely on anti-immigration policies and became notorious for the extremely racist slogan "If you want a nigger for a neighbour, vote Labour" which was used throughout the campaign. As in Handsworth the housing situation was at the root of much of the anti-immigrant feeling in the town, with many working-class white people believing that immigrants were being given preferential treatment in the allocation of council houses. Griffiths exploited this anxiety and also encouraged the same prejudice and animosity as was being shown by the white residents of Birmingham, Alabama towards those with a different coloured skin. Joe Street notes how Griffiths 'even warned local teachers to tell their schoolchildren not to enter houses occupied by immigrants, for they would be in "grave moral danger." Invariably, he linked immigration with violence, crime, and disease and maintained that Smethwick's supposed race problem was far worse than that of other British towns'.[15] At his adoption meeting he had told local conservatives that 'we believe that unrestricted immigration into this town has caused a deterioration in public morals'.[16]

In the 1964 election the Conservatives in Smethwick overturned a Labour majority of more than 3,000 with the largest swing towards the Conservatives in the country, an event made even more significant by the fact that in the nation as a whole Labour were returned to power in Westminster for the first time in thirteen years. After the election Griffiths designed a plan to be implemented by the Conservative-run Smethwick council in which the council would compulsorily purchase houses which came on the market in a rundown street in the north of the town called Marshall Street. White residents of this street assisted with this plan by sending a petition to the council demanding that the houses they purchased would only be let to white families ensuring that Marshall Street would be immigrant free. In order to carry out this plan the council required a loan from the government but when this was requested the Labour Minister for Housing and Local Government, Richard Crossman, angrily retorted that 'Griffiths's politics were grossly offensive' and the loan was refused'.[17] This somewhat futile attempt to establish a zoned housing system such as that found in Birmingham, Alabama was consequently unsuccessful and in 1968 the amended Race Relations Act made discrimination in housing unlawful.

In February 1965, just a few months after the election of Peter Griffiths as its Member of Parliament, Malcolm X, the American black rights activist, made an unexpected visit to Smethwick. He had been intending to make a speech in Paris but was refused entry to France and after diverting to London where he spoke at the London School of Economics he was persuaded to meet up with a television crew in Smethwick who were hoping to engineer a meeting with Peter Griffiths. Joe Street notes that 'Griffiths – perhaps aware of Malcolm X's stellar debating skills and the potential for embarrassing himself on national television – withdrew at short notice, leaving Malcolm X and the BBC with a few hours to kill. They visited Marshall Street, where Malcolm X inspected the "for sale" signs'.[18] Reporters asked him why he had come to this small town and he replied, 'I have heard that the blacks . . . are being treated in the same way as the Negroes were treated in Alabama – like Hitler treated the Jews.'[19] Malcolm X urged local black people to organise themselves and assert their identity as non-whites using force if necessary, a message that had not endeared him to members of the Civil Rights movement in America which aimed to bring an end to discrimination by peaceful, non-violent means. The mayor of Smethwick, Clarence Williams, was outraged at Malcolm X's words and the fact that he had been allowed into the country at all, claiming that he was trying 'to turn Smethwick into Birmingham Alabama'. After giving a press conference in Birmingham and speaking to Muslim students at Birmingham University, Malcolm X flew back to the United States and nine days after his visit was shot dead by several members of the Nation of Islam in a ballroom in Manhattan.

One person who followed Peter Griffiths's campaign with particular interest was the Member of Parliament for Wolverhampton South West, Enoch Powell, who in the early 1960s was Minister of Health in the Conservative government. He had been born and brought up in Birmingham and his constituency was only about ten miles from Smethwick. As Housing Minister in the late 1950s he had advocated immigration controls and although he welcomed immigrant nurses and doctors when he became Health Minister this was conditional on their being temporary and returning to their countries of origin after training. His message in the 1964 General Election was that it was essential to introduce control over the number of immigrants allowed into the country and he was particularly impressed with the fact that Peter Griffiths won his seat by appealing to the fears of white working class voters. In 1967 Powell and his wife visited the United States and spent two weeks in New York where they witnessed the increasing racial tension and violence which came after desegregation. Believing, as Joe Street observes, that 'integration was a myth perpetuated by liberal elites', Powell 'became convinced that the United Kingdom – and Birmingham in particular, which was regularly presented in the press as a British version of Harlem – was facing an eerily similar future'.[20] On April 20, 1968 Powell delivered a speech to the West Midlands Conservative Association at the Midland Hotel in Birmingham, beginning with the words 'The supreme function of statesmanship is to provide against preventable evils'.[21] His audience might have been expecting to hear of 'evils' such as war, crime, hunger, disease or poverty, but instead Powell proceeded to warn of the dangers associated with the introduction of 'an alien element' into the country. This alien element consisted of 'Commonwealth immigrants and their descendants', and it became clear that he was only referring to those immigrants with black or brown skins. He describes an encounter with one of his constituents, a middle-aged, working-class white man, who says to him 'If I had the money to go, I wouldn't stay in this country . . . In this country in 15 or 20 years' time the black man will have the whip hand over the white man'. Powell views the idea of 'integration' as a 'dangerous delusion' for to become integrated into a society he says is to become 'indistinguishable from its other members' and 'where there are marked physical differences, especially of colour' integration is almost impossible.

Powell makes it clear that he is not simply concerned with the number of immigrants entering the country but with the number of their descendants born in England, after all the Commonwealth Immigrants Act passed by the Conservative government in 1962 had tightened regulations, allowing only those with employment vouchers issued by the government to enter the country. This was fiercely opposed by the Labour Party who referred to it as 'cruel and brutal anti-colour legislation'. It is significant that the year in which this Act was passed was the year in which Jamaica gained independence and its citizens were no longer entitled to a British passport. In his speech Powell proposed that the only way to bring about a reduction in the number of immigrants and their descendants was by 'stopping or virtually stopping, further inflow, and by promoting the maximum outflow' which would be achieved by 'the encouragement of re-emigration'. Both processes he maintained were 'part of the official policy of the Conservative Party', and 'generous assistance ' would be given to those who 'chose either to return to their countries of origin or to go to other countries anxious to receive the manpower and the skills they represent'. Powell manages to subvert the anti-discrimination legislation recently introduced by maintaining that 'the discrimination and the deprivation, the sense of alarm and of resentment, lies not with the immigrant population but with those among whom they have come and are still coming'. In other words it is the native inhabitants of this country who are suffering from discrimination, not the immigrants. He explains further, 'while to the immigrant, entry to this country was admission to privileges and opportunities eagerly sought, the impact upon the existing population was very different. For reasons which they could not comprehend . . . on which they were never consulted, they found themselves made strangers in their own country'. It becomes clear that the 'privileges and opportunities' which Powell seems to begrudge the new citizens include the right to vote, to be treated under the National Health Service, to have somewhere to live, to have school places for their children and to earn a decent wage. He seems to ignore the fact that up to 1962 when Jamaica gained its independence its citizens held British passports and were legally permitted to live and work in Britain. The fact that many of them wished to leave Jamaica to find employment in Britain was, as described in the previous chapter, the result of lack of opportunities and bad governance when their country was under British rule.

Clem Jones, the editor of the *Wolverhampton Express and Star* describes in an interview how several incidents described by Powell in the speech were myths generated by the local branch of the National Front and could not be verified.[22] Powell's account of the elderly pensioner who was the only remaining white resident in her street and was tormented and harassed by her 'Negro' neighbours is typical of stories circulated by the National Front, as was the story of a white constituent who was worried because his daughter was the only white child in her class at primary school. Jones, whose newspaper had received many similar anonymous letters, checked nearly every school in the constituency and could not find the one described in the report. Powell ends his speech by comparing the current situation in Britain with that in America, saying,

> That tragic and intractable phenomenon which we watch with horror on the other side of the Atlantic but which there is interwoven with the history and existence of the States itself, is coming upon us here by our own volition and our own neglect.

He overlooks the fact that the black people from the West Indies had a history as closely interwoven with that of Britain as those in America had with the current United States.

Although Powell was sacked by the Prime Minister from the opposition front bench and censured by many for his comments a poll taken after the speech suggested that 74 percent of the population supported his suggestion of repatriation. The day after his sacking a group of London dockers marched on Parliament in his support and there were marches in the Midlands towns with large immigrant populations. Racist groups such as the National Front which formed in the late 1960s, continued their activities throughout the 1970s and 80s, increasing racial tension. Most of the unrest during these decades was the result of conflict between the police and usually young black men, a situation which Augustine John had examined in his detailed study of Handsworth.

In 1976 an update to the Race Relations Act of 1968 was passed by Parliament which prevented any discrimination on the grounds of race. The Act made it 'unlawful to treat a person less favourably than others on racial grounds. These cover grounds of race, colour, nationality and national or ethnic origin . . . in the fields of employment, education, training, housing, and the provision of goods, facilities and services'. Of course this legislation did not prevent discrimination and this seemed to be particularly relevant in the case of the relationship between the police and black men in inner city areas. The powers of 'stop and search' were based on a 'sus' or suspected person law which formed part of the 1824 Vagrancy Act and was still part of British law. Under this Act a police officer could stop, search and arrest a person who they considered to be wandering with intent to commit an offence, a law reminiscent of vagrancy laws enacted in Alabama and in Jamaica in the aftermath of abolition. There was considerable opposition to this law, particularly when it became apparent that it was being used to target young, black men, and was actually a contributory factor to rioting which often occurred when innocent people were targeted by the police. The law was eventually repealed in August 1981 but unfortunately this was too late to prevent the riots which broke out that summer in London, Birmingham, Manchester, Liverpool and other cities. The first of these riots occurred in April 1981 in Brixton, an area of London where many Afro-Caribbean immigrants had settled since the 1950s, and where, as in other inner city areas, there was high unemployment and inadequate housing. Earlier in the year the police had initiated 'Operation Swamp '81', the intention being to send large numbers of police into the area to target men believed to be involved in criminal activity. The choice of name for this initiative was rather unfortunate for as the academic Paul Gilroy observed 'it seemed they were remembering the things Mrs Thatcher said just before the election two years ago when she said, "People are really rather frightened they might be swamped by those of a different culture". This is, in a sense, a sort of revenge swamping'.[23] Relatively minor clashes with the police on 10 April escalated during the following few days resulting in 299 police and 65 members of the public being injured, vehicles being destroyed and many business premises being burned, damaged and looted. Exactly three months later rioting broke out in Handsworth, Birmingham, and the following year a detailed study into the possible causes of and the degree of participation in the riots by the local population, was made by Peter Southgate as part of a Home Office Research Study.[24] He describes how

> 'on the first night tension had built up in Handsworth around a rumour that a National Front march was about to take place through the area . . . This march never took place, but crowds gathered and violence exploded at about 10 pm beginning with an attack on the local police superintendent who had been trying to dispel the rumours. Within the next hour the police station and fire station were attacked. There then followed attacks on vehicles, premises and police officers, throwing of

fire bombs, looting and other disorder, which continued until the early hours'.[25]

It was estimated that only about 250 to 300 people took part in the riot which was easily broken up by the 400 police officers deployed. Police records suggest that half of those arrested were white, a third of West Indian origin and the remainder Asian. Four out of five were aged between 16 and 24 and they were nearly all male. After the riots Southgate interviewed over 500 men between the ages of 16 and 34 comprising whites and those of West Indian and Asian origin, all of whom had been observers of the disturbances. When asked what they thought were the causes of the rioting, the cause mentioned most often was unemployment closely followed by boredom, the two obviously being closely related. Many mentioned the 'copycat' theory, that the rioters had been influenced by the riots in Brixton and Toxteth in Liverpool, and blame was also assigned to political agitators from outside the area. Racial tension between different groups in the community was only mentioned by one in ten of those interviewed 'suggesting that it was not seen as a major problem in the area'. Although police harassment was not mentioned by the majority of those who had been observers of the riot, it was given as a major cause by a quarter of those who were actively involved. It is significant that among those aged 16–24, 41 percent of West Indians and 36 percent of whites said they had been stopped and searched in the past twelve months. This indicates that in a more racially diverse area such as Handsworth stop and search powers were not being used exclusively against black youths. This was not of course the case in Brixton which was a predominantly Afro-Caribbean community and where increased use of the 'sus' law during 'Operation Swamp '81' was aimed mainly at black youths and was thought to be the main contributory factor in the outbreak of riots.

As a result of the Brixton riot an enquiry was set up under the leadership of Lord Scarman who found evidence of the 'disproportionate and indiscriminate use of stop and search powers by the police against black people'. After the report the 'sus' law was repealed and in 1984 was replaced by the Police and Criminal Evidence Act which gave the police powers to stop and search only if they had grounds to believe that a person had been involved in a crime or was in possession of a prohibited item such as drugs, weapons or stolen property. Scarman had stressed the importance of improving relationships between the community and the police and in 1985 a Police Complaints Authority was set up. In the autumn of the same year riots again broke out in Handsworth, this time with more serious consequences than the riot of 1981. The riot started when police put a fine notice on an illegally parked car with a missing tax disc outside a café in Lozells Road. The arrested man fled into the café and the police were pelted with stones and bottles. The violence rapidly escalated with buildings and vehicles being set on fire and shops being looted. The Birmingham *Evening Mail* of 10 September, the day after the riot, reported that

> cars on Archibald Road were overturned and a barricade was set up by the rioters who also set fire to police vehicles. In Heathfield Road a mob of mainly West Indian teenagers pelted police with petrol bombs but none of the officers were hurt. One rioter advanced petrol bomb in hand but instead of throwing at the police line hurled it through the window of a building contractor's office. Within seconds the building was blazing.[26]

A local West Indian councillor and community leader, James Hunte, reports in the newspaper that the young black man whose motoring offence had precipitated the riot was 'handcuffed, beaten up and threatened with being pushed under a bus during the arrest'. He recounts how he went to the police station where the man was being held and warned officers to free the man after charging him if they wanted to avoid trouble. He adds 'this riot could have been avoided if we had police who were more understanding'. The West Midlands Chief Constable, Geoffrey Dear had received criticism for his hardline tactics particularly in relation to drug dealers who operated in the area and many residents complained about heavy-handed drugs raids in sensitive areas. However, after the riots Geoffrey Dear did admit that the root causes were 'massive social deprivation, inadequate housing, unsuccessful education, mass unemployment and racial discrimination'.[27]

As noted above most of the violence was directed towards shops and businesses in the area, the majority of these being owned by

Asian immigrants. The worst incident resulting from the riot was the death of two Asian brothers who ran a Post Office and who decided to stay to protect their property instead of fleeing to safety. They were burnt to death when the building was set on fire by a crowd of black youths. The significance of this horrific incident needs to be considered in an attempt to provide one explanation for this and other riots occurring in British cities in the 1980s and 1990s. Augustine John (now known as Gus John) who wrote the 1970 report 'Race in the Inner City', comments on the 1985 riot saying that at the time he wrote his report 'Handsworth was a very different place'.[28] In the 1960s the majority ethnic group was white English and the second largest African-Caribbean who as he reported had to contend with hostility from many of the local population and from the police. During the 1970s and 1980s increasing numbers of immigrants arrived from Asia, the majority from Pakistan and Bangladesh and these closely knit communities soon established dominance in businesses and retail outlets. African-Caribbean businesses declined and there was high unemployment amongst young black men. It was estimated that fewer than 5 percent of young black people leaving school in 1985 had found jobs. Gus John comments that 'one of the main causes of African-Caribbean resentment is that they are seldom employed in these Asian retail outlets or warehouses, even when what is on sale are goods that only African people purchase, for example hair products'. He believes that the black community resented the fact that financial establishments 'tend to the view that there is a culture of entrepreneurship among Asians that African-Caribbeans do not share', and they began to feel unrepresented in the local community.[29] Racial tension between the different groups in the community which Southgate's survey had concluded was insignificant during the 1981 riot, certainly seemed to play a significant role in 1985. It does seem however that it was the combination of unemployment and feelings that they had no role to play in society that led many young black men to react with violence against the communities in which they lived and which they felt had done little to improve their situation. As Ellis Cashmore points out 'decisions aren't made to recruit more blacks into industry and commerce, or to implement procedures for boosting their chances of promotion or arranging for changes in education to make it more adequate for a multicultural society'.[30] These were exactly the changes that Lord Scarman had suggested were necessary in his report on the Brixton riots when he concluded that 'complex political, social and economic factors' created a 'disposition towards violent protest'.

To conclude this part of the story it is necessary to move from the city of Birmingham to the South-East of London where on 22 April 1993 an eighteen-year-old college student, Stephen Lawrence, was stabbed to death by a gang of white youths while he and his friend were waiting for a bus home. Five years after this killing a public enquiry was set up, led by Sir William Macpherson, in an attempt to determine why no-one had so far been convicted for this crime. Stephen's parents were Jamaican and had emigrated to the UK in the 1960s. Five white suspects who were well known in the area for racist behaviour and violence were reported to the police and after a delay of four days, during which time they were able to dispose of clothing and other evidence, they were arrested and questioned but not charged due to lack of evidence. In June five suspects were arrested and two were identified by Stephen's friend, Duwayne Brooks, and charged with murder. However, the charges were dropped when Brooks' evidence was said to be unreliable. Many errors were shown to have been made by the police in conducting the investigation and it was also alleged that a smear campaign was carried out against Stephen's family in order to discredit them. In 1997 the Police Complaints Authority ruled that there had been 'significant weaknesses, omissions and lost opportunities' shown by the police but that there was no racism. In 1999 the Macpherson report accused the police of being 'institutionally racist' in their investigation of Stephen's murder, and put forward proposals to rectify this racism, not only in the police service but in all national institutions. It proposed that,

> The Government will establish performance indicators to monitor the handling of racist incidents, levels of satisfaction with the police service among ethnic minorities, training of family and witness liaison officers, racial awareness training, stop and search procedures, recruitment of ethnic minorities and complaints about racism in police forces.[31]

It recommended that there should be 'a review and revision of racial awareness training in police forces', and that all proven 'racist words or acts' should lead to disciplinary proceedings. An important recommendation was that the Government should consider the introduction of a revised national curriculum for schools, 'to prevent racism and value cultural diversity'.[32]

Stephen Lawrence was killed because he was black, and because he was black the police did not make sufficient effort to prosecute those who had been responsible for his death. Two months after his death Stephen's body was taken to Jamaica where he was buried in the land of his ancestors, ancestors who had endured unimaginable suffering at the hands of their British masters. Perhaps the legacy of this past was still being felt in the streets of London and Birmingham at the end of the twentieth century.

PART TWO Birmingham, Alabama

On May 4, 1961 two interstate buses left Washington D.C. at the start of a journey that would take them through Virginia, North and South Carolina, Georgia and Alabama, aiming to end up in New Orleans about two weeks later. Unfortunately for most of the passengers their journey would come to a violent end in Birmingham Alabama on May 15. The Freedom Ride, as the journey became known, had been organised by members of the Congress of Racial Equality (CORE) joined by members of the Student Nonviolent Coordinating Committee (SNCC). In most Southern states segregation ordinances had been passed in defiance of Supreme Court rulings against segregation. This meant that there was still segregated seating on buses and segregated waiting areas, restrooms and refreshment facilities in bus terminals. The twelve Freedom Riders, both white and black, boarded two buses ensuring that one black rider sat in a seat normally reserved for whites and that at least one interracial pair sat in adjoining seats. This defiance of Jim Crow conventions initially provoked only minor hostilities at stopping points until the bus crossed the border into South Carolina. On stopping in the town of Rock Hill, John Lewis one of the youngest SNCC riders made for the 'White' waiting room and was immediately attacked by a group of young white men. Two other riders went to his assistance and they were also attacked. Lewis suffered from bad cuts to his face but insisted on rejoining the bus pointing out that 'the Freedom Riders had passed their first major test, refusing to strike back against an unprovoked assault'.[33] It was known that the Ku Klux Klan held a particularly strong position in Rock Hill and because the Freedom Riders had made no secret of their plans the Klan members were aware of their arrival well in advance. Details of their journey had been sent to the Birmingham Police Department by the FBI, and the chief commissioner, Eugene "Bull" Connor working closely with an 'avid Klan Supporter', Police Sergeant Tom Cook, set about providing the KKK with 'detailed information on the Ride, including a city-by-city itinerary'.[34] Connor agreed with Cook that when the Freedom Riders arrived at the Greyhound bus terminal in Birmingham sixty Klansmen 'would be selected to take care of the integrationists, thirty at the bus depot and thirty reinforcements stationed nearby'. Diane McWhorter continues,

> Connor would give them fifteen to twenty minutes to work over the Freedom Riders before any officers arrived. Police headquarters were virtually across the street from the Greyhound bus terminal. If Negroes went into the restrooms, Connor advised, the Klansmen were to beat them till they "looked like a bulldog got ahold of them". Then, Connor said, take the "nigger's" clothing off and carry it away so that he would have to walk into the depot naked, he would be immediately arrested and sent to the penitentiary.[35]

However, on May 14, the day the buses were due to arrive in Birmingham events did not proceed according to plan for Connor and Cook. Just before midday the Atlanta FBI wired to inform them that the Greyhound bus had left Atlanta and would arrive in Birmingham at 3.30, with the second Trailways bus arriving at 4.05. The Rev. Shuttlesworth had also received a call from one of the Freedom Riders, James Peck, a white, pacifist, NewYorker who had long been involved with the civil rights struggle. After crossing into Alabama the first stop was in Anniston, about sixty miles from Birmingham, but on arriving in the town they found the bus terminal closed and an angry crowd gathered in the surrounding streets.

The Anniston Klan had not wanted to leave all the action to Klan members in Birmingham and as the bus parked outside the station it was surrounded by a large mob carrying metal pipes, clubs and chains. The windows of the bus were smashed, the sides dented and the tyres slashed. Throughout this attack there was no sign of the Anniston police and when they did eventually arrive no arrests were made, the police officers just chatting with members of the crowd and then telling the driver to move on away from the station. As the bus left Anniston it was accompanied by a long line of cars and trucks with two slow moving vehicles at the head of the line. Six miles out of the town the driver was forced to stop in an attempt to find replacement tyres but as he did so the occupants of the accompanying vehicles surrounded the bus, smashing in the remaining windows and attempting to turn the vehicle on its side. The Riders remained in their seats and eventually two members of the mob set fire to a petrol soaked bundle of rags and threw it through a window. The bus was filled with smoke and flames and the occupants heard members of the mob shouting "Burn them alive" and "Fry the goddamn niggers".[36] The passengers managed to squeeze through smashed windows and one door on the opposite side of the bus and eventually the mob retreated when they feared that the whole bus might explode. All the Riders survived but some were badly injured and lay on the ground bleeding and choking. Arsenault relates how one twelve-year-old white girl who lived nearby 'supplied the choking victims with water, filling and refilling a five-gallon bucket while braving the insults and taunts of Klansmen. Later ostracized and threatened for this act of kindness, she and her family found it impossible to remain in Anniston in the aftermath of the bus bombing'.[37] None of the police patrolmen who arrived at the scene made any attempt to arrest those responsible or even to call an ambulance and when one eventually did arrive the driver refused to take any of the black Riders. He eventually relented when the white Riders already in the ambulance dismounted refusing to leave their black friends behind. The Riders received little attention at the Anniston hospital and when a crowd of Klansmen gathered threatening to burn the hospital down, hospital officials ordered the Riders to leave. A frantic call was made to the Rev. Fred Shuttlesworth in Birmingham who organized a convoy of cars to go to Anniston to pick up the stranded riders.

Meanwhile the second Trailways bus had stopped briefly at Anniston where they heard about the attack on their friends. Eight young white men boarded the bus and ordered Charles Person, a young black Freedom Rider to go to the back of the bus saying 'You ain't up north. You're in Alabama, and niggers ain't nothing here'. James Peck and Walter Bergman, a sixty-one year-old white college professor from Michigan got up from their seats to reason with the attackers and 'were battered to the floor with Coke bottles' and stamped on, leaving Bergman with permanent brain damage. The injured Riders were dragged to the back of the bus and McWhorter notes 'A policeman boarded the bus, smiled at the batterers, and said, "Don't worry about no lawsuits. I ain't seen a thing'.[38] The bus set off for Birmingham arriving at the Trailways station which was filled with waiting Klansmen. They knew that the police would give then fifteen minutes before interfering and as soon as the badly injured Peck and Person got off the bus and made their way to the white waiting room they were grabbed and pushed into a dimly lit corridor where they were attacked by 'more than a dozen whites, some armed with lead or iron pipes ... punching and kicking them repeatedly'.[39] Person managed to escape and 'eventually found his way to Fred Shuttlesworth's parsonage' but Peck was left unconscious on the floor of the bus station in a pool of blood. When he regained consciousness he staggered into the waiting room where he was found by Walter Bergman and the two of them 'finally found a black cab driver brave enough to drive them to Shuttlesworth's parsonage'.[40] Alarmed at the seriousness of Jim Peck's wounds Shuttlesworth called for an ambulance but it was several hours before he found one willing to transport a Freedom Rider to hospital. While they were waiting several police cars arrived and threatened to arrest the interracial group for 'violating local segregation laws'. Bull Connor himself telephoned Shuttlesworth, ordering him to give the Riders up to the police but he refused to comply. Peck was eventually taken to hospital where he underwent surgery on his head wounds and as he recovered his bed was soon surrounded by local reporters asking him about his experiences and taking photographs of his wounds. Press reporters and photographers had been present at the Trailways bus station when the Freedom Riders bus arrived but much of their film of the attack was grabbed and destroyed by the

Klansmen. News of the situation in Birmingham did gradually reach the North, eventually coming to the attention of the President and his brother, the Attorney-General, Robert Kennedy, both of whom were angered by the fact that the FBI had not informed them of the plot to disrupt the Freedom Rides. The President was very much involved in Cold War negotiations and was not happy to be diverted by racial conflicts in the Southern States of his own country. However as more reports and images of the events appeared in newspapers such as the *New York Times* and *Washington Post* it became clear that such atrocities could not be ignored. As Arsenault writes,

> Nothing, it seems, had prepared Americans for the image of the burning bus outside of Anniston, or of the broken bodies in Birmingham... Citizens of all persuasions found themselves pondering the implications of the violence and dealing with the realization that a group of American citizens had knowingly risked their lives to assert the right to sit together on a bus.[41]

The suffering that the Freedom Riders had been willing to endure for the sake of their cause played a large part in the eventual defeat of Jim Crow laws. In November 1961 the Interstate Commerce Commission (ICC) issued a ruling prohibiting racial segregation on interstate buses. However this did not mean that the ruling was universally enforced and it was some years before all white people in states like Alabama were prepared to tolerate mixed race facilities in bus stations.

Martin Luther King had not participated in the Freedom Rides despite being requested to do so by SNCC members. However, towards the end of 1961 he went to Albany in Georgia to support members of the Albany Movement in their campaign to end segregation and introduce voting rights. Various factors, including disagreements between King's SCLC and the SNCC concerning the tactics to be employed, and the refusal of the city's white leaders to make any concessions in the face of black demands particularly with regard to voting rights, meant that the Albany campaign was unsuccessful. King was determined to learn from the mistakes of this campaign and decided that Birmingham, with its reputation as being the most racially segregated city in the Southern States would be the ideal place to conduct his new campaign. The failure of Bull Connor to prevent the attacks on the Freedom Riders at the Trailways bus station meant that the whole country, both North and South, had been made aware of the racist violence carried out by the Ku Klux Klan in Birmingham and the lack of any attempt by the authorities to combat this violence. King was also encouraged by the presence in Birmingham of the Rev. Fred Shuttlesworth and the organisation of which he was president, the 'Alabama Christian Movement for Human Rights' (ACMHR) with which King's SCLC was affiliated. The campaign began on April 3, 1963, when a small group of demonstrators entered the Britling Cafeteria in Birmingham, sat at the whites only lunch counter and asked to be served. After the expected refusal they staged a sit-in, tactics which were repeated in segregated businesses throughout the city. Bringing about the desegregation of lunch counters and public facilities and the removal of 'white only' and 'black only' signs was not the only aim of the protest. Even more important was the establishment of 'fair hiring practices' in all city departments as well as in stores. The black people of Birmingham wanted access to 'whites only' jobs such as policemen and bus drivers and full integration into the employment system. This meant 'removal of the 'race wage' that paid black workers less by limiting them to inferior positions in the city's economy'.[42]

These early demonstrations did not meet with as much success as King and Shuttlesworth had hoped for, mainly due to the reluctance of many black people to take part in direct action and also to Connor's initial policy of choosing to ignore the demonstrators. He had recently been defeated in local elections by Albert Boutwell but refused to give up his position until his original term of office elapsed. Possibly wanting to avoid a repeat of the criticism he had received after the Trailways bus station violence he had instructed the Ku Klux Klan not to intervene in the demonstrations. However, on 9 April a march through the city attracted a large crowd of black supporters and Connor's policemen came out with dogs to control the crowd. King and his friend the Rev. Ralph Abernathy decided to lead a march on Good Friday, 12 April, realising that as a result they would probably be arrested and sent to jail. Soon after beginning the march the two men together with fifty demonstrators were indeed arrested and driven straight to the city jail where King was placed in solitary confinement. It was during the week that he spent in jail that King wrote his 'Letter from Birmingham Jail' in which he defended the use of non-violent, direct action in the face of racial injustice, segregation and police brutality. In an attempt to justify his methods to those who might criticise them he observes that 'History is the long and tragic story of the fact that privileged groups seldom give up their privileges voluntarily'. He continues,

> I guess it is easy for those who have never felt the stinging darts of segregation to say "wait". But when you have seen vicious mobs lynch your mothers and fathers at will and drown your sisters and brothers at whim; when you have seen hate-filled policemen curse, kick, brutalize, and even kill your black brothers and sisters with impunity; when you see the vast majority of your twenty million Negro brothers smothering in an airtight cage of poverty in the midst of an affluent society... when you take a cross-country drive and find it necessary to sleep night after night in the uncomfortable corners of your automobile because no motel will accept you; when you are humiliated day in and day out by nagging signs reading "white" and "colored"; when your first name becomes "nigger" and your middle name becomes "boy" (however old you are) . . . when you are forever fighting a degenerating sense of "nobodyness" – then you will understand why we find it difficult to wait.[43]

King and Abernathy were released from jail after SCLC supporters helped to raise their bail money but with so many demonstrators in jail and others unwilling to risk arrest for fear of losing their jobs it became clear that a new source of volunteers would have to be found if the demonstrations were to continue. Civil Rights campaigners in Mississippi had noticed the enthusiasm shown by young high school students to take part in non-violent direct action, and James Bevel and Diane Nash were invited by King to come to Birmingham to organise training sessions in Birmingham schools. Despite the children's enthusiasm much opposition was expressed to the idea of allowing children to take part in demonstrations, but with no obvious alternative if the campaign was to continue on Thursday, 2 May students left their classrooms to 'march for justice'. They gathered in 16th Street Baptist Church and as described by an eyewitness 'in disciplined groups of 50, children singing freedom songs march out two-by-two. When each group is arrested, another takes its place. There are not enough cops to contain them, and police reinforcements are hurriedly summoned. By the end of the day almost 1,000 kids have been jailed'.[44] *Time* magazine captured the image of a 'little Negro girl splendid in a newly starched dress looking at the armed officers and calling to her friend "Hurry up Lucille. If you stay behind you won't get arrested with our group"'.[45] On the following day a thousand students assembled and as the jails were already filled to capacity Connor decided to use high-pressure fire hoses in an attempt to disperse them. The students were knocked off their feet many being 'washed tumbling down the street like leaves in a flood' while 'hundreds of Black on-lookers . . . threw rocks and bottles at the cops and firemen'. To further intimidate the demonstrators Connor brought up his 'K9 Corps of eight vicious attack dogs' and John Lewis later recalled 'we were witnessing police violence and brutality Birmingham-style: unfortunately for Bull Connor, so was the rest of the world'. Television and newspapers showed images of 'young children marching up to snarling police dogs, cops clubbing women to the ground, and high-pressure hoses sweeping young bodies into the street'.[46] By Saturday as demonstrations continued and the jail and its yard could hold no more, children were placed in a stockade at the state fair ground.

On Monday, 6 May a young black lawyer and civil rights worker, Len Holt, arrived in Birmingham and wrote an account of what he saw. As he drove out of the downtown area he saw that 'on the roofs of the three and four story buildings surrounding Kelly-Ingram Park were clusters of policemen with short-wave radios over their shoulders. At the four intersections surrounding the park were dozens of white-helmeted officers . . . Pressing on each cop were the eyes of 4,000 Negro spectators – women, men, boys, girls and mothers with babies . . . they didn't talk much, just looked . . . and waited'. From inside the 16th Street Baptist Church came the sound of more than 2,000 school students singing songs of freedom such as '*We Shall Overcome*'. A minister standing near Holt commented 'At any moment those cops expect 300 years of hate to spew forth from that church'.[47] Holt continues, 'the time was 1.10 p.m. Four fire engines arrived at the intersections and set themselves up for "business". Each disgorged its high-pressure hoses, and nozzle mounts were set up in the street'. As students left the church marching two abreast and singing freedom songs, they were met by policemen with sticks and ushered into yellow school buses which carried them to the already full jail. Holt and his fellow workers from SNCC were at least grateful that the police dogs had not been employed and that violence had been limited. However Holt records, 'at 6pm. word got back to the motel that the 1,000 students arrested earlier had neither been housed nor fed. With Jim Forman of SNCC I drove to the jail. There were youths throwing candy bars over the fence to the students . . . while we were there it began to rain. The students got soaked . . . there was no shelter for the kids . . . That night the weather turned cool. We learned that the students were still in the jail yard, unsheltered and unfed. The same message got to the others in the Negro community. An estimated 500 cars and 1,200 people drove to the jail with blankets and food. The police responded by bringing up dogs and fire hoses' but eventually 'the food and blankets were given to the kids'.[48]

The student leaders decided to change their tactics for the following day, 7 May, and instead of starting their demonstrations at 1pm when the police usually arrived, they would begin to demonstrate earlier, giving them a chance to reach the downtown area before being arrested. Holt records, 'that night five of us slept in a motel room designed for two. We were crowded, but so were the 2,000 students crammed 75 or more in cells for eight in the city jail. Our room was hot that night, but not as hot as the unventilated sweat boxes in which Cynthia Cook, 15, and other girls were placed as punishment by the jail personnel when they refused to say "sir". Before 10am on the following morning, 600 students had gathered in the church and were transported by cars to downtown where they immediately began to picket department stores. Police were hurriedly called to report for duty by a furious Bull Connor but when they arrived in the area, knowing that the jails were full, all they could do was tell the students to go home. They returned to 16th Street Baptist Church where more demonstrators were waiting and more than 2,000 again marched downtown where their numbers were doubled by cheering spectators. They marched back to the church which was soon surrounded by 300 policemen with dogs and fire hoses. Holt recalls seeing '3,000 Negroes encircled in the Kelly-Ingram Park by policemen swinging clubs . . . the firemen used the hoses to knock down the students . . . they were directed at everyone with a black skin, demonstrators and non-demonstrators'. The Rev. Fred Shuttlesworth was one of those thrown against the church wall by the power of the water, resulting in internal injuries. It was reported that 'As he is rushed to hospital by ambulance, Bull Connor tells a reporter: "*I wish he'd been carried away in a hearse*".[49] Holt ponders 'I wondered how long it would be before some Negro lost his restraint. It had almost happened Monday, the day before, when cops flung a Negro woman to the ground and two of them had put their knees in her breast and twisted her arm. This was done in the presence of the woman's 19-year-old son and thousands of Negro spectators. Four 200-pound Negro men barely managed to restrain the son'.[50] Throughout the demonstration on 7 May speakers from the church spoke to the people on a public address system stressing the importance of nonviolent resistance, a policy which was maintained despite immense provocation.

As images of police brutality were viewed throughout the world and public pressure grew, President Kennedy could no longer turn a blind eye to the situation in Birmingham. He sent a Justice Department official, Burke Marshall to the city in an attempt to persuade King to bring a halt to the demonstrations but King refused to give in. On the evening of 7 May the Birmingham authorities eventually agreed to hold talks with leaders of the black community and King declared a temporary truce. George Wallace who had been elected Governor of Alabama the previous year and had ended his inaugural speech with the words 'I say segregation now, segregation tomorrow, segregation forever', condemned all attempts to end segregation in Birmingham and sent in a small army of Alabama State Troopers to carry out military drills in Kelly Ingram park, while Bull Connor ordered the doors of 16th Street church to be padlocked. Despite calls from Shuttlesworth and others to renew protests, on 9 May an initial agreement was made to bring an end to segregation in Birmingham. Before King would agree to the settlement he insisted that all demonstrators should be released from jail and the Kennedys managed to persuade sympathetic labour unions in the north to raise sufficient funds to bail out all those imprisoned. Another condition insisted on by white businessmen was that Boutwell should be allowed to take over control of the city government from Bull Connor. On 10 May the terms of the 'Birmingham Truce Agreement', which was to be phased in over sixty days, were announced. Public facilities such as waiting rooms would be desegregated, segregation signs on washrooms, restrooms and drinking fountains would be removed and the desegregation of lunch counters would begin. Finally non-discriminatory hiring practices would be introduced ensuring that there was at least one black employee in each shop or business. However, as Bruce Hartford observes 'employers resisted hiring and promotion of Blacks into "white" jobs for years to come, and job discrimination remains a reality to this day'.[51]

Throughout the demonstrations of April and May it was noticed that the Ku Klux Klan had remained surprisingly quiet, leaving the men of Bull Connor's police and fire departments to demonstrate their brutal methods of control. This was not to last for on the night of Saturday, 11 May the Klan's angry reaction to the terms of the settlement manifested itself in violent, bombing attacks on two buildings associated with the Civil Rights Movement. The first was the Gaston Motel which SNCC and SCLC members had used as their headquarters during the campaign, the target being the room which King had occupied and had vacated only a few hours previously. The second attack was on the home of King's brother, Rev. A.D. King. Fortunately no one was injured but an angry crowd gathered in Kelly Ingram Park and stones and bottles were thrown at the police. There was a suspicion that Governor Wallace's Alabama state troopers who had been guarding the area around the Gaston Motel had conveniently disappeared before the explosion. Kirk observes that shortly afterwards 'President Kennedy decided to federalise the Alabama National Guard to prevent its possible use by Governor Wallace'.[52] Following the bombings King spent time in Birmingham hoping to prevent further violence and assisting with the process of desegregation. It was obvious however that the Ku Klux Klan would oppose any attempt to bring about integration and this acquired particular significance in August 1963 when the Birmingham Board of Education approved a desegregation plan. This plan was not particularly ambitious, stating that formerly white schools would admit 'no more than five black children', but even Robert Kennedy was prompted to ask how many troops he would need to send to

Birmingham to enforce order. On 20 August, the day after the approval of the plan, Klan members held a meeting and that evening a bomb was exploded outside the house of Arthur Shores, the NAACP lawyer, in an attempt to show their opposition to school desegregation. Three white schools were to be integrated on 4 September and with state troops on standby police lines were formed around the schools. Members of the Ku Klux Klan and the National States Rights Party (NSRP) formed a motorcade to West End High School only to find that the three black students due to enrol had been told not to report for another two days. At another school two students arrived to chants of 'Keep Alabama White' and 'Close Mixed Schools', but they were escorted in through a side door and became the first black children to legally enter a white Birmingham public school. The next day Governor George Wallace 'issued an executive order forbidding the integration of the public schools, "for the sole and express purpose of preserving the peace . . . "'[53]

That afternoon Robert Chambliss, member of the Robert E. Lee klavern of the Ku Klux Klan and known locally as 'Dynamite Bob', drove out of Birmingham to a local mining community and bought 140 sticks of dynamite from a store that supplied explosives to local mines. Although it was supposedly going to be used to clear land the Klan had just bought to build a new Klan hall, Leon Negron, the owner of the store 'drew his own conclusions about Chambliss's plans for the dynamite. "If you are going to blow up some niggers, I will throw in a few extra sticks", he said'.[54] Some of this dynamite was soon to be put to use when that night a second explosion occurred at the home of Arthur Shores. Neither Shores nor his wife were seriously injured but a crowd soon gathered and heavily armed police arrived to be met by black residents throwing bricks and bottles. A young black man John Coley was caught in the police gunfire and another Thomas Lymon was beaten with a rifle butt by a policeman who told him 'All you black bastards need to be dead; we ain't got no use for you anyway'.[55] Lymon survived the attack but John Coley was found to be dead on arrival at hospital. Later that night two Klan members were instructed to collect the case of dynamite from Chambliss's house and guessed by the rattling that some sticks were missing. Two years later Chambliss admitted that he had used some of the sticks on Shores' house. The men who had collected the case of dynamite drove out of the city and hid it in woods under vegetation. It would be moved to various destinations in Birmingham before its contents eventually arrived at Sixteenth Street Baptist Church in the early hours of Sunday, 15 September.

This Sunday was to be a special Youth Day organised by the minister the Rev. John Cross and members of the youth choir were attending Sunday school classes in the basement of the church. Two of the singers, eleven-year-old Denise McNair and fourteen-year-old Cynthia Wesley, both daughters of school teachers, left their class to go to the women's lounge to 'freshen up' before the church service. Here they met up with fourteen-year-old Carole Robertson and sisters Addie Mae and Sarah Collins. McWhorter records events as reported by those who were present in the church. 'At 10.22 there was a resonant thud, as if someone had hit the world's largest washtub, followed by a ripping blast that sent a streak of fire above the church. Closed doors flew open, and the walls shook. As a stale-smelling white fog filled the church, a blizzard of debris – brick, stone, wire, glass – pelted the neighborhood . . . In the basement, Sarah Collins lay in darkness, surrounded by rubble. The last thing she had seen was Addie by the restroom window, tying the sash of Denise McNair's purple plaid winter-cotton dress'.[56] The Rev. Cross and others who had rushed to the scene walked through the 'seven-by-seven foot hole in the wall of what had been the women's lounge . . . and began digging into the wreckage'. After removing several layers of bricks and concrete slabs they uncovered four bodies which appeared to them to be old women. It was only when Denise's grandfather recognized the black patent-leather shoes that his granddaughter had been wearing that they realised the bodies were those of young girls. They found Sarah Collins alive but terribly wounded. She was rushed to hospital and the ambulance driver then returned to pick up the body of her sister, Addie May.

Four girls were murdered and twenty other people were badly injured, but they were not the only victims that day. A thirteen-year-old boy, Virgil Ware, whose father was an unemployed black coal miner was riding on a bicycle with his older brother when two white boys who had been attending a segregationist rally and were carrying a Confederate flag passed them. One of the boys, Larry Sims, pulled out a pistol and shot and killed Virgil. The boys who attended a prestigious private school were convicted of second degree manslaughter and Larry was sentenced to six months in a juvenile detention centre. However, the judge, who considered the shooting to be merely "a lapse" in judgement on the part of the boys, suspended their sentences, and for the cold-blooded, violent murder of a black child they were placed on probation for two years. Another victim was a black sixteen-year-old, Johnnie Robinson who was shot in the back by an Officer as he ran down an alley after throwing stones at a car painted with the slogan 'Negroes, go back to Africa'. Robinson was dead on arrival at hospital but no action was taken against the policeman who had shot him.

On Monday, 16 September, the day after the church bombing, a young, white Birmingham lawyer, Charles Morgan gave a speech at the Birmingham Young Men's Business Club in which he spoke powerfully and eloquently about the events of the previous day. In the speech which was reproduced in *The Atlantic* on the fiftieth anniversary of the bombing, he said,

> Four little girls were killed in Birmingham yesterday. A mad, remorseful worried community asks, "Who did it? Who threw that bomb? Was it a Negro or a white?" The answer should be, "We all did it." ... the "who" of "Who did it" is really rather simple ... The "who" is every little individual who talks about the "niggers" and spreads the seeds of his hate to his neighbor and his son. The jokester, the crude oaf whose racial jokes rock the party with laughter ... It is every senator and every representative who in the halls of Congress stands and with mock humility tells the world that things back home aren't really like they are ... It is all the Christians and all their ministers who spoke too late in anguished cries against violence ... We are a mass of intolerance and bigotry and stand indicted before our young.
>
> Yesterday while Birmingham ... was attending worship services, a bomb went off and an all-white police force moved into action ... a police force which has solved no bombings. A police force which many Negroes feel is perpetrating the very evils we decry. And why would Negroes think this? ... There are no Negro policemen; there are no Negro Sheriff's deputies. Few Negroes have served on juries; few have been allowed to vote; few have been allowed to accept responsibility, or granted even a simple part to play in the administration of justice ...

Birmingham is a city where four little Negro girls can be born into a second-class school system, live a segregated life, ghettoed into their own little neighbourhoods, restricted to Negro churches, destined to ride in Negro ambulances, to Negro wards of hospitals or to a Negro cemetery.

And who is really guilty? Each of us. Each citizen who has not consciously attempted to bring about peaceful compliance with the decisions of the Supreme Court of the United States, every person in this community who has in any way contributed ... to the popularity of hatred, is at least as guilty, or more so, than the demented fool who threw that bomb.

What's it like living in Birmingham? No one ever really has known and no one will until this city becomes part of the United States. Birmingham is not a dying city, it is dead.

It is hardly surprising that after delivering this speech Morgan was forced to close down his law practice and move his family out of Birmingham. Constant threats were made against himself and his family with comments such as 'Nigger-lovers don't live long in Alabama'.

Morgan spent the rest of his life working as a civil rights lawyer, one of his achievements being to successfully sue the University of Alabama for refusing to admit two black men. Andrew Cohen who reproduced and commented on Morgan's speech in *The Atlantic*, noted that 'there is no monument or commemoration of the speech in Birmingham. Last time I was in the Birmingham Civil Rights Museum, I did not see any reference to Morgan's speech'. He suggests that one reason for this is that 'it is very hard for anyone today, in Birmingham and elsewhere, to genuinely understand how often and how many good white people kept silent in the face of rank injustice and racial violence in the South during the era of Jim Crow'.[57]

The police force which according to Morgan 'had solved no bombings' during the years of violent attacks in Birmingham, did try to give the appearance of making an attempt to find those responsible. They arrested a few Klan members and charged them with the possession of dynamite but they were released after the payment of a fine. Most of the police were either members or supporters of the Ku Klux Klan and as Klan members had made no secret of their involvement in the bombing it was clear that the police knew the identity of those responsible. On the day before the bombing Chambliss had boasted to his niece that he had 'enough stuff put away to flatten half of Birmingham' adding 'you just wait till after Sunday morning, they will beg us to let them segregate'.[58]

The White House was deluged with demands from the public that the perpetrators should be brought to justice and the FBI, under J. Edgar Hoover, agreed to take on the investigation. It was well known that Hoover was a racist who supported segregation and who believed that Martin Luther King and the Civil Rights movement were under Communist control. He had no interest in solving the murder of four black girls from Birmingham. Several witnesses had seen cars belonging to Chambliss and his Klan associate Thomas Blanton parked close to 16th Street church in the early hours of 15 September and one witness had had a clear view of one of four white men sitting in a parked car. Relatives of the bombers had overheard conversations in which the bomb plot was discussed and some of them would have been willing to testify. The bombers however had constructed various alibis as to their whereabouts on the night before the bombing and it would be another fourteen years before one of the bombers, Robert Chambliss was arrested and convicted of murder. At the time it was considered by many that FBI agents investigating the case had sufficient evidence to obtain a prosecution but were instructed by Hoover to conceal this evidence from the Justice Department. In 1971 Alabama Attorney General, Bill Baxley reopened the case but could make little progress until, under pressure from the media, the FBI were forced to release some of the hidden evidence. Some evidence had been obtained by the use of phone taps and the installation of microphones in the homes of suspected Klan members, both methods being considered illegal and Hoover had refused a request from the Justice Department to release this evidence. Eventually in 1977 sufficient evidence was produced to convict Robert Chambliss of murder and he died in prison in 1985. Towards the end of the century, long after the death of Hoover and under the Clinton administration, the FBI finally released all the evidence relating to the 1963 bombing and the case was reopened under U.S. Attorney, Doug Jones. Thomas Blanton was convicted of murder in 2001 and fellow Klansman, Bobby

Frank Cherry in 2002. A fourth bomber, Herman Cash, had died in 1994.

Following the 'Birmingham Truce Agreement' of May 1963 the Civil Rights Act, first proposed by President Kennedy in June 1963 a few months before his assassination, was signed into law by President Lyndon Johnson on July 2nd. 1964. The Act aimed to end segregation in public places and banned discrimination on the basis of race, colour, religion, sex or national origin. The Voting Rights Act followed in 1965 stating that the right to vote cannot be denied on the basis of race or colour and prohibiting the imposition of devices such as literacy tests which might restrict the ability of racial or language minorities to cast their vote. Both Acts although obviously welcomed by the Civil Rights organizations which had worked so hard and suffered so much to bring then about, did not result in an immediate end to segregation, as evidenced by the number of court cases brought in attempts to avoid the enforcement of the law. This was particularly evident in the case of desegregation in education. Laws introduced by senator Albert Boutwell in 1955 and 1956 such as the 'pupil placement law' and 'freedom of choice law'[59] allowed segregation to continue and there was a sharp increase in the number of whites-only private schools. In 1967 these 'Boutwell' laws were invalidated in a legal case and all non-integrated public schools in Alabama were ordered to admit black students, a decision which led to even more court cases. Despite numerous desegregation orders being issued in the 1970s there were still areas where 'conservative white parents pulled their children out of schools in large numbers, enrolling them in the segregation academies that were immune to court orders'.[60]

By 1980 most schools in Alabama were desegregated but this did not apply to schools in cities like Birmingham where resegregation started to occur. Despite the end of residential zoning laws in the 1960s, a study published in 1980 found that residential segregation between blacks and whites actually increased in Birmingham during the 1970s.[61] This was mainly due to the increasing numbers of African Americans moving into the city for employment and settling in areas previously occupied by whites. The consequence of this was that large numbers of white people moved out to the suburbs creating new housing areas with 'whites-only' schools.

Bobby Wilson in his study of racial segregation trends in the 1980s comments 'this racial polarity is creating racial homogeneity not only among schools, but also among community contacts, stores, and other community facilities'.[62] The consequences of this were being felt well into the next century as will be discussed in the following chapter.

The Voting Rights Act of 1965 aimed to eliminate all the devices which had been introduced since the beginning of the century which made it almost impossible for African Americans to be registered to vote. Under the act the supervision of voting was taken away from state authorities and given to the federal government which meant that any proposed changes in voting laws had to be approved by the federal court before being enacted. Southern state authorities were furious at this infringement of their powers and proceeded to devise various schemes whereby the new act could be frustrated without actually breaking the law. These schemes accelerated and became more devious when it was revealed that since the passing of the act black voter registration had increased dramatically, rising from 24 to 57 percent in Alabama between 1964 and 1968. The fear was that in areas with large numbers of black voters, increasing numbers of African American officials would be elected taking power away from the white minority. To avoid this some states changed voting district boundaries producing wider voting areas and thus diluting the black vote. During the 1980s the main tactic adopted by Southern state authorities was to accuse African Americans of voter fraud particularly in relation to the use of absentee ballots. In 1985 three civil rights workers in Alabama were charged with 'forging or changing and then mailing bogus absentee ballots.' One of these, Albert Turner Sr. who had worked closely with Martin Luther King had noticed 'that despite the VRA, and despite the large number of African Americans in the state's Black Belt counties, whites consistently won every election'. He discovered that a large number of absentee ballots were being sent in by people who owned land in these counties but lived elsewhere and had been 'strongly and actively encouraged by election officials in the Black Belt . . . to use absentee ballots to keep the political power in white hands'.[63]

In her detailed analysis of 'voter suppression' Anderson notes that despite the 'potential for an actual thriving, viable democracy' arising from the passage of the VRA, it in fact 'set the stage for a backlash that would gain momentum and velocity in the ensuing decades', [64] and to some extent still continues.

7

Into the Twenty-First Century

The story of the West Indian and American descendants of the people who were forcibly removed from their African homelands more than two hundred years ago does not of course end with the start of the new millennium. In the 1950s and 1960s many people travelled to Britain from the West Indies in order to find employment and at the same time, to contribute to the financial recovery of Britain after World War Two. Many of these new immigrants were children who had travelled with their parents or in some cases had remained in the West Indies with relatives and then travelled to Britain once their parents had settled and obtained employment. All of them were legally entitled to enter and stay in the country and as they grew up, went to school and obtained employment they never doubted that they were British citizens. This confidence in their British identity was to be broken in 2012 as a result of the government's proposal to create 'a hostile environment' for illegal migration a move which it considered would be popular with voters. The original intention was to identify those who had arrived in the country legally but had failed to return to their country of origin after their visas expired. This meant that anyone suspected of being in the country illegally had to produce documentary evidence to prove that they had a right to be here. Unless this evidence was produced they were denied access to work, housing, health care, benefits, education and all public services. Due to the large amount of time and effort involved in making these checks the Home Office required landlords, doctors, teachers, council workers and hospital staff to carry out checks on their behalf and report anyone who could not provide evidence of their legal status. Fines were imposed on businesses employing illegal immigrants and landlords were obliged to verify the immigration status of new tenants. This resulted in landlords being particularly reluctant to rent accommodation to anyone who appeared foreign, particularly those with a black skin. As a result of the 2014 Immigration Act more aggressive measures were introduced with an emphasis on the production of documents with particular importance being attached to the possession of a passport. In the words of Amelia Gentleman, 'anyone who could not produce a British passport was deemed to have violated immigration rules until they could prove that they hadn't. It was not up to the Home Office to disprove entitlement but up to the individual to show that they qualified'.[1] These inflexible requirements meant that a particular group of British citizens found themselves targeted solely because they were non-white, had been born in the West Indies and had arrived in Britain during the 1950s and 1960s before the enactment of the Immigration Act in 1973. The stories of two people, born in Jamaica, who received assistance from the Wolverhampton, Walsall and Birmingham branch of The Refugee and Migrant Centre (RMC), will help to reveal the inhumane treatment handed out to citizens who for various reasons were unable to produce the documents deemed necessary to prove that they were indeed British. The RMC received increasing requests for assistance when the Home Office started to outsource the tracking down of suspected illegal immigrants to a private company called Capita who were paid according to the number of people they succeeded in removing from the country. Needless to say they used increasingly aggressive techniques including phone calls and text messages to frighten people into leaving the country or face imprisonment and forced deportation. One person who suffered badly from this harassment was Gladstone Wilson who arrived in Britain from Jamaica in 1968 at the age of twelve to join his parents who had already settled in Wolverhampton. Wilson had worked for many years as a security guard and was currently employed at New Cross Hospital in Wolverhampton. In 2014 he received messages from Capita informing him that he was suspected of being in the UK illegally and that he no longer had a right to remain. He was no longer allowed to work and he had his security guard licence revoked. Like many others Wilson had lost the passport with which he had legally entered Britain nearly fifty years previously. His parents had returned to retire in Jamaica and when his mother died in 2014 he had attempted to apply for a new passport so that he could attend her funeral. It appears that this brought him to the attention of the Immigration Enforcement department and he was placed on the illegal migrants list. He had to report to the Solihull Immigration Centre at regular intervals or face six months in jail and a £5,000 fine, all the time having the threat hanging over him of being removed from the country.

Between 2014 and 2018 many other black British citizens were detained and threatened with deportation. Another resident of Wolverhampton who was assisted by the RMC was Paulette Wilson who had arrived in Britain from Jamaica in 1968 at the age of ten to live with her grandparents. She had worked as a cook for thirty-four years including some time in the House of Commons restaurant and had paid taxes and national insurance contributions. In 2015 she received a letter from the Home Office informing her that she had no right to remain in the UK and had six months to leave the country. Her housing and sickness benefits were stopped and she was forced to depend on her daughter Natalie who had a flat nearby in Wolverhampton. Paulette was confused and shocked having lived her life knowing that she was a British citizen but unfortunately having no passport or other documents to prove it. After several house moves her Jamaican passport stamped with her date of arrival into the UK proving her legal immigration status had been lost. Like Gladstone Wilson she was told that she had to report every fortnight to the Solihull Immigration Centre which was twenty-four miles away involving several train changes. Natalie struggled for two years to persuade the Home Office that an error had been made but as Amelia Gentleman so clearly points out, 'anyone who has tried to take on the Home Office will know that it is an unequal battle, with confused and frightened individuals spending hours held in automated telephone queuing systems, waiting to speak to government employees who read from scripts and have scant discretion to listen to or to divulge any helpful information'.[2] In 2017 Paulette was detained at the Solihull centre and taken in a secure van to Yarl's Wood detention centre to 'await deportation to Jamaica'. After six days she was moved to the immigration removal centre at Heathrow and it was only due to last-minute intervention from the RMC in

Wolverhampton and her local Member of Parliament, Emma Reynolds, that her removal from the country was prevented.

Amelia Gentleman had visited Paulette and her daughter in Wolverhampton and on 28 November 2017 she wrote an article in *The Guardian* newspaper in which she described in detail the nightmarish experiences to which Paulette had been subjected over the past few years. There was a huge public reaction to this article which five months later resulted in an admission from the Home Secretary, Amber Rudd, that the way in which undocumented Commonwealth citizens had been treated 'has been appalling – and I am sorry . . . I would not want anyone who has made their life in the UK to feel unwelcome or to be in any doubt of their right to remain here'. She added 'I am concerned that the Home Office has become too concerned with policy and strategy and sometimes loses sight of the individual'.[3] She failed to admit that it was the 'hostile environment' policy of the previous Home Secretary, Theresa May that had been responsible for the distress and hardship suffered by so many black British citizens.

Gladstone Wilson was granted British citizenship in August 2018 at a ceremony at the Civic Centre in Wolverhampton which means he now has a passport and can travel to Jamaica to visit the grave of his mother. He said 'I've got the right to be here. It's been a big weight off my shoulders . . . I get on with the people of Wolverhampton. I'm proud to be a citizen of Wolverhampton and I can't see any problem with being a citizen here'.[4] It is interesting to surmise what Enoch Powell, Member of Parliament for Wolverhampton South West in the 1960s, who in 1968 spoke of the 'dangerous delusion' that the black man can become integrated into this country, would have made of the affection shown towards Gladstone fifty years later by the citizens of Wolverhampton who were 'proud to have him as a citizen'.

In the Handsworth district of Birmingham tension continued to exist between young men of Caribbean origin and those of Asian origin which had been partly responsible for the riot in 1985. In October 2005 this ethnic tension resulted in a conflict which was based on a still unsubstantiated rumour that a fourteen-year-old black girl had been raped by a gang of Pakistani men after being accused of shoplifting in a beauty store owned by the men. The men naturally denied the rumour and the girl never came forward supposedly because she was afraid of being deported as she was in the country illegally. The rumour was circulated on a local pirate radio station and on the night of Saturday 22 October rioting occurred during which shops were attacked, cars set on fire and four people were stabbed one of them being a local black man, Isaiah Young-Sam who died later in hospital. The fact that such violence could occur as a result of an incident for which there was no evidence and no apparent victim suggests that deeper reasons lay behind this outbreak of hatred between two groups of people. These reasons have been discussed in the previous chapter and result from the assumption that Afro-Caribbean people resented the way in which more recent immigrants from Pakistan and Bangladesh had established dominance in local businesses and refused to employ people from the black community.[5] This meant that the location of the supposed incident in an Asian owned beauty shop selling products mainly bought by black women would have particularly angered local black people. In reality of course, both groups were disadvantaged with few employment opportunities, low incomes and inadequate housing, After the riots of the 1980s many white people together with Afro-Caribbeans who had obtained employment and earned a reasonable income moved away from Handsworth to other areas of Birmingham, their places being taken by an increasing number of immigrants from Africa and more recently Eastern Europe. In a study carried out in 2005 it was estimated that over a third of the population of Birmingham belonged to ethnic minorities and that although these minorities were disadvantaged in important areas the local authority 'has made some genuine efforts to ensure that all its citizens are provided equality of opportunity'.[6] One of the main areas benefitting from increased funding and resources was education with marked improvement in outcomes for Afro-Caribbean and Asian children in Birmingham schools.

In Birmingham, Alabama increasing polarisation of black and white communities led to an increase in the number of predominantly white schools in the new suburbs. These areas were part of Jefferson County where desegregation orders were in place but laws existed which allowed towns with more than 5,000 residents to vote for their own school system. This process known as secession had been adopted by a number of white communities and in 2015 residents of the town of Gardendale, ten miles to the north of Birmingham city centre, started to campaign for secession believing that their bid would not be challenged. Gardendale is 88 percent white but some black children were bussed in from the North Smithfield area of Birmingham meaning that the schools were 25 percent black. Arguments based on racial identity could obviously not be used in the bid but a ruling which only allowed students who lived in Gardendale to attend its schools would mean that the schools would be virtually all white. Campaigners argued that the schools would be run better under local control and the local council voted to introduce a property tax to fund the new system. In order to obtain secession Gardendale's plans had to be approved by the federal court in Birmingham but the hearing, which commenced in December 2016, did not go as smoothly as the Gardendale lawyers had expected. Those who opposed secession were represented by the black lawyer U.W.Clemon who, as a young law-school graduate had been successful in obtaining desegregation orders in Jefferson County in the 1960s and 1970s. He was born just outside Birmingham city where his father worked as a labourer in a steel works and he attended Dolomite Colored School which 'was inferior in every way to the gleaming modern school the white students in town attended'.[7] He graduated from an all-black college but was not able to proceed to law school at the University of Alabama which was still refusing to admit black students. Instead, in order to comply with federal law, the state paid for Clemon to attend the prestigious law school at Columbia University expecting that he and others like him would not return to Alabama after graduating. Clemon though, did return and worked throughout his career to bring about desegregation in Jefferson County schools. Since his retirement as a federal judge in 2008, Clemon had become increasingly concerned about the increasing number of schools who were reintroducing segregation, partly because 'mostly-white well-off communities are separating themselves from diverse and poorer school systems'.[8]

The Gardendale Board of Education lawyers insisted that there was no element of racism motivating their case simply that the citizens of Gardendale had raised their own taxes to enable them to operate their own school system 'for the sake of their children's education'. Various witnesses were called including Rickey Reeves, a black army veteran from North Smithfield whose thirteen year-old granddaughter attended a middle school in Gardendale. She loved her school and her teachers and Reeves could not bear the thought of her having to leave the school if it only accepted children from the predominantly white Gardendale. Another person who testified was the newly appointed superintendent of schools in Gardendale, Patrick Martin, who admitted that in nearly two decades in education 'he had never hired a single black person for any position, nor worked with a single black teacher'.[9] The judge presiding over the case, Madeline Hughes Haikala, reminded Martin of the *Brown v. Board of Education* decision from 1954 which he shamefacedly had to admit that he had not read. Haikala read a section of the decision out loud to the court,

> Segregation of white and colored children in public schools has a detrimental effect upon the colored children. The impact is greater when it has the sanction of the law. For the policy of separating the races is usually interpreted as denoting the inferiority of the negro group. A sense of inferiority affects the motivation of a child to learn.

Clemon, who admitted being moved to tears by the judge's action was convinced that the secession bid would be defeated and in April 2017 when the judge's ruling was published that did initially appear to be the case. Despite Gardendale's assertion that their secession bid was not about segregation or racism Haikala's report stated 'the Court finds that race was a motivating factor in Gardendale's decision to separate from the Jefferson County public school system', adding that they clearly wished to prevent black children travelling from Jefferson County to Gardendale schools as was permissible under the present desegregation laws. However, towards the end of the report she states that a number of 'practical considerations' prevent the court from denying Gardendale's bid to secede. She decided to allow Gardendale to take over two elementary schools for the coming year provided they appointed a black school board member and came up with a desegregation plan for the new district. She added that after three years she would reconsider their bid for full separation. It appears that Haikala was concerned that if secession was disallowed angry Gardendale residents would blame black students who would continue to be bussed in and racism would increase. Haikala's decision was not however the end of the story for her ruling was appealed by the NAACP, lawyers acting on behalf of black school children and former federal judge, U.W.Clemon and the case was taken to the Court of Appeal which in February 2018 overruled the order that Gardendale should be allowed to form its own school system. Their decision was based on Haikala's own admission that race was the motivating factor in the case, that it was an attempt to exclude black children from Gardendale schools and that in so doing would impede the progress of desegregation in Jefferson County.

In March 2019 in a letter to Jefferson County Board of Education, the Gardendale Board of Education stated that it had given up its plan to operate its own school system and would not appeal the Court's decision. The hope that this case would see the end of attempts to bring about re-segregation of schools has unfortunately not been borne out by recent trends. A study published by the American Educational Research Association in September 2019 suggests that a rise in the creation of smaller, separate school districts, usually mainly white and more affluent, is resulting in schools which are increasingly segregated.[10]

Just as school boards devised secession schemes to reintroduce segregation in education, various schemes have been introduced in Southern states in an attempt to frustrate the Voting Rights Act and make it more difficult for African Americans to cast their vote. This is particularly important in Republican states with a large black population the supposition being that African Americans are more likely to vote for the Democratic candidate. Concerns about voter suppression and racial discrimination in the 2000 presidential election led to the introduction of a bill intended to 're-instill the American public's confidence in the electoral system'.[11] This was the 2002 Help America Vote Act (HAVA) under which an Election Assistance Commission was set up to 'help standardise voting systems'. However, the Republican Senator Bond, who oversaw the passage of the bill insisted that it should contain a requirement for everyone to have identification in order to vote. The type of ID required by the bill covered a fairly wide range of documents but it soon became evident that individual states were introducing their own more stringent requirements which would adversely affect the ability of members of disadvantaged groups to cast their vote even though they were on the electoral register. In 2011 Alabama passed a photo ID law which forbade the use of documents such as utility bills or social security cards insisting on the production of government issued photo ID such as passports or driving licenses which were possessed by a greater proportion of white Republican voters than black, mainly Democrat voters. The NAACP Legal Defense Fund estimated that 'more than 100,000 registered voters in Alabama can't vote because they don't have the photo identification require by the state', but Anderson observes that other sources give a far higher figure than this. Other measures taken in the state were to close down a number of driver's license offices in areas with a large number of black voters and 'with no viable public transportation, no access to vehicles, and the closest licence office sometimes nearly fifty miles away and open for only a few days a month, many Black Belt county residents were simply and completely disfranchised'. Anderson concludes 'the goal of all the GOP (Republican) voter ID laws is to reduce significantly the demographic and political impact of a growing share of the American electorate. To diminish the ability of blacks, Latinos, and Asians, as well as the poor and students to choose government representatives and the types of policies they support. Unfortunately, it's working'.[12]

There was, however one recent occasion on which it did not work. In December 2017 a U.S. Senate special election was held in the state of Alabama and it was presumed by all involved that the Republican candidate, Judge Roy Moore would win the seat. Moore was a self-proclaimed racist who considered that the last time America was truly great was during slavery. Moore's Democratic opponent was Doug Jones, the U.S. Attorney who in 2001 had reopened the 16th Street Baptist Church bombing case, resulting in the conviction of Thomas Blanton and Frank Cherry. The Republicans utilised all the voter suppression techniques they had devised in order to make it as difficult as possible for African Americans to get to the polling stations, particularly in counties with majority black populations. However, one important factor they had not anticipated was the influence still exerted in the state by the NAACP, who along with other local groups mounted a fierce campaign to mobilize black communities to exert their right to vote. They provided legal assistance and aid, checks on voter registration status and eligibility to vote, and help with filling out forms, as well as information on the location of polling stations and the provision of transport where necessary. As a result of their efforts the turnout in the central Black Belt counties was over 50 percent and in two of these counties, Macon and Greene, Jones received nearly 90 percent of the votes. In the state as a whole the result was 49.9 percent for Jones and 48.4 percent for Moore with most of Moore's votes coming from the mainly white, rural states. In Birmingham Jones won a large majority of 83,213 votes, 68.1 percent of the total and similar results were obtained in Montgomery, Mobile, Tuscaloosa and Huntsville, suggesting that a considerable number of white city dwellers were also voting for Jones. Moore naturally blamed voter fraud for his defeat unable to admit that on this occasion Republican voter suppression tactics had not been successful.[13]

Despite Doug Jones's success in the 2017 Alabama election it is believed that techniques designed to reduce the number of African Americans and other ethnic minorities casting their votes are still being implemented in many states when it is believed that their votes would be likely to produce the 'wrong' result.

The story of black slavery is the story of millions of people who were taken by force from their homelands so that white people could accumulate wealth and power and it is also the story of their descendants who well over a hundred years after abolition are still experiencing the effects of white privilege. This study of slavery and its aftermath reveals how certain attitudes became accepted and entrenched in societies that were involved in slavery. In late eighteenth-century Britain many of those campaigning to end the trade in slaves believed that slavery itself was a natural part of life and most members of the Church of England considered that members of the 'black races' were inferior to white Europeans. In some parts of the USA this belief was taken even further with the theory of polygenesis which maintained that black people actually belonged to a separate and inferior branch of the human race, thus justifying their position as slaves. Even ardent abolitionists like Joseph Sturge found it difficult to accept former black slaves as equal human beings, expecting them to be docile, respectable and grateful to their liberators. They certainly believed in the superiority of European culture and considered difference to be an indication of inferiority. In Britain attitudes towards people of other races were predominantly formed as a result of the colonial relationship whereas in the Southern United States white and black people had been living closely together in the same country for many years with the white planter class having complete dominance over their black slaves, a position of power which they did not intend to relinquish after abolition. Aided by white supremacist groups such as the Ku Klux Klan they struggled for nearly a hundred years to maintain segregation and ensure that black people were unable to advance in society. In 1968 a British Member of Parliament delivered a speech which although not actively encouraging violence displayed racist views as virulent as any of those put forward by white supremacists in the United States, views supported at the time by many members of the public.

David Olusoga writes that the West Indian population of Britain 'has amalgamated and assimilated more successfully than perhaps any other immigrant group of modern times' but he adds that 'disadvantages are still entrenched and discrimination remains rife'.[14] These disadvantages are revealed in the Equality and Human Rights Commission report of 2018 which revealed that black people are more likely to be employed in low-paid occupations and to live in poor quality housing. Black and mixed ethnicity children are more likely than white to be excluded from school and only a small number of black students are awarded places at top universities. In 2017 David Lammy's Review of the criminal justice system revealed 'racial discrimination at every stage' of the system with 12 percent of those detained in prison being of black Caribbean origin while making up only 3 percent of the population.

In America many people still live in voluntarily segregated areas with their children attending segregated schools. Unemployment for black and other ethnic minorities is double that for whites and black people make up 38 percent of the prison population when the black population in the country as a whole is 12.6 percent. Police brutality against black people is acknowledged to be common and many people see a direct link between this and the days of slavery and its aftermath. In 2019 the Pew Research Center on Social and Demographic Trends carried out a survey into how Americans saw the state of race relations in their country. They conclude that 'most U.S. adults say that the legacy of slavery continues to have an impact on the position of black people in American society today' and that 'there is some scepticism, particularly among blacks, that black people will ever have equal rights with whites in the U.S.'[15]

It would be a pity to have to end this story on a pessimistic note and it is no doubt true that many residents of Britain and the United States whose ancestors were taken into slavery are leading happy and successful lives, contributing to society and receiving friendship and respect from their white colleagues and neighbours. People of Caribbean descent in Britain are now Members of Parliament, actors, television newsreaders, Olympic athletes and highly paid footballers, but they are still likely to suffer from discrimination in employment, particularly in securing senior positions in large companies, financial institutions and in the legal and criminal justice systems. In the United States various initiatives have been adopted which help to ensure that African Americans are able to progress to the top in their chosen careers. Unfortunately, the situation for most black people in America, particularly in the Southern States is not as hopeful. Racially motivated incidents in Alabama are common and the success of a recent legal case aimed at overturning a Birmingham ordinance which discriminated against the city's majority black population showed that the fight for civil rights is not yet over. Birmingham fast-food workers had brought a lawsuit against the state of Alabama charging them with barring a citywide minimum wage increase, an action which discriminated against black people which make up 74 percent of the population. The case was initially dismissed with the claim that racial discrimination could not be proved. However in July 2018 the Court of Appeals agreed that the state's action did have a 'discriminatory effect on the city's majority black population' and that their claim was legally valid. Lucas Guttentag concludes that 'this case . . . originating in a town where America's history of racial violence faced some of its most pivotal confrontations . . . could now open the door for communities of color across the country to challenge racially discriminatory laws that deny localities the power to improve the lives of people of color'.[16]

At the beginning of the twentieth century W.E.B. Du Bois wrote,

Actively we have woven ourselves with the very warp and woof of this nation – we fought their battles, shared their sorrow, mingled our blood with theirs, and generation after generation have pleaded with a headstrong, careless people to despise not Justice, Mercy, and Truth, lest the nation be smitten with a curse. Our song, our toil, our cheer, and warning have been given to this nation in blood-brotherhood. Are not these gifts worth the giving? Is not this work and striving?
Would America have been America without her Negro people?[17]

Although the evil of slavery will never be forgotten it must be hoped that it will cease to cast its shadow over the lives of people today and in the future.

Notes

1 Guns Sugar and Cotton

1. Marvin T. Smith, Jon Marcoux, Erin Gredell and Gregory Waselkov, 'A Seventeenth-century trade gun and associated collection from Pine Island, Alabama', *Southeastern Archaeology*, 2016, http://dx.doi.org/10.1080/0734578X.2016.1257237
2. Ibid., pp. 1–6.
3. Barbara M.D. Smith, 'The Galtons of Birmingham: Quaker Gun Merchants and Bankers, 1702–1831', *Business History*, IX, 2 (1967), p. 133.
4. W.A. Richards, *The Birmingham Gun Manufactory of Farmer and Galton and the Slave Trade in the Eighteenth Century*, submitted for Master of Arts degree of the Faculty of Commerce and Social Sciences, University of Birmingham, 1972, pp. 47–???.
5. Eric Williams, *Capitalism and Slavery* (London: André Deutsch, 1964), p. 47.
6. Hugh Thomas, *The Slave Trade: The History of the Atlantic Slave Trade, 1440–1870* (London: Papermac, 1998), p. 324.
7. Smith, p. 139.
8. Letter from S.Galton to J. Galton, September 1756, Galton Papers ref. MS 3101/C/D/15/1, Archives and Collections, Library of Birmingham.
9. Thomas, p. 371.
10. Paul Edwards, ed., *Equiano's Travels: The Interesting Narrative of the Life of Olaudah Equiano, or Gustavus Vassa the African, Written by Himself, first published 1789* (Oxford: Heinemann, 1996).
11. *Equiano's Travels*, pp. 6–8.
12. Ibid., pp. 14–18.
13. Mungo Park, *Travels in the Interior of Africa* (Hertfordshire: Wordsworth Editions Limited, 2002), p. 296.
14. *Equiano's Travels*, p. 28.
15. Galton Papers, Archives and Collections, Library of Birmingham.
16. Richards, p. 123.
17. Ibid., p. 124.
18. Ibid., p. 124.
19. Thomas, p. 303.
20. Smith, p. 138.
21. Richards, pp. 7-8.

22 Ibid., p. 114. See Galton Papers, letter from S.Galton to Peter Farmer, Feb. 16, 1757.
23 Smith, p. 135.
24 See Eric Williams, p. 101.
25 Letter from S.Galton to Freame and Barclay, March 1755, Galton Papers, MS 3101/C/D/15/1
26 Smith, p. 146.
27 Eric Williams, p. 83.
28 See Richard S. Dunn, *Sugar and Slaves: The Rise of the Planter Class in the English West Indies, 1624–1713* (The University of North Carolina Press, 1972), pp. 190–195, for an account of the sugar making process.
29 D. Watts, *The West Indies, Patterns of Development, Culture and Environmental Change since 1492* (Cambridge, 1917), p. 180, quoted in Jennifer Tann, 'Steam and Sugar: The Diffusion of the Stationary Steam Engine to the Caribbean Sugar Industry, 1770–1840' *History of Technology*, Vol. 19, 1997, p. 64.
30 Tann, p. 64.
31 Dunn, p. 192.
32 Tann, p. 65.
33 See Veront M. Satchell, 'Steam for Sugar-Cane Milling: The Diffusion of the Boulton and Watt Stationary Steam Engine to the Jamaican Sugar Industry, 1809–1830', in *Jamaica in Slavery and Freedom: History, Heritage and Culture,* eds. Kathleen Monteith, Glen Richards (University of West Indies Press, 2001), p. 246.
34 William Pulteney to Boulton and Watt, I May 1776, Boulton and Watt Collection, Library of Birmingham Archive. Quoted in Tann, p. 67.
35 Lord Penryhn to Boulton and Watt, 30 Jan. 1786, 13 Feb. 1787, Boulton and Watt Collection, Library of Birmingham Archive. Quoted in Tann, p. 67.
36 John Dawson to Boulton and Watt, 9 November 1790, Boulton and Watt Collection, Library of Birmingham Archive, ref. MS 3147/3/88/9.
37 Tann, p. 64.
38 Ibid., p. 77.
39 Satchell, p. 252.
40 Samuel Whitbread to Boulton and Watt, 13 May, 1789, quoted in Tann, p. 69.
41 Mary Anne Galton, quoted in Revolutionary Players, Commerce, Slavery and Anti-Slavery, http://www.revolutionaryplayers.org.uk.
42 James Watt to Beguye and Co. of Nantes, 31 Oct. 1791, Boulton and Watt Collection, Library of Birmingham Archive, ref. MS 3147/3/88, p. 119.
43 Josiah Wedgwood to James Watt, 14 Feb. 1788, from the papers of James Watt, Library of Birmingham Archive, ref. MS 3219/4/95/20.

44 Jenny Uglow, *The Lunar Men: The Friends who made theFuture, 1730–1810* (London: Faber and Faber, 2003), p. 260.
45 Uglow, p. 414.
46 Boulton to Watt, 19 April 1783.
47 Uglow, p. 414.
48 See Robert Woods, 'A Turn of the Crank Started the Civil War', *Mechanical Engineering*, Sept. 2009.
49 Charles C. Mitchell, 'The Development of Cotton from the Old World to Alabama: Chronological Highlights in Alabama Cotton Production'.
50 Gloria Jahoda *The Trail of Tears: The Story of the American Indian Removals, 1813–1855* (New York: Wings Books, 1995), p. 16.
51 Thomas, p. 568.
52 Kolchin, p. 96.
53 Kolchin, p. 97.
54 See John Morse, https://birminghamhistorycenter.wordpress.com/2011/04/22.
55 https://www.bhamwiki.com/w/Alington_Antebellum_Home.
56 Jesse Chambers, http:/blog.al.com/spotnews/2013/06/arlington_antebellum_home_in_w.html.
57 James Oakes, *The Ruling Race: A History of American Slaveholders* (New York: W.W.Norton and Company, Inc., 1998), p. 72.
58 Oakes, p. 72.
59 Oakes, p. 73.
60 The Library of Congress, *Born in Slavery: Slave Narratives from the Federal Writers' Project, 1936–1938, Alabama Narratives, Volume1*, Aarons-Young, https//www.loc.gov/collections/slave-narratives-from–the-federal-writers-project-1936-to-1938/.
61 Walter Calloway, interviewed by W.P.Jordan, Library of Congress Manuscript Division, ID mesnp 010051.
62 Simon Phillips, interviewed by Morgan Smith, Library of Congress Manuscript Division, ID mesn 010/318312.
63 Kolchin, p. 130.
64 Thomas, p. 596.
65 Sven Beckert, *Empire of Cotton*, https://www.theatlantic.com/business/archive/2014/empire-of-cotton/383660/, p. 3.
66 Beckert, p. 4.
67 Gene Dattel, 'Cotton, the Oil of the Nineteenth Century', *The International Economy*, Winter, 2010.

2 Abolition

1 *A century of Birmingham life: or, A chronicle of local events, from 1741 to 1841/ compiled and edited by John Alfred Langford* (Birmingham: E.C. Osborne; London: Simpkin, Marshall and Co., 1868)

2 See http://calmview.birmingham.gov.uk, p. 4.
3 Joseph Priestley, L.L.D. F.R.S., *Sermon on the Slave Trade*, reproduced on http://www.revolutionaryplayers.org.uk, pp. 1–12.
4 Priestley, p. 9
5 Barry R. Weingast, *Persistent Inefficiency: Adam Smith's Theory of Slavery and its Abolition in Western Europe*, Stanford University, December, 2016. https://web.stanford.edu/group/mcnollgast/cgi-bin/wordpress/wp-content/uploads/2016/01.
6 See Adam Smith, *Lectures on Jurisprudence (A)*, 1762–3, Glasgow edn., pp. 112–14, 185–6.
7 Priestley, p. 9.
8 Michael Jordan, *The Great Abolition Sham: The True Story of the End of the British Slave Trade* (Stroud: The History Press, 2010), p. 85.
9 Ibid.
10 Priestley, p. 7.
11 Abraham Lincoln, Lincoln-Douglas Debates (Ottawa, 21 August, 1858), http://bartleby.com/251/1006.
12 Erasmus Darwin, *The Economy of Vegetation*, Canto II, lines 421–430
13 Erasmus Darwin, *The Loves of the Plants*, Canto III, lines 439–456, https://francoistremblay.wordpress.com/2013/01/14/erasmus-darwin-on-slavery/.
14 Patricia Fara, 'Grandfather Erasmus Darwin: written out of history', http://blog.oup.com/2012/09/erasmus-darwin—who-invented-evolution. Fara's biography is *Erasmus Darwin: Sex, Science and Serendipity* (Oxford: Oxford University Press, 2012).
15 Adam Hochschild, *Bury the Chains: The British Struggle to Abolish Slavery* (London: Macmillan, 2005), p.68.
16 Hochschild, p. 193.
17 Quoted in Uglow, p. 446.
18 Jordan, p. 114.
19 Jordan, p. 192.
20 The official title was 'The Society for the Mitigation and Gradual Abolition of Slavery Throughout the British Dominions'.
21 See http://calmview.birmingham.gov.uk, p. 6.
22 Clare Midgley, *Women Against Slavery: The British Campaigns, 1780–1870* (London: Routledge, 1995), pp. 45–6.
23 R. Isaac Wilberforce and S. Wilberforce, *The Correspondence of William Wilberforce* (London:John Murray, 1838), Vol. II, pp. 493–4. Quoted in Midgley, p. 48.
24 Midgley, p. 70.
25 Birmingham Anti-Slavery Society Minute Book, MS3058/1, Archives and Collections, Library of Birmingham.

26 Richard Henry, *Memoirs of Joseph Sturge*, 1864, L78.1 STU, Archives and Collections, Library of Birmingham.
27 Birmingham Anti-Slavery Society Minute Book.
28 Elizabeth Heyrick, *Immediate, not Gradual Abolition: or, an Inquiry into the Shortest, Safest and Most Effectual Means of Getting Rid of West Indian Slavery*. Quoted in Hochschild, pp. 324–5.
29 Fowell Buxton, *Parl. Deb.*, new series, vol. IX, f.257 ff. Quoted in Jordan, p. 189.
30 Elizabeth Heyrick, quoted in Hochschild, p. 325.
31 Hochschild, p. 326.
32 David Brion Davis, *Inhuman Bondage: The Rise and Fall of Slavery in the New World* (Oxford: Oxford University Press, 2006), p. 246.
33 By 1810 the slave population of the North had fallen from 40,000 to about 27,000 but in the South it had increased from 717,000 to almost 1,200,000.
34 D. Laurence Rogers, *Apostles of Equality: The Birneys, the Republicans, and the Civil War* (Michigan: Michigan State University Press, 2011), p. 15.
35 See Rogers, p. 17.
36 Rogers, p. 50.
37 Rogers, p. 52.
38 Thomas McAdory Owen, *Transactions of the Alabama Historical Society* (Montgomery, AL: Brown Printing Co., 1899), Vol. 3: 154–157. Quoted in Rogers, p. 53.
39 Rogers, p. 58.
40 Sarah Grimké, quoted in Mark Perry, *Lift Up Thy Voice* (New York: Viking, 2001), p. 2.
41 Alabama Slave Codes, www.en.wikiperia.org/wiki/slave_codes.
42 Rogers, p. 90.
43 Ibid., p. 108.
44 Rev. William T. Allan, in Theodore Dwight Weld, *American Slavery As It Is: Testimony of a Thousand Witnesses*, Personal Narratives, Part II, pp. 45–6, https://docsouth.unc.edu/neh/weld/weld.html.
45 Ibid., p. 47.
46 Ibid., p. 46.
47 Ibid.
48 J.C. Furnas, *The Road to Harper's Ferry* (New York: William Sloane Associates, 1959), p. 319, quoted in Rogers, *Apostles of Equality*, p. 46.
49 Angelina Grimké, quoted in Mark Perry, *Sarah and Angelina Grimké: On Slavery and Abolitionism* (New York, Penguin Books, 2014), p. xii.
50 Mark Perry, p. xiii.
51 Ibid.
52 Angelina Grimké, quoted in Perry, p. ix.
53 Ibid.

54 Abraham Lincoln, quoted at http://www.abrahamlincolnonline.org/lincoln/speeches/house.htm.
55 See https://rogerjnorton.com/Lincoln95.html.
56 Abraham Lincoln, quoted in W.E.B. Du Bois, *Black Reconstruction in America* (New York: The Free Press, 1998), p. 146.
57 See Ira Berlin, Barbara J. Fields, Steven F. Miller, Joseph P. Reidy and Leslie S. Rowland, eds., *Free At Last: A Documentary History of Slavery, Freedom, and the Civil War* (New York: The New Press, 1992), pp. 4–5, 134–5.
58 Ibid., pp. 44–5.
59 Berlin et al., pp. 536–7.
60 https://www.law.cornell.edu/amendmentxiii.
61 Clare Midgley, *Women Against Slavery: The British Campaigns, 1780–1870* (London: Routledge, 1992), p. 123. Midgley's chapter 'The Transatlantic Sisterhood' has provided much useful information for this section.
62 Elizabeth Barrett Browning, 'The Runaway Slave at Pilgrim's Point', verse II.

3 The Aftermath, Jamaica

1 Mary Reckord, 'The Jamaica Slave Rebellion of 1831' in *Past and Present*, Vol. 40, Issue 1, 1July 1968, pp. 108–125.
2 Taylor Memorandum, pp. 54–5, quoted in Thomas C. Holt, *The Problem of Freedom: Race, Labor, and Politics in Jamaica and Britain, 1832–1938* (London: The Johns Hopkins Press Ltd. 1992), p. 45.
3 The three men who accompanied Joseph Sturge were Thomas Harvey, William Lloyd and John Scoble.
4 Diana Paton, Introduction to *A Narrative of Events since the first of August, 1834, by James Williams, An Apprenticed Labourer in Jamaica* (Durham: Duke University Press, 2001), p. xxi.
5 James Williams, *A Narrative of Events*, p. 5.
6 Ibid., pp. 5–8.
7 Ibid., p. 9.
8 Joseph Sturge and Thomas Harvey, *The West Indies in 1837: Being the Journal of a Visit to Antigua, Montserrat, Dominica, St. Lucia, Barbados and Jamaica; Undertaken for the Purpose of Ascertaining the Actual Condition of the Negro Population of those Islands* (London: Hamilton, Adams, and Co. Paternoster Row). Printed by B. Hudson, Birmingham, 1838. Kissinger Legacy Reprints.
9 Henrice Altink, 'Slavery by Another Name' in *Representations of Slave Women in Discourses on Slavery and Abolition, 1780–1838* (Routledge Studies in Slave and Post – slave Societies and Cultures, Book 3, 2007), p. 147.
10 Williams, *A Narrative of Events*, p. 10.

180 | Notes

11 Sturge and Harvey, p. 204.
12 Ibid., p. 205.
13 Ibid., pp. 206–7.
14 Williams, *A Narrative of Events*, p. 12.
15 Ibid., p. 14.
16 Altink, p. 147.
17 A full account of the Report of Evidence can be found in 'A Narrative of Events', pp. 47–93.
18 Letters sent from Sturge to Clark can be found in the Additional Documents section of ' A Narrative of Events', pp. 95–105.
19 Ibid., p. 97.
20 Catherine Hall, *Civilising Subjects : Metroplole and Colony in the English Imagination 1830–1867* (Cambridge:Polity Press, 2002), p. 321.
21 Sturge to Clark letters, p. 98.
22 Ibid., p. 104.
23 Diana Paton, Introduction to *A Narrative of Events*, p. xlv.
24 Catherine Hall, p. 322.
25 Charles H. Wesley, 'The Abolition of Negro Apprenticeship in the British Empire', *The Journal of Negro History*, Vol. 23, No. 2 (Apr. 1938), p. 184.
26 Hall, p. 324.
27 Ibid., p. 325.
28 Holt, p. 105.
29 Henry Taylor, *Autobiography of Henry Taylor, 1800–1875* (London: Longmans, Green, 1885), Vol. 1, p. 246, quoted in Holt, p. 108.
30 Holt, pp. 73–4.
31 Holt, p. 147.
32 John Clark, *Anti-Slavery Reporter*, 1 March, 1852, quoted in Catherine Hall, p. 355.
33 Midgley, p. 186.
34 Holt, p. 165.
35 Ibid., p. 184.
36 Eyre to Cardwell, 6 August 1864, quoted in Holt, p. 273.
37 The *Birmingham Daily Gazette*, Monday, 13 November, 1865, https://www.britishnewspaperarchive.co.uk.
38 The *Birmingham Daily Gazette*, Friday 17 November, 1865, https://www.britishnewspaperarchive.co.uk.
39 *The Globe*, 13 December, 1865, https://www.britishnewspaperarchive.co.uk.
40 The *Birmingham Journal*, 18 November, 1865, https://www.britishnewspaperarchive.co.uk.
41 The *Birmingham Journal*, 6 January, 1866, quoted in Hall, p. 409.
42 LNFS, *41st Report* (Hudson, Birmingham, 1866), quoted in Catherine Hall, p. 410.

43 Thomas Harvey and William Brewin, *Jamaica in 1866, A Narrative of a Tour through the Island with Remarks on its Social, Educational and Industrial Condition*, https://google.co.uk, pp. 4–5.
44 Ibid., p. 5.
45 William Morgan,The *Anti-Slavery Reporter*, 1 October, 1866, quoted in Hall, p. 414
46 Ibid., 1 May, 1866, quoted in Hall, p. 415.
47 Hoskinson to Seward, in Despatches from US Consuls in Kingston, Jamaica, 1796–1906, US Consular Papers, in Holt, p. 340.
48 Sir H. Hocking, *Correspondence relevant to the Question of Punishment by Flogging*, May 1900, Colonial Office, in Holt, p. 340.
49 William Adlington Cadbury, *Notes on Voyage to West Indies, Dec. 16, 1896 to Feb. 2, 1897*. MS 466A/537-8, Archives and Collections, Library of Birmingham.

4 The Aftermath, Alabama

1 Zora Neale Hurston, *Barracoon: The Story of the Last Slave* (London: Harper Collins, 2018), pp. 62–5.
2 W.E.B. Du Bois, *Black Reconstruction in America, 1860–1880*, first published 1935 (New York: The Free Press, 1998), p. 140.
3 Peter Kolchin, *First Freedom: The Responses of Alabama's Blacks to Emancipation and Reconstruction* (Tuscaloosa: The University of Alabama Press, 1972), p. 5.
4 Peter Kolchin, *American Slavery, 1619–1877* (New York: Hill and Wang, 1993), p. 211.
5 Kolchin, *First Freedom*, p. 6.
6 *Acts of Alabama 1865–1866*, quoted in Jonathan M. Wiener, *Social Origins of the New South: Alabama, 1860–1885* (Louisiana State University Press, 1978), p. 59.
7 Wiener, p. 61.
8 See Chapter 1, pp. 23–27 and Chapter 2, p. 56.
9 *Ku Klux Conspiracy*, X, 1757, quoted in Kolchin, *First Freedom*, p. 18.
10 The Freedmen's Bureau Online, *Records of the Assistant Commissioner for the State of Alabama*, National Archives Publication M809 Roll 23, 'Miscellaneous Papers'. http://freedmensbureau.com/alabama/affidavit-1.htm.
11 Freedmen's Bureau List of Murders in the District of Alabama 1866, *Records of the Assistant Commissioner for the State of Alabama*, National Archives Publication M809 Roll 23, http://freedmensbureau.com/alabama/alaoutrages.htm.
12 Wiener, p. 62
13 Ibid., p. 65.

14 Quoted in Eric Foner, *Reconstruction: America's Unfinished Revolution, 1863–1877* (New York: Harper and Row, 1988), p. 288.
15 Foner, p. 363.
16 Kolchin, *First Freedom*, p. 81.
17 Report of Wager Swayne, 31 October,1866, US, Congress. Quoted in Kolchin, p. 84.
18 Quoted in Kolchin, p. 83.
19 Eugene Feldman, 'James T. Rapier, Negro Congressman from Alabama', *The Phylon Quarterly*. Vol. 19, No. 4 (4th Qtr., 1958), pp. 418. Published by Clark Atlanta University.
20 Ibid., p. 417.
21 Foner, p. 534.
22 Feldman, p. 422.
23 Ibid., p. 422.
24 Foner, p. 608.
25 Wiener, pp. 137–8.
26 Nicolas Barreyre, 'The Politics of Economic Crises: The Panic of 1873, the End of Reconstruction, and the Realignment of American Politics', *The Journal of the Gilded Age and Progressive Era*, Vol. 10, No. 4 (October, 2011), pp. 418–20.
27 Foner, p. 550.
28 www.encyclopediaofalabama.org/article/h-2390.
29 As related by Randolph Johnson, 'Born in Slavery: Slave Narratives from the Federal Writers' Project 1936–1938', The Library of Congress, Alabama Narratives, Volume 1, p. 232.
30 *New York Times*, Dec. 17, 1882, quoted in Mary Ellen Curtin, *Black Prisoners and Their World, Alabama, 1865–1900* (Charlottesville: University Press of Virginia, 2000), p. 70.
31 Frederick Douglass, 'Convict Lease System', 1893. Frederick Douglass Papers at the Library of Congress: Manuscript Division.
32 See Douglas A. Blackmon, *Slavery by Another Name: The Re-Enslavement of Black Americans from the Civil War to World War II* (New York: Anchor Books, 2008), p. 56.
33 W.E.B. Du Bois, *Black Reconstruction in America: 1860–1880*, pp. 698–9.
34 Report on convict leasing system, Alabama Federation of Women's Clubs, 1923, www.usprisonculture.com.
35 Foner, pp. 588–9.
36 See Jeremy W. Richter, 'Alabama's Anti-Miscegenation Statutes', *Alabama Review*, The University of Alabama Press, Volume 68, Number 4, October 2015, pp. 345–365.
37 *Congressional Globe*, 39th Congress, 1st Session, Part 1, p. 127, quoted in W.E.B. Du Bois, *Black Reconstruction in America*, p. 232.

38 Foner, p. xxv.
39 Du Bois, p. 30.

5 The Twentieth Century, 1900–1960

1 Report of the West India Royal Commission (1897), quoted in Holt, p. 312.
2 Holt, p. 316.
3 https://api.parliament.uk/historic-hansard/commons/1898/mar/14/west-india-grant.
4 Catherine Hall, *Civilising Subjects: Metropole and Colony in the English Imagination 1830–1867* (Cambridge: Polity Press, 2002), p. 432.
5 Oswald 'Columbus' Denniston, quoted in Mike Phillips and Trevor Phillips, *Windrush: The Irresistable Rise of Multi-Racial Britain* (London: HarperCollins, 1998), p. 9.
6 David Olusoga, *Black and British: A Forgotten History* (London: PanMacmillan, 2017), pp. 434–5.
7 Dr Finlayson McKenzie, quoted in Holt, p. 373.
8 Holt, p. 374.
9 Holt, p.384.
10 *West India Royal Commission Report* (London: HMSO, June 1945), p. 35.
11 Sam King, quoted in Mike Phillips and Trevor Phillips, *Windrush*, p. 17.
12 Sahadeo, Basdeo, 'Walter Citrine and the British Caribbean Workers Movement during the Commission Hearing, 1938–39', *Journal of Caribbean History* 18 (1983), p. 54.
13 Claire Brennan, *Soldiers of the Caribbean: Britain's forgotten war heroes* (BBC News, 13 May 2015).
14 https://TheConversation.com/ *Black Troops were welcome in Britain, but Jim Crow wasn't*, 22 June 2018.
15 Lloyd King, quoted in Peter L. Edmead, ed. Kathryne Wray and Martin Flynn, *The Divisive Decade: A History of Caribbean Immigration to Birmingham in the 1950s* (Birmingham Library Services, 1999), p. 7.
16 *Daily Express*, Tuesday 8 June 1948, quoted in Mike Phillips and Trevor Phillips, *Windrush*, p. 59.
17 Letter to Ivor Cummings, Colonial Office, 29 May 1948, Privy Council Office, PRO CO 876/88.
18 Letter from Privy Council Office to Colonial Office, 15 June 1948, PRO CO 876/88.
19 Letter from Clement Attlee, Prime Minister, in reply to a letter from a group of backbenchers, 5 July 1948, PRO CO 876/88
20 Linda McDowell, 'How Caribbean migrants helped to rebuild Britain', *Windrush Stories*, (British Library, 4 Oct. 2018)
21 Peter L. Edmead, *The Divisive Decade: A History of Caribbean Immigration to Birmingham in the 1950s* (Birmingham Library Services, 1999), p. 18.

22 Edmead, p. 21.
23 Ibid., p. 23.
24 Henry Gunter, 'Impressions of Britain and its workers', *Jamaica Arise*, June 1949, MS 2165/2/1, Birmingham Archives and Collections.
25 Henry Gunter, *Caribbean News*, February 1953, MS 2165/2/4, Birmingham Archives and Collections.
26 Henry Gunter, 'A Man's a Man: A Study of the Colour Bar in Birmingham – and An Answer', p. 5, published by The Communist Party, Birmingham, 1954, MS 2165/2/5, Birmingham Archives and Collections.
27 Ibid., p. 6.
28 Ibid., pp. 8–9.
29 Ibid., p. 10.
30 Ibid., p. 11.
31 Edmead, p. 30.
32 Birmingham Mail 12/9, 'Coloured people in Great Britain: Summary of press news and comment', September 1958 (UK/43), Warwick University Library, Modern Records Centre
33 Edmead, p. 32.
34 Z. Layton-Henry, *The Politics of Race in Britain* (London: Allen and Unwin, 1984), p. 35, quoted in Edmead, p. 32.
35 Edmead, p. 32.
36 Quoted in Edmead, p. 31.
37 Booker T. Washington, letter to John B. Knox, May 23, 1901, Alabama Dept. Of Archives and History
38 Carol Anderson, *One Person, No Vote: How Voter Suppression Is Destroying Our Democracy* (New York: Bloomsbury Publishing, 2018), p. 5.
39 Blaine A. Brownell, 'Birmingham, Alabama: New South City in the 1920s', *The Journal of Southern History*, Vol. 38, No. 1 (Feb., 1972), pp. 22–29.
40 *Wyatt v. Adair*, Supreme Court of Alabama, Dec 16, 1926, https://casetext.com.
41 Birmingham Racial Segregation Ordinances, Birmingham Civil Rights Institute, civil rights digital library, crdl.usg.edu.
42 See Glenn T. Eskew, '"Bombingham": Black Protest in Postwar Birmingham, Alabama', *The Historian*, Vol. 59, No. 2 (Winter 1997), pp. 371–390. I am indebted to Eskew for much of the information contained in the following pages on specific incidents occurring in Smithfield, Birmingham during the 1940s and 1950s.
43 Eskew, p. 377.
44 Brownell, pp. 39–40
45 Eskew, p. 377.
46 Eskew, p. 381.
47 Eskew, p. 386.

6 The Twentieth Century, 1960–2000

1. See Chapter 1, pp. 15–18.
2. See Augustine John, *Race in the Inner City: A Report from Handsworth, Birmingham,* (London: The Runnymede Trust, 1970).
3. John, p. 3
4. John, p. 3.
5. John, p. 4.
6. John, p. 20.
7. John, p. 20.
8. John, pp. 6, 7.
9. John, pp. 7, 8.
10. John, p. 10.
11. John, p. 13.
12. John, p. 14.
13. John, p. 18.
14. John, p. 18.
15. Joe Street, 'Malcolm X, Smethwick, and the Influence of the African American Freedom Struggle on British Race Relations in the 1960s', *Journal of Black Studies,* Volume 38, Number 6, July 2008, pp. 935–6.
16. Peter Griffiths, quoted in Street, p. 936.
17. Street, p. 938.
18. Street, p. 939.
19. Malcolm X, reported in the *Birmingham Post,* February 13, back page, in Street, p. 939.
20. Street, p. 933.
21. Full text of Powell's speech published in 'The Telegraph', 6 Nov. 2007, telegraph.co.uk/comment/3643823/Enoch-Powells-Rivers-of-Blood-speech.html.
22. Clem Jones, quoted in Mike Phillips and Trevor Phillips, 'Windrush', p. 250.
23. Paul Gilroy, quoted in Phillips and Phillips, p. 358.
24. Peter Southgate, 'The Disturbances of July 1981 in Handsworth, Birmingham: a survey of the views and experiences of male residents', in Simon Field and Peter Southgate *Public Disorder: a review of research and a study in one inner city area* (London: Her Majesty's Stationery Office, 1982).
25. Southgate, p. 42.
26. Birmingham *Evening Mail,* 10 September 1985, p. 2.
27. birmingham.co.uk/news/local-news/the-handsworth-riots-25-years-on-131492.
28. Gus John, 'This conflict has been 30 years in the making', *The Guardian,* 26 October 2005.
29. Gus John, 2005.

30 E. Ellis Cashmore, 'The Handsworth Riots, *Marxism Today*, October, 1985.
31 Macpherson report summary in *The Guardian*, 24 February 1999.
32 In 2005 the 'double jeopardy' law by which suspects could not be tried twice for the same offence was scrapped. In 2007, using new technology, Stephen's DNA was found on the clothes of the two suspects previously identified by Duwayne Brooks and in 2011 they were charged with murder and sentenced to life imprisonment.
33 Raymond Arsenault, *Freedom Riders: 1961 and the Struggle for Racial Justice* (New York: Oxford University Press, 2011), p. 81.
34 Ibid., p. 90.
35 Diane McWhorter, *Carry Me Home: Birmingham, Alabama, The Climactic Battle of the Civil Rights Revolution* (New York: Touchstone, 2002), p. 197.
36 Arsenault, p. 97.
37 Ibid., p. 98.
38 McWhorter, p. 204.
39 Arsenault, p. 107.
40 Arsenault, p. 110.
41 Arsenault, p. 115.
42 Glenn T. Eskew, *But for Birmingham: The Local and National Movements in the Civil Rights Struggle* (Chapel Hill, NC: The University of North Carolina Press, 1997), p. 7.
43 Martin Luther King, Jr., 'Letter from Birmingham Jail', *The Atlantic Monthly, August 1963: The Negro is Your Brother:* Volume, 212, No. 2: pp. 78–88.
44 Bruce Hartford, Civil Rights Movement Veterans website, crmvet.org/tim/timhis63.htm#1963bham.
45 Eskew, p. 5.
46 See Hartford's account, crmvet.org/tim/timhis63.htm#1963bham.
47 Len Holt, 'Eyewitness: The Police Terror at Birmingham', *National Guardian* newsweekly, 16 May 1963. As reprinted from *Black Protest:350 Years of History, Documents and Analyses,* by Joanne Grant, Ed. (Fawcett: 1968), Civil Rights Movement Veterans website, crmvet.org/ nars/bhamholt.htm
48 Ibid.
49 Bruce Hartford, Civil Rights Movement Veterans website, crmvet.org/tim/timhis63.htm#1963bham.
50 Holt, crmvet.org/nars/bhamholt.htm .
51 Hartford, crmvet.org/tim/timhis63.htm#1963bham.
52 John A. Kirk, *Martin Luther King Jr.* (Harlow: Pearson Education Limited, 2005), p. 88.
53 Diane McWhorter, *Carry Me Home: Birmingham, Alabama: The Climactic Battle of the Civil Rights Revolution* (New York: Touchstone, 2001), p. 496.

54 Ibid., p. 497.
55 Ibid., p. 500.
56 McWhorter, p. 522.
57 Andrew Cohen, 'The Speech That Shocked Birmingham the Day After the Church Bombing', *The Atlantic*, https://www.theatlantic.com>national>archive>2013/09.
58 McWhorter, p. 510.
59 See Chapter 5, p. 125.
60 Gordon Harvey, 'Public Education in Alabama After Desegregation', *Encyclopedia of Alabama*, 8 March 2013,
61 Jerry W. Fly and George R. Reinhart, 'Racial Separation during the 1970s: The Case of Birmingham', *Social Forces*, Vol. 58, No. 4 (June, 1980), pp. 1255–1262.
62 Bobby M. Wilson, 'Racial Segregation Trends in Birmingham, Alabama', *Southeastern Geographer*, Vol. 25, No. 1 (May, 1985), pp. 30–43.
63 Carol Anderson, *One Person, No Vote* (New York: Bloomsbury Publishing, 2018), pp. 32–3.
64 Ibid., p. 23.

7 Into the Twenty-First Century

1 Amelia Gentleman, *The Windrush Betrayal: Exposing the Hostile Environment* (London: Guardian Faber, 2019), p. 138.
2 Amelia Gentleman, p. 19. See Gentleman's book for a full account of Paulette's story.
3 Amber Rudd, speech in Parliament, 16 April 2018,
4 Gladstone Wilson, quoted in *Wolverhampton Express and Star*, 13 August 2018.
5 See Chapter 6, pp. 139–40.
6 See Tahir Abbas and Muhammad Anwar, 'An Analysis of Race Equality Policy and Practice in the City of Birmingham, UK', *Local Government Studies*, Volume 31, 2005 – Issue 1, pp. 53–68.
7 Nikole Hannah-Jones, 'The Resegregation of Jefferson County: What one Alabama town's attempt to secede from its school district tells us about the fragile progress of racial integration in America'. *The New York Times Magazine,* The Education Issue, 6 September 2017.
8 Ibid.
9 Hannah-Jones.
10 Kendra Taylor, Erica Frankenberg, Genevieve Siegel-Hawley, 'Racial Segregation in the Southern Schools, School Districts, and Counties Where Districts Have Seceded', *AERA Open*, 4 September 2019.
11 Carol Anderson, p. 51.
12 Carol Anderson, p. 70.

13 See Carol Anderson, *One Person, No Vote: How Voter Suppression Is Destroying Our Democracy* (New York: Bloomsbury Publishing, 2018) for a detailed analysis of the 2017 election.
14 David Olusoga, *Black and British: A Forgotten History* (London: Macmillan, 2016), p. 525.
15 For the full survey see Juliana Menasie Horowitz, Anna Brown and Kiana Cox, 'Pew Research Center. Social and Demographic Trends. Race in America 2019', pewsocialtrends.org/2019/04/09/how-americans-see-the-state-of-race-relations/.
16 Lucas Guttentag, the founder and former national director of the American Civil Liberties Union Immigrants' Rights Project, in *The New York Times*, 20 Aug. 2018.
17 W.E.B. Du Bois, *The Souls of Black Folk*, 1903 (Millennium Publications, 2014), p. 122.

Bibliography

Abbas, Tahir and Anwar Muhammad 'An Analysis of Race Equality Policy and Practice in the City of Birmingham, UK', *Local Government Studies,* Volume 31, 2005 – Issue 1.

Altink, Henrice, 'Slavery by another name: Apprenticed women in Jamaican workhouses in the period 1834–81', *Social History,* Volume 26, 2001 – Issue 1.

Anderson, Carol, *One Person, No Vote: How Voter Suppression is Destroying Our Democracy* (New York: Bloomsbury Publishing, 2018).

Arsenault, Raymond, *Freedom Riders: 1961 and the Struggle for Racial Justice* (New York: Oxford University Press, 2011).

Berlin, Ira, *The Long Emancipation: The Demise of Slavery in the United States* (Cambridge, Massachusetts: Harvard University Press, 2015).

Berlin, Ira, Fields, Barbara J., Miller, Steven F., Reidy, Joseph P., Rowland, Leslie S., eds. *Free at Last: A Documentary History of Slavery, Freedom and the Civil War* (New York: The New Press, 1992).

Blackburn, Robin, *The Overthrow of Colonial Slavery: 1776–1848* (London: Verso, 1988).

Blackmon, Douglas A., *Slavery by Another Name: The Re-Enslavement of Black Americans from the Civil War to World War II* (New York: Anchor Books, 2009).

Brownell, Blaine A., 'Birmingham, Alabama: New South City in the 1920s', *The Journal of Southern History,* Vol. 38, No. 1 (Feb., 1972).

Carson, Clayborne, ed., *The Autobiography of Martin Luther King, Jr.* (London: Abacus, 2000).

Connerly, Charles E., *The Most Segregated City in America: City Planning and Civil Rights in Birmingham, 1920–1980* (Charlottesville: University Press of Virginia, 2005).

Davis, David Brion, *Inhuman Bondage: The Rise and Fall of Slavery in the New World* (New York: Oxford University Press, 2006).

Deerr, Noel and Brooks, Alexander, 'The Early Use of Steam Power in the Cane Sugar Industry', *Transactions of the Newcomen Society,* Volume 21, 1940 – Issue 1.

Douglass, Frederick, *The Portable Frederick Douglass* (New York: Penguin Books, 2016).

Dunn, Richard S., *Sugar and Slaves: The Rise of the Planter Class in the English West Indies, 1624–1713* (Chapel Hill: The University of North Carolina Press, 1972).
Du Bois, W.E.B., *Black Reconstruction in America, 1860–1880* (New York: The Free Press, 1998).
Du Bois, W.E.B., *The Souls of Black Folk* (Millenium Publications, 2014).
Edwards, Paul, ed., *Equiano's Travels* (Oxford: Heinemann Educational, 1996).
Edmead, Peter L., *The Divisive Decade: A History of Caribbean Immigration to Birmingham in the 1950s* (Birmingham City Council, 1999).
Eskew, Glenn T., '"Bombingham": Black Protest in Postwar Birmingham, Alabama', *The Historian*, Vol. 59, No. 2 (Winter 1997).
Eskew, Glenn T., *But for Birmingham: The Local and National Movements in the Civil Rights Struggle* (Chapel Hill, NC: The University of North Carolina Press, 1997).
Fara, Patricia, *Erasmus Darwin: Sex, Science and Serendipity* (Oxford: Oxford University Press, 2012).
Feldman, Eugene, 'James T. Rapier, Negro Congressman from Alabama', *The Phylon Quarterly*, Vol. 19, No. 4, 1958.
Field, Simon and Southgate, Peter, 'Public Disorder: a review of research and a study in one inner city area', *Home Office Research Study No. 72* (London: HMSO, 1982).
Fitzgerald, Michael W., *Splendid Failure: Postwar Reconstruction in the American South* (Chicago: Ivan R. Dee, 2007).
Fly, Jerry W. and Reinhart, George R., 'Racial Separation during the 1970s: The Case of Birmingham', *Social Forces*, Vol. 58, No. 4 (June, 1980).
Foner, Eric, *Reconstruction: America's Unfinished Revolution, 1863–1877* (New York: Harper and Row, 1988).
Gentleman, Amelia, *The Windrush Betrayal: Exposing the Hostile Environment* (London: Guardian Faber, 2019).
Grimke, Sarah and Angelina, *On Slavery and Abolitionism* (New York: Penguin Books, 2014).
Grosvenor, Ian, Rita McLean, Sian Roberts, *Making Connections* (Black Pasts, Birmingham Futures Group, 2002).
Hall, Catherine, *Civilising Subjects: Metropole and Colony in the English Imagination, 1830–1867* (Cambridge: Polity Press, 2002).
Harris, W. Edward, *Miracle in Birmingham: A Civil Rights Memoir, 1954–1965* (Indianapolis: Stonework Press, 2004).
Harrold, Stanley, *American Abolitionists* (Harlow: Pearson Education Limited, 2001).
Hochschild, Adam, *Bury the Chains: The British Struggle to Abolish Slavery* (London: Macmillan, 2005).
Holt, Thomas C., *The Problem of Freedom: Race, Labor, and Politics in Jamaica*

and Britain, 1832–1938 (Maryland: The Johns Hopkins University Press, 1992).

Hurston, Zora Neale, *Barracoon: The Story of the Last Slave* (London: Harper Collins Publishers Ltd., 2018).

Jahoda, Gloria, *The Trail of Tears: The Story of the American Indian Removals, 1813–1855* (New York: Random House, 1995).

John, Augustine, *Race in the Inner City: A Report from Handsworth, Birmingham* (London: The Runnymede Trust, 1970).

Jordan, Michael, *The Great Abolition Sham: The True Story of the End of the British Slave Trade* (Stroud, Gloucestershire: The History Press, 2005).

Kirk, John, A., *Martin Luther King Jr.* (Harlow: Pearson Education Limited, 2005).

Kolchin, Peter, *First Freedom: The Responses of Alabama's Blacks to Emancipation and Reconstruction* (Tuscaloosa: The University of Alabama Press, 1972).

Kolchin, Peter, *American Slavery, 1619–1877* (New York: Hill and Wang, 1993).

Langford, John, Alfred, *A Century of Birmingham life: or, A chronicle of local events, from 1741to 1841, compiled and edited by John Alfred Langford* (Birmingham: E.C. Osborne; London: Simpkin, Marshall and Co., 1868).

London Anti-Slavery Society, *Statements and Observations on the Working of the Laws for the Abolition of Slavery Throughout the British Colonies and on the Present State of the Negro Population* (Cornell University Library Digital Collections).

McWhorter, Diane, *Carry Me Home: Birmingham, Alabama: The Climactic Battle of the Civil Rights Revolution* (New York: Touchstone, 2002).

Midgley, Clare, *Women Against Slavery: The British Campaigns, 1780–1870* (London: Routledge, 1992).

Oakes, James, *The Radical and the Republican: Frederick Douglas, Abraham Lincoln and the Triumph of Antislavery Politics* (New York: W.W. Norton and Company, 2008).

Oakes, James, *The Ruling Race: A History of American Slaveholders* (New York: W.W. Norton and Company, 1998).

Olusoga, David, *Black and British: A Forgotten History* (London: Pan Macmillan, 2017).

Park, Mungo, *Travels in the Interior of Africa* (Ware: Wordsworth Editions Limited, 2002).

Phillips, Mike and Phillips, Trevor, *Windrush: The Irresistible Rise of Multi-Racial Britain* (London: HarperCollins, 1998).

Reckord, Mary, 'The Jamaica Slave Rebellion of 1831', *Past and Present*, Volume 40, Issue 1, 1 July 1968.

Richards, W.A., *The Birmingham Gun Manufactory of Farmer and Galton and the Slave Trade in the Eighteenth Century,* submitted for Master of Arts of

the Faculty of Commerce and Social Sciences, University of Birmingham, 1972.
Rogers, D. Laurence, *Apostles of Equality: The Birneys, the Republicans, and the Civil War* (Michigan: Michigan State University Press, 2011).
Satchell, Veront M., 'Early Use of Steam Power in the Jamaican Sugar Industry, 1768–1810', *Transactions of the Newcomen Society*, Volume 67, 1995, Issue 1.
Smith, Barbara M. D., 'The Galtons of Birmingham: Quaker Gun Merchants and Bankers, 1702–1831', *Business History*, Vol. 9, No. 2, 1967.
Smith, Marvin T., Marcoux Jon, Gredell Erin, Waselkov, Gregory, 'A Seventeenth-century trade gun and associated collection from Pine Island, Alabama', *Southeastern Archaeology*, 2016.
Street, Joe, 'Malcolm X, Smethwick, and the Influence of the African American Freedom Struggle on British Race Relations in the 1960s', *Journal of Black Studies*, Volume 38, Number 6, July 2008.
Sturge, Joseph and Harvey, Thomas, *The West Indies in 1837: Being the Journal of a Visit to Antigua, Montserrat, Dominica, St. Lucia, Barbados and Jamaica* (London: Hamilton, Adams, and Co., 1838), reprinted by Kessinger Publishing.
Tann, Jennifer, 'Steam and Sugar: The Diffusion of the Stationary Steam Engine to the Caribbean Sugar Industry, 1770–1840', *History of Technology*, Vol. 19, 1997.
Taylor, Kendra, Frankenberg, Erica, Siegel-Hawley, Genevieve, 'Racial Segregation in the Southern Schools, School Districts, and Counties Where Districts Have Seceded', *American Educational Research Association*, AERA Open, 4 September 2019.
Thomas, Hugh, *The Slave Trade: The History of the Atlantic Slave Trade 1440–1870* (London: Picador, 1997).
Uglow, Jenny, *The Lunar Men: The Friends who made the Future, 1730–1810* (London: Faber and Faber Ltd., 2002).
Wiener, Jonathan M., *Social Origins of the New South: Alabama 1860–1885* (Baton Rouge: Louisiana State University Press, 1978).
Williams, Eric, *Capitalism and Slavery* (London: André Deutsch, 1964).
Williams, James, *A Narrative of Events, since the first of August, 1834, by James Williams, an Apprenticed Labourer in Jamaica* (Durham: Duke University Press, 2001).
Williams, Patricia J., *Seeing a Colour-Blind Future: The Paradox of Race, The 1997 Reith Lectures* (London: Virago Press, 1997).
Wilson, Bobby M., 'Racial Segregation Trends in Birmingham, Alabama', *Southeastern Geographer*, Vol. 25, No. 1 (May, 1985).

Index

Abernathy, Rev. Ralph, 147–8
Alabama Christian Movement for Human Rights (ACMHR), 147
Alabama Constitution (1901), 98, 116, 118, 121
Alabama slave codes, 48
Albany Movement, 146
American Anti-Slavery Society, 47, 49, 50
American Colonization Society, 46, 50
American troops in Britain, 107–8
Anniston, 143–6
anti-miscegenation law, 97–8
apprenticeship system, 59–69, 71, 80, 83

Beecher, Catherine, 46
Birmingham, Al, Truce Agreement (1963), 152, 158
Birmingham, Al, Zoning Ordinance (1926), 3, 119, 122, 124, 158
Birmingham Anti-Slavery Society, 38–9, 60, 67, 70, 76, 80
Birmingham and Midland Freedmen's Aid Association, 103
Birmingham Ladies' Negro's Friend Society, 38, 103, 57, 70
Birney, James, 43–51, 53
Black Codes, 83, 93–4, 99
Bogle, Paul, 73
Boulton, Matthew, 13–19, 30, 126
Boutwell, Albert, 147, 151, 158
British and Foreign Anti-Slavery Society, 57, 77
British West Indies Regiment, 104, 107
Brixton riots, 137–8, 141

Cadbury, William Adlington, 79
Chamberlain, Joseph, 101–3
Chamblis, Robert E., 123, 153, 157
Christianity, 30, 35, 58, 80, 96
Citrine, Sir Walter, 107
Civil Rights Act (1964), 3, 125, 158

Civil Rights Movement, 124–5, 133, 152, 157
Civil War, 22–8, 46–7, 54, 56, 74, 90–4
Clark, John, 61, 65–6, 70
Clarkson, Thomas, 30, 31, 35, 38, 40
Clay, Clement Corner, 45–6
Clay, Henry, 49, 53
Colonial Office, 60, 68–9, 71–2, 75–6, 79, 81, 106, 108–9
Commonwealth Immigrants Act, 134
Congress of Racial Equality (CORE), 142
Connor, Eugene "Bull", 124, 143, 145, 147, 149–52
convict lease system, 94, 96, 99
cotton gin, 20, 24
Creek Indians, 4, 5, 20–2, 45

Darwin, Erasmus, 18, 34–6, 38
Douglas Frederick, 82
Du Bois, W.E.B., 96, 99, 100, 172

Edmead, Peter, 110–11, 115–16
Elyton Land Company, 23–4, 9
Equality and Human Rights Commission Report (2018), 171
Equiano, Olaudah, 9, 10, 19
Eyre, Governor, 72–3, 76–7

Farmer, James, 6–8, 10–12
Federal Writers' Project, 2, 25, 92
Female Society for Birmingham, 38–9
Fifteenth Amendment (1870), 98
Fourteenth Amendment (1868), 86, 97–8
Freedmen's Bureau, 2, 82, 84–7
Freedom Ride, 142–3, 145–7

Galton, Samuel, 6–8, 10–13, 16, 18, 19
Mary Anne, 18, 36, 38
Gardendale, school secession, 166–68
Garrison, William Lloyd, 47, 52–3, 58
Gentleman Amelia, 162–4

194 | Index

Glenelg, Lord, Colonial Secretary, 60, 65, 67, 69, 71
Griffiths, Peter, 131–4
Grimké, Sarah and Angelina, 47, 50, 52
Gunter, Henry, 2, 111–14

Handsworth, Birmingham, 16, 18, 34, 116, 126–32, 136–40, 164–5
Hawkins, William, 22–3, 56
Help America Vote Act, HAVA (2002), 168
Heyrick, Elizabeth, 40–1, 58
Holt, Len, 149
Hoover, J. Edgar, 157

Immigration Act, UK (2014), 162
Indian Removal Act (1830), 20
industrialization, Birmingham, Al, 90–93

Jackson, Andrew, 21, 45, 46
Jamaican Assembly, 70, 76, 81
Jim Crow laws, 96, 100, 107, 114, 142, 146, 156
John, Augustine, 127, 131, 136, 140
Jones, Doug, 157, 169

Kennedy, President John F., 151–2, 158
    Robert, 146, 152
King, Martin Luther, Jr., 146–7, 151–2, 157, 159
    Letter from Birmingham Jail, 148
Knox, John B., 116–17
Ku Klux Klan, 84, 86, 89, 91, 100, 122–3, 125, 143, 147, 152–3, 156, 171

Lawrence, Stephen, 141–2
Lewis, Cudjo, 81
Lewis John, 142, 149
Liberator newspaper, 47, 52
Liberty Party, 53
Lincoln, Abraham, 33, 53–4, 56, 73, 81
Lincoln-Douglas debates, 33, 54
literacy tests, 117–18
Lloyd, Samuel, 38–9
Lunar Society, 13, 16, 18, 30, 33, 35–6, 38

Macpherson report, 141
Malcolm X, 133
Manesty, Joseph, 7
Manley, Norman, 104
McAdory, Thomas, 23

Montego Bay uprising, 59
Moore, Ray, 169–70
Morant Bay rebellion, 73, 75–6, 103
Morgan, Charles, B'ham speech (1963), 155–6
Morgan, William, 70, 76–8, 80
Mosley, Oswald, 116
Moyne Report (1945), 108
Mudd, William, 23–4, 27, 56, 93

National Association for the Advancement of Colored People (NAACP), 122–4, 153, 168–9
National Front, 135–7
Native Americans, 4, 19, 21, 29, 44

Parks, Rosa, 124–5
Peck, James, 143, 145
Philanthropist, The, newspaper, 48–9
polygenesis, 44, 170
Populist Party, 99
Powell, Enoch, 133–36, 164
Presidential Reconstruction, 82
Priestley, Joseph, 18, 19, 30–33, 35–8

Quakers, 11, 12, 30, 42–3, 61, 77

Race Relations Acts, UK (1965/68/76), 127, 132, 136
Rachman, Peter, 115
Racial Segregation Ordinances (1944), Al, 116, 120, 124
Radical Reconstruction, 86, 88, 94, 100
Rapier, James T., 88–90
Redemption, 91, 96
Red Sticks, 21
Royal Africa Company, 6, 7
Royal Commissions on Jamaica (1897), 102–3, (1945), 106–7

Sadler, Isaac, 23
Segregation Regulation Ordinances, 116, 119–20, 124, 142
Sharp, Granville, 30, 31
Sharpe, Samuel, 59
Shores, Arthur, 122–3, 153
Shuttlesworth, Rev. Fred L., 124–5, 143–5, 147, 151
Sixteenth Street Baptist Church, 123, 148–9, 150, 154, 169
Slavery Abolition Act (1833), 41, 57
Smethwick, 131–33
Smith, Adam, 32

Society of Friends, 12, 42
Soho Works, 16, 126
Southern Christian Leadership Conference (SCLC), 146–8, 152
stationary steam engine, 13
'stop and search', 130, 136, 138, 141
Student Non-Violent Coordinating Committee (SNCC), 142, 146, 150, 152
Sturge, Joseph, 39–41, 57, 60, 61, 63–8, 70, 75–7, 80, 101, 170
  Sophia, 41
Swayne, Wager, 82, 87

Tate and Lyle, 78, 105
Taylor, Henry, Colonial Office, 60, 68, 76
Thirteenth Amendment (1865), 29, 73
Townsend, Lucy, 38
Trans-Atlantic slave trade, 6, 20, 21, 25, 29, 42
treadmill, 62–6, 68, 79
Turner, Nat, 47

University of Alabama, 46, 156, 166

Union League, 86

Vagrancy Act, US, 71, 83
  UK, 136–7
voter suppression, 3, 159, 168–70
Voting Rights Act (1965), 3, 158–9, 168

Wallace, George, 151–3
Washington, Booker T., 116–17
Watt, James, 13–19, 126
Wedgwood, Josiah, 18, 19, 31, 35–6, 38
  Sarah, 38
Weld, Rev. Theodore, 47, 49, 50
West Indian Sugar Company (WISCO), 105
Whitney, Eli, 20
Wilberforce, William, 30, 36, 39, 40
Williams, James, 61–7
Wilson, Gladstone, 162–4
Wilson, Paulette, 163
Windrush, *SS Empire*, 103, 106, 108–9
World War I, 104, 107
World War II, 105, 107, 161
Wyatt v. Adair, 119, 121